THE ISLÂMIC WORLD

THE ISLÂMIC WORLD

Edited by

WILLIAM H. McNEILL

and

MARILYN ROBINSON WALDMAN

New York
OXFORD UNIVERSITY PRESS
London   1973   Toronto

Preface

Islâm is the youngest and in a sense also the most coherent of the world's great civilizations. It arose on the basis of Allâh's revelations to the Prophet Muhammad, and quickly established its sway in the ancient Near Eastern lands and throughout the southern and eastern coastlands of the Mediterranean. These initial territorial conquests guaranteed that Islâmic civilization would inherit much from ancient Greece and Rome as well as from the cosmopolitanism of the ancient Near East, where Semitic and Persian traditions were especially strong. Yet these complex and indeed contradictory inheritances were all subordinated to and reorganized around the Prophet Muhammad's revelation. Only elements compatible with that revelation could fit comfortably within the new order of Islâm. A tremendous effort was made, especially in the first Muslim centuries, to reject all that did not fit, and to reduce obedience to God's will to the precise prescriptions of codified Sacred Law.

Subsequently, of course, new peoples, new ideas and ideals, and new institutions arose. Islâm expanded from its initial heartland into the Balkans, across the steppelands of Asia and Europe, into sub-Saharan Africa and throughout the seacoasts of the Indian Ocean and southeast Asia. Rival sects and rival states arose, dividing the community of the faithful into jarring fragments; and since about 1700 a long series of defeats at the hands of Europeans reversed earlier military patterns which, on the whole, had given Muslims the upper hand in collisions with neighbors of every kind, whether in Europe, India, or central Asia.

Yet these changes, far reaching though they were, never erased the fact that Islâm was built around belief in Allâh and

obedience to His commands as revealed through Muhamma
and spelled out by the early generations of experts in the Sacre
Law. Hence any study of Islâm must concentrate especial atter
tion on the Prophet himself and on the community of the Faitl
ful that formed around him, as well as on the first centurie
when his followers had suddenly to come to terms with th
Graeco-Roman and Persian (Sassanian) cultural traditions. Th
readings which follow conform to this principle by devotin
about one-third of the available space to this early "classical
period of Islamic history.

Muslims and many Western scholars have, however, tendeι
to see changes that occurred in Islâmic civilization and societ
after about 1000 as deplorable departures from the attainment
of the classical period. This judgment depends on accepting th
dogmatic idea that any departure from patterns of Muhammad':
time is deplorable, or on viewing the importance of Islâmic civi
lization as resting on its role in transmitting elements of ancien1
Greek learning from a decaying antiquity to the Christian West.
which became capable of accepting and reacting to that inheritance soon after the year 1000. But Islâm, surely, did not
exist to serve the West, even though Muslim learning did in fact
irrigate and illuminate the intellectual life of medieval Europe
in important ways. But this was a by-product of Islâmic achievements, not, as nineteenth-century European scholars tended to
assume, the *raison d'être* of Islâm in world history.

Anyone who attempts to understand Islâmic civilization as an
historical phenomenon with a value and character of its own
cannot disregard and should not denigrate the varied changes
that came to the realm of Islâm after 1000. We have therefore
devoted most of this volume to readings that illustrate and point
up some of these changes.

In this connection it is worth emphasizing that until quite recently the expansion of Islâm in Europe, Asia, and Africa was a
leading fact of world history. Other civilizations were either on
the defensive, losing ground to the followers of Muhammad (in
Europe and India), or expanded far more slowly (in the Far
East). Moreover, the consolidation of the Islâmic heartlands into

three great empires—the Ottoman, Safavid, and Mughal—that occurred between 1400 and 1600, gave Islam a firmer political-military framework than it had enjoyed since the collapse of the early caliphate. Islâm, in short, continued to enjoy spectacular success in late medieval and early modern times. Only since about 1700 has the balance between an expansive, aggressive western European civilization and a no less expansive, aggressive Islâmic civilization shifted sharply against Muslims; and even in the nineteenth and twentieth centuries, Islâmic missionaries often prevailed over Christian missionaries in appealing to Africans and a few remote Asian peoples emerging from paganism.

This history of political-military success, combined with the dogmatic basis of Islâm upon a revelation believed to be superior to and intended by God to supersede Jewish and Christian error, explains the extraordinary difficulty Muslims had and continue to have in coming to terms with world patterns of the nineteenth and twentieth centuries. Modernization of the sort required to achieve political and military power in our own time seems incompatible with much of the Muslim heritage. As a result, successful combination of old and new, such as that the Japanese hit upon more than a century ago, has yet to be found. On the other hand, outright repudiation of Islâm, which occurred in Turkey after World War I, has not proved very stable, nor has it attracted other Muslims.

The fevered situation in the contemporary Near East complicates the task of understanding the heirs of Islâmic civilization. Obviously, ancient feuds and hatreds are far from dead. The clash of doctrine that arose from Muhammad's revelation, reinforced by centuries of warfare between Muslims and Christians, built up a wall of prejudice on both sides which has yet to show signs of crumbling.

Under such circumstances, historical study cannot by itself do much to diminish hostility; on the contrary it is often conducted in such a way as to inflame animosity. Yet if approached in a spirit of detachment, seeking to understand both sides of contemporary as well as of more ancient conflicts, study of the past can, perhaps, diminish ill will. Such study is also likely to make public and private action a little more effective than it can be when mutual ignorance as well as mutual dislike govern behavior. The editors of these readings hope that students will explore them in such a spirit, finding a special challenge in coming to grips with a cultural tradition that is both so close and so alien to our own.

Chicago, Illinois   W. H. M.
October 1972

Editorial Note

The texts in this volume have been reproduced exactly as they stand in the sources indicated except for (1) cuts made necessary for comprehensibility or by limitations of space (such cuts are indicated by ellipses); (2) the expansion of the symbol "Q" to "Qur'ân"; (3) the addition of short explanatory comments in brackets. Many important sources are not included, either because of space limitations or unavailability in English.

The editors have made no attempt to standardize spelling within the texts as between English and American usage or in the transliteration of foreign terms into English. An attempt has been made, however, to standardize (1) dating, deleting Muslim "Hijrî" dates (see Note on Muslim Chronology) in favor of Common Era dates unless otherwise specified; (2) the format of Qur'ân citation (Roman numerals for chapter, Arabic for verse); and (3) transliterations of Arabic words in the footnotes and headings, following the system employed by the *Journal of the Royal Asiatic Society.* It should be added that where the symbol "b." appears in a Muslim name, it indicates usually "ibn," "son of," and occasionally "bint," "daughter of."

The editors are responsible for the introductions and in general for the footnotes, which seek to place the various selections in historical context and make them more easily comprehensible to the non-specialist. In many instances, material provided by the translator has been a source of valuable information for the notes; notes reprinted verbatim (or changed only for consistency of dating or Qur'ân citation) are followed by "(Tr.)." Other

notes have been added to identify terms or explain unfamiliar
allusions, provide supplementary background information, call
attention to particular items, or point out similarities or con-
trasts between the passage at hand or some other passage or
source. Technical discussions and scholarly references have
been almost entirely omitted.

Note on Islâmic Chronology

The Muslim calendar year has twelve lunar months and lasts about 354 days; so for every thirty solar years, thirty-one lunar years elapse. The first Muslim year began July 16, 622, of the Common or Christian Era,* when the founder of the Muslim community, Muhammad, emigrated from his native town of Mecca to the nearby Yathrib (later to be known as Medina). This emigration was called the *hijra,* so a year of the Muslim calendar is referred to as A.H., after the *hijra.* The entire system of dating is called *hijrî* dating.

The sources used in this book often employ double dates, e.g., 31/652, the smaller being the *hijrî* year, the larger, the Common Era. Sometimes the *hijrî* date is linked to two Common Era years, e.g., 1387/1967-68, because the Muslim year 1387 ran from April 11, 1967, to March 31, 1968. Where possible in this volume, however, the editors have attempted to use only C.E. dates to avoid confusion. Though there is no rigid or generally accepted dynastic chronology for all of Islâmic history, it is common for scholars to divide the early history of the Muslim lands according to the following dynasties of caliphs (rulers of the Muslim community after Muhammad): "Rightly-Guided," 632-661; Umayyad, 661-750; 'Abbâsid, 750-1258. The lack of a central Islâmic political authority after the end of the caliphate in 1258 makes it impossible to use a single dynastic division of time to cover all Muslim lands.

* Because of the religious implications, Muslims as well as many scholars do not find it appropriate to use A.D. (in the year of our Lord) and B.C. (before Christ) when talking about Islâmic civilization. Many prefer to use C.E. to signify Common or Christian Era and B.C.E. to signify before the Common or Christian Era.

Note on Islâmic Transliteration
and Pronunciation

This book uses a symbol-equivalent transliteration system for Arabic with two exceptions: (1) common spellings like Mecca and Medina are left unchanged, and (2) we could not reproduce the five articulated and aspirated letters, hâ', sâd, dâd, tâ', zâ', so they are transliterated simply h, s, d, t, and z. Persian and Turkish words and names are generally spelled in their most common forms, e.g., Selîm rather than Salîm; if no common form exists the Arabic system has been used.

The transliteration systems of the original sources have been left intact, but the editors have brought headings, added words and phrases, and notes into conformity with the system described above.

The equivalents used in this book are as follows (pronunciation is similar to English unless otherwise indicated):

hamza	'	glottal stop, as in "*a a*pple"
âlif	a	
bâ'	b	
tâ'	t	
thâ'	th	as in "*th*ink"
jîm	j	
hâ'	h	(aspirated)
khâ'	kh	as in German "na*ch*t"
dâl	d	
dhâl	dh	as in "*th*is"
râ'	r	
zay	z	
sîn	s	
shîn	sh	as in "*sh*oe"

sâd	s	(articulated)
dâd	d	(articulated)
tâ'	t	(articulated)
zâ'	z	(articulated)
'ayn	'	a consonant similar to *hamza*
ghayn	gh	as in throaty French "r"
fâ'	f	
qâf	q	as "k," not "kw"
kâf	k	
lâm	l	
mîm	m	
hâ'	h	
wâw	w	
yâ'	y	
alif yâ'	ai	(diphthong)
alif wâw	aw	(diphthong)
tâ' marbûta	a	

Unmarked (short) vowels are

    a as in had
    i as in sit
    u as in fruit
    s as in set
    o as in auto

Vowels with a circumflex above are long, i.e., held longer by the voice:

    â as in aah
    î as in eee
    û as in ooo

These vowels should be lightly stressed, as should be syllables before double consonants, as in Mecca, where the first syllable is stressed.

Contents

I   THE FORMATIVE YEARS   600-750

Introduction   3
Pre-Islâmic Arabia   5
    Thâbit: *The Death of the Knight Rabia, Called
        Boy Longlocks*   6
    Khansâ: "A Sister's Grief"   8
    Ibn al-Kalbî: From *The Book of Idols*   9
Life of Muhammad   13
    Ibn Ishâq: From *Biography of the Messenger of God*   14
Revelation   27
    Selections from the Qur'ân   29
Conquest and Expansion   67
    Balâdhurî: From *Opening Up of the Lands*   68
Crisis and Compromise   75
    Tabarî: "The Death of 'Uthmân," from *The History
        of Prophets and Kings*   76
    Ziyâd ibn Abîhî: "Inaugural Speech"   79
    Hasan al-Basrî: Letter to 'Umar II   79

II   "THE GOLDEN AGE"   750-1000

Introduction   85
Life Styles   86
    Tanûkhî: From *Ruminations and Reminiscences*   86
Essays   110
    Jâhiz: From "The Merits of the Turks"
        and Other Essays   111
Law   134
    Shâfi'î: From *The Treatise*   136

History   142
    Tabarî: From *The History of Prophets and Kings*   143
Theology   151
    Ash'arî: From *The Elucidation of Islâm's Foundation*   152
Philosophy   166
    Farâbî: From *The Attainment of Happiness*   167
Poetry   171
    Mutanabbî: Four Poems   172
Abbâsid Decline   177
    Ibn Miskawaih: From *The Experiences of the Nations*   178

III   POLITICAL FRAGMENTATION AND
      CULTURAL FLORESCENCE   1000-1400

Introduction   183
Crusades   184
    Usâma: Memoirs   185
The New Mysticism: Theology   206
    Ghazâlî: From *That Which Delivers From Error*   207
The New Mysticism: Poetry   239
    From Rûmî: *Dîvân-i Shams-i Tabrîz*   241
Mongols   248
    Ibn al-Athîr: From *Great History*   249
    Juvainî: From *The History of the World Conqueror*   253
Expansion of Islâm   273
    Ibn Batûta: From *Travels*   274

IV   THE ERA OF THE THREE EMPIRES   1400-1800

Introduction   311
Ottoman Conquest of Constantinople   312
    Kritovoulos: From *History of Mehmed the Conqueror*   312
The Safavid Challenge   337
    Letters from Selîm and Ismâ'îl   338
Portraits of Three Monarchs   344
    I. The Ottoman Sulaymân   344
        Busbecq: From *The Turkish Letters*   345

II. The Mughal Akbar · 353
   Abû'l-Fazl: From *The Book of Akbar* · 354
III. The Safavid ʿAbbâs · 373
   Report of the Carmelite Mission · 373

V THE CRISIS OF MODERNIZATION
19th and 20th Centuries

Introduction · 395
The Plight of Islâm: Poetry · 396
   Iqbâl: From *Complaint and Answer* · 396
The Plight of Islâm: Prose · 407
   Hussein: From *The Stream of Days* · 407
   Hussein: From *The Future of Culture in Egypt* · 407
Revival · 423
   Afghânî: "Commentary on the Commentator" · 423
Nationalism: The Case of Turkey · 431
   Atatürk: From "Speech to the Assembly, October, 1924" · 432
Nationalism: The Case of Pakistan · 449
   From Jinnah: Presidential Address, December, 1938 · 450
      Speech Broadcast on Îd Day, 13th November, 1939 · 453
      Presidential Address, March, 1940 (?) · 457
Reform in the Hinterland · 461
   The Mahdî: From Letters and Proclamations · 463

I

The Formative Years
(600-750)

Introduction

The Islâmic religion was formed mainly in Arabia, and throughout its history the Muslim faith continued to bear a strong Arabic imprint. Most of what we know about Arabia in the time of Muhammad (*ca.* 572-632) is derived from investigations and traditions recorded by early generations of Muslims who felt a need to pass on what they knew or could find out about the Arabic past. This literature included stories about tribal struggles and customs from the pre-Islâmic period, but devoted most attention to the Prophet himself and to the circle of his friends and companions. Any scrap of information about these men seemed of special value to later generations of Muslims, for here could be found the purest and most authentic models of conduct pleasing to God.

The Arabia in which Muhammad was born was not an empty desert. Broad territories were inhabited by semi-nomadic Bedouin tribes, living by raising camels, sheep, and other livestock, and constantly divided into warring fragments. But there were also a number of important cities in Arabia, chief among them Mecca, where Muhammad began his life as a humble member of the dominant tribe, the Quraysh. Mecca was a center for the caravan trade that ran from south Arabia to the settled lands of Syria and Palestine. It was also an important religious center, where a pagan cult, presided over by the Quraysh, attracted reverence from Arabs of many different tribes. Through contacts with the civilized lands to the north many of the peoples of Arabia, like the merchants of Mecca, had also become familiar with the major monotheistic traditions, Christianity, Judaism, and Zoroastrianism.

Muhammad himself was a trader. When, at about forty years of age, he withdrew from his occupation and began to prophesy in the name of Allâh, few of his fellow Meccans were ready to believe his message. Muhammad's revelation, after all, required the abandonment of pagan rites and beliefs, thus threatening one of the bases of Mecca's prosperity. He attracted few followers until after 622, when, with a few companions, he left Mecca secretly by night and went to

3

Yâthrib (later known as Medîna), another oasis city some two hundred miles to the north, where rival tribes had invited him to act as arbiter among them.

Muhammad's emigration (in Arabic, *hijra*) from Mecca came to be counted a short time after his death as the start of the Muslim era, and not without reason, for in Medîna the Muslim community grew very rapidly. Muhammad's revelations provided guidelines for belief and conduct that transcended old tribal customs and duties, making cooperation possible, even among rival tribes. These guidelines were particularly appropriate for urban living and therefore met a pressing need among the Arabs of Muhammad's day. In addition, a series of successes in battle against the Meccans convinced Bedouin tribesmen that Allâh was on Muhammad's side, and in 630 Muhammad and his followers were able to return to Mecca in triumph. There they threw down the old idols and made the Ka'ba, where the idols had stood, the most holy shrine of the new faith. Soon all of Arabia united under Muhammad's leadership, and after his death the Muslims began massive raiding of the settled lands of Palestine and Syria.

Muhammad's death in 632 raised the difficult problem of choosing a suitable successor. At first, a rough consensus among the most important Muslims sufficed, and a series of splendid and surprising military victories kept morale among the Muslims high. Later, the principle of "hereditary" succession prevailed and the office of caliph ("successor" to the Prophet) was passed on in the houses of two Quraysh families, first the Umayyads, then the 'Abbâsids.

Having conquered Syria, Egypt, and Irâq (634-50), the Muslims, still organized as tribes, could live as conquerors in their new lands. But they sought to remain loyal to the rules of godly behavior Muhammad had revealed to their forefathers. This desire called for careful recording of Muhammad's inspired utterances, collected into the Qur'ân, in Muslim eyes the only holy book, for here were to be written the words of Allâh as delivered to Muhammad. It called also for researches into all aspects of the Prophet's life, researches which gradually amassed a large store of miscellaneous information about the society into which it had pleased God to call his Prophet.

Pre-Islâmic Arabia

The next three selections reflect different aspects of pre-Islâmic life in Arabia which continued to influence the Muslim community in its formative years. The first is a story of tribal rivalry and heroism. Such tales had been transmitted orally from generation to generation and tended to keep ancient grudges alive and vivid in each tribesman's memory. This account was written down by Thâbit, son of Jâbir of the Fahm clan, nicknamed "The Man with Mischief under his Arm." Nothing is known of his life, but it seems fairly clear that he shared most of the values that inspired the warriors whose violent deeds he recorded. Part of the secret of Islâm's early victories lay in the ability of Muhammad and his successors to turn the Arabs' warring skills against an outside foe and at the same time maintain peace among the tribes themselves.

The second selection is a sample of Arabic poetry, composed by a woman named Khansâ. Living in the time of Muhammad, she had accepted Islâm. The Prophet in turn expressed admiration for her poetry, even though it was the fruit of a long tradition of oral composition unaffected by the new revelation he had brought. After Muhammad's time this oral tradition gradually dried up, but for many generations men continued to recite and admire the old verses. Eventually some were written down, and they have been preserved to the present.

The third selection describes the pagan religious practices of Mecca in Muhammad's day. The author, Hishâm ibn Muhammad al-Kalbî (d. ca. 817), lived in Kûfa, Irâq, and used both written and oral sources for his book. Some scholars of his own age attacked him as a forger, but modern experts believe his information is generally accurate. The passages reproduced here deal with matters particularly important for later Muslims. The goddess Al-'Uzza, because she was mentioned in the Qur'ân, needed to be explained to later generations of pious inquirers. Similarly, the ritual of circumambulating the Ka'ba, which became a religious duty and a key ceremony for Muslims making the pilgrimage to Mecca, required comment. This account, like the preceding selections, allows us to see how Islâm adjusted itself to and purified pagan customs; or, conversely, how pre-Islâmic traditions survived within the new context created by Muhammad's revelation.

THÂBIT: THE DEATH OF THE KNIGHT RABIA, CALLED BOY LONGLOCKS

Rabia espied far way the stir of dust. Ride on fast! said he to the womenfolk with him; this is no friendly troop that follows us, I fear. Keep straight to the road; I will wait here till the dust clear and I spy who they be. If I see cause to fear aught for you women, I'll fall on them in yonder covert of trees, and draw them away from the road. We'll meet again at the Pass of Ghazal, or Usfan in Kadid; or if I do not meet you there, at least you will have won to our own country.

He mounted his mare, and rode back toward the dust. He shewed himself to the pursuers riding forth from the trees, as they were searching the tracks of his company; and when they saw him, they came on against him in a body, taking it for sure the women were beyond him. Now Longlocks was a famous archer; and he began to ply his arrows, till he had slain and disabled a good few men. So having given them something to do, he spurred his mare after the fleeing women; and when he came up with them bade press on faster still. But the clansmen of Sulaym followed him up; so he turned a second time to encounter them. And so he continued, urging on the women and turning to face his enemies, until his arrows all were spent. They won to the country of Kadid even as the sun was sinking.

But the horses black with sweat followed fast behind, and the riders in hate and rage, feverish for revenge. Then he turned once more, with spear and sword, and did great slaughter among them. But here Nubaysha son of Habib bore down on him and thrust him through with his lance. That thrust stopped him.

The two selections that follow are from *Muhammad's People: A Tale by Anthology*, by Eric Schroeder, Portland, Maine: The Bond Wheelwright Company, 1955, pp. 7-10. Reprinted by permission.

I have slain him! Nubaysha cried.

Thy mouth lies, Nubaysha, said Rabia. But Nubaysha smelt at the blade of his lance, and said: Thou art the liar; I surely smell the smell of thy vitals!

At this Rabia turned his mare, and galloped in spite of his wound until he came up with the women, in the mouth of the Pass of Ghazal. He cried to his mother: Drink! Give me to drink!

O my son! she answered him; if I give thee any drink, thou'lt die straightway, even here in this place; and we shall be taken. Endure then—we may escape them yet.

So: Bind up my wound, then, he said. She bound it with her veil; and while she worked he spoke a verse:

> Bind the binding on me fast!
> Ye lose a knight like burning gold:
> A hawk who drove a troop like birds,
> And stooped, and struck forehand and back.

His mother answered:

> We are of Malik's stock, and Tha'laba's,
> We are the world's tale without end.
> Our folk fall, man after man;
> Our life is loss, day after day.

Now go; and while thy strength lasts, smite!

So he turned back to face them once again, at the head of the pass, while the women hurried on with all the speed they might. Longlocks sat upright on his mare, barring the road; and when he felt his death coming on him, he stayed himself upon his spear; so he stood in the twilight. When the men of Sulaym descried him there, still sitting his mare, they flinched from another onset, and halted a long while, thinking not but that he was still a living man. At last Nubaysha, watching him steadily, said: His head droops on his neck! Yon's a dead man, I swear!

He bade a clansman of Khuza'a who rode with them shoot an arrow at the mare. The man shot; and the mare shied. Right forward on his face Boy Longlocks fell. So they came up and spoiled his body. But they were afraid to follow the women any further; for by this time they must be safe home, near the dwellings of their own people. A man of Sulaym rode close.

Thou foughtest for thy women in life and death both! he said; and so saying thrust the heel of his lance into Rabia's eye.

KHANSÂ: "A SISTER'S GRIEF"

The rising sun reminds me: Him!
I remember him every setting sun.

.   .   .   .

In the cleft of the rocks below Sala lies
One slain. That dripping blood's avenged. . . .

Many we were held on through noonheat;
Through nightfall still held on; at daybreak
Halted—keen-set as belted iron,
Blades once drawn that lightened like levin.
They were tasting sleep in sips, and nodding;
Down came Terror! and they were scattered.
We had our revenge: of the two kindreds
There got away what a pitiful few!

Though Clan Hudhayl broke his sword in the end,
How often he notched it on Hudhayl!
How many a dawn he fell on their camp,
And after good slaughter came plunder and spoil.

Hudhayl is burned! I burned them! I fearless!
I unwearied when they were weary—
Whose spear drank a deep first draught, and liked it,
And drank again, deep, of unfriendly blood.
I swore off wine till the deed should be done;
With no light labor I loosed that vow.
Reach me a cup at last, my cousin;
Fret for slain kin has wasted me.
We reached them a cup: the draught was Death;
The dregs Disgrace, Shame, and Dishonor!
Hyena laughs at slain Hudhayl!
Wolf grins at what's left of them;
Heavy-belly vultures flap their vans,
Trampling the dead, trying to fly,
Too full to fly!

Never shaykh[1] of us died quiet in his bed.
Never unavenged was blood of us shed.
Others may say, and we can say No.
None can naysay when we say So!

1. *Shaikh:* Arabic for elder, chief. Here "clan leader" is meant.

IBN AL-KALBÎ: FROM THE BOOK OF IDOLS

Al-'Uzza

They [Quraysh][1] then adopted al-'Uzza[1] as their goddess.
She is, in point of time, more recent than either Allât or
Manâh,[2] since I have heard that the Arabs named their children
after the latter two before they named them after al-'Uzza.

. . . .

. . . The Arabs as well as the Quraysh were wont to name
their children 'Abd-al-'Uzza. Furthermore al-'Uzza was the
greatest idol among the Quraysh. They used to journey to her,
offer gifts unto her, and seek her favours through sacrifice.

/We have been told that the Apostle of God once mentioned
al-'Uzza saying, "I have offered a white sheep to al-'Uzza, while
I was a follower of the religion of my people."

The Quraysh were wont to circumambulate the Ka'bah and
say:

> "By Allât and al-'Uzza,
>   And Manâh, the third idol besides,
>   Verily they are the most exalted females
>   Whose intercession is to be sought."

These were also called "the Daughters of Allah,"[3] and were

From *The Book of Idols*, by Hishâm ibn al-Kalbî, trans. from the Arabic by
Nahim Amin Faris. Copyright 1952 by Princeton University Press; Series
Princeton Oriental Studies, pp. 16-17, 19-20, 23-24, 27-29. Reprinted by per-
mission of Princeton University Press.

1. Muhammad's tribe.
2. Two other female goddesses discussed previously.
3. This use of "Allâh" to refer to a pre-Islâmic Arabian religious concept
suggests, as have some modern scholars, that a concept of God existed along-
side worship of the idols. Some have even theorized that the words "Allâh"
and "Allât" (the idol) are related to one another.

supposed to intercede before God. When the Apostle of God was
sent, God revealed unto him [concerning them] the following:

"Have you seen Allât and al-'Uzza, and Manâh the third
idol besides? What? Shall ye have male progeny and God
female? This indeed were an unfair partition! These are
mere names: ye and your fathers named them thus: God
hath not sent down any warranty in their regard."[4]

.   .   .   .

The Quraysh were wont to venerate her above all other idols.
For this reason Zayd ibn-'Amr ibn-Nufayl, who, during the
Jâhilîyah days,[5] had turned to the worship of God and re-
nounced that of al-'Uzza and of the other idols, said:

/ "I have renounced both Allât and al-'Uzza,
For thus would the brave and the robust do.
No more do I worship al-'Uzza and her two daughters,
Or visit the two idols[6] of the banu-Ghanm;
Nor do I journey to Hubal[7] and adore it,
Although it was our lord when I was young."

.   .   .   .

/Al-'Uzza continued to be venerated until God sent His
Prophet who ridiculed her together with the other idols and forbade her worship. At the same time a revelation concerning her
came down in the Koran.[8]

.   .   .   .

The Quraysh had also several idols in and around the Ka'bah.[9]
The greatest of these was Hubal. / It was, as I was told, of red
agate, in the form of a man with the right hand broken off. It
came into the possession of the Quraysh in this condition, and
they, therefore, made for it a hand of gold. . . .

4. Qur'ân LIII: 19-20. (Tr.)
5. "The Days of Ignorance," the phrase used by Muslims to refer to pre-
Islâmic times.
6. Unidentified. (Tr.)
7. See paragraph 2 below.
8. Qur'ân LIII: 19. (Tr.)
9. Ka'ba: The sacred small stone building in Mecca containing the Black
Stone. The Ka'ba was an object of pilgrimage before Islâm as well as after.

It stood inside the Ka'bah. In front of it were seven divination arrows. . . . On one of these arrows was written "pure," . . . and on another "consociated alien." . . . Whenever the lineage of a new-born was dobted, they would offer a sacrifice to it [Hubal] and then shuffle the arrows and throw them. If the arrows showed the word "pure," the child would be declared legitimate and the tribe would accept him. If, however, the arrows showed the words "consociated alien," the child would be declared illegitimate and the tribe would reject him. The third arrow was for divination concerning the dead, while the fourth was for divination concerning marriage. The purpose of the three remaining arrows has not been explained. Whenever they disagreed concerning something, or purposed to embark upon a journey, or undertake some project, they would proceed to it [Hubal] and shuffle the divination arrows before it. Whatever result they obtained they would follow and do accordingly.

It was before [Hubal] that 'Abd-al-Muttalib[10] shuffled the divination arrows [in order to find out which of his ten children he should sacrifice in fulfilment of a vow he had sworn], and the arrows pointed to his son 'Abdullâh, the father of the Prophet. Hubal was also the same idol which abu-Sufyân ibn-Harb[11] addressed when he emerged victorious after the battle of Uhud,[12] saying:

"Hubal, be thou exalted" (i.e. may thy religion triumph);

To which the Prophet replied:

"Allâh is more exalted and more majestic."

.   .   .   .

When, on the day he conquered Mecca [630], the Apostle of God appeared before the Ka'bah, he found the idols arrayed around it. Thereupon he started to pierce their eyes with the point of his arrow saying, "Truth is come and false-

10. Grandfather of the Prophet. . . . (Tr.)
11. One of "those whose hearts are reconciled" to Islâm, namely Arab chiefs with whom the Prophet made terms after the battle of Hunayn, 629, in order to secure their aid. . . . His son, Mu'âwiya, who later founded the Umayyad dynasty, was another. (Tr.)
12. In this battle, 625, the Meccans defeated Muhammad and his followers.

hood is vanished. Verily, falsehood is a thing that vanisheth."[13]
He then ordered that they be knocked down, after which they
were taken out and burned.

In this connection, Râshid ibn-'Abdullâh al-Sulami said:

"She asked me to speak, but I said, 'No.
Neither God nor Islam would approve our speech.
Hast thou not seen Muhammed and his men
On the day of victory, when the idols were demolished?
Then the light of God shone with all its brilliance,
And polytheism was submerged in a sea of darkness.' "

. . . .

[Abu-al-Mundhir] also said: Every family in Mecca had at
home an idol which they worshipped. Whenever one of them
purposed to set out on a journey, his last act before leaving the
house would be to touch the idol in hope of an auspicious journey; and on his return, the first thing he would do was to touch
it again in gratitude for a propitious return.

/ When God sent His Prophet, who came preaching the
Unity of God and calling for His worship alone without any
associate, [the Arabs] said, "Maketh he the god to be but one
god? A strange thing forsooth is this."[14] They had in mind the
idols.

The Arabs were passionately fond of worshipping idols. Some
of them took unto themselves a temple around which they centered their worship, while others adopted an idol to which they
offered their adoration. The person who was unable to build
himself a temple or adopt an idol would erect a stone in front of
the Sacred House or in front of any other temple which he
might prefer, and then circumambulate it in the same manner
in which he would circumambulate the Sacred House. The
Arabs called these stones baetyls. . . . Whenever these stones
resembled a living form they called them idols . . . and images. . . . The ace of circumambulating them they called
circumrotation. . . .

Whenever a traveler stopped at a place or station [in order

13. Qur'ân XVII: 83. (Tr.)
14. Qur'ân XXXVIII:4. (Tr.)

to rest or spend the night] he would select for himself four stones, pick out the finest among them and adopt it as his god, and use the remaining three as supports for his cooking-pot. On his departure he would leave them behind, and would do the same on his other stops.

The Arabs were wont to offer sacrifices before all these idols, baetyls, and stones. Nevertheless they were aware of the excellence and superiority of the Ka'bah, to which they went on pilgrimage and visitation. What they did on their travels was a perpetuation of what they did at the Ka'bah, because of their devotion to it.

Life of Muhammad

The commanding figure of Muhammad, the Prophet of God, began to attract curiosity during his lifetime, and after his death stories about him excited lively attention among Muslims. The author of *Biography of the Messenger of God*, Muhammad ibn Ishâq ibn Yasâr (d. *ca.* 768), was the first to gather stories about the Prophet into a coherent narrative, aimed at demonstrating Muhammad's right to rank as the last authentic prophet of God. To accomplish this purpose Ibn Ishâq traced the history of prophecy from Abraham on as preface to a compilation of everything he could ascertain as true about Muhammad's life and the events immediately after his death.

Ibn Ishâq was not himself of Arab descent, but like other converts from former Roman and Persian territory he steeped himself in Arabic literary traditions as part of his education in the faith. Hence his tales of Muhammad's battles echo pre-Islâmic literary forms, such as those sampled in our first selection. Another influence playing upon the author was the tendency to invent miraculous stories about Muhammad similar to stories Christians attributed to Christ and the saints. Our first selection, dealing with the Prophet's birth, reflects this tendency clearly.

Muslims usually resisted the temptation to make the Prophet superhuman, and the major criticism they leveled against Christians was that Christians mistakenly called the prophet Jesus the Son of God. Learned Muslims were always alert to prevent a similar corruption of the true faith as transmitted by Muhammad. This emphasis on the humanness of Muhammad is reflected in our second selection, which explains with circumstantial detail exactly how he was called to prophecy and how the words of Allâh reached him.

The final excerpt shows another aspect of Muhammad's role in the early Muslim community. As judge, administrator, and lawgiver he had to cope with family and tribal jealousies, expressed through rumor and backbiting. Holding the community together depended in no small measure on Muhammad's wisdom and restraint amid such pettiness, as is convincingly illustrated by this case.

IBN ISHÂQ: FROM BIOGRAPHY OF THE MESSENGER OF GOD

I

OF THE WOMAN WHO OFFERED HERSELF IN MARRIAGE TO 'ABDULLAH B. 'ABDU'L-MUTTALIB

Taking 'Abdullah by the hand Abdul'l-Muttalib[1] went away and they passed—so it is alleged—a woman . . . who was at the Ka'ba. When she looked at him she asked, "Where are you going Abdullah?" He replied, "With my father." She said, "If you will take me you can have as many camels as were sacrificed in your stead." "I am with my father and I cannot act against his wishes and leave him," he replied.

'Abdu'l-Muttalib brought him to . . . the leading man of B. Zuhra[2] in birth and honour, and he married him to his daughter Âmina, she being the most excellent woman among the Quraysh in birth and position at that time. . . .

Adapted from *The Life of Muhammad*, trans. from Ishâq's *Sîrat Rasûl Allâh* (*Biography of the Messenger of God*), with introduction and notes by A. Guillaume, Lahore: Oxford University Press, 1955, pp. 68-72, 104-7, 493-97. Reprinted by permission.
  1. Muhammad's father and grandfather, respectively.
  2. B. equals Banû, "sons of," meaning here a tribe.

It is alleged that 'Abdullah consummated his marriage immediately and his wife conceived the apostle of God. Then he left her presence and met the woman who had proposed to him. He asked her why she did not make the proposal that she made to him the day before; to which she replied that the light that was with him the day before had left him, and she no longer had need of him. She had heard from her brother Waraqa b. Naufal, who had been a Christian and studied the scriptures, that a prophet would arise among this people.

My father Ishâq b. Yasâr told me that he was told that 'Abdullah went in to a woman that he had beside Âmina d. Wahb when he had been working in clay and the marks of the clay were on him. She put him off when he made a suggestion to her because of the dirt that was on him. He then left her and washed and bathed himself, and as he made his way to Âmina he passed her and she invited him to come to her. He refused and went to Âmina who conceived Muhammad. When he passed the woman again he asked her if she wanted anything and she said "No! When you passed me there was a white blaze between your eyes and when I invited you you refused me and went in to Âmina, and she has taken it away."

It is alleged that that woman of his used to say that when he passed by her between his eyes there was a blaze like the blaze of a horse. She said: "I invited him hoping that that would be in me, but he refused me and went to Âmina and she conceived the apostle of God." So the apostle of God was the noblest of his people in birth and the greatest in honour both on his father's and his mother's side. God bless and preserve him!

WHAT WAS SAID TO ÂMINA WHEN SHE HAD CONCEIVED
THE APOSTLE

It is alleged in popular stories (and only God knows the truth) that Âmina d. Wahb, the mother of God's apostle, used to say when she was pregnant with God's apostle that a voice said to her, "You are pregnant with the lord of this people and when he is born say, 'I put him in the care of the One from the evil of every envier; then call him Muhammad.'" As she was pregnant with him she saw a light come forth from her by which she could see the castles of Busrâ in Syria. Shortly afterwards 'Abdullah the apostle's father died while his mother was still pregnant.

THE BIRTH OF THE APOSTLE AND HIS SUCKLING

The apostle was born on Monday, 12th Rabî'u'l-awwal, in the year of the elephant. . . .

. . . .

After his birth his mother sent to tell his grandfather 'Abdu'l-Muttalib that she had given birth to a boy and asked him to come and look at him. When he came she told him what she had seen when she conceived him and what was said to her and what she was ordered to call him. It is alleged that 'Abdu'l-Muttalib took him . . . in the . . . Ka'ba, where he stood and prayed to Allah thanking him for his gift. Then he brought him out and delivered him to his mother, and he tried to find foster-mothers for him.

. . . .

Jahm b. Abû Jahm the client of al-Hârith b. Hâtib al-Jumahî on the authority of 'Abdullah b. Ja'far b. Abû Tâlib or from one who told him it as from him, informed me[3] that Halîma the apostle's foster-mother used to say that she went forth from her country with her husband and little son whom she was nursing, among the women of her tribe, in search of other babies to nurse. This was a year of famine when they were destitute. She was riding a dusky she-donkey of hers with an old she-camel which did not yield a drop of milk. They could not sleep the whole night because of the weeping of her hungry child. She had no milk to give him, nor could their she-camel provide a morning draught, but we were hoping for rain and relief. "I rode upon my donkey which had kept back the other riders through its weakness and emaciation so that it was a nuisance to them. When we reached Mecca, we looked out for foster children, and the apostle of God was offered to everyone of us, and each

3. This series of authorities comprises an *isnâd*, the basic method used by early Islâmic historians to validate their information. The editors have simplified the use of *isnâd*s in this selection to ensure readability, but it is important to remember that authors like Ibn Ishâq might offer the reader several versions of an event under different *isnâd*s.

woman refused him when she was told he was an orphan,[4] because we hoped to get payment from the child's father. We said,
'An orphan! and what will his mother and grandfather do?', and
so we spurned him because of that. Every woman who came
with me got a suckling except me, and when we decided to depart I said to my husband: 'By God, I do not like the idea of
returning with my friends without a suckling; I will go and
take that orphan.' He replied, 'Do as you please; perhaps God
will bless us on his account.' So I went and took him for the sole
reason that I could not find anyone else. I took him back to my
baggage, and as soon as I put him in my bosom, my breasts over-
flowed with milk which he drank until he was satisfied, as also
did his foster-brother. Then both of them slept, whereas before
this we could not sleep with him. My husband got up and went
to the old she-camel and lo, her udders were full; he milked it
and he and I drank of her milk until we were completely satisfied, and we passed a happy night. In the morning my husband
said: 'Do you know, Halîma, you have taken a blessed creature?'
I said, 'By God, I hope so.' Then we set out and I was riding my
she-ass and carrying him with me, and she went at such a pace
that the other donkeys could not keep up so that my companions
said to me, 'Confound you! stop and wait for us. Isn't this the
donkey on which you started?' 'Certainly it is,' I said. They replied, 'By God, something extraordinary has happened.' Then
we came to our dwellings in the Banû Sa'd country and I do not
know a country more barren than that.

When we had him with us my flock used to yield milk in
abundance. We milked them and drank while other people had
not a drop, nor could they find anything in their animals' udders,
so that our people were saying to their shepherds, 'Woe to you!
send your flock to graze where the daughter of Abû Dhuayb's
shepherd goes.' Even so, their flocks came back hungry not yielding a drop of milk, while mine had milk in abundance. We
ceased not to recognize this bounty as coming from God for a
period of two years, when I weaned him. He was growing up as

4. The Qur'ân repeatedly insists on protecting the orphan: Muhammad, an
orphan himself, was very familiar with the kind of treatment orphans received in pre-Islâmic Arabia.

none of the other children grew and by the time he was two he was a well-made child. We brought him to his mother, though we were most anxious to keep him with us because of the blessing which he brought us. I said to her: 'I should like you to leave my little boy with me until he becomes a big boy, for I am afraid on his account of the pest in Mecca.' We persisted until she sent him back with us.

Some months after our return he and his brother were with our lambs behind the tents when his brother came running and said to us, 'Two men clothed in white have seized that Qurayshî brother of mine and thrown him down and opened up his belly, and are stirring it up.' We ran towards him and found him standing up with a livid face. We took hold of him and asked him what was the matter. He said, 'Two men in white raiment came and threw me down and opened up my belly and searched therein for I know not what.'[5] So we took him back to our tent.

His father said to me, 'I am afraid that this child has had a stroke, so take him back to his family before the result appears.' So we picked him up and took him to his mother who asked why we had brought him when I had been anxious for his welfare and desirous of keeping him with me. I said to her, 'God has let my son live so far and I have done my duty. I am afraid that ill will befall him, so I have brought him back to you as you wished.' She asked me what happened and gave me no peace until I told her. When she asked if I feared a demon possessed him, I replied that I did. She answered that no demon had any power over her son who had a great future before him, and then she told how when she was pregnant with him a light went out from her which illumined the castles of Busrâ in Syria, and that she had borne him with the least difficulty imaginable. When she bore him he put his hands on the ground lifting his head towards the heavens. 'Leave him then and go in peace,' she said."

Thaur b. Yazîd from a learned person who I think was Khâlid b. Ma'dân al Kalâ'î told me that some of the apostle's companions asked him to tell them about himself. He said: "I am what

5. Cf. Qur'ân XCIV:1. (Tr.)

Abraham my father prayed for and the good news of . . . Jesus. When my mother was carrying me she saw a light proceeding from her which showed her the castles of Syria. I was suckled among the B. Sa'd b. Bakr, and while I was with a brother of mine behind our tents shepherding the lambs, two men in white raiment came to me with a gold basin full of snow. Then they seized me and opened up my belly, extraced my heart and split it; then they extracted a black drop from it and threw it away; then they washed my heart and my belly with that snow until they had thoroughly cleaned them. Then one said to the other, weigh him against ten of his people; they did so and I outweighed them. Then they weighed me against a hundred and then a thousand, and I outweighed them. He said, 'Leave him alone, for by God, if you weighed him against all his people he would outweigh them.' "

The apostle of God used to say, There is no prophet but has shepherded a flock. When they say, "You, too, apostle of God?", he said "Yes."

II

THE PROPHET'S MISSION

When Muhammad the apostle of God reached the age of forty God sent him in compassion to mankind, "as an evangelist to all men."[6] Now God had made a covenant with every prophet whom he had sent before him that he should believe in him, testify to his truth and help him against his adversaries, and he required of them that they should transmit that to everyone who believed in them, and they carried out their obligations in that respect. God said to Muhammad, "When God made a covenant with the prophets (He said) this is the scripture and wisdom which I have given you, afterwards an apostle will come confirming what you know that you may believe in him and help him." He said, "Do you accept this and take up my burden?" i.e. the burden of my agreement which I have laid upon you. They said, "We accept it." He answered, "Then bear witness and I am a witness with you."[7] Thus God made a covenant with all

6. Qur'ân XXXIV: 27. (Tr.)
7. Qur'ân III:75. (Tr.)

the prophets that they should testify to his truth and help him
against his adversaries and they transmitted that obligation to
those who believed in them among the two monotheistic religions.

. . . .

. . . The apostle would pray in seclusion on Hirâ',[8] every year
for a month to practise *tahannuth* as was the custom of Quraysh
in heathen days. *Tahannuth* is religious devotion.

. . . .

Wahb b. Kaisân told me that 'Ubayd said to him: Every year
during that month the apostle would pray in seclusion and give
food to the poor that came to him. And when he completed the
month and returned from his seclusion, first of all before entering his house he would go to the Ka'ba[9] and walk round it seven
times or as often as it pleased God; then he would go back to his
house until in the year when God sent him, in the month of
Ramadân[10] in which God willed concerning him what He willed
of His grace, the apostle set forth to Hirâ' as was his wont, and
his family with him. When it was the night on which God honoured him with his mission and showed mercy on His servants
thereby, Gabriel brought him the command of God. "He came
to me," said the apostle of God, "while I was asleep, with a
coverlet of brocade whereon was some writing, and said, 'Read!'
I said, 'What shall I read?' He pressed me with it so tightly that
I thought it was death; then he let me go and said, 'Read!' I said,
'What shall I read?' He pressed me with it again so that I
thought it was death; then he let me go and said 'Read!' I said,
'What shall I read?' He pressed me with it the third time so that
I thought it was death and said 'Read!' I said, 'What then shall
I read?'—and this I said only to deliver myself from him, lest he
should do the same to me again. He said:

> 'Read in the name of thy Lord who created,
> Who created man of blood coagulated.

8. Hirâ': mountain near Mecca.
9. Stone building containing Meccan idols, including the Black Stone.
10. Ramadân: the ninth month of the Muslim calendar and the one set
aside in the Qur'ân for daylight fasting.

> Read! Thy Lord is the most beneficent,
> Who taught by the pen,
> Taught that which they knew not unto men.'[11]

So I read it, and he departed from me. And I awoke from my sleep, and it was as though these words were written on my heart. (T.[12] Now none of God's creatures was more hateful to me than an (ecstatic) poet or a man possessed: I could not even look at them. I thought, Woe is me poet or possessed—Never shall Quraysh say this of me! I will go to the top of the mountain and throw myself down that I may kill myself and gain rest. So I went forth to do so and then) when I was midway on the mountain, I heard a voice from heaven saying, 'O Muhammad! thou art the apostle of God and I am Gabriel.' I raised my head towards heaven to see (who was speaking), and lo, Gabriel in the form of a man with feet astride the horizon, saying, 'O Muhammad! thou art the apostle of God and I am Gabriel.' I stood gazing at him, (T. and that turned me from my purpose) moving neither forward nor backward; then I began to turn my face away from him, but towards whatever region of the sky I looked, I saw him as before.[13] And I continued standing there, neither advancing nor turning back, until Khadîja sent her messengers in search of me and they gained the high ground above Mecca and returned to her while I was standing in the same place; then he parted from me and I from him, returning to my family. And I came to Khadîja and sat by her thigh and drew close to her. She said, 'O Abû'l-Qâsim,[14] where hast thou been? By God, I sent my messengers in search of thee, and they reached the high ground above Mecca and returned to me.' (T. I said to her, 'Woe is me poet or possessed.' She said, 'I take refuge in God from that O Abû'l-Qâsim. God would not treat you thus since

11. Qur'ân XCVI:1-5. (Tr.) "Recite" would have been a better translation of the Arabic root "QR'"; Muhammad was being asked to "recite" after Gabriel, not to "read" something written.

12. T indicates variations in quotations from Ibn Ishâq found in the work of another historian, Tabarî (d. 923).

13. This reluctance to accept the Call to Prophecy is reminiscent of Moses to whom Muhammad compared himself in many ways.

14. The *kunya*, or "name of honor," of Muhammad. Khadîja: his first wife.

he knows your truthfulness, your great trustworthiness, your fine character, and your kindness. This cannot be, my dear. Perhaps you did see something.' 'Yes, I did,' I said.) Then I told her of what I had seen; and she said, 'Rejoice, O son of my uncle, and be of good heart. Verily, by Him in whose hand is Khadîja's soul, I have hope that thou wilt be the prophet of this people.' " Then she rose and gathered her garments about her and set forth to her cousin Waraqa b. Naufal b. Asad b. 'Abdu'l-'Uzzâ b. Qusayy, who had become a Christian and read the scriptures and learned from those that follow the Torah and the Gospel.[15] And when she related to him what the apostle of God told her he had seen and heard, Waraqa cried, "Holy! Holy! Verily by Him in whose hand is Waraqa's soul, if thou hast spoken to me the truth, O Khadîja, there hath come unto him the greatest Nâmûs . . . who came to Moses aforetime, and lo, he is the prophet of this people. Bid him be of good heart." So Khadîja returned to the apostle of God and told him what Waraqa had said. (T. and that calmed his fears somewhat.) And when the apostle of God had finished his period of seclusion and returned (to Mecca), in the first place he performed the circumambulation of the Ka'ba, as was his wont.[16] While he was doing it, Waraqa met him and said, "O son of my brother, tell men what thou hast seen and heard." The apostle told him, and Waraqa said, "Surely, by Him in whose hand is Waraqa's soul, thou art the prophet of this people. There hath come unto thee the greatest Nâmûs, who came unto Moses. Thou wilt be called a liar, and they will use thee despitefully and cast thee out and fight against thee. Verily, if I live to see that day, I will help God in such wise as He knoweth." Then he brought his head near to him and kissed his forehead; and the apostle went to his own house.

.   .   .   .

15. The religious composition of the Hijâz was rich and varied. As is apparent in the selections from the Qur'ân to follow, Muhammad (and many of his contemporaries) were familiar with Jewish and Christian scriptures.
16. This pre-Islâmic ritual was purified and adopted for Islâm by Muhammad. It became a well-known part of the pilgrimage to Mecca.

III

THE LIE THAT WAS UTTERED ON THE RAID OF B. AL-MUSTALIQ[17]

According to what a man I do not suspect told me from al-Zuhrî from 'Urwa from 'Â'isha[18] the apostle had gone forward on that journey of his until he was near Medina, 'Â'isha having been with him on the journey, when the liars spoke about her.

. . . .

. . . She said: "When the apostle intended to go on an expedition he cast lots between his wives which of them should accompany him. He did this on the occasion of the raid on B. al-Mustaliq and the lot fell on me, so the apostle took me out. The wives on these occasions used to eat light rations; meat did not fill them up so that they were heavy. When the camel was being saddled for me I used to sit in my howdah; then the men who saddled it for me would come and pick me up and take hold of the lower part of the howdah and lift it up and put it on the camel's back and fasten it with a rope. Then they would take hold of the camel's head and walk with it.

"When the apostle finished his journey on this occasion he started back and halted when he was near Medina and passed a part of the night there. Then he gave permission to start and the men moved off. I went out for a certain purpose having a string of Zafâr beads on my neck. When I had finished, it slipped from my neck without my knowledge, and when I returned to the camel I went feeling my neck for it but could not find it. Meanwhile the main body had already moved off. I went back to the place where I had been and looked for the necklace until I found it. The men who were saddling the camel for me came up to the place I had just left and having finished the saddling they took hold of the howdah thinking that I was in it as I normally was, picked it up and bound it on the camel, not

17. 626. This is the incident referred to in the Qur'ânic selection from Sûra al-Nûr (XXIV).
18. Al-Zuhrî and 'Urwa: Very early (third generation) Muslim authorities. 'Â'isha: Muhammad's youngest wife, one of the wives he took after Khadîja's death.

doubting that I was in it. Then they took the camel by the head and went off with it. I returned to the place and there was not a soul there. The men had gone. So I wrapped myself in my smock and then lay down where I was, knowing that if I were missed they would come back for me, and by Allah I had but just lain down when Safwân b. al-Mu'attal al-Sulamî passed me; he had fallen behind the main body for some purpose and had not spent the night with the troops. He saw my form and came and stood over me. He used to see me before the veil was prescribed for us,[19] so when he saw me he exclaimed in astonishment 'The apostle's wife' while I was wrapped in my garments. He asked me what had kept me behind but I did not speak to him. Then he brought up his camel and told me to ride it while he kept behind. So I rode it and he took the camel's head going forward quickly in search of the army, and by Allah we did not overtake them and I was not missed until the morning. The men had halted and when they were rested up came the man leading me and the liars spread their reports and the army was much disturbed. But by Allah I knew nothing about it.

"Then we came to Medina and immediately I became very ill and so heard nothing of the matter. The story had reached the apostle and my parents, yet they told me nothing of it though I missed the apostle's accustomed kindness to me. When I was ill he used to show compassion and kindness to me, but in this illness he did not and I missed his attentions. When he came in to see me when my mother was nursing me (740), all he said was, 'How is she?'[20] so that I was pained and asked him to let me be taken to my mother so that she could nurse me. 'Do what you like,' he said, and so I was taken to my mother, knowing nothing of what had happened until I recovered from my illness some twenty days later. Now we were an Arab people: we did not have those privies which foreigners have in their houses; we loathe and detest them. Our practice was to go out into the open

19. Muhammad veiled his women as befitting the wives of someone in his position, but the general practice of veiling and secluding women was not an Arab custom and came into vogue much later under different influences.
20. The form used indicates the plural and, to some extent, the speaker's indifference. (Tr.)

spaces of Medina. The women used to go out every night, and
one night I went out with Umm Mistah d. Abû Ruhm b. al-
Muttalib b. 'Abdu Manâf. Her mother was d. Sakhr b. 'Âmir b.
Ka'b b. Sa'd b. Taym aunt of Abû Bakr.[21] As she was walking
with me she stumbled over her gown and exclaimed, 'May Mistah stumble,' Mistah being the nickname of 'Auf.[22] I said, 'That
is a bad thing to say about one of the emigrants who fought at
Badr.' She replied, 'Haven't you heard the news, O daughter of
Abû Bakr?' and when I said that I had not heard she went on to
tell me of what the liars had said, and when I showed my astonishment she told me that all this really had happened. By Allah,
I was unable to do what I had to do and went back. I could not
stop crying until I thought that the weeping would burst my
liver.[23] I said to my mother, 'God forgive you! Men have spoken
ill of me (T. and you have known of it) and have not told me
a thing about it.' She replied 'My little daughter, don't let the
matter weigh on you. Seldom is there a beautiful woman married to a man who loves her but her rival wives gossip about her
and men do the same.'

"The apostle had got up and addressed the men, though I
knew nothing about it. After praising God he said: 'What do
certain men mean by worrying me about my family and saying
false things about them? By Allah, I know only good of them,
and they say these things of a man of whom I know naught but
good, who never enters a house of mine but in my company.'

. . . .

As for 'Alî[24] he said: 'Women are plentiful, and you can easily change one for another. Ask the slave girl, for she will tell
you the truth.' So the apostle called Burayra to ask her, and
'Alî got up and gave her a violent beating, saying, 'Tell the
apostle the truth,' to which she replied, 'I know only good of her.
The only fault I have to find with 'Â'isha is that when I am

21. I.e., 'Â'isha's great aunt.
22. 'Auf: relative of Abû Bakr, the first Caliph, and an early convert.
23. Arabic and Persian commonly use "liver" where "heart" would be appropriate in English.
24. 'Alî: son-in-law and early follower of Muhammad, later to become
fourth Caliph.

kneading dough and tell her to watch it she neglects it and falls asleep and the sheep . . . comes and eats it!'[25]

"Then the apostle came in to me. My parents and a woman of the Ansâr were with me and both of us were weeping. He sat down and after praising God he said, ' 'A'isha, you know what people say about you. Fear God and if you have done wrong as men say then repent towards God, for He accepts repentance from His slaves.' As he said this my tears ceased and I could not feel them. I waited for my parents to answer the apostle but they said nothing. By Allah I thought myself too insignificant for God to send down concerning me a Quran which could be read in the mosques and used in prayer, but I was hoping that the apostle would see something in a dream by which God would clear away the lie from me, because He knew my innocence, or that there would be some communication. As for a Quran coming down about me by Allah I thought far too little of myself for that. When I saw that my parents would not speak I asked them why, and they replied that they did not know what to answer, and by Allah I do not know a household which suffered as did the family of Abû Bakr in those days. When they remained silent my weeping broke out afresh and then I said: 'Never will I repent towards God of what you mention. By Allah, I know that if I were to confess what men say of me, God knowing that I am innocent of it, I should admit what did not happen; and if I denied what they said you would not believe me.' Then I racked my brains for the name of Jacob and could not remember it, so I said, 'I will say what the father of Joseph said: "My duty is to show becoming patience and God's aid is to be asked against what you describe." '[26]

"And, by God, the apostle had not moved from where he was sitting when there came over him from God what used to come over him and he was wrapped in his garment and a leather cushion was put under his head. As for me, when I saw this I felt no fear or alarm, for I knew that I was innocent and that God would not treat me unjustly. As for my parents, as soon as

25. The homeliness of Ibn Ishâq's *Sîra* is evident here and throughout and seems to correspond to the actual flavor of Muhammad's environment.
26. Qur'ân XII:18. (Tr.)

the apostle recovered I thought that they would die from fear
that confirmation would come from God of what men had said.
Then the apostle recovered and sat up and there fell from him
as it were drops of water on a winter day, and he began to wipe
the sweat from his brow, saying, "Good news, 'Â'isha! God has
sent down (word) about your innocence.' I said, 'Praise be to
God,' and he went out to the men and addressed them and recited to them what God had sent down concerning that. . . .[27]

"My father Ishâq b. Yasâr told me from some of the men of
B. al-Najjâr that the wife of Abû Ayyûb Khâlid b. Zayd said to
him, "Have you heard what people are saying about 'Â'isha?'
'Certainly, but it is a lie,' he said. 'Would you do such a thing?'[28]
She answered 'No, by Allah, I would not.' He said, 'Well,
'Â'isha is a better woman than you.' "

'Â'isha continued: When the Qur'ân came down with the
mention of those of the slanderers who repeated what the liars
had said, God said: "Those who bring the lie are a band among
you. Do not regard it as a bad thing for you; nay it is good for
you. Every man of them will get what he has earned from the
sin, and he who had the greater share therein will have a painful
punishment,"[29] meaning Hassân b. Thâbit and his companions
who said what they said.

27. Descriptions of how Muhammad's revelations actually took place are
rare.
28. I.e., what 'A'isha was accused of.
29. Qur'ân XXIV:11. (Tr.)

Revelation

The Qur'ân (literally "recitations") is the name given to the collection of Muhammad's inspired utterances. Muslims regard it as
the word of God. Others find it difficult to appreciate adequately,
for two reasons. First, the language of the Qur'ân is poetic, and
poetry, which depends for its full effect upon word music and the

multiple nuances of meaning, can never be translated fully. Second, the Qur'ân, compiled under the Caliph 'Uthmân (reigned 644-656), was designed to ensure authenticity and to facilitate memorization. But by placing the longest *sûra*s (chapters) first, the compilers of the Qur'ân more or less reversed the order in which the revelations had been received (in general the earlier the *sûra*, the shorter it is). Moreover, Muhammad's later revelations sometimes referred to previous ones, even revising them. Hence if read from beginning to end the Qur'ân abounds in repetitions and jumbles subjects in a way that beginners are bound to find confusing.

Three phases or stages of Muhammad's revelation can be distingushed. His earliest messages (represented, for example, by Sûras LXXIII, LXXV, LXXVI, LXXXI, LXXXII, LXXXIV, which follow) announced an impending Day of Judgment and Resurrection, at which time all men would be judged by God on the basis of what each had done while on earth. This vision of the human condition contradicted the tenets of Meccan paganism, which was based on propitiation of the gods through prayer and sacrifice.

After Muhammad's first messages failed to win more than a few converts among the people of Mecca, new revelations were forthcoming; they enumerated the signs of Allâh's wisdom and power and recited precedents from Jewish and Christian history to confirm the doctrines Muhammad preached. Abraham was identified as the first Muslim and the first prophet, and Muhammad identified himself as one of the succession of prophets, each of whom had delivered the same message to unbelieving mankind and each of whom had been misunderstood; the distortion of their messages had produced the errors and contradictions of existing Jewish, Christian, and pagan faiths. This second group of *sûra*s was also characterized by repeated encouragement to the faithful, as, for example, in Sûra VIII.

The third phase of Muhammad's revelation came after the emigration to Medîna, when the Prophet became head of a growing community. Revelations in this peri d sometimes dealt with everyday rules of behavior. A small body of lawgiving thus entered the Qur'ân, and appears especially in the longer *sûra*s.

In the early Muslim community, every word and phrase of the Qur'ân was enormously important, being God's own authentic utterance designed for man's salvation and support. As a guideline for everyday conduct, the Qur'ân was later used as the basis for the elaboration of codes of Sacred Law—the principal intellectual creation of the first Muslim centuries. Its other principal use was as a text for worship—to be recited in public gatherings and to be mem-

orized for personal guidance and religious instruction. In this capacity the Qur'ân proved supremely effective in binding together
Muslims everywhere. Mastering the Arabic language to grasp the
Qur'ân's meaning and learning it by heart became the necessary
first step of initiation into the nascent civilization of Islâm.

SELECTIONS FROM THE QUR'ÂN

LXXIII
Enwrapped

In the name of God, the Merciful, the Compassionate

O thou enwrapped in thy robes,
keep vigil the night, except a little
(a half of it, or diminsh a little,
or add a little), and chant the Koran
very distinctly.[1]
5   Behold, We shall cast upon thee a weighty word;
surely the first part of the night is heavier in
tread, more upright in speech,
surely in the day thou hast long business.
And remember the Name of thy Lord, and devote thyself
very devoutly.   [unto Him
Lord of the East and the West;
there is no god but He;
so take Him for a Guardian.
10 And bear thou patiently what they say,
and forsake them graciously.
Leave Me to those who cry lies,[2]

From *The Koran Interpreted*, trans. by Arthur J. Arberry, London: George
Allen and Unwin, Ltd., © 1955, vol. II: pp. 308-9, 313-17, 326-28, 331;
vol. I: pp. 197-206, 330-38, 82-83; vol. II: pp. 46-47, 50-52, 284-86; vol. I:
pp. 100-101. Reprinted by permission of The Macmillan Company and
George Allen and Unwin, Ltd.

1. The night vigil was an important part of early Muslim observance.
Muhammad emphasized it in his own behavior and it was practiced in particular by those with mystical leanings.

2. Though this is a high-numbered *sûra* in the standard 'Uthmânian arrangement, it belongs to the Meccan period when Muhammad's message was
being rebuffed by most of his fellow Quraysh.

those prosperous ones, and respite them a little,
for with Us there are fetters, and a furnace, and
food that chokes, and a painful chastisement,
upon the day when the earth and the mountains shall quake
and the mountains become a slipping heap of sand.

15   Surely We have sent unto you a Messenger
as a witness over you, even as We sent to
        Pharaoh a Messenger,
but Pharaoh rebelled against the Messenger,
        so We seized him remorselessly.
If therefore you disbelieve, how will you
guard yourselves aaginst a day that shall make
        the children grey-headed?
Whereby heaven shall be split, and its promise
        shall be performed.
        Surely this is a Reminder; so let
        him who will take unto his Lord
                a way.

Thy Lord knows that thou keepest vigil
nearly two-thirds of the night, or a half
of it, or a third of it, and a party of
those with thee; and God determines
the night and the day. He knows that you
will not number it, and He has turned
towards you. Therefore recite of the Koran
so much as is feasible. He knows that some
of you are sick, and others journeying
in the land, seeking the bounty of God,
and others fighting in the way of God. So
recite of it so much as is feasible.
And perform the prayer, and pay the alms,[3]
and lend to God a good loan. Whatever
good you shall forward to your souls'

3. Two of the five duties prescribed in the Qur'ân. The other three are fasting
during the month of Ramadân, pilgrimage to Mecca, and the profession of
faith.

account, you shall find it with God as
better, and mightier a wage. And ask
God's forgiveness; God is All-forgiving,
All-compassionate.

LXXV
The Resurrection
In the Name of God, the Merciful, the Compassionate

No! I swear by the Day of Resurrection.
No! I swear by the reproachful soul.
What, does man reckon We shall not gather his bones?
Yes indeed; We are able to shape again his fingers.
5   Nay, but man desires to continue on as a libertine,
asking, "When shall be the Day of Resurrection?"[4]

But when the sight is dazed
and the moon is eclipsed,
and the sun and moon are brought together,
10   upon that day man shall say, "Whither to flee?"
No indeed; not a refuge!
Upon that day the recourse shall be to thy Lord.
Upon that day man shall be told his former deeds and his
nay, man shall be a clear proof against himself,   [latter;
15   even though he offer his excuses.

Move not thy tongue with it
to hasten it;
Ours it is to gather it, and to recite it.
So, when We recite it, follow thou its recitation.
Then Ours it is to explain it.

20   No indeed; but you love the hasty world,
and leave be the Hereafter.

---

4. Acceptance of the Day of Resurrection and its implications for how life
should be lived is central to the Qur'ân's demands. After this *sûra*, there
follow some of the dramatic and graphic descriptions of the Day which
characterize Muhammad's early Call.

Upon that day faces shall be radiant,
gazing upon their Lord;
and upon that day faces shall be scowling,
25 thou mightiest think the Calamity has been wreaked on
[them.

No indeed; when it reaches the clavicles
and it is said, "Who is an enchanter?"
and he thinks that it is the parting
and leg is intertwined with leg,
upon that day unto thy Lord shall be the driving,

30 For he confirmed it not, and did not pray,
but he cried it lies, and he turned away,
then he went to his household arrogantly.

Nearer to thee and nearer
35 then nearer to thee and nearer!
What, does man reckon he shall be left to
roam at will?
Was he not a sperm-drop spilled?
Then he was a blood-clot, and He created and formed,
and he made of him two kinds, male and female.
40 What, is He not able to quicken the dead?

LXXVI
Man

In the Name of God, the Merciful, the Compassionate

Has there come on man a while of time
when he was a thing unremembered?

We created man of a sperm-drop, a mingling, trying him;
and We made him hearing, seeing.
Surely We guided him upon the way
whether he be thankful or unthankful.
Surely We have prepared for the unbelievers
chains, fetters, and a Blaze.
5 Surely the pious shall drink of a cup
whose mixture is camphor,
a fountain whereat drink the servants of God,

making it to gush forth plenteously.
They fulfil their vows, and fear a day whose evil is
upon the wing;
they give food, for the love of Him, to the needy,
the orphan, the captive:
"We feed you only for the Face of God;
we desire no recompense from you, no
thankfulness;
10   for we fear from our Lord a frowning day,
inauspicious."
So God has guarded them from the evil of
that day, and has procured them radiancy
and gladness,
and recompensed them for their patience
with a Garden, and silk;
therein they shall recline upon couches,
therein they shall see neither sun nor
bitter cold;
near them shall be its shades, and its clusters hung
meekly down,
15 . and there shall be passed around them vessels of
silver, and goblets of crystal,
crystal of silver that they have measured
very exactly.
And therein they shall be given to drink a cup whose
mixture is ginger,
therein a fountain whose name is called Salsabil.
Immortal youths shall go about them;
when thou seest them, thou supposest them
scattered pearls,
20   when thou seest them then thou seest bliss
and a great kingdom.
Upon them shall be green garments of silk
and brocade; they are adorned with
bracelets of silver, and their Lord shall
give them to drink a pure draught.
"Behold, this is a recompense for you, and
your striving is thanked."

Surely We have sent down the Koran on thee,
  a sending down;
so be thou patient under the judgment of thy Lord,
and obey not one of them, sinner or unbeliever.
25   And remember the Name of thy Lord
        at dawn and in the evening[5]
and part of the night; bow down before Him
and magnify Him through the long night.

Surely these men love the hasty world, and
  leave behind them a heavy day.
We created them, and We strengthened their
joints; and, when We will, We shall exchange
        their likes.

Surely this is a Reminder; so he
who will, takes unto his Lord
        a way.
30   But you will not unless God wills;
    surely God is ever All-knowing,
        All-wise.
For He admits into His mercy
whomsoever He will; as for the
evildoers, He has prepared for them
        a painful chastisement.

LXXXI
The Darkening
In the Name of God, the Merciful, the Compassionate

When the sun shall be darkened,
  when the stars shall be thrown down,
  when the mountains shall be set moving,
when the pregnant camels shall be neglected,
5   when the savage beasts shall be mustered,
    when the seas shall be set boiling,
    when the souls shall be coupled,

5. These are the only two prayers prescribed in the Qur'ân. The other three
came to be added in imitation of Muhammad's own practice.

when the buried infant shall be asked for what sin she was
10   when the scrolls shall be unrolled,   [slain,
when heaven shall be stripped off,
when Hell shall be set blazing,
when Paradise shall be brought nigh,
then shall a soul know what it has produced.

15   No! I swear by the slinkers,
the runners, the sinkers,
by the night swarming,
by the dawn sighing,
truly this is the word of a noble Messenger
20   having power, with the Lord of the Throne secure,
obeyed, moreover trusty.

Your companion is not possessed;
he truly saw him on the clear horizon;
he is not niggardly of the Unseen.[6]

25   And it is not the word of an accursed Satan;
where then are you going?

It is naught but a Reminder
unto all beings,
for whosoever of you who would go straight;
but will you shall not, unless God wills,
the Lord of all Being.

LXXXII
The Splitting
In the Name of God, the Merciful, the Compassionate

When heaven is split open,
when the stars are scattered,

---

6. This refers to Muhammad's initial encounter with Gabriel (see Ibn Ishâq's *Sîra*, page 23). Muhammad's fellow Quraysh at first charged him with being simply a madman rather than accepting him as a man blessed with revelation.

when the seas swarm over,
when the tombs are overthrown,
5   then a soul shall know its works, the former and the latter.

O Man! What deceived thee as to thy generous Lord
who created thee and shaped thee and wrought thee in
                                        ⸌ [symmetry
and composed thee after what form He would?

No indeed; but you cry lies to the Doom;
10   yet there are over you watchers
noble, writers
who know whatever you do.

Surely the pious shall be in bliss,
and the libertines shall be in a fiery furnace
15   roasting therein on the Day of Doom,
nor shall they ever be absent from it.

And what shall teach thee what is the Day of Doom?
Again, what shall teach thee what is the Day of Doom?
A day when no soul shall possess aught to succour another
                                        [soul;
that day the Command shall belong unto God.

LXXXIV
The Rending
In the Name of God, the Merciful, the Compassionate

When heaven is rent asunder
and gives ear to its Lord, and is fitly disposed;
when earth is stretched out
and casts forth what is in it, and voids itself,
5   and gives ear to its Lord, and is fitly disposed!

O Man! Thou art labouring unto thy Lord laboriously,
and thou shalt encounter Him.
Then as for him who is given his book in his right hand,

>   he shall surely receive an easy reckoning
>   and he will return to his family joyfully.
10   But as for him who is given his book behind his back,
>   he shall call for destruction
>   and he shall roast at a Blaze.
>   He once lived among his family joyfully;
>   he surely thought he would never revert
15   Yes indeed; his Lord had sight of him.

>   No! I swear by the twilight
>   and the night and what it envelops
>   and the moon when it is at the full,
>   you shall surely ride stage after stage.

20   Then what ails them, that they believe not,
>   and when the Koran is recited to them they do not bow?
>   Nay, but the unbelievers are crying lies,
>   and God knows very well what they are secreting.

>   So give them good tidings of a painful chastisement,
25   except those that believe, and do righteous deeds—
>   theirs shall be a wage unfailing.

VIII

The Spoils[7]

In the Name of God, the Merciful, the Compassionate
They will question thee concerning
the spoils. Say: "The spoils belong to
God and the Messenger; so fear you God,
and set things right between you, and
obey you God and His Messenger,
     if you are believers."
Those only are believers who, when God
is mentioned, their hearts quake, and

---

7. This is a low-numbered *sûra*, but actually dates from after the *Hijra* and specifically from after the battle of Badr (624) in which Muhammad won an important military victory over the Meccans.

when His signs are recited to them, it
increases them in faith, and in their Lord
     they put their trust,
those who perform the prayer, and expend of
     what We have provided them,
those in truth are the believers; they have
degrees with their Lord, and forgiveness,
     and generous provision.

5   As thy Lord brought thee forth from thy house
with the truth, and a part of the believers
     were averse to it,
disputing with thee concerning the truth
after it had become clear, as though
they were being driven into death with
     their eyes wide open.
And when God promised you one of the two
parties should be yours, and you were wishing
that the one not accoutred should be yours;
but God was desiring to verify the truth
by His words, and to cut off the unbelievers
     to the last remnant,
and that He might verify the truth and
prove untrue the untrue, though the sinners
     were averse to it.
When you were calling upon your Lord for
succour, and He answered you, "I shall
reinforce you with a thousand angels
     riding behind you."[8]

10   God wrought this not, save as good tidings
and that your hearts thereby might be at rest;
help comes only from God; surely God is
     All-mighty, All-wise.
When He was causing slumber to overcome you
as a security from Him, and sending

8. This passage and what follows it assert the presence of divine aid during
the flight to Medîna and the subsequent battle of Badr.

down on you water from heaven, to purify
you thereby, and to put away
from you the defilement of Satan,
and to strengthen your hearts, and to
    confirm your feet.
When thy Lord was revealing to the angels,
"I am with you; so confirm the believers.
I shall cast into the unbelievers' hearts
terror; so smite above the necks, and smite
    every finger of them!"
That, because they had made a breach
with God and with His Messenger; and
whosoever makes a breach with God and with
His Messenger, surely God is terrible
    in retribution.
That for you; therefore taste it; and
that the chastisement of the Fire is
    for the unbelievers.

15   O believers, when you encounter
the unbelievers marching to battle, turn
    not your backs to them.
Whoso turns his back that day to them,
unless withdrawing to fight again
or removing to join another host,
he is laden with the burden of God's
anger, and his refuge is Gehenna—
    an evil homecoming!

You did not slay them, but God slew them;
and when thou threwest, it was not
thyself that threw, but God threw, and

that He might confer on the believers
a fair benefit; surely God is
    All-hearing, All-knowing.
That for you; and that God weakens the
    unbelievers' guile.

If victory you are seeking, victory
has already come upon you; and if
you give over, it is better for you.
But if you return, We shall return,
and your host will avail you nothing
though it be numerous; and that God is
    with the believers.

20   O believers, obey God and His Messenger,
and do not turn away from Him, even
    as you are listening;
and be not as those who say, "We hear,"
    and they hear not.
Surely the worst of beasts in God's sight
are those that are deaf and dumb and
    do not understand.
If God had known of any good in them
He would have made them hear; and if
He had made them hear, they would have turned
    away, swerving aside.
O believers, respond to God and the Messenger
when He calls you unto that which will
give you life; and know that God stands
between a man and his heart, and that to Him
    you shall be mustered.

25   And fear a trial which shall surely not
smite in particular the evildoers
among you; and know that God is terrible
    in retribution.
And remember when you were few and
abased in the land, and were fearful
that the people would snatch you away;
but He gave you refuge, and confirmed you
with His help, and provided you
with the good things, that haply
    you might be thankful.
O believers, betray not God and the

Messenger, and betray not your trusts
    and that wittingly;
and know that your wealth and your children
are a trial, and that with God is
    a mighty wage.
O believers, if you fear God, He will assign
you a salvation, and acquit you of your
evil deeds, and forgive you; and God is
    of bounty abounding.

30   And when the unbelievers were devising
against thee, to confine thee, or slay thee,
or to expel thee, and were devising,
and God was devising; and God is
    the best of devisers.[9]
And when Our signs were being recited to
them, they said, "We have already heard;
if we wished, we could say the like of
this; this is naught but the fairy-tales
    of the ancients."
And when they said, "O God, if this be
indeed the truth from Thee, then rain down
upon us stones out of heaven, or bring us
    a painful chastisement."
But God would never chastise them, with thee
among them; God would never chastise them as
    they begged forgiveness.
But what have they now, that God should
not chastise them, when they are barring from
the Holy Mosque, not being its protectors?
Its only protectors are the godfearing; but
    most of them know not.[10]
And their prayer at the House is nothing
but a whistling and a clapping of hands—

9. The Meccans allegedly carried out an unsuccessful assassination attempt against Muhammad the night he fled to Medîna. Muhammad had learned of the plan and arranged for someone else to be in his bed.
10. I.e., the Ka'ba in Mecca.

therefore taste you now the chastisement
    for your unbelief!
35 The unbelievers expend their wealth
to bar from God's way, and still they will
expend it, till it is an anguish for them,
    then be overthrown,
and the unbelievers will be mustered
    into Gehenna,
that God may distinguish the corrupt
from the good, and place the corrupt
one upon another, and so heap them up
all together, and put them in Gehenna;
    those are the losers.

Say to the unbelievers, if they give over
He will forgive them what is past; but
if they return, the wont of the ancients
    is already gone!
40 Fight them, till there is no persecution
and the religion is God's entirely;
then if they give over, surely God sees
    the things they do;
but if they turn away, know that God is
your Protector—an excellent Protector,
    an excellent Helper!

Know that, whatever booty you take, the
fifth of it is God's, and the Messenger's,
and the near kinsman's, and the orphans',
and for the needy, and the traveller,
if you believe in God and that We
sent down upon Our servant on the day
of salvation, the day the two hosts
encountered; and God is powerful
    over everything;
when you were on the nearer bank, and they
were on the farther bank, and the cavalcade
was below you; and had you made tryst

together, you would have surely failed
the tryst; but that God might determine a
    matter that was done,
that whosoever perished might perish
by a clear sign, and by a clear sign
he might live who lived; and surely God is
    All-hearing, All-knowing.

45 When God showed thee them in thy dream
as few; and had He shown them as many
you would have lost heart, and quarrelled
about the matter; but God saved; He knows
    the thoughts in the breasts.
When God showed you them in your eyes as
few, when you encountered, and made you
few in their eyes, that God might determine
a matter that was done; and unto God all
    matters are returned.

O believers, whensoever you
encounter a host, then stand firm, and
remember God frequently; haply
    so you will prosper.
And obey God, and His Messenger,
and do not quarrel together, and
so lose heart, and your power depart;
and be patient; surely God is
    with the patient.
Be not as those who went forth from
their habitations swaggering boastfully
to show off to men, and barring
from God's way; and God encompasses
    the things they do.

50 And when Satan decked out their deeds
fair to them, and said, "Today no man
shall overcome you, for I shall be
your neighbour." But when the two hosts
sighted each other, he withdrew upon
his heels, saying, "I am quit of you;

for I see what you do not see.
I fear God; and God is terrible
    in retribution."

When the hypocrites, and those in whose
hearts was sickness, said, "Their religion
has deluded them"; but whosoever
puts his trust in God, surely God is
    All-mighty, All-wise.
If thou couldst only see when the angels
take the unbelievers, beating their faces
and their backs: "Taste the chastisement
    of the burning—
that, for what your hands have forwarded,
and for that God is never unjust
    unto His servants."
Like Pharaoh's folk, and the people before him,
who disbelieved in God's signs; God seized them
because of their sins; God is strong, terrible
    in retribution.
55 That is because God would never change His favour
that He conferred on a people until they changed
what was within themselves; and that God is
    All-hearing, All-knowing.
Like Pharaoh's folk, and the people before him,
who cried lies to the signs of their Lord,
so We destroyed them because of their sins,
and We drowned the folk of Pharaoh; and
    all were evildoers.[11]

Surely the worst of beasts in God's sight
are the unbelievers, who will not believe,
those of them with whom thou hast made compact
then they break their compact every time,
    not being godfearing.

11. Throughout the Qur'ân, Old and New Testament stories—or the version of them Muhammad was acquainted with—are reworked to express his message. Moses' experience with Pharaoh is a favorite prototype.

So, if thou comest upon them anywhere
in the war, deal with them in such wise
as to scatter the ones behind them; haply
    they will remember.

60 And if thou fearest treachery any way
at the hands of a people, dissolve it
with them equally; surely God loves
    not the treacherous.

And thou art not to suppose that they who
disbelieve have outstripped Me; they cannot
    frustrate My will.

Make ready for them whatever force and
strings of horses you can, to terrify thereby
the enemy of God and your enemy, and others
besides them that you know not; God knows them.
And whatsoever you expend in the way
of God shall be repaid you in full;
    you will not be wronged.

And if they incline to peace, do thou incline
to it; and put thy trust in God; He is
    the All-hearing, the All-knowing.

And if they desire to trick thee, God is
sufficient for thee; He has confirmed thee
with His help, and with the believers, and
brought their hearts together. Hadst thou
expended all that is in the earth, thou couldst
not have brought their hearts together; but
God brought their hearts together; surely He is
    All-mighty, All-wise.

65 O Prophet, God suffices thee, and the believers
    who follow thee.

O Prophet, urge on the believers to fight.
If there be twenty of you, patient men,
they will overcome two hundred; if there be
a hundred of you, they will overcome
a thousand unbelievers, for they are a people
    who understand not.

Now God has lightened it for you, knowing

that there is weakness in you. If there be
a hundred of you, patient men, they will
overcome two hundred; if there be of you
a thousand, they will overcome two thousand
by the leave of God; God is with the patient.

It is not for any Prophet to have prisoners
until he make wide slaughter in the land.
You desire the chance goods of the present world,
and God desires the world to come; and God is
      All-mighty, All-wise.
Had it not been for a prior prescription from
God, there had afflicted you, for what you took,
      a mighty chastisement.

70   Eat of what you have taken as booty, such as
is lawful and good; and fear you God; surely
God is All-forgiving, All-compassionate.

O Prophet, say to the prisoners in your hands:
"If God knows of any good in your hearts
He will give you better than what has been taken
from you, and He will forgive you; surely
God is All-forgiving, All-compassionate."

And if they desire treachery against thee,
they have tricked God before; but He has
given thee power over them; and God is
      All-knowing, All-wise.

Those who believe, and have emigrated
and struggled with their possessions
and their selves in the way of God,
and those who have given refuge and help—
those are friends one of another.
And those who believe, but have not
emigrated—you have no duty of friendship
towards them till they emigrate; yet if
they ask you for help, for religion's sake,

it is your duty to help them, except
against a people between whom and you
there is a compact; and God sees
    the things you do.
As for the unbelievers, they are friends
one of another. Unless you do this,
there will be persecution in the land
    and great corruption.
75   And those who believe, and have emigrated
and struggled in the way of God.
those who have given refuge and help—
those in truth are the believers,
and theirs shall be forgiveness
    and generous provision.
And those who have believed afterwards
and emigrated, and struggled with you—
they belong to you; but those related
by blood are nearer to one another
in the Book of God; surely God has knowledge
    of everything.

XIX
Mary

In the Name of God, the Merciful, the Compassionate

Kaf Ha Ya Ain Sad

The mention of thy Lord's mercy
unto His servant Zachariah;
when he called upon his Lord
    secretly
saying, "O my Lord, behold
the bones within me are feeble
and my head is all aflame with
    hoariness.
And in calling on Thee, my Lord,
I have never been hitherto
    unprosperous.
5   And now I fear my kinsfolk

after I am gone; and my wife
is barren. So give me, from Thee,
    a kinsman
who shall be my inheritor
and the inheritor of the House
of Jacob; and make him, my Lord,
    well-pleasing."
"O Zachariah, We give thee
good tidings of a boy, whose name
    is John.
No namesake have We given him
    aforetime."
He said, "O my Lord, how
shall I have a son, seeing
my wife is barren, and I
have attained to the declining
    of old age?"

10   Said He, "So it shall be; thy
Lord says ,"Easy is that for
Me, seeing that I created
thee aforetime, when thou wast
    nothing.' "
He said, "Lord, appoint to me
some sign." Said He, "Thy sign
is that thou shalt not speak to
men, though being without fault,
    three nights."
So he came forth unto his
people from the Sanctuary,
then he made signal to them,
"Give you glory at dawn and
    evening."
"O John, take the Book forcefully";
and We gave him judgment, yet a
    little child,
and a tenderness from Us,
and purity; and he was
godfearing, and cherishing

his parents, not arrogant,
    rebellious.
15   "Peace be upon him, the day
he was born, and the day he
dies, and the day he is raised
    up alive!"

And mention in the Book Mary
when she withdrew from her people
    to an eastern place,
and she took a veil apart from them;
then We sent unto her Our Spirit
that presented himself to her
    a man without fault.
She said, "I take refuge in
the All-merciful from thee!
    If thou fearest God. . . ."
He said, "I am but a messenger
come from thy Lord, to give thee
    a boy most pure."
20   She said, "How shall I have a son
whom no mortal has touched, neither
    have I been unchaste?"
He said, "Even so they Lord has said:
"Easy is that for Me; and that We
may appoint him a sign unto men
and a mercy from Us; it is
    a thing decreed.' "
So she conceived him, and withdrew with him
    to a distant place.
And the birthpangs surprised her by
the trunk of the palm-tree. She said,
"Would I had died ere this, and become
    a thing forgotten!"
But the one that was below her
called to her, "Nay, do not sorrow;
see, thy Lord has set below thee
    a rivulet.

25   Shake also to thee the palm-trunk,
and there shall come tumbling upon thee
      dates fresh and ripe.
Eat therefore, and drink, and be
comforted; and if thou shouldst see
      any mortal,
say, "I have vowed to the All-merciful
a fast, and today I will not speak
      to any man.' "
Then she brought the child to her folk
carrying him; and they said,
"Mary, thou hast surely committed
      a monstrous thing!
Sister of Aaron, thy father was not
a wicked man, nor was thy mother
      a woman unchaste."

30   Mary pointed to the child then;
but they said, "How shall we speak
to one who is still in the cradle,
      a little child?"
He said, "Lo, I am God's servant;
God has given me the Book, and
      made me a Prophet.
Blessed He has made me, wherever
I may be; and He has enjoined me
to pray, and to give the alms, so
      long as I live,
and likewise to cherish my mother;
He has not made me arrogant,
      unprosperous.
Peace be upon me, the day I was born,
and the day I die, and the day I am
      raised up alive!"

35   That is Jesus, son of Mary,
in word of truth, concerning which
      they are doubting.
It is not for God to take a son
unto Him. Glory be to Him! When He

decrees a thing, He but says to it
   "Be," and it is.
Surely God is my Lord, and your
Lord; so serve you Him. This is
   a straight path.

But the parties have fallen into variance among themselves;
then woe to those who disbelieve for the scene of a dreadful
                                         [day.
How well they will hear and see on the day they come to Us!
But the evildoers even today are in error manifest.
40 Warn thou them of the day of anguish, when the matter
shall be determined, and they yet heedless and unbelieving.
Surely We shall inherit the earth and all that are upon it,
and unto Us they shall be returned.[12]

And mention in the Book Abraham;
surely he was a true man, a Prophet.
When he said to his father, "Father,
why worshippest thou that which neither
hears nor sees, nor avails thee anything?
Father, there has come to me knowledge
such as came not to thee; so follow me,
and I will guide thee on a level path.
45 Father, serve not Satan; surely Satan
is a rebel against the All-merciful.
Father, I fear that some chastisement
from the All-merciful will smite thee,
so that thou becomest a friend to Satan."
Said he, "What, art thou shrinking
from my gods, Abraham? Surely, if thou
givest not over, I shall stone thee;
so forsake me now for some while."
He said, "Peace be upon thee!
I will ask my Lord to forgive thee;

12. This passage refers to the claim of Islâm to set the other monotheistic
religions back on the right track, one of their "errors" having been the at-
tribution of divinity to Jesus.

surely He is ever gracious to me.
Now I will go apart from you
and that you call upon, apart from
God; I will call upon my Lord,
and haply I shall not be, in calling
upon my Lord, unprosperous."
50   So, when he went apart from them
and that they were serving, apart
from God, We gave him Isaac and
Jacob, and each We made a Prophet;
and We gave them of Our mercy,
and We appointed unto them
a tongue of truthfulness, sublime.

And mention in the Book Moses;
he was devoted, and he was
    a Messenger, a Prophet.
We called to him from the right side
of the Mount, and We brought him
    near in communion.
And We gave him his brother Aaron, of
    Our mercy, a Prophet.

55   And mention in the Book Ishmael;
he was true to his promise, and he was
    a Messenger, a Prophet.
He bade his people to pray
and to give the alms, and he was
    pleasing to his Lord.

And mention in the Book Idris;[13] he was
    a true man, a Prophet.
We raised him up to a high place.

These are they whom God has blessed
    among the Prophets
of the seed of Adam, and of those

13. Idrîs = Enoch, one of the apocryphal books of the Old Testament.

We bore with Noah, and of the seed of
    Abraham and Israel,
and of those We guided and chose.
When the signs of the All-merciful were
    recited to them,
they fell down prostrate, weeping.

60   Then there succeeded after them a succession
who wasted the prayer, and followed lusts; so
    they shall encounter error
save him who repents, and believes, and
does a righteous deed; those—they shall
enter Paradise, and they shall not
    be wronged anything;
Gardens of Eden that the All-merciful
promised His servants in the Unseen; His
    promise is ever performed.
There they shall hear no idle talk, but only
"Peace." There they shall have their provision
    at dawn and evening.
That is Paradise which We shall give
as an inheritance to those of Our servants
    who are godfearing.

65 We came not down, save at the commandment of thy Lord.
    To Him belongs
all that is before us, and all that is behind us, and all
    between that.
    And thy Lord is never forgetful,
Lord He of the heavens and earth and all that is between
                   [them.
    So serve Him,
and be thou patient in His service; knowest thou any that
    can be named with His Name?

Man says, "What, when I am dead
shall I then be brought forth alive?"
Will not man remember that We created
him aforetime, when he was nothing?

Now, by thy Lord, We shall surely muster them, and the
[Satans,

then We shall parade them about Gehenna hobbling on their
[knees.

70   Then We Shall pluck forth from every party whichever of
[them

was the most hardened in disdain of the All-merciful;

then We shall know very well those most deserving to burn
[there.

Not one of you there is, but he
shall go down to it; that for thy Lord
is a thing decreed, determined.
Then We shall deliver those that were
godfearing; and the evildoers We shall
leave there, hobbling on their knees.
When Our signs are recited to them
as clear signs, the unbelievers say
to the believers, "Which of the two parties
is better in station, fairer in assembly?"
75   And how many a generation We
destroyed before them, who were fairer
in furnishing and outward show!
Say: "Whosoever is in error, let the
All-merciful prolong his term for him!
Till, when they see that they were threatened,
whether the chastisement, or the Hour,
then they shall surely know who is worse
in place, and who is weaker in hosts."

And God shall increase those who were guided in guidance;
and the abiding things, the deeds of righteousness,
are better with thy Lord in reward, and better in return.

80   Hast thou seen him who disbelieves
in Our signs[14] and says, "Assuredly

14. The "signs" are not "miracles" in the usual sense but rather naturally
existing evidences of God's power and wisdom, such as the wonders of nature. The only miracle was the Qur'ân itself.

I shall be given wealth and children?"
What, has he observed the Unseen, or
taken a covenant with the All-merciful?
No, indeed! We shall assuredly
write down all that he says, and We shall
prolong for him the chastisement;
and We shall inherit from him that
he says, and he shall come to Us alone.

And they have taken to them other gods
apart from God, that they might be for them
     a might.
85   No, indeed! They shall deny their
service, and they shall be against them
     pitted.
Hast thou not seen how We sent the
Satans against the unbelievers, to
     prick them?
So hasten thou not against them;
We are only numbering for them a
     number.
On the day that We shall muster
the godfearing to the All-merciful
     with pomp
and drive the evildoers into Gehenna
     herding,
90   having no power of intercession, save
those who have taken with the All-merciful
     covenant.

And they say, "The All-merciful
has taken unto Himself a son."
You have indeed advanced something
     hideous!
The heavens are wellnigh rent of it
and the earth split asunder, and
the mountains wellnigh fall down
     crashing
for that they have attributed

to the All-merciful a son; and it
behoves not the All-merciful to take
            a son.

None is there in the heavens and earth
but he comes to the All-merciful
as a servant; He has indeed counted
them, and He has numbered them
            exactly.
Every one of them shall come to Him
upon the Day of Resurrection, all
            alone.
Surely those who believe and do deeds
of righteousness—unto them
the All-merciful shall assign
            love.

95

Now We have made it easy by thy tongue
that thou mayest bear good tidings
thereby to the godfearing, and warn a people
            stubborn.
And how many a generation We
destroyed before them! Dost thou perceive
so much as one of them, or hear of them a
            whisper?

III
The House of Imran

.   .   .   .

Say: "People of the Book! Come now to a word
common between us and you, that we serve
none but God, and that we associate not
aught with Him, and do not some of us take
others as Lords, apart from God." And if
they turn their backs, say: "Bear witness that
we are Muslims."[15]

---

15. The Trinity was also considered one of the deviations of Christianity
from true and original monotheism.

People of the Book! Why do you dispute
concerning Abraham? The Torah was not sent
down, neither the Gospel, but after him. What,
    have you no reason?
Ha, you are the ones who dispute on what you
know; why then dispute you touching a matter
of which you know not anything? God knows,
    and you know not.
60   No; Abraham in truth was not a Jew,
neither a Christian; but he was a Muslim
and one pure of faith; certainly he was never
    of the idolaters.[16]
Surely the people standing closest to Abraham
are those who followed him, and this Prophet,
and those who believe; and God is the Protector
    of the believers.

.   .   .   .

XXIV
Light
In the Name of God, the Merciful, the Compassionate

A sura that We have sent down
and appointed; and We have sent down
in it signs, clear signs, that haply
    you will remember.[17]

The fornicatress and the fornicator—
scourge each one of them a hundred stripes,
and in the matter of God's religion
let no tenderness for them seize you

16. This assertion is critical to Islâm's claim to be returning to the primal
monotheism.
17. The event (626) which gave rise to these revelations was the slander of
'A'isha already narrated in the selections from Ibn Ishâq's *Sîra*. This *sûra*
is remarkable for its combination of mundane, almost sordid rule-giving
(which is rare in the Qur'ân) with the Qur'ân's most sublime passage (verses
35 ff.), the sublimity itself emphasizing the holy purpose of the rules just
promulgated.

if you believe in God and the Last Day;
and let a party of the believers
        witness their chastisement.
The fornicator shall marry none but
a fornicatress or an idolatress.
and the fornicatress—none shall marry her
but a fornicator or an idolator;
that is forbidden to the believers.

And those who cast it up on women in
wedlock, and then bring not four witnesses,
scourge them with eighty stripes, and do not
accept any testimony of theirs ever; those—
        they are the ungodly,
5   save such as repent thereafter and
make amends; surely God is All-forgiving,
        All-compassionate.
And those who cast it up on their wives
having no witnesses except themselves,
the testimony of one of them shall be
to testify by God four times that he
        is of the truthful,
and a fifth time, that the curse of
God shall be upon him, if he should
        be of the liars.
It shall avert from her the chastisement
if she testify by God four times that he
        is of the liars,
and a fifth time, that the wrath of
God shall be upon her, if he should
        be of the truthful.

10   But for God's bounty to you and His mercy
and that God turns, and is All-wise—

Those who came with the slander are a
band of you; do not reckon it evil
for you; rather it is good for you.

Every man of them shall have the sin
that he has earned charged to him; and
whosoever of them took upon himself
the greater part of it, him there awaits
                a mighty chastisement.

·   ·   ·   ·   ·   ·   ·   ·   ·   ·   ·   ·   ·

Marry the spouseless among you, and your
slaves and handmaidens that are righteous;
if they are poor, God will enrich them
of His bounty; God is All-embracing,
                All-knowing.
And let those who find not the means to
marry be abstinent till God enriches them
of His bounty. Those your right hands own
who seek emancipation, contract with
them accordingly, if you know some good
in them; and give them of the wealth of God
that He has given you. And constrain not
your slavegirls to prostitution, if they
desire to live in chastity, that you may
seek the chance goods of the present life.
Whosoever constrains them, surely God,
after their being constrained, is All-forgiving,
                All-compassionate.[18]

Now We have sent down to you signs
making all clear, and an example
of those who passed away before you,
and an admonition for the godfearing.

35   God is the Light of the heavens and the earth;
                the likeness of His Light is as a niche
                        wherein is a lamp
                        (the lamp in a glass,
                the glass as it were a glittering star)
                        kindled from a Blessed Tree,

18. All of this represents a totally new kind of personal morality and integrity.

an olive that is neither of the East nor of the West
whose oil wellnigh would shine, even if no fire touched it;
                Light upon Light;
            (God guides to His Light whom He will.)
            (And God strikes similitudes for men,
            and God has knowledge of everything.)
in temples God has allowed to be raised up,
            and His Name to be commemorated therein;
therein glorifying Him, in the mornings and the evenings,
            are men whom neither commerce nor trafficking
                diverts from the remembrance of God
            and to perform the prayer, and to pay the alms,
fearing a day when hearts and eyes shall be turned about,
that God may recompense them for their fairest works
                and give them increase of His bounty;
and God provides whomsoever He will, without reckoning.

            And as for the unbelievers,
their works are as a mirage in a spacious plain
            which the man athirst supposes to be water,
till, when he comes to it, he finds it is nothing;
                there indeed he finds God,
and He pays him his account in full; (and God is swift
                at the reckoning.)
40   or they are as shadows upon a sea obscure
                    covered by a billow
                    above which is a billow
                    above which are clouds,
            shadows piled one upon another;
when he puts forth his hand, wellnigh he cannot see it.
            And to whomsoever God assigns no light,
                    no light has he.

Hast thou not seen how that whatsoever is in the heavens
            and in the earth extols God,
                and the birds spreading their wings?
Each—He knows its prayer and its extolling; and God knows
                the things they do.

To God belongs the Kingdom of the heavens and the earth,
and to Him is the homecoming.
Hast thou not seen how God drives the clouds, then com-
then converts them into a mass, [poses them,
then thou seest the rain issuing out of the midst of them?
And He sends down out of heaven mountains, wherein is
[hail,
so that He smites whom He will with it, and turns it aside
from whom He will;
wellnigh the gleam of His lightning snatches away the sight.
God turns about the day and the night;
surely in that is a lesson for those who have eyes.
God has created every beast of water,
and some of them go upon their bellies,
and some of them go upon two feet,
and some of them go upon four; God
creates whatever He will; God is powerful
over everything.

45 Now We have sent down signs making all
clear; God guides whomsoever He will
to a straight path.
They say, "We believe in God and the
Messenger, and we obey." Then after that
a party of them turn away; those—
they are not believers.
When they are called to God and His Messenger[19]
that he may judge between them, lo, a party of them
are swerving aside;
but if they are in the right, they will come to
him submissively.
What, is there sickness in their hearts,
or are they in doubt, or do they fear
that God may be unjust towards them
and His Messenger? Nay, but those—
they are the evildoers.

19. Rasûl Allâh, Messenger of God, is one of the most common designations
of Muhammad in the Qur'ân.

50   All that the believers say, when they
are called to God and His Messenger, that he
may judge between them, is that they say,
"We hear, and we obey"; those—
    they are the prosperers.
Whoso obeys God and His Messenger,
and fears God and has awe of Him, those—
    they are the triumphant.
They have sworn by God the most earnest oaths,
if thou commandest them they will go forth.
Say: "Do not swear; honourable obedience
is sufficient. Surely God is aware of
    the things you do."
Say: "Obey God, and obey the Messenger;
then, if you turn away, only upon
him rests what is laid on him, and
upon you rests what is laid on you.
If you obey him, you will be guided.
It is only for the Messenger to deliver
    the manifest Message."

God has promised those of you who believe
and do righteous deeds that He will surely
make you successors in the land, even as He
made those who were before them successors,
and that He will surely establish their
religion for them that He has approved for them,
and will give them in exchange, after
their fear, security: "They shall serve Me,
not associating with Me anything."
Whoso disbelieves after that, those—
    they are the ungodly.
55   Perform the prayer, and pay the alms,
and obey the Messenger—haply so
    you will find mercy.
Think not the unbelievers able to frustrate
God in the earth; their refuge is the Fire—
    an evil homecoming.

LXV
Divorce
In the Name of God, the Merciful, the Compassionate

O Prophet, when you divorce women, divorce them
when they have reached their period. Count the
period, and fear God your Lord.[20] Do not expel
them from their houses, nor let them go forth,
except when they commit a flagrant indecency.
Those are God's bounds; whosoever trespasses
the bounds of God has done wrong to himself.
Thou knowest not, perchance after that God will
      bring something new to pass.
Then, when they have reached their term, retain
them honourably, or part from them honourably.
And call in to witness two men of equity from
among yourselves; and perform the witnessing
to God Himself. By this then is admonished
whosoever believes in God and the Last Day.
And whosoever fears God, He will appoint for him
a way out, and He will provide for him from
      whence he never reckoned.

    And whosoever puts his trust in God,
    He shall suffice him. God attains his
    purpose. God has appointed a measure
      for everything.

As for your women who have despaired of further
menstruating, if you are in doubt, their period
shall be three months, and those who have not
menstruated as yet. And those who are with child,
their term is when they bring forth their burden.

20. To ensure against divorcing a pregnant woman and leaving her unborn
child unprotected. This kind of family "legislation" was important in aiding
the ongoing transition from nomadic to settled life and in ameliorating
the social confusion which had ensued. These particular rules counter the
importance of birth order and gender in determining a child's future.

Whoso fears God, God will appoint for him, of His
        command, easiness.
5   That is God's command, that He has sent down
unto you. And whosoever fears God, He will
acquit him of his evil deeds, and He will give him
        a mighty wage.
Lodge them where you are lodging, according to
your means, and do not press them, so as to
straiten their circumstances. If they are with
child, expend upon them until they bring forth
their burden. If they suckle for you, give them
their wages, and consult together honourably.
If you both make difficulties, another woman shall
        suckle for him.
Let the man of plenty expend out of his plenty.
As for him whose provision is stinted to him,
let him expend of what God has given him. God
charges no soul save with what He has given him.
God will assuredly appoint, after difficulty,
        easiness.

        How many a city turned in disdain
        from the commandment of its Lord
        and His Messengers; and then We
        made with it a terrible reckoning
        and chastised it with a horrible
            chastisement.
        So it tasted the mischief of its
        action, and the end of its affair
          was loss.
10   God prepared for them a terrible
        chastisement. So fear God, O men
          possessed of minds!

        Believers, God has sent down to you, for a
        remembrance, a Messenger reciting to
        you the signs of God, clear signs, that
        He may bring forth those who believe
        and do righteous deeds from the shadows

into the light. Whosoever believes in
God, and does righteousness, He will
admit him to gardens underneath which
rivers flow; therein they shall dwell
for ever and ever. God has made for him
a goodly provision.

It is God who created seven heavens, and of earth their like,
between them the Command descending,
that you may know that God is powerful over everything
and that God encompasses everything in knowledge.

IV
Women
In the Name of God, the Merciful, the Compassionate

Mankind, fear your Lord, who created you
of a single soul, and from it created
its mate, and from the pair of them scattered
abroad many men and women; and fear God
by whom you demand one of another,
and the wombs; surely God ever
watches over you.

Give the orphans their property, and do not
exchange the corrupt for the good; and devour
not their property with your property; surely
that is a great crime.
If you fear that you will not act justly
towards the orphans, marry such women
as seem good to you, two, three, four;
but if you fear you will not be equitable,
then only one, or what your right hands own;
so it is likelier you will not be partial.
And give the women their dowries as a gift
spontaneous; but if they are pleased
to offer you any of it, consume it
with wholesome appetite.

But do not give to fools their property
that God has assigned to you to manage;
provide for them and clothe them out of it,
and speak to them honourable words.
5   Test well the orphans, until they reach
the age of marrying; then, if you perceive
in them right judgment, deliver to them
their property; consume it not wastefully
       and hastily
ere they are grown. If any man is rich,
let him be abstinent; if poor, let him
       consume in reason.
And when you deliver to them their property,
take witnesses over them; God suffices
       for a reckoner.

To the men a share of what parents and kinsmen
leave, and to the women a share of what
parents and kinsmen leave, whether it be
little or much, a share apportioned;
and when the division is attended by
kinsmen and orphans and the poor,
make provision for them out of it,
and speak to them honourable words.
10   And let those fear who, if they left
behind them weak seed, would be afraid
on their account, and let them fear
God, and speak words hitting the mark.
Those who devour the property of orphans
unjustly, devour Fire in their bellies,
and shall assuredly roast in a Blaze.

God charges you, concerning your children:
to the male the like of the portion
of two females, and if they be women
above two, then for them two-thirds
of what he leaves, but if she be one
then to her a half; and to his parents

to each one of the two the sixth
of what he leaves, if he has children;
but if he has no children, and his
heirs are his parents, a third to his
mother, or, if he has brothers, to his
mother a sixth, after any bequest
he may bequeath, or any debt.
Your fathers and your sons—you know not
which out of them is nearer in profit
to you. So God apportions; surely God is
All-knowing, All-wise.

. . . .

Conquest and Expansion

The initial Muslim conquests of Syria, Egypt, and Irâq were achieved with amazing speed; at the time, it appeared that Allâh indeed favored the community Muhammad had created. Soon Muslims began to compose brief accounts of Muhammad's raids and of the conquests carried out in his name. But it was not until some generations later, when the need for rules to administer the newly conquered lands became apparent, that men set themselves to write continuous narratives of the conquests.

One of the earliest of such narratives is represented here in excerpts from *Opening Up of the Lands*, written by a learned Irâqî, Ahmad ibn Yahyâ al-Balâdhurî (d. 892). His history started with creation, then hurried through the intervening centuries as preface to a full treatment of Islâmic times. Our selections have been chosen because they cast light on the way the victorious Muslims defined their relations with the other "People of the Book," that is, with Jews and Christians who also shared God's revelation, however much they had allowed human error to contaminate the original purity which had now, of course, been restored (and for the last time) by Muhammad.

BALÂDHURÎ: FROM OPENING UP OF THE LANDS

Khaibar

The capitulation of Khaibar. The Prophet invaded Khaibar in the year 7.[1] Its people contended with him, delayed him and resisted the Moslems. So the Prophet besieged them for about one month. They then capitulated on the terms that their blood would not be shed, and their children be spared, provided that they evacuate the land, which he permitted the Moslems to take together with the gold and silver and arms—except what was on the person of the banu-Khaibâr,[2] and that they keep nothing secret from the Prophet. They then told the Prophet, "We have special experience in cultivation and planting palm-trees," and asked to be allowed to remain in the land. The Prophet granted them their request and allowed them one-half of the fruits and grains produced saying: "I shall keep you settled so long as Allah keeps you."

.   .   .   .

The division of Khaibar.[3] 'Amr an-Nâkid from Bushair ibn-Yasâr:—The Prophet divided Khaibar into thirty-six shares and each share into a hundred lots. One-half of the shares he reserved for himself to be used in case of accident or what might befall

From *The Origins of the Islamic State, Being a Translation from the Arabic Accompanied with Annotations, Geographic and Historic Notes of the Futûh al-Buldân* [*Opening Up of the Lands*] of al Imâm Abu-l 'Abbas Ahmad ibn Jâbir al Balâdhurî, trans. by Philip K. Hitti, Khayats (Beirut), 1966, pp. 42, 45-48, 98-102. Reprinted by permission of P. K. Hitti.

1. 628-29. Khaibar: oasis twenty miles north of Medîna, to which Jews had been immigrating since the first century.
2. I.e., the inhabitants of Khaibar.
3. Balâdhurî's method of describing the division of Khaibar in characteristic of at least the first three centuries of Muslim historical scholarship: he presents conflicting traditions intact, each with a different *isnâd* or chain of sources, and leave it to the reader to choose. This material should show why it was so difficult for the Muslims after Muhammad's death to codify the rules of their society. The Qur'ân itself had not provided enough "rules." Even Muhammad had had to supplement them during his lifetime.

him, and the other half he distributed among the Moslems. According to this, the Prophet's share included ash-Shikk with an-Natât and whatever was included within them. Among the lands turned into *wakf*[4] were al-Katîbah and Sulâlim. When the Prophet laid his hands on these possessions, he found that he had not enough *'âmils*[5] for the land. He therefore turned it over to the Jews on condition that they use the land and keep only one-half of its produce. This arrangement lasted throughout the life of the Prophet and abu-Bakr. But when 'Umar was made caliph, and as the money became abundant in the lands of the Moslems, and the Moslems became numerous enough to cultivate the land, 'Umar expelled the Jews to Syria and divided the property among the Moslems.[6]

Bakr ibn-al-Haitham from az-Zuhri:—When the Prophet conquered Khaibar the fifth share of it [reserved for himself] was al-Katîbah; as for ash-Shikk, an-Natât, Sulâlim and al-Watîh they were given to the Moslems. The Prophet left the land in the hands of the Jews on condition that they give them one-half of the produce. Thus the part of the produce assigned by Allah to the Moslems was divided among the Moslems until the time of 'Umar who divided the land itself among them according to their shares.

Abu-'Ubaid from Maimûn ibn-Mihrân:—The Prophet besieged the inhabitants of Khaibar between twenty and thirty days.

Al-Husain ibn-al-Aswad from Bushair ibn-Yasâr:—The Prophet divided Khaibar into thirty-six shares—eighteen for the Prophet to meet the expenses of accidents, visitors, and delegates,

4. Unalienable legacy to the Muslim general community. (Tr.) An important concept still in use today.

5. Governors whose chief function it was to collect taxes and conquer more lands. (Tr.)

6. Abû Bakr: Muhammad's successor and first Caliph (632-634); 'Umar, second Caliph (634-644). This passage underscores the fact that Muhammad's own arrangements were not felt to be binding by his immediate successors who continually adapted rules for the benefit of the Muslim community in light of changing circumstances. Balâdhurî in compiling his administrative history did not view these changes critically, though many under Muslim rule protested them.

and the remaining eighteen shares to be divided each among one hundred men.

Al-Husain from Bushair ibn-Yasâr:—Khaibar was divided into thirty-six shares, each one of which was subdivided into one hundred lots. Eighteen of these shares were divided among the Moslems including the Prophet, who had in addition eighteen shares to meet the expenses of visitors and delegates and accidents that might befall him.

'Abdallâh ibn-Rawâhah estimates the produce. 'Amr an-Nâkid and al-Husain ibn-al-Aswad from ibn-'Umar:—The Prophet sent ibn-Rawâhah to Khaibar who made a conjectural estimation of the palm-trees and gave the people their choice to accept or refuse, to which they replied: "This is justice; and upon justice have heaven and earth been established."[7]

The sons of abu-l-Hukaik put to death. Ishâk ibn-abi-Isrâ'il from an inhabitant of al-Madînah:—The Prophet made terms with the sons of abu-l-Hukaik stipulating that they conceal no treasure. But they did conceal; and the Prophet considered it lawful to shed their blood.

Abu-'Ubaid from Maimûn ibn-Mihrân:—The people of Khaibar were promised security on their lives and children on condition that the Prophet get all that was in the fort. In that fort were the members of a family strongly opposed to the Prophet. To them the Prophet said: "I am aware of your enmity to Allah and to his Prophet, but this is not to hold me from granting you what I granted your companions. Ye, however, have promised me that if ye conceal a thing your blood will become lawful to me. What has become of your utensils?" "They were all"—they replied, "used up during the fight." The Prophet then gave word to his *Companions* to go to the place where the utensils were. The vessels were disinterred and the Prophet struck off their heads.

. . . .

The Jews of Khaibar expelled. 'Abd-al-A'la ibn-Hammâd an-Narsi from ibn-Shihâb:—The Prophet said: "There can be no two religions at the same time in the Arabian peninsula." 'Umar

7. This may have been the Muslim idea of what the Banû Khaibar should have thought.

ibn-al-Khattâb investigated until he found it certain and assured
that the Prophet had said, "There can be no two religions at the
same time in the Arabian peninsula." Accordingly, he expelled
the Jews of Khaibar.

The Capitulation of Najrân

The terms agreed upon. Bakr ibn-al-Haitham from az-
Zuhri:—There came to the Prophet the military chief and the
civil chief, delegated by the people of Najrân in al-Yaman,[8] and
asked for terms which they made on behalf of the people of Najrân, agreeing to offer two thousand robes—one thousand in Safar
and one thousand in Rajab[9]—each one of which should have the
value of one ounce, the ounce weighing 40 *dirhams*.[10] In case the
price of the robe delivered should be more than one ounce, the
surplus would be taken into consideration; and if it were less, the
deficiency should be made up. And whatever weapons, horses,
camels or goods they offered, should be accepted instead of the
robes, if they are the same value. Another condition was made
that they provide board and lodging for the Prophet's messengers for a month or less, and not detain them for more than a
month. Still another condition was that in case of war in al-
Yaman, they are bound to offer as loan thirty coats of mail,
thirty mares and thirty camels, and whatever of these animals
perish, the messengers [of the Prophet] guarantee to make up
for them. To this effect, the Prophet gave them Allah's covenant
and his promise. Another condition was that they be not allured
to change their religion or the rank they hold in it, nor should
they be called upon for military service or made to pay the tithe.
The Prophet made it a condition on them that they neither take
nor give usury.

The two monks of Najrân and the Prophet. Al-Husain ibn-al-
Aswad from al-Hasan:—There came to the Prophet two monks
from Najrân. The Prophet proposed Islâm to them, and they
replied, "We embraced Islâm before thou didst." To this the

8. Southern Arabia. Najrân was a Christian settlement south of Mecca.
9. The second and seventh months of the Muslim calendar, respectively.
10. *Dirham:* the silver unit of the Arab monetary system, weighing around
3 grams.

Prophet replied, "Ye have told a lie. Three things keep you from
Islâm: pork eating, cross-worship and the claim that Allah has a
son." "Well then," said they, "who is 'Îsa's[11] father?" Al-Hasan
adds that the Prophet was never too quick but always waited for
Allah's command. Hence the text revealed by his Lord:[12] "These
signs and this wise warning do we rehearse to thee. Verily, Jesus
is as Adam in the sight of Allah. He created him of dust: He
then said to him, 'Be'—and he was," etc. to "on those who lie."

This the Prophet repeated to them and then asked them to
join with him in imprecating the curse of Allah upon whichever
of them was wrong, taking hold of the hands of Fâtimah, al-
Hasan and al-Husain.[13] At this, one of the two monks said to the
other, "Climb the mountain and do not join with him in imprecating the curse, for if thou shouldst, thou wouldst return with
the curse on thee." "What shall we do then?" asked the other.
"I believe," said the former, "we had better give him the kharâj[14]
rather than join with him in imprecating the curse."

A statement of the treaty. Al-Husain from Yahya ibn-Âdam
who said:—"I copied the statement of the Prophet to the people
of Najrân from that of a man who took it from al-Hasan ibn-
Sâlih. These are the words:

"In the name of Allah, the compassionate, the merciful. The
following is what the Messenger of Allah, Muhammad, wrote to
Najrân, at whose disposal[15] were all their fruits, their gold, silver
and domestic utensils, and their slaves, but which he benevo-
lently left for them, assessing on them two thousand robes each
having the value of one *aukiyah*, one thousand to be delivered
in Rajab of every year, and one thousand in Safar of every year.
Each robe shall be one *aukiyah*; and whatever robes cost more

11. Jesus.
12. Qur'ân III:51. (Tr.)
13. Muhammad's daughter and her two sons, by 'Alî.
14. *Kharâj* here means tax on non-Muslims. For the so-called "Ahl al-Kitâb,"
"People of the Book," the sword was not the only alternative to conversion
to Islâm. The protection of Christian and Jewish minorities (not to the exclusion of occasional persecution, however) was a principle of Muslim society. It reached its fullest systematization under the Ottoman empire in the
sixteenth century.
15. The text here is probably corrupt. . . . (Tr.)

or less than one *aukiyah*, their overcost or deficiency shall be taken into consideration; and whatever coats of mail, horses, camels or goods they substitute for the robes shall be taken into consideration. It is binding on Najrân to provide board and lodging for my messengers[16] for one month or less, and never to detain them for more than a month. It is also binding on them to offer as loan thirty coats of mail, thirty mares and thirty camels, in case of war in al-Yaman due to their rebelling. Whatever perishes of the horses or camels, lent to my messengers, is guaranteed by my messengers and is returned by them. Najrân and their followers[17] are entitled to the protection of Allah and to the security of Muhammad the Prophet, the Messenger of Allah, which security shall involve their persons, religion, lands and possessions, including those of them who are absent as well as those who are present, their camels, messengers and images.[18] The state they previously held shall not be changed, nor shall any of their religious services or images be changed. No attempt shall be made to turn a bishop from his office as a bishop, a monk from his office as a monk, nor the sexton of a church from his office, whether what is under the control of each is great or little. They shall not be held responsible for any wrong deed or blood shed in pre-Islamic time. They shall neither be called to military service nor compelled to pay the tithe. No army shall tread on their land. If some one demands of them some right, then the case is decided with equity without giving the people of Najrân the advantage over the other party, or giving the other party the advantage over them. But whosoever of them has up till now received usury, I am clear of the responsibility of his protection. None of them, however, shall be held responsible for the guilt of the other. And as a guarantee to what is recorded in this document, they are entitled to the right of protection from Allah, and to the security of Muhammad the Prophet, until Allah's order is issued, and so long as they give the right counsel [to Moslems] and render whatever dues are bound on them, provided they are not asked to do anything unjust. Witnessed by abu-Sufyân ibn-

16. Sent to bring the *kharâj*. (Tr.)
17. . . . Jews. . . . (Tr.)
18. . . . Crosses and pictures used in churches. (Tr.)

Harb, Ghailân ibn-'Amr, Mâlik ibn-'Auf of banu-Nasr, al-Akra'
ibn-Hâbis al-Hanzali and al-Mughîrah. Written by—' "[19]

Yaha ibn-Âdam adds, "I have seen in the hands of the people
of Najrân another statement whose reading is similar to that of
this copy, but at the close of it the following words occur: Written by 'Ali ibn-abu-Tâlib.' Concerning this I am at a loss to
know what to say."

'Umar expels them. When abu-Bakr as-Siddîk became caliph
he enforced the terms agreed upon and issued another statement
similar to that given by the Prophet. When 'Umar ibn-al-Khattâb became caliph, they began to practise usury, and became so
numerous as to be considered by him a menace to Islâm. He
therefore expelled them and wrote to them the following statement:

"Greetings! Whomever of the people of Syria and al-'Irâk
they happen to come across, let him clear for them tillable land;
and whatever land they work, becomes theirs in place of their
land in al-Yaman." Thus the people of Najrân were dispersed,
some settling in Syria and others in an-Najrânîyah in the district of al-Kûfah, after whom it was so named. The Jews of
Najrân were included with the Christians in the terms and went
with them as their followers.[20]

---

19. At this point one tradition supplies the name of the son of Abû Bakr, the
grst Caliph, whereas the tradition reported in the following paragraph mentions 'Ali, the fourth Caliph. This discrepancy reflects the conflict between the
partisans of 'Ali and Abû Bakr over who should become first Caliph. 'Alid par-
tisanship and its development into the sectarian group known as the Shî'a
pervaded even early traditions. Like many historians, Balâdhurî leaves the
choice to the reader.
20. The text of this chapter continues for several pages to trace the fluctuat-
ing fortunes of this group in the course of the next two hundred years.

Crisis and Compromise

Between 632 when Muhammad died and 656 when the third caliph, 'Uthmân ibn 'Affân, was assassinated, the Muslim community conquered an enormous territory. The religious conviction Muhammad's prophecy had created among them had been maintained at white heat. But sudden worldly success brought problems: How were the rich new provinces to be ruled? How was succession to the Prophet to be agreed upon? How should men set out to follow God's will when the Prophet was no longer at hand to answer new questions?

The three selections that follow illustrate critical aspects of these crises. The first is an account of Caliph 'Uthmân's assassination, and of the bitter quarrels within the Islâmic community that followed it. The excerpt comes from *The History of Prophets and Kings*, a universal history written by Ibn Jarîr al-Tabarî (838-923), a resident of Baghdâd in its days of greatness. (More will be said of Tabarî's life and opinions in the next section, where other excerpts from his history are reproduced.)

The second selection is a speech attributed to the incoming governor of Irâq, Ziyâd ibn Abîhî, who had been appointed by Mu'âwîya (reigned 661-680), the first Umayyad caliph (that is, of the Umayya sub-clan of Quraysh). During the struggles that followed 'Uthmân's death, Irâq had supported Mu'âwîya's defeated rival, 'Alî. Hence Ziyâd expected opposition, and his truculent tone makes clear how he intended to deal with it.

Yet a government that depended on brutality and terror to suppress opposition was in conflict with the ideals or practice of the early Muslim community. How could true religion flourish when the successors to the Prophet were so utterly unworthy? A letter written by Hasan al-Basrî to the Caliph 'Umar II (r. 717-720) reflects the views of those who were unwilling to compromise in their search for holiness and, unable to find satisfaction in the world about them, had turned to mystical exercises and association with like-minded athletes of religion.

A compromise between hard-fisted rulers and warriors on the one hand and those who whole-heartedly sought holiness in the other was not achieved under the Umayyads. Workable resolution of the tensions arising from Islâm's sudden success was achieved only after 750, when a new family of rulers, the 'Abbâsids, relocated the capital from Damascus to Baghdâd and inaugurated a "Golden Age" for Islâm.

TABARÎ: "THE DEATH OF 'UTHMÂN," FROM THE HISTORY OF PROPHETS AND KINGS

Then Muhammad b. Abû Bakr came to 'Uthmân.[1] He threatened Ibn al-Zubayr and Marwân, and they fled;[2] Muhammad b. Abû-Bakr then came to 'Uthmân and seized him by his beard. He said, "Let go of my beard—your father did not take hold of it." Muhammad let it go. But the people rushed upon him, some striking him with the iron tips of their scabbards, others striking him with their fists. A man came at him with a broad iron-tipped arrow and stabbed the front of his throat, and his blood fell on the Koran.[3] Yet (even) when they were in that state they feared killing him. 'Uthmân was old and he fainted. Others came in and when they saw that he had fainted they dragged him by the legs and (his wife) Nâ'ila and his daughters wailed loudly. Al-Tujîbî[4] came, drawing his sword to thrust it into his belly. When Nâ'ila protected ('Uthmân), he cut her hand. Then he leaned with his sword upon his chest; and 'Uthmân (Allah bless him) was killed before sundown. A crier went about calling that his blood and property were forbidden. But the people sacked everything and then proceeded to the public treasury. . . .

From *Introduction to Islamic Civilization: Course Syllabus and Selected Readings*, edited by Marshall G. S. Hodgson, vol. I (revised), University of Chicago Press, 1964, pp. 34-36. Reprinted by permission of the Syllabus Division, University of Chicago Press.

1. Muhammad b. Abû Bakr: son of the first Caliph Abû Bakr (r. 632-634).
2. Meccan companions of 'Uthmân.
3. Variant spelling of "Qur'ân."
4. One of the assassins, probably one of a group of Arab tribesmen from Egypt who felt they had been double-crossed by 'Uthmân.

Muhammad said: Al-Zubayr b. 'Abd-Allâh related to me from Yûsuf b. 'Abd-Allâh b. Salâm,[5] who said:

" 'Uthmân looked upon the people while he was under siege and they were surrounding the house in every direction, and he said: 'I beseech you by Allâh (to Him belong glory and power), do you know that when the Commander of the Faithful, 'Umar b. al-Khattâb[6] (Allâh bless him), was (fatally) wounded, you prayed to Allâh asking Him to bless you and unite you in choosing the best among us (to succeed him)? What do you think of Allâh? Do you say that you were of so little consequence to Him, that he did not heed your prayer at a time when you were the only upholders of His truth among his creatures, and had not yet disagreed about it? Glory to Allâh! Allâh is far above such imperfection! Or do you say that His religion was of so little value to Him that He did not care who had charge of it, at a time when the religion is the way that people unite in worshipping Allâh? Submit yourselves to Allâh or you will be vanquished and punished. Or do you say that the selection was not done through consultation—you are very proud!—and that God appointed the community to act, if it disobeyed him!—and that you did not take counsel in choosing the *imâm*[7] and did not exert yourselves to learn his weaknesses? Or do you say that Allâh did not know how I would conduct my affairs? In some of my acts I did good and the Faithful approved. Since then, in the conduct of my affairs I have not committed any acts which you condemn that Allah did not know of on the day that he chose me and clothed me with the robe of His glory (glory to Allâh! Allâh is far from such imperfection). I beseech you by Allâh, do you know that Allâh has made me witness over his Truth (and to

5. The transmitters in this chain (*isnâd*) would have been sympathetic to 'Uthmân.

6. 'Umar b. al-Khattâb: the second Caliph (r. 634-644) who had appointed the *shûra* or council which chose 'Uthmân. 'Umar did so on his deathbed, having himself been stabbed by a madman.

7. *Imâm*: originally indicating the leader of Muslim prayer, it came to mean the leader of the community with the implication of religious authority. During the time of the first four Caliphs, it was synonymous with Caliph.

fight for Allâh against His enemies is the Truth), which every man coming after me should confess that I possess? Do not kill me. For killing is allowed in only three cases: a man may be killed for committing adultery, for disbelieving after accepting Islâm, or for murdering another person except in retaliation. If you kill me you will be putting your necks under a sword which Allâh (to Him belong glory and power) will not remove from you until the Day of Judgment. Do not kill me, for if you kill me you will never pray together again after I am gone, and you will never divide the booty among you again, after I am gone, and Allâh will never settle your disagreement again.'

"They replied. 'As for what you have mentioned concerning the people's appeal for Allâh's guidance (to Him belong glory and power) in appointing a guardian to succeed 'Umar (Allâh bless him) and your selection with Allâh's guidance, we answer that all the actions of Allâh are the best of actions, but Allâh (glory to Allâh! Allâh is above imperfection) has sent your case upon His people as a trial. As for what you have mentioned concerning your seniority, and priority with the Messenger of Allâh (Allâh's blessing and peace upon him), you used to have seniority and precedence with him and were worthy of the highest office; but since then you have changed and have innovated in the way you already know. As for what you have mentioned concerning the affliction which would befall us if we killed you, the fear of a rebellion ought not to sway us from upholding the truth against you. As for your belief that killing is forbidden except on three grounds only, we find in the Book of Allâh [i.e., the Qur'ân] other lawful killings than those which you have named—the killing of one who has spread corruption in the land; the killing of one who swerves from the path of justice and prevents its execution and fights against it and scorns it. You acted in tyranny; and you have prevented the executions of justice and have swayed from its path and been scornful of it, refusing to punish yourself in recompense for those whom you have deliberately oppressed. You have held fast to the Caliphate over us, and you have gone astray in your rule and your oath. You claim that you did not treat us with scorn and that those who defended you and prevented us from reaching you were fighting without your command. But they are fighting because of your tenacious hold upon the Caliphate. If you had abdicated they would not have fought to defend you.' "

ZIYÂD IBN ABÎHÎ: "INAUGURAL SPEECH"

You allow kinship to prevail and put religion second, you excuse and hide your transgressors and tear down the orders which Islam has sanctified for your protection. Take care not to creep about in the night; I will kill every man found on the streets after dark. Take care not to appeal to your kin. I will cut off the tongue of every man who raises that call. . . . I rule you with the omnipotence of God and maintain you with God's wealth (i.e. the state's); I demand obedience from you, and you can demand uprightness from me. However much I may lag behind my aims I will not fail in three things: I will at all times be there for every man to speak to me, I will always pay your pension punctually and I will not send you into the field for too long a time or too far away. Do not be carried away by your hatred and anger against me, it would go ill with you. I see many heads rolling; let each man see that his own head stays upon his shoulders.

From *Classical Islam*, by Gustave E. Von Grunebaum, Chicago: Aldine Press, 1971, pp. 70-71. Reprinted by permission of George Allen & Unwin, Ltd. and Aldine-Atherton, Inc.

HASAN AL-BASRÎ: LETTER TO 'UMAR II

Beware of this world with all wariness; for it is like to a snake, smooth to the touch, but its venom is deadly. Turn away from whatsoever delights thee in it, for the little companioning thou wilt have of it; put off from thee its cares, for that thou hast seen its sudden chances, and knowest for sure that thou shalt be parted from it; endure firmly its hardships, for the ease that

From *Sufism*, by Arthur J. Arberry, London: Allen & Unwin, 1950, pp. 33-35. Reprinted by permission.

shall presently be thine. The more it pleases thee, the more do thou be wary of it; for the man of this world, whenever he feels secure in any pleasure thereof, the world drives him over into some unpleasantness, and whenever he attains any part of it and squats him down upon it, the world suddenly turns him upside down. And again, beware of this world, for its hopes are lies, its expectations false; its easefulness is all harshness, muddied its limpidity. And therein thou art in peril: or bliss transient, or sudden calamity, or painful affliction, or doom decisive. Hard is the life of a man if he be prudent, dangerous if comfortable, being wary ever of catastrophe, certain of his ultimate fate. Even had the Almighty not pronounced upon the world at all, nor coined for it any similitude, nor charged men to abstain from it, yet would the world itself have awakened the slumberer, and roused the heedless; how much the more then, seeing that God has Himself sent us a warning against it, an exhortation regarding it! For this world has neither worth nor weight with God; so slight it is, it weighs not with God so much as a pebble or a single clod of earth; as I am told, God has created nothing more hateful to Him than this world, and from the day He created it He has not looked upon it, so much He hates it. It was offered to our Prophet with all its keys and treasures, and that would not have lessened him in God's sight by so much as the wing of a gnat, but he refused to accept it; and nothing prevented him from accepting it—for there is naught that can lessen him in God's sight—but that he knew that God hated a thing, and therefore he hated it, and God despised a thing, and he abased it. Had he accepted it, his acceptance would have been a proof that he loved it; but he disdained to love what his Creator hated, and to exalt what his Sovereign had debased. As for Muhammad, he bound a stone upon his belly when he was hungry; and as for Moses, the skin of his belly shewed as green as grass because of it all: he asked naught of God, the day he took refuge in the shade, save food to eat when he was hungered, and it is said of him in the stories that God revealed to him, "Moses, when thou seest poverty approaching, say, Welcome to the badge of the righteous! and when thou seest wealth approaching, say, Lo! a sin whose punishment has been put on aforetime." If thou

II

"The Golden Age"
(750-1000)

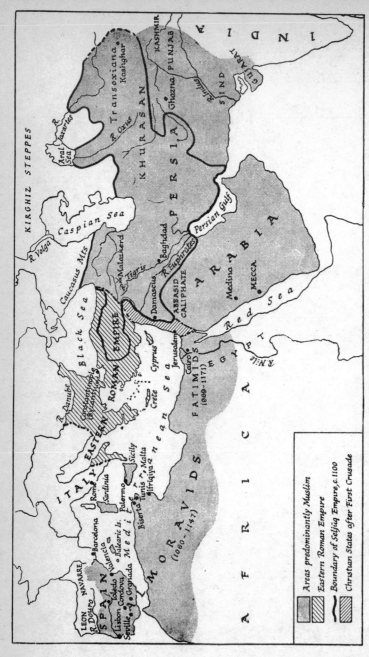

From *The Social Structure of Islam* by Reuben Levy (1971) by permission of Cambridge University Press.

Introduction

In 744 the Umayyad power, centered upon Damascus in Syria, was overthrown; after six years of strife, a new ruling family, the 'Abbâsids, won general recognition as caliphs and set up their capital at Baghdâd in Irâq. The dynasty lasted nominally until 1258, but actual power disintegrated after 945.

During the first two centuries of 'Abbâsid rule, the Muslim world became the seat of great cultural activity. A tacit compromise between seekers after holiness and the 'Abbâsid rulers was achieved: the caliph and his court busied themselves with the defense of Islâm, while experts in holiness prescribed godly conduct to less learnèd Muslims on the basis of carefully worked out codes of Sacred Law. Partially secret sectarian movements, most often associated with the name of 'Alî, Muhammad's son-in-law and the defeated rival to the founder of the Umayyad dynasty, were numerous; these Shî'î and 'Alid, groups, as they were called, sometimes espoused social protest and revolution.

Cultural activities in the 'Abbâsid empire were rich and varied. Not all of the aspects of this multifold activity are reflected in the samples of anecdote, essay, history, theology, philosophy, and poetry that follow. But from them some understanding of the preoccupations of the age ought to emerge, even though other genres—mysticism, geography, biography, Shî'î thought—have had to be omitted.

The authors represented here reflect the cosmopolitanism of the 'Abbâsid period. Some were Arab, many were of Persian or other non-Arab descent. Some were rich, others poor. Many lived their active lives in Baghdâd, but some migrated, especially toward the end of the period, to the courts of various provincial rulers and upstarts. Nearly all reflect tensions within what may be called the official form of Islâm—between the so-called Sunnî form and the dissenting Shî'î tradition. In addition, they reflect tensions between reason and revelation as sources of truth, and between indulgence of the senses and their repression in the interest of a more perfect holiness. Richness and variety, subtlety and seriousness were the hallmarks of the time which Muslims soon began to look back upon as "The Golden Age."

Life Styles

The author of the following anecdotes and character sketches, Abû 'Alî al-Muhassin al-Tanûkhî, was born in Irâq about 940 and died in 994. The son of a learnèd Muslim judge from Basra, Tanûkhî followed in his father's footsteps and become a judge in the capital, at Baghdâd. Toward the end of his life, however, he was driven from office and suffered various hardships and persecutions.

Though he made his living as a judge and administrator of the Sacred Law, Tanûkhî made his reputation as a writer, compiling three collections of literary sketches. Extracts from one of them, reproduced here, suggest the variety of personality types and the divergent ways of pursuing happiness that urban life in the 'Abbâsid society accommodated. A light, witty style made his works popular in his own time. Even in translation, Tanûkhî's words convey an educated man's tolerance of, and perhaps pity for, the foibles and weaknesses of mankind.

TANÛKHÎ: FROM RUMINATIONS AND REMINISCENCES

Acts of Piety

I was told by the Qâdi Abû Bakr Mohammed b. 'Abd al-Rahmân that he had been informed by a steward of Abu'l-Mundhir Nu'mân b. 'Abdallâh how it was the latter's custom at

From *The Table Talk of a Mesopotamian Judge*, edited and trans. by D. S. Margoliouth, London: Royal Asiatic Society, 1922, pp. 64-67, 164-68, 135-37, 293, 289-92, 86-87, 31, 160, 97-101, 172-73, 84-86, 204-6. Reprinted by permission.

1. Qâdî: judge.

shouldst wish, thou mightest name as a third the Lord of the
Spirit and the Word (Jesus), for in his affair there is a marvel;
he used to say, "My daily bread is hunger, my badge is fear, my
raiment is wool, my mount is my foot, my lantern at night is the
moon, my fire by day is the sun, and my fruit and fragrant
herbs are such things as the earth brings forth for the wild beasts
and cattle. All the night I have nothing, yet there is none richer
than I!" And if thou shouldst wish, thou mightest name as a
fourth David, who was no less wonderful than these; he ate barley bread in his chamber, and fed his family upon bran meal,
but his people on fine corn; and when it was night he clad himself in sackcloth, and chained his hand to his neck, and wept
until the dawn; eating coarse food, and wearing robes of hair.
All these hated what God hates, and despised what God despises;
then the righteous thereafter followed in their path and kept
close upon their tracks.

the close of the winter season to collect all the poplin, wool,
blankets, stoves and other appliances for winter which he had
been using and sell them by auction; he would then send to the
Qâdî's prison and find out what prisoners were there in consequence of their own confessions (not of evidence brought against
them, and were without means. He would pay their debts out of
the price obtained for these goods, or else would make a settlement permitting of their release, if the debt was heavy. He
would then turn his attention to small dealers such as confec-
tioners and pedlars, people whose business capital was from one
to three dinars, and give them some sum such as ten dinars or a
hundred dirhems as additional capital. He would also turn his
attention to those who were selling in the market such things as
kettles, pots, torn shirts, etc. which would probably only be sold
owing to extreme need, and to old women who were selling their
spinning, give them many times the value of the articles, and
allow them to retain them. Many more things of this sort would
he do, and order me to carry out, expending the price of his
goods on these objects. When winter came he would similarly
collect his *dabîqî*,[2] gold and silver network, matting, water-cool-
ers, and other appliances for summer, and deal with them in the
same way. When next summer or winter came, he would get in
fresh supplies of everything he wanted. When I grew tired of
this procedure on his part, I said to him: Sir, you are crippling
yourself without achieving any profitable result; for you are
buying these garments, instruments and furniture at abnormally
high prices at the times when there is a demand for them,
whereas you sell them at the season when there is no demand
for them, and get in consequence no more than half price.
Thereby you lose a vast sum. If you will permit, I will put all
you want sold up to auction, and when they are about to be
knocked down, will buy them in for you at a higher price, reserve them for you for the summer or winter, and devote out of
your estate an amount equal to that for which they were
knocked down to these objects.—He said: I do not want this
done. These are goods which God has permitted me to enjoy
throughout my summer or winter, and He has brought me to

2. A type of cloth.

the time wherein I can dispense with them. I have no assurance
that I shall live to the time when I shall need them again. Possibly I may have offended God either for them or with them. I
prefer to sell the articles themselves, and devote the actual price
to these objects, by way of thanking God for having brought me
to the time wherein I no longer need them, and as compensation
for any offence which I may have committed in connexion with
them. Then if God spare me for the time when I shall require
them, they will not be very costly and I shall have no difficulty
in purchasing the like, renewing my stock and enjoying the new
articles. There is a further advantage about my selling them
cheap and buying them dear, which is that the poorer dealers
from whom I buy and to whom I sell will get the profit from
me, whereas this will not affect my fortune.

The Qâ*d*î added that this agent told him how when any rare
dainty or sweet was served up before Nu'mân, he did not like to
eat much of it, but would order it to be given away as it was to
mendicants. Every day too he used to order what was taken
away from his table with such of his slaves' rations as remained
over in his kitchen to be given away, whence a great number of
mendicants assembled at his gate every day. One day, he said, a
Hâshimite[3] friend was eating at Nu'mân's table, and some
dainty dish was served up. Before they had finished Nu'mân
ordered it to be given to the mendicants. A fatted kid was then
served, and before they had enjoyed it, he ordered it to be removed and given to the mndicants. There was served up a dish
of almond made up with pistachio-nuts, of which Nu'mân was
fond, and for a glass of which according to the size he paid fifty
dirhems, five dinars, more or less. They had only eaten a little
of it when he said: Hand it over to the mendicants. The Hâshimite held the glass fast, and said: My friend, imagine us to be
the mendicants, and let us enjoy our food; why do you hand on
to mendicants everything for which you have a taste? What has
a mendicant to do with this? They can do very well on beef and
date-cake; so please, do not let it be removed. Nu'mân replied:
My friend, what you see is a custom of mine. A bad custom it

3. Hâshimite: member, follower, or supporter of 'Abbâsid house.

is, he said; we shall not endure it. If the mendicants must have it, then order a similar dish to be prepared for them; let us enjoy this, and pay them its value in money. Nu'mân replied: I will counter-order and have a similar dish prepared for them; but as for money—a mendicant would not have the heart or spirit to prepare a dish of this sort, even if many times its value were paid him; when he gets the coins, he spends them on other things, on supplying more immediate needs, nor would he have the skill either to prepare such a dish. Now I like to share my pleasures. Addressing his slave, he bade him have a dish similar to theirs prepared at once and distributed to the mendicants. It was done; and after this occasion, when he was entertaining any one whom he respected, he ordered dishes similar to those which were to be served to be prepared and bestowed in charity, and only ordered them to be removed from his table when the guests had had sufficient.

I was told by the qâdî Abu'l-Hasan Mohammed son of the qâdî 'Abd al-Wâhid Hâshimî that a large sum was owed to a leading tradesman by one of the generals, who deferred paying; and, said the tradesman, I made up my mind to appeal to Mu'-tadid,[4] because whenever I went to the general, he had the door shut against me and let his slaves revile me, whereas if I tried mild methods and used mediation, it was useless. . . . Then one of my friends said to me: I will recover your money, and you need not appeal to the Caliph. Come with me at once.—So, said he, I arose and he brought me to a tailor in Tuesday Street, an old man who was seated, sewing and reading the Quran. Telling him my story, he asked him to call on the general, and see me righted. The general's residence was near the tailor's, and the latter started with us. As we were walking, I lagged behind and said to my friend: You are exposing this aged man, yourself, and me to serious annoyance. When he comes to the door of my debtor, he will be cuffed, and you and I with him. For the general paid no attention to the remonstrances of So-and-so, and So-and-so, nor even troubled about the vizier. Is he likely to trouble about our friend here?—My friend laughed and said:

4. Mu'tadid: 'Abbâsid Caliph (r. 892-902).

Never mind, walk on and keep quiet.—We arrived at the general's door, and when his slaves saw the tailor, they treated him with reverence, and rushed to kiss his hand, which he would not permit. Then they said: What has brought you, sir? The master is riding, and if it be something which we can do, we shall do it at once; but if not, then come in and sit down till he comes.— This encouraged me, and we went inside and sat down. Presently the man came, and when he saw the tailor, he was most respectful, and said: Before I change my clothes you must give me your orders. The tailor then spoke to him about my affair. He assured the tailor that he had not in his house more than five thousand dirhems, but begged him to take those and his silver and gold harness as pledges for the rest which he would pay within a month. I readily assented, and he produced the dirhems and the harness to the value of the remainder; of this I took possession, and made the tailor and my friend attest the arrangement whereby the pledge for the remainder of the money was to remain in my possession for a month, and if this term were exceeded I was at liberty to sell it and recoup myself from the proceeds. After obtaining their attestations I left with them; and when we reached the tailor's place I flung down the money before him, saying: Sir, through you God has restored me my property, and I shall be pleased if you will accept a quarter, a a third, or a half of it, which I gladly offer.—Friend, he replied, you are indeed in a hurry to return evil for good! Take yourself off with your property, with the blessing of God!—I said that I had one more request.—When he bade me utter it, I asked him to tell me the reason why the general had yielded to him, when he had treated the greatest men in the empire with contempt. Sir, he replied, you have got what you wanted, so please do not interrupt me in the occupation by which I earn my livelihood. When I insisted, he said: I have been a leader of prayer and have been teaching the Quran in this mosque for forty years, earning my living by tailoring which is the only trade I know. A long time ago, after saying the sunset prayer, as I was going homewards I passed by a Turk, who was in this house. Suddenly a woman of fair countenance passed by, and the Turk who was drunk seized hold of her, trying to drag her into the house, while she resisted and called for help, which was not forthcoming, no one coming forward to rescue her from the Turk in spite of her cries. Among other things she was saying that her husband had sworn he would divorce her if she spent a night away from his house, and if the Turk compelled her to disobey this he would ruin her home in addition to the crime which he could be committing, and the disgrace which he would bring upon her. I went up to the Turk and stopped him, requesting him to let the woman go, but he struck me on the head with a club that was in his hand, giving me a painful wound, and forced the woman to enter the house. I went home, washed off the blood, bound up the wound, and when the pain had eased went out to say the evening prayer. When that was over I said to the congregation: Come with me to this godless Turk, to remonstrate with him, and not leave him until we make him release the woman. They rose up, and we went and made a great noise at his door, and presently he came out at the head of a number of his slaves, raining blows upon us, and he singled me out, striking me a blow of which I nearly died. My neighbours carried me to my dwelling in a dying condition. My family treated my wounds, and I slept, but very slightly owing to the pain, and I woke up at midnight and could sleep no longer as I thought about the affair. Then I said to myself: The fellow must have been drinking all night, and will not know the time; if I sound the call to prayer, he will suppose that the dawn has commenced, and will release the woman so that she can reach her house before dawn. She will thus escape from one of the two disasters, and her home will not be ruined in addition to what has befallen her. So I went out to the mosque walking as best I could, and mounting the minaret, sounded the call, and then sat down and looked out upon the street, waiting to see the woman come out; if she did not come out, I would start prayer, that there might be no doubt in the Turk's mind that it was morning and he might release her. Only a little while elapsed and the woman was still with him when the street became filled with horse and foot, with torches, and men crying: Who is it who has just been calling to prayer? Where is he?—At first I was too terrified to speak, but then I thought I would address them and perhaps get help for the woman. So I called out from the minaret: I was the person.—They said to me: Come down and answer the Commander of the Faithful.—Thinking to myself that deliverance was near, I descended, and went with them, and found them to be a company of guards with Badr, who brought me before Mu'tadid. When I saw him, I shook and trembled, but he encouraged me, and then asked me what had induced me to alarm the Moslems[5] by sounding the call to prayer at a wrong time, so that people who had business would go about it prematurely, and those who meant to fast would restrain themselves at a time when they were allowed to break their fast. I said: If the Commander of the Faithful will grant me amnesty, I will tell the truth.—He told me my life was safe. I then recounted to him the story of the Turk, and showed him the marks upon me, and he ordered Badr at once to bring the soldier and the woman. I was taken apart, and after a short time the soldier and the woman were produced, and Mu'tadid proceeded to ask her about the affair, which she narrated as I had done. Mu'tadid then ordered Badr to send her at once to her husband with a trustworthy escort, who should bring her into her house and explain the affair to her husband, with a request from the Caliph to him not to send her away, but to treat her kindly. He then summoned me, and while I stood listening, he began to question the soldier as follows: How much, fellow, is your allowance? He gave the amount. Your pay?—So much.—Your perquisites?—So much.—Then he began to enumerate the gratuities which the man received, and the Turk acknowledged to an enormous amount. Then he asked him how many slave-girls he possessed. He gave the number. The Caliph said to him: Were not these and the ample fortune which you enjoyed sufficient for you, but you must needs violate the commands of God, and injure the majesty of the Sultan, and not only perpetrate this offence, but in addition assault the person who tried to make you do right? The soldier was conscience-smitten and could make no reply. The Caliph then ordered them to fetch a sack, some cement-makers' pestles, bonds and fetters. The man was bound and fettered, and put into the sack, and the attendants were then ordered to pound him with the pestles.

5. Variant spelling of Muslim.

This was done in my sight, and for a time the man screamed, then his voice stopped as he was dead. The Caliph ordered the body to be thrown into the Tigris, and told Badr to seize the contents of his dwelling. Then he said to me: Sir, whenever you see any kind of wrong committed, great or small, or anything of the sort great or small, then order it to be righted and remonstrate about it, even with him (pointing to Badr); and if anything befalls you and you are not listened to, then the sign between us is that you sound the call to prayer at about this time; I, hearing your voice, will summon you and will do this to any one who refuses to listen to you, or injures you.—I invoked a blessing on him and departed; then the rumour spread among the Dailemites[6] and the Turks, and I have never asked any one to right another or to desist from wrongdoing, but he has obeyed me to my satisfaction for fear of Mu'tadid, so that up to this time I have not had to sound the call.

I was told by my father that when Abu Yûsuf cultivated the society of Abû Hanîfah[7] in order to learn law, he was very poor, and his attendance on his teacher prevented him from earning his livelihood. So he used to return at the end of the day to short rations in an ill-appointed establishment. This went on a long time, his wife resorting to various expedients in order to maintain herself day by day. At last her patience was exhausted, and when one day he had gone to the lecture-room, spent the whole day there, and returned at night to ask for his meal, she produced a covered dish; when he removed the cover he found it to contain some note-books. To his question what this meant, she replied that it was what he was occupied with the whole day, so he had better eat it at night. Deeply affected, he went without food that night, and stayed away from the lecture next morning until he had secured some food for the household. Coming then to Abû Hanîfah, and being asked why he was so late, he told the truth. Why, asked Abû Hanîfah, did you not tell me, so that

6. Dailemites: mercenaries of the 'Abbâsids, who came from Gîlân on the Caspian coast.

7. Abû Yûsuf: famous jurist (731-798) of Hanafite school of law; Abû Hanîfa: founder of Hanafite school of law (699-767).

I might have helped you? You need not be anxious; if your life is preserved your legal earnings will enable you to feast on almond paste and shelled pistachios.—Abû Yûsuf stated that when he had entered the service of Rashîd,[8] and enjoyed his favour, one day a dish of almond paste and pistachios was brought to the imperial table. When I tasted it, he said, tears came to my eyes, as I remembered Abû *H*anîfah.—When Rashîd asked me the reason of my emotion, I told him this story.

The occasion, said my father, of Abû Yûsuf entering the service of Rashîd was that one of the generals had forsworn himself, and wished to consult a jurist on the matter. Abû Yûsuf, being fetched, gave it as his opinion that he had not forsworn himself; and the general presented him with some dinars,[9] took a house for him near his own, and attached him to himself. One day when the general visited Rashîd, he found him depressed, and, inquiring the reason, was told that the Caliph was troubled by a religious question, and requested him to fetch a jurist whom he might consult. The general brought Abû Yûsuf. Abû Yûsuf narrated as follows: Entering a corridor between the apartments, I saw a handsome lad with the marks of royalty upon him, imprisoned in one of the chambers which opened on the corridor. The lad made a sign to me with his finger, to implore my assistance, but I did not understand his meaning. I was then taken into the presence of Rashîd, and when I appeared before him, I saluted and stood. He asked me my name, to which I replied. Ya'qûb, God prosper the Commander of the Faithful.—He then said: What say you of a sovereign who witnesses a man committing a mortal sin? Must he inflict the penalty?—Not necessarily, I replied. When I said this, Rashîd prostrated himself, and it occurred to me that he must have seen one of his own sons committing that offence and that the person who had signalled to me for assistance was the adulterous son. Presently Rashîd raised his head and asked me my authority. Because, I replied, the Prophet said: *Avert penalties by doubts*, and there is here a doubt which invalidates the penalty.—What doubt is there, he

8. Hârûn al-Rashîd: 'Abbâsid Caliph (r. 786-809).
9. Dînâr: gold coin weighing about 4.25 grams.

asked, when there is ocular evidence?—Ocular evidence, I replied, does not necessitate it any more than knowledge of the occurrence would necessitate it; and the law does not inflict penalties from mere knowledge.—Why? he asked.—Because, I replied, the penalty is a right of God, which the sovereign is commanded to maintain, so that it becomes as it were his own right; and no person may exact his right by virtue of his own knowledge, nor himself enforce it. The Moslems are agreed that the penalty requires for its enforcement confession or evidence. They are not agreed that knowledge is sufficient to necessitate its enforcement.—Thereupon Rashîd prostrated himself a second time, and ordered that I should be given a vast sum as well as a monthly allowance among the jurists, and that I should be attached to the Palace. Before I had got outside I received a gift from the young man and another from his mother, and others from his followers, and thereby I got the foundation of a fortune. The Caliph's allowance was added to the allowance which I was receiving from the general, and, being attached to the Palace, I was asked for an opinion by one servant and for advice by another, and by giving opinions and advice I gained authority with them and won their respect, and presents kept reaching me from them, so that my position strengthened. Then the Caliph summoned me to a lengthy interview, to ask my opinion concerning an emergency, and treated me with cordiality; and I proceeded to advance in his favour until he made me judge.

Mystical Ecstasy

I saw in Baghdad a one-eyed Sûfî,[10] named Abu'l-Fath, who was chanting the Qur'an beautifully in a gathering arranged by Abû 'Abdallâh Ibn al-Buhlûl. A lad read the text (Qur'ân xxxv: 34) *Did we not give you length of life sufficient for a man to take warning in?* The Sûfî cried out *Aye, aye* many times and fainted, remaining unconscious during the whole of the meeting. He had not recovered when the congregation dispersed, the meeting having been held in the court of a house which I inhabited. I left him where he was, and he did not come to himself till about the afternoon, when he arose. After some days I

10. Muslim mystic.

inquired about him, and learned that he had been present in Karkh[11] when a singing-woman was performing to the lute, and heard her repeat the lines in which comes the passage

> The day when each man brings his plea,
> Thy blessed face shall plead for me.

This affected him so much that he shouted and beat his breast and at last fell down in a fit. When the entertainment was over they moved him and found that he was dead. He was taken away for burial and the affair got noised abroad. The verses whence this is taken are by 'Abd al-Ṣamad b. al-Mu'adhdhal; they were dictated by Ṣûlî after him by a chain recorded in my records of traditions which I have heard; they were:

> Author of ways which fascinate,
> Thou art the sovereign of our fate.
> A house with thee for habitant
> Needeth not an illuminant.
> If e'er release from thy control
> I crave, may God not save my soul!
> The day when each man brings his plea,
> Thy blessed face shall plead for me.

Religious Trickery

The following was told me by Abu'l-Ṭayyib Ibn 'Abd al-Mu'min: An accomplished knight of industry went from Baghdad to Ḥims, accompanied by his wife, and when he had got to the latter place, he said to her: This is a foolish and wealthy town, and I wish to bring off a stunner (a phrase used by these people whereby they mean a great piece of knavery), for which I want your help and endurance.—She accorded it willingly. He told her she was to remain in her place and not pass by his at all, only each day to take two-thirds of a *ratl*[12] of raisins and the same quantity of almond-paste, to knead them together and place it at midday on a clean tile in a certain lavatory near the mosque where he would find it. That was absolutely all she was to do, and she was not to approach his quarters. She agreed, and

11. Karkh: important quarter of old Baghdâd.
12. Unit of weight varied from time to time and place to place.

then he produced a tunic and breeches of wool which he had brought, and a veil to put over his head, and took up his station by a pillar in the mosque before which most of the people passed. Here he remained praying the whole day and the whole night, except at the time wherein prayer is forbidden, and when he sat down to rest he kept counting his beads and did not utter a word. For a time he was unnoticed; then he began to attract attention, and he was watched for a space and talked about and observed; it was found that he never ceased praying, and never tasted food. The people of the town were astonished at him, as he never left the mosque save once at midday, when he went to the lavatory and made his way to the marked tile whereon the paste was laid, which had changed colour and looked like dried and discoloured dung, which those who came in and out supposed it to be. This he would eat to support life, after which he would come back and drink as much water as he required, when he was washing for the nightly prayer and during the night. The people of *H*ims supposed that he tasted neither water nor food, and that he maintained a complete fast during the whole period; and this they thought extraordinary, and admirable. Many approached him and addressed him, but he returned no answer; when they surrounded him he took no notice, and however hard they tried to get him into conversation, he maintained silence and his line of conduct, so that he won their profound respect; and indeed when he went for purification, they went to the place which he had been occupying and rubbed their hands thereon or carried away the dust from the places where he had walked; and they brought to him the sick that he might lay his hands on them. When a year had passed in this performance, and he perceived what respect he had won, he had a meeting with his wife in the lavatory, where he told her on the following Friday when the people were praying, to come, seize hold of him, and smite him on the face, and say to him: You enemy of Allah, you scoundrel, after killing my son in Baghdad, have you come here to play the devotee? May your face be smitten with your devotion!—You are not, he said, to let me go, but pretend that you want to slay me to avenge your son; the people will gather against you, but I will see that they do you no harm, as

I shall admit that I have killed him, and pretend that I have come to this town to do penance, and practise devotion in order to expiate my offence. You are then to demand that I be driven out of the mosque and brought to the magistrate for execution; the people will then offer to pay blood-money, but you are not to accept less than ten times the legal amount or what, from the eagerness with which they raise their bids, you gather that they are prepared to pay. When the bidding has reached a point beyond which they seem to you unlikely to go in their efforts to redeem my life, then accept the ransom, collect it and leave the town at once for the Baghdad road; I will escape and follow you. —The next day the woman came to the mosque, and when she saw him, she did what he had bidden her, buffeted him on the face and recited the speech which he had taught her. The people of the town rose up wishing to kill her, saying: Enemy of Allah, this is one of the chief saints, one of the maintainers of the world, the Pole[13] of the time, the lord of the age, and so on.—He signalled to them to be patient and not to hurt her, shortened his prayer, said the benediction, then rolled for a long time on the ground, and then asked the people whether since he had been living among them they had heard him speak a word. They were delighted to hear his voice, and a loud cry of No! gave the answer to his question. He then said: The reason is that I have been living among you to do penance for the crime she mentioned; I was a man who erred and ruined himself murdering this woman's son; but I have repented and came here to practise devotion. I was thinking of going back to her and looking for her that she might demand my blood, fearing lest my penitence might not be true; and I have constantly been praying God to accept my penitence and put me into her power until at last my prayer has been answered, and it is a sign that God has accepted my prayer that he has brought us together and put it into her power to obtain retaliation; suffer her therefore to slay me and I commit you to the care of God.—Cries and lamentations then arose, and one after another implored him to pray for him. The woman advanced in front of him as he moved, walking slowly and deliberately to the door of the mosque, with the in-

13. The Pole, or Quṭb, is a central concept in Ṣûfî cosmology.

tention of going thence to the palace of the governor of the place,
that the latter might order him to be executed for the murder of
her son. Then the sheikhs said: Citizens, why have you forgotten
to remedy this disaster and protect your country by the presence
of this saint? Deal gently with the woman and ask her to accept
the blood-money, which we shall pay out of our purses.—The
woman said: I refuse.—They said: Take twice the legal amount.
—She said: One hair of my son's head is worth a thousand times
the legal amount!—They went on bidding until they had
reached ten times the amount; then she said: Collect the money,
and when I have seen it, if I feel that I can accept it and acquit
the murderer, I will do so; if not, then I shall slay the slayer.—
They agreed to do this. Then said the man to her: Rise up, God
bless you and take me back to my place in the mosque.—She declined and he said: As you will.—The congregation went on
collecting money until they had got together a hundred thousand dirhems, which they asked her to accept. But she said: I
will take nothing but the death of my son's murderer; so deeply
has it affected my soul!—Thereupon the people began to fling
down their coats and cloaks and rings, the women their ornaments and every man some of his possessions, any one who was
unable to bear part of the ransom being in a terrible state, and
feeling like an outcast from society. At last she took what was
offered, acquitted the man and went off. The man remained in
the mosque a few days—long enough for her to get to a safe
distance—and himself decamped one night. When he was
sought the next day he could not be found nor was he heard of
until a long time after when they discovered that the whole affair had been a plot.

I was informed by Abu'l-Hasan Ahmad b. Yûsuf al-Azraq as
follows. I had heard, he said, how Husain b. Mansûr al-Hallâj[14]
would eat nothing for a month or so though he was under close
inspection. I was amazed thereat, and since there was a friendship between me and Abu'l-Faraj Ibn Rauhân the Sûfî, who was
a pious and devout traditionalist, and whose sister was married

14. Hallâj: a famous mystic who was executed (922) for publicly proclaim-
ing his unity with God.

to Qaṣrî, attendant of Ḥallâj, I asked him about this; he replied:
I do not know how Ḥallâj managed, but my brother-in-law
Qaṣrî, his attendant, practised abstinence from food for years
and by degrees got to be able to fast for fifteen days, more or
less. He used to manage this by a device which had escaped me,
but which he divulged when he was imprisoned with the other
followers of Ḥallâj.[14] If a man, he said, be strictly watched for
some length of time, and no trickery be discovered, the scrutiny
becomes less strict, and continues to slacken as fraud fails to
appear, until it is quite neglected, and the person watched can
do what he likes. These people have been watching me for fifteen
days wherein they have seen me eat nothing, and that is the limit
of my endurance of famine; if I continue to fast for one day more
I shall perish. Do you take a *ratl* of raisins of Khorasan and another of almonds and pound them into the consistency of oil-
dregs, then make them into thin leaf. When you come to me
to-morrow place it between two leaves of a note-book, which you
are to carry openly in your hand, so rolled up that its contents
may not break nor yet be seen. When you are alone with me and
see that no-one is watching, then put it under my coat-tails and
leave me; then I shall eat the cake secretly, and drink the water
with which I rinse my mouth for the ceremonial washing, and
this will suffice me for another fifteen days, when you will bring
me a second supply in the same style. If these people watch me
during the third fortnight, they will find that I eat nothing in
reality until you pay your periodical visit with supplies, when
I shall again escape their notice when I eat them, and this will
keep me alive. The narrator added that he followed these instructions the whole time the man was in prison.

Torture and Endurance

Among stories of extraordinary endurance is the following:—
when Bâbak al-Khurramî[15] and his colleague Mâziyâr were
brought before Mu'taṣim,[16] the latter said to the former: Bâbak,
you have perpetrated what no-one before has perpetrated, now

15. Bâbak: leader of a socio-religious rebellion against the 'Abbâsids (817-838).
16. Mu'taṣim: 'Abbâsid Caliph (r. 833-841).

exhibit unparalleled endurance.—Bâbak said: You shall see.—
When they were brought into the presence of Mu'tasim, the
Caliph ordered their hands and feet to be amputated before him.
The executioner commenced with Bâbak, whose right hand was
amputated; as the blood began to flow, Bâbak began to smear
therewith the whole of his face, until it was entirely disfigured
thereby. Mu'tasim bade them ask Bâbak why he did this. Being
asked, he replied: Tell the Caliph thus: You have ordered my
four limbs to be amputated, and are determined on my death;
you are doubtless not going to cauterize the stumps, but will
allow the blood to flow until I am decapitated. I was afraid the
blood might flow out to such an extent that my face would be
left pale, in which case those present might conclude from this
paleness that I was afraid of death, supposing this rather than
the loss of blood to be its cause; hence I smeared the blood all
over my face that no such paleness might be seen. Mu'tasim
said: Were it not that his crimes do not permit his being par-
doned, he would deserve to be spared for this heroism.—He then
ordered the executioner's work to continue. After the four limbs
had been amputated he was beheaded, the severed members
were then placed on the trunk, naphtha was then poured upon
them, and the whole set on fire. The same was done to his colleague and not one of them uttered a cry or a groan.

A Wazîr and a Qâdî

'Alî b. 'Îsâ[17] was anxious to display his superiority to every
one else in gravity of demeanour. Several people have told me
how in one of his vizierates he received a visit from the qâdî
Abû 'Umar, who had on him a magnificent dabîqî robe of Shustar manufacture. 'Alî b. 'Îsâ, wishing to make him ashamed of
himself, said to him: Abû 'Umar, at how much the piece did you
buy the material of your tunic?—Two hundred dinars was the
reply. 'Alî b. 'Îsâ said: Oh, the material out of which this
durrâ'ah[18] of mine was cut with the tunic underneath cost
twenty dinars!—Abû 'Umar answered without hesitation, as
though he had got his reply ready: *The vizier (God exalt him)*

17. Wazîr to 'Abbâsid Caliphs off and on from 913 to 928.
18. Outer garment.

*beautifies his clothes, and is therefore in no need of extravagance
therein, whereas we are beautified by ours, and in consequence
have to be extravagant. We come in contact with the lower
classes, whom we have to impress with our dignity; whereas the
vizier is served by the upper classes rather than by the lower,
and it is known that he neglects this parade while well able to
indulge in it.*—His reply made 'Alî b. 'Îsâ feel uncomfortable,
and he kept silent.

Acts of Prodigality

Mutawakkil[19] desired that every article whereon his eye
should fall on the day of a certain drinking-bout should be coloured yellow. Accordingly there was erected a dome of sandal-
wood covered and furnished with yellow satin, and there were
set in front of him melons and yellow oranges and yellow wine
in golden vessels; and only those slave-girls were admitted who
were yellow with yellow brocade gowns. The dome was erected
over a tesselated pond, and orders were given that saffron should
be put in the channels which filled it in sufficient quantities to
give the water a yellow colour as it flowed through the pond.
This was done, and as the drinking-bout was protracted their
supplies of saffron were exhausted and safflower was used as a
substitute, they supposing that he would be intoxicated before
this was exhausted, or they could incur reproach. It was exhausted, and when only a little remained they informed him,
fearing that he would be angry if the supply stopped, while the
want of time made it impossible for them to purchase more from
the market. When they told him, he blamed them for not having
laid in a large stock; and telling them that if the yellow water
ceased, his day would be spoiled, he bade them take fabrics that
were dyed yellow with *qasab* (?) and soak them in the channel
that the water might be coloured by the dye which they contained. This was done, and all the fabrics of this sort in the
treasury were exhausted by the time he was intoxicated. The
value of the saffron, safflower and ruined fabrics was estimated
and came to fifty thousand dinars.

19. Mutawakkil: 'Abbâsid Caliph (r. 847-860).

Another, I am told, was in a hurry to get rid of his money, and when only five thousand dinars were left, said he wanted to have done with it speedily in order that he might see what he would do afterwards. . . . Then one of his friends advised him to buy cut glass with the whole sum, all but five hundred dinars, spread the glass, which should be of the finest, out before him and expend the remaining dinars in one day on the fees of sing- ing women, fruit, scent, wine, ice, and food. When the wine was nearly drained he should set two mice free in the glass, and let a cat loose after them. The mice and the cat would fight amid the glass and break it all to pieces, and the remains would be plun- dered by the guests. The man aproved the notion, and acted upon it. He sat and drank and when intoxicated called out Now! and his friend let loose the two mice and the cat, and the glass went crashing to the amusement of the owner, who dropped off to sleep. His friend and companions then rose, gathered together the fragments, and made a broken bottle into a cup, and a broken cup into a pomade jar, and pasted up what was cracked; these they sold amongst themselves, making up a goodly num- ber of dirhems,[20] which they divided between them; they then went away, leaving their host, without troubling further about his concerns. When a year had passed the author of the scheme of the glass, the mice and the cat said: Suppose I were to go to that unfortunate and see what has become of him. So he went and found that the man had sold his furniture and spent the proceeds and dismantled his house and sold the materials to the ceilings so that nothing was left but the vestibule, where he was sleeping, on a cotton sheet, clad in cotton stripped off blankets, and bedding which had been sold, which was all that was left for him to put under him and keep off the cold. He looked like a quince ensconced between his two cotton sheets. I said to him: Miserable man, what is this?—What you see, he replied.—I said: Have you any sorrow? He said he had. I asked what it was. He said: I long to see some one—a female singer whom he loved and on whom he had spent most of his wealth. His visitor pro- ceeds: As the man wept, I pitied him, brought him garments from my house which he put on, and went with him to the

20. *Dirham*: silver coin weighing approximately 3 grams.

singer's dwelling. She, supposing that his circumstances had improved, let us enter, and when she saw him treated him respectfully, beamed on him, and asked how he was doing. When he told her the truth, she at once bade him rise, and when he asked why, said she was afraid her mistress would come, and finding him destitute, be angry with her for letting him in. So go outside, she said, and I will go upstairs and talk to you from above. —He went out and sat down expecting her to talk to him from a window on the side of the house which faced the street. While he was sitting, she emptied over him the broth of a stewpan, making an object of him, and burst out laughing. The lover however began to weep and said: O sir, have I come to this? I call God and I call thee to witness that I repent.—I began to mock him, saying: What good is your repentance to you now?— So I took him back to his house, stripped him of my clothes, left him folded in the cotton as before, took my clothes home and washed them, and gave the man up. I heard nothing of him for three years, and then one day at the *Tâq* Gate seeing a slave clearing the way for a rider, raised my head and beheld my friend on a fine horse with a light silver-mounted saddle, fine clothes, splendid underwear and fragrant with scent—now he was of a family of clerks and formerly in the days of his wealth, he used to ride the noblest chargers, with the grandest harness, and his clothes and accoutrements were of the magnificent style which the fortune inherited by him from his parents permitted. When he saw me, he called out: Fellow!—I, knowing that his circumstances must have improved, kissed his thigh, and said: My lord, Abû so-and-so!—He said Yes!—What is this? I asked. He said: God has been merciful, praise be to Him! Home, home. —I followed him till he had got to his door, and it was the old house repaired, all made into one court with a garden, covered over and stuccoed though not whitewashed, one single spacious sitting-room being left, whereas all the rest had been made part of the court. It made a good house, though not so lordly as of old. He brought me into a recess where he had in old times sought privacy, and which he had restored to its pristine magnificence, and which contained handsome furniture, though not of the former kind. His establishment now consisted of four slaves, each

of whom discharged two functions, and one old functionary
whom I remembered as his servant of old, who was now re-estab-
lished as porter, and a paid servant who acted as *sâ'is*. He took
his seat, and the slaves came and served him with clean plate of
no great value, fruits modest both in quantity and quality, and
food that was clean and sufficient, though not more. This we proceeded to eat, and then some excellent date-wine was set before
me, and some date jelly, also of good quality, before him. A
curtain was then drawn, and we heard some pleasant singing,
while the fumes of fresh aloes, and of *nadd* rose together. I was
curious to know how all this had come about, and when he was
refreshed he said: Fellow, do you remember old times?—I said
I did.—I am now, he continued, comfortably off, and the knowledge and experience of the world which I have gained are preferable in my opinion to my former wealth. Do you notice my
furniture? It is not as grand as of old, but it is of the sort which
counts as luxurious with the middle classes. The same is the case
with my plate, clothes, carriage, food, dessert, wine,—and he
went on with his enumeration, adding after each item "if it is
not super-fine like the old, still it is fair and adequate and sufficient." Finally he came to his establishment, compared its present with its former size, and added: This does instead. Now I
am freed from that terrible stress. Do you remember the day
the singing-girl—plague on her—treated me as she did, and how
you treated me on the same day, and the things you said to me
day by day, and on the day of the glass?—I replied: That is all
past, and praise be to God, who has replaced your loss, and delivered you from the trouble in which you were! But whence
comes your present fortune and the singing-girl who is now
entertaining us? He replied: She is one whom I purchased for a
thousand dinars, thereby saving the singing-women's fees. My
affairs are now in excellent order.—I said: How do they come
to be so?—He replied that a servant of his father and a cousin
of his in Egypt had died on one day, leaving thirty thousand
dinars, which were sent to him and arrived at the same time,
when he was between the cotton sheets, as I had seen him. So, he
said, I thanked God, and made a resolution not to waste, but to
economize, and live on my fortune till I die, being careful in my

expenditure. So I had this house rebuilt, and purchased all its present contents, furniture, plate, clothing, mounts, slaves male and female, for 5000 dinars; five thousand more have been buried in the ground as a provision against emergencies. I have laid out ten thousand on agricultural land, producing annually enough to maintain the establishment which you have seen, with enough over each year to render it unnecessary for me to borrow before the time when the produce comes in. This is how my affairs proceed and I have been searching for you a whole year, hearing nothing about you, being anxious that you should see the restoration of my fortunes and their continued prosperity and maintenance, and after that, you infamous scoundrel, to have nothing more to do with you. Slaves, seize him by the foot! And they *did* drag me by the foot right out of the house, not permitting me to finish my liquor with him that day. After that when I met him riding in the streets he would smile if he saw me, and he would have nothing to do either with me or any of his former associates.

Royal Authority

I was told by the qâdî Abu'l-Hasan Mohammed b. 'Abd al-Wâhid Hâshimî a story which he had heard from Abû 'Alî Hasan b. Ismâ'îl b. Ishâq, the qâdî, who was a companion of Mu'tadid[21] and allowed to take liberties with him. One day, he said, we were drinking with Mu'tadid, until Badr presented himself, and said: Sire, they have brought the draper from Birket Zalzal. Mu'tadid thereupon left the drinking-room, and retired to a chamber behind it, so close that we could see and hear. A curtain was then let down so as to screen it, the Caliph put on a qabâ[22] and, taking a spear in his hand, sat down with the expression of a man enraged and anxious to inspire terror. Hence we, notwithstanding our familiarity with him, were alarmed. A feeble old man was introduced, whom the Caliph questioned in a terrible voice: Are you the draper who said that yesterday?— The man fainted, and was ordered to be taken away until he had recovered his senses. He was then brought back and the Caliph

21. R. 892-902.
22. An outer garment with full-length sleeves.

said: What, does a man like you dare to say "the Moslems have no one to look after their interests"? Where do I come in, and what is my business?—He said: Commander of the Faithful, I am a tradesman, who understand nothing but thread and cotton, and how to talk to women and common people. A man passed by, with whom we did business buying his goods, and when we found his weight short, I said that, meaning the Censor[24] and no one else; I swear that I only referred to the Censor, and promise never to say the like again.—The Caliph said: The Censor shall be summoned and severely reprimanded for neglecting to interfere in such a matter, and shall be told to set it right, and to look after the travellers and tradesmen and bring them into order.— He then told the old man to go, and that no harm should befall him. He returned to us amused and diverted, and recommenced his potations. Under the influence of the wine I said: Sire, you know how inquisitive I am; have I permission to make a remark?—When he had given it, I said: Your majesty was agreeably occupied in drinking, but left it off to go and talk to a vulgar cur, for whom it would have been sufficient to be shouted at by one of the infantry of the district magistrate; not satisfied with letting this creature come into your majesty's presence, you changed your costume, armed yourself and personally examined him: all for the sake of a phrase commonly uttered by the vulgar, who do not even assign it any particular meaning.— Hasan, he replied, you do not know what may be the consequences of such a saying. If that sort of thing circulates among the people, one takes it up from another, they are emboldened to repeat it, get into the habit of uttering it until it becomes to them like the moral law. Such a thing easily instils disaffection towards the government and the religion, and the stirring up of revolts against the Sultan. The most effective mode of dealing with such a case is to stop the evil at its source.

Crime and Fraud

The following is a curious device put in pratice by a thief in our time. I was informed by Abu'l-Qasim 'Ubaidallah b. Mo-

23. I.e., the *muhtasib*, the officer who supervised markets and bazaars, as well as public morality in general.

hammed the Shoemaker that he had seen a thief caught and
charged with picking the locks of small tenements supposed to
be occupied by unmarried persons. Entering the house he would
dig a hole such as is called "the well" in the *nard* game, and
throw some nuts into it as though some one had been playing
with him, and leave by the side a handkerchief containing some
two hundred nuts. He would then proceed to wrap up as many
of the goods in the house as he could carry, and if he passed un-
observed, he would depart with his burden. If, however the master of the house came on the scene, he would abandon the booty
and endeavour to fight his way out. If the master of the house
proved doughty, sprung upon him, held him, tried to arrest him,
and called out Thieves!, and the neighbours assembled, he would
address the master of the house as follows: You are really wanting in humour. Here have I been playing nuts with you for
months, and, though you beggared me and took away all I possessed, I made no complaint, nor did I shame you before your
neighbours; and now that I have won your goods, you begin to
charge me with larceny, you mean and wretched creature! Between us is the gambling-house, the place where we became
acquainted. State in the presence of the people there or of the
people here that I have cheated, and I will leave you your goods.
The man might continue to assert that the other was a thief, but
the neighbours supposed that he was unwilling to be branded as
a gambler, and in consequence charged the other with theft;
whereas in reality he was a gambler and the other man was
speaking the truth. They would endeavour to make peace between the two, presently the thief would walk away with his
nuts, and the master of the house would be defamed.

He informed me that he knew of another whose plan was to
enter the residences of families, especially those in which there
were women whose husbands were out. If he succeeded in getting anything he would go away; if he were perceived and the
master of the house came, he would suggest that he was a friend
of the wife, and some officer's retainer; and ask the master to
keep the matter quiet from his employer for the sake of both;
displaying a uniform, and suggesting that if the master chose to

dishonour his household, he could not bring him before the Sultan on a charge of adultery. However much the master might shout Thief!, he would repeat his story, and when the neighbours assembled, they would advise the master of the house to hush the matter up. When the master objected, they would attribute his conduct to marital affection and help the thief to escape from his hand. Sometimes they would compel the master to let the thief go. Likewise the more the wife denied and swore with tears that the man was a thief, the more inclined would they be to let him go; so he would get off, and the master would afterwards divorce his wife, and part from his children's mother. This thief thus ruined more than one home and impoverished others, until he went into a house where there was an old woman aged more than ninety years; he not knowing of this. Caught by the master of the house he tried to make his usual insinuation; the master said to him: Scoundrel, there is on one in the house but my mother, who is ninety years old and for more than fifty of them she has spent her nights in prayer and her days in fasting; do you maintain that she is carrying on an amour with you or you with her? So he hit him on the jaw and when the neighbours came together and the thief told them the same story they told him he lied, they knowing the old lady's piety and devoutness. Finally he confessed the facts and was taken off to the magistrate.

I was told by Abu Mohammed 'Abdallâh b. 'Umar al-*H*arithî, on the authority of a professional connoisseur of stones with peculiar properties, who was of Khorasan, the following story. I passed, he said, by a pedlar in Egypt, and noticed that he had a stone with which I was acquainted, pretty to look at and weighing five drachms. He had put it in front of him among his goods. I was aware that it possessed the property of driving away flies, and had been on the look out for it for many years. When I saw it, I made a bid for it, and when he demanded five dirhems, I did not beat him down, but gave him the coins in good money. When they were in his possession and the stone in mine, he began to indulge in mirth at my expense, saying: How easily we can gull these asses who do not know what they give or what they take! I assure you I saw this pebble only a few days ago in the hands of a child, and gave him one sixth of a dirhem for it; and here has this fool been giving me five dirhems for it!—I turned back and said to him: I would have you know that you are the fool, not I.—How so, he asked.—Come with me, I said, and I will show you.—So I made him come, and presently we came to a huckster who was selling dates out of a dish, and the flies were buzzing all about. Bidding the man stand at a little distance from the dish, I placed the stone upon it, and when it was there all the flies flew away and left it, and for a time there was not a single fly there. Presently I took the stone away and the flies returned; then I replaced the stone and the flies flew off. I did this three times, then I concealed the stone, and said: Fool, this is the flystone, in search of which I have come the whole way from Khorasan. Among us, kings place it on their tables, and the flies will not come near, whence no fans nor fly-flaps are required. Had you asked five hundred dinars for it, I should have given them you. The man heaved a deep sign, so deep that I thought his end had come; after a time he recovered, and we parted. After some days I went off to Khorasan, having in my possession the stone, which I sold to Nasr b. Ahmad the governor for ten thousand dirhems.

Essays

A popular literary exercise of the 'Abbâsid age was known as *adab*. The term is not easily translated: it means a way of dealing gracefully with a topic, not too seriously or dryly, but in an urbane and sophisticated way. *Adab* was also used to refer to the qualities and ideal of life—a Muslim version of England's eighteenth-century gentility—that found expression in such writing.

Abû 'Uthmân 'Amr ibn Bahr al-Fuqaimî al-Basrî al-Jâhiz (776-869), the author of the following selection, was a master of this form of art. Born of an obscure non-Arab family and educated in Basra, Jâhiz soon attracted the attention of the Caliph Ma'mûn (r. 813-833) through his talent for writing. For the rest of his life he wrote industriously, apparently living on the gifts of rich patrons. In all, Jâhiz was credited with more than two hundred books.

Many of the subjects Jâhiz touched upon carried a good deal of dynamite and fascinated 'Abbâsid society. His essay "The Merits of the Turks and of The Imperial Army as a Whole" addressed itself to one such controversial matter. At the time the Turks were threatening military preponderance in Baghdâd and cultivated Arabs were inclined both to despise and to fear them. Jâhiz' essays also skirted questions of faith, challenging the religious enthusiasts of 'Abbâsid society more by a light, disengaged tone than by direct contradiction or overt expression of disbelief.

JÂHIZ: "FROM THE MERITS OF THE TURKS" AND OTHER ESSAYS

I Semi-Political, Semi-Theological Works
The Merits of the Turks and of the Imperial Army as a Whole

This epistle is addressed to al-Fath b. Khâqân, the Caliph's favourite and himself a Turk. After declaring that knowledge must precede action, the author expresses his admiration for the loyalty and zeal with which al-Fath defends his master against the

ENEMIES OF AUTHORITY

. . . The monarch has no lack of people in whom disfavour has aroused resentment, base fellows spoilt by royal favour, impatient ones who, having received double their due, suppose, in their ignorance of their true worth and their narrowminded in-

From *The Life and Works of Jahiz*, by Charles Pellat (trans. by D. M. Hawkes). Originally published by the University of California Press, 1969, pp. 91-97, 106-8, 195-97, 239-43, 251, 257-58, 265-67. Reprinted by permission of the Regents of the University of California Press and Routledge & Kegan Paul Ltd.

gratitude, that their proper share is larger and their right to it better founded than it really is; malcontents who deserve rather to be reminded of their monarch's earlier favours and past kindnesses to them, but who have been led astray by the tolerance shown them, made insolent by a long spell of good fortune, and spoilt by long-standing freedom from material cares; revolutionaries unknown in the community but mighty in disorder, who thrive on commotion: having been driven away by the power of the monarch, restored to favour by the educational instrument of *adab*, and humbled and brought low by the rule of law, they now make defamation their sole [defence], are satisfied only when engaging in seditious talk, find their peace only in wild dreams, and associate only with agitators, impostors and suspected lunatics; and men of ambition but no merit, unworthy opponents, who on the strength of some matter earlier put down to their credit, or a service actually rendered by someone else, seek to be placed on a par with men of merit and set above the supporters of the régime.

THE UNITY OF THE IMPERIAL ARMY

You tell me that at a gathering attended by members of the Imperial army of various nationalities, descendants of 'Abbâsid propagandists, old men belonging to the Shî'ite élite, seasoned sons of high officials, and men known for their loyalty and the sincerity of their religious convictions . . . , you heard a man in the body of the audience, one of the last category of those present, make an ex-tempore speech of remarkable authority and independence of thought, without kowtowing to the great men or being overawed by the orators present. Expressing strong views in outspoken language, he declared that the Imperial army at present consisted of five groups: Khurâsânîs,[1] Turks, *mawâlî*,[2] Arabs and Abnâ'[3]; and he gave thanks to God for uniting men so different, races so varied and ambitions so disparate under the same allegiance.

1. Khurâsânîs: Arab tribesmen from the Persian province of Khurâsân, important supporters in bringing 'Abbâsids to the throne originally; comprised separate unit in 'Abbâsid army.
2. Mawâlî: emancipated slaves, clients. (Tr.)
3. Abnâ': the descendants of the Persian immigrants in the Yemen. (Tr.)

You say that you challenged this extraordinary speaker, this affected orator, who had set up these subdivisions and distinguished these groups, contrasting their racial origins, differentiating between them on ethnic grounds and emphasizing the disparity of their antecedents. You upbraided him severely for his words and heaped abuse on him, saying that the Imperial army ought to be described as united, or virtually so, and that you did not approve of the introduction of racial distinctions between its various groups, or any loosening of the ties that bound them together.

Al-Fath had reinforced his argument by declaring that the army could really be regarded as composed entirely of Khurâsânîs, and that there were no sharp distinctions between the various groups. In an endeavour to bring them together, he had also said that the Turks already formed part and parcel of the Arab community, but that the orator in question had simply omitted to mention them. Jâhiz accordingly proposes to deal with the Turks and compare their merits with those of the other groups, with a view to conciliating them. The author bases himself on evidence from friends of his who have taken part in discussions about the virtues of the various groups within the army; he reports that the officers tend to regard the Khârijites as more formidable than the Turks—except a certain Humaid, whose views he proceeds to retail.

THE TURK AS A HORSEMAN

A Khârijite[4] at close quarters relies entirely on his lance. But the Turks are as good as the Khârijites with the lance, and in addition, if a thousand of their horsemen are hard-pressed they will loose all their arrows in a single volley and bring down a thousand enemy horsemen. No body of men can stand up against such a test.

Neither the Khârijites nor the Bedouins are famous for their prowess as mounted bowmen. But the Turk will hit from his saddle an animal, a bird, a target, a man, a couching animal, a

---

4. Khârijite: religious sect opposed to Shî'ites and Sunnites, which engaged in repeated warfare. (Tr.)

marker post or a bird of prey stooping on its quarry. His horse may be exhausted from being galloped and reined in, wheeled to right and left, and mounted and dismounted: but he himself goes on shooting, loosing ten arrows before the Khârijite has let fly one. He gallops his horse up a hillside or down a gully faster than the Khârijite can make his go on the flat.

The Turk has two pairs of eyes, one at the front and the other at the back of his head.

One of the criticisms of the Khârijite concerns his way of disengaging from combat, and of the Khurâsânî his method of engaging. The weakness of the Khurâsânîs is that as soon as they come up with the enemy they wheel round: if pursued they then take flight, and return again and again to the charge. These are reckless tactics, which may encourage the enemy to keep on their heels. When the Khârijites break off an engagement, it is broken off for good: once they withdraw they do not return to the charge, unless by chance. The Turk does not wheel round like the Khurâsânî, indeed if he turns his horse's head it is deadly poison and certain death, for he aims his arrow as accurately behind him as he does in front of him. Especially formidable is his trick of using his lasso to throw a horse and unseat its rider, all at full gallop. . . . He also commonly resorts to another trick with his lasso: he aims it nowhere near his adversary, and the fool takes this for clumsiness on the Turk's part or adroitness on his own!

They train their horsemen to carry two or even three bows, and spare bowstrings in proportion. Thus in the hour of battle the Turk has on him everything needful for himself, his weapon and the care of his steed. As for their ability to stand trotting, sustained galloping, long night rides and cross-country journeys, it is truly extraordinary. In the first place the Khârijite's horse has not the staying-power of the Turk's pony; and the Khârijite has no more than a horseman's knowledge of how to look after his mount. The Turk, however, is more experienced than a professional farrier, and better than a trainer at getting what he wants from his pony. For it was he who brought it into the world and reared it from a foal; it comes when he calls it, and follows behind him when he runs. . . .

If the Turks' daily life were to be reckoned up in detail, he would be found to spend more time in the saddle than on the ground.

The Turk sometimes rides a stallion, sometimes a brood mare. Whether he is going to war, on a journey, out hunting or on any other errand, the brood mare follows behind with her foals. If he gets tired of hunting the enemy he hunts waterfowl. If he gets hungry, jogging up and down in the saddle, he has only to lay hands on one of his animals. If he gets thirsty, he milks one of his brood mares. If he needs to rest his mount, he vaults on to another without so much as putting his feet to the ground.

Of all living creatures he is the only one whose body can adapt itself to eating nothing but meat. As for his steed, leaves and shoots are all it needs; he gives it no shelter from the sun and no covering against the cold.

As regards ability to stand trotting, if the stamina of the border fighters, the posthorse outriders, the Khârijites and the eunuchs were all combined in one man, they would not equal a Turk.

The Turk demands so much of his mount that only the toughest of his horses is equal to the task; even one that he had ridden to exhaustion, so as to be useless for his expeditions, would outdo a Khârijite's horse in staying-power, and no Tukhâri pony could compare with it.

The Turk is at one and the same time herdsman, groom, trainer, horse-dealer, farrier and rider: in short, a one-man team.

When the Turk travels with horsemen of other races, he covers twenty miles to their ten, leaving them and circling around to right and left, up on to the high ground and down to the bottom of the gullies, and shooting all the while at anything that runs, crawls, flies or stands still. The Turk never travels like the rest of the band, and never rides straight ahead. On a long, hard ride, when it is noon and the halting-place is still afar off, all are silent, oppressed with fatigue and overwhelmed with weariness. Their misery leaves no room for conversation. Everything round them crackles in the intense heat, or perhaps is frozen hard. As the journey drags on, even the toughest and most resolute begin to wish that the ground would open under their feet. At the sight of a mirage or a marker post on a ridge they are transported with joy, supposing it to be the halting-place. When at last they reach it, the horsemen all drop from the saddle and stagger about bandy-legged like children who have been given an enema, groaning like sick men, yawning to refresh themselves and stretching luxuriously to overcome their stiffness. But your Turk, though he has covered twice the distance and dislocated his shoulders with shooting, has only to catch sight of a gazelle or an onager near the halting-place, or put up a fox or a hare, and he is off again at a gallop as though he had only just mounted. It might have been someone else who had done that long ride and endured all that weariness.

At a gully the band bunches together at the bridge or the best crossing-place; but the Turk, digging his heels into his pony, is already going up the other side like a shooting star. If there is a steep rise, he leaves the track and scrambles straight up the hillside, going where even the ibex cannot go. To see him scaling such slopes anyone would think he was recklessly risking his life: but if that were so he would not last long, for he is always doing it. . . .

. . . The Khârijite's lance is long and heavy, the Turk's a hollow pike; and short hollow lances have greater penetrating power and are lighter to carry. This is why the Îrânîs keep long lances only for their foot-soldiers: these are the weapons used by the Persians of Iraq for fighting at the entries to trenches and from behind barricades. Not that they are to be compared with the Turks or the Khurâsânîs; in most cases they use them only at the entries to trenches or from behind barricades. The others are horsemen and riders, and horses and riders are the pivot of an army. They it is who withdraw and return to the charge, who fold the battalions around themselves as a letter is folded, and then scatter them like hair. No ambush, advance-guard or rear-guard duty but is always entrusted to the best of the mounted troops. Theirs are the glorious days, the famous battles, the vast conquests. Without them there could be no squadrons or battle formations. They it is who carry the standards and banners, the kettledrums, bells and trappings. Theirs are the neighing, the dust flying, the spurring on, the cloaks and weapons flapping in the wind, and the thunder of hooves; they are the unerring in pursuit, the unattainable when pursued.

The author continues his eulogy of the Turks, quoting sundry traditions borrowed from the man Humaid. Then he considers their psychology, pointing out that they are characterized by great home-sickness for their own country and exceptional fondness for moving about. From this he passes on to a consideration of

NATIONAL CHARACTERISTICS

. . . Know that every nation, people, generation or tribe that shows itself outstanding in craftsmanship or pre-eminent in eloquence, the various branches of learning, the establishment of empires or the art of war, only attains the peak of perfection because God has steered it in that direction and given it the means and the special aptitudes appropriate to those activities. Peoples of varying habits of thought, different opinions and dissimilar characters cannot attain perfection unless they fulfill the conditions needed to carry on an activity, and have a natural aptitude for it. Good examples are the Chinese in craftsmanship, the Greeks in philosophy and literature, the Arabs in fields that we mean to deal with in their proper place, the Sâsânians[5] in imperial administration, and the Turks in the art of war. Do you not see that the Greeks, who studied theory, were not merchants, artisans, sowers, farmers, builders, fruit-farmers, hoarders of treasure or men bent on making money by hard work? Their rules absolved them from the necessity to work by providing for their needs; and hence they were free to engage in research, and (thanks to their single-mindedness, ingenuity and imaginativeness) to invent machines, tools and musical instruments—music which brings peace to the soul, relaxation after travail, and blessed balm for the ulcer of anxiety. They built for men's profit and edification scales, balances, astrolabes, hourglasses and other [instruments], and invented medicine, mathematics, geometry, music and engines of war such as the mangonel, etc.

5. Sâsânians: Persian dynasty overthrown by early Muslim conquests.

They were thinkers, not doers: they designed the machine, made
a template and drew a model of the tool, but could not use it;
they confined themselves to giving directions about instruments,
without handling them themselves. They loved science, but
shrank from its application.

The Chinese for their part are specialists in smelting, casting
and metalworking, in fine colours, in sclupture, weaving and
drawing; they are very skilful with their hands, whatever the
medium, the technique or the cost of the materials. The Greeks
are theoreticians rather than practitioners, while the Chinese
are practitioners rather than theoreticians; the former are thinkers, the latter doers.

The Arabs, again, were not merchants, artisans, physicians,
farmers—for that would have degraded them—, mathematicians
or fruit-farmers—for they wished to escape the humiliation of
the tax; nor were they out to earn or amass money, hoard possessions or lay hands on other people's; they were not of those
who make their living with a pair of scales, or [by giving
short measure] in dried foods, and knew neither the *qîrât*[6] nor
the *dânaq*,[7] they were not poor enough to be indifferent to learning, pursued neither wealth, that breeds foolishness, nor good
fortune, that begets apathy, and never tolerated humiliation,
which was dishonour and death to their souls. They dwelt in the
plains, and grew up in contemplation of the desert. They knew
neither damp nor rising mist, neither fog nor foul air, nor a
horizon bounded by walls. When these keen minds and clear
brains turned to poetry, fine language, eloquence and oratory, to
physiognomy and astrology, genealogy, navigation by the stars
and by marks on the ground, and knowledge of *anwâ'*,[8] to horse-
breeding, weaponry and engines of war, to memorizing all that
they heard, pondering on everything that caught their attention
and discriminating between the glories and the shames of their
tribes, they achieved perfection beyond the wildest dreams. Cer-

6. *Qîrât*: weight of about 0.2 grams. (Tr.)

7. *Dânaq*: Coin and weight equivalent to one-sixth of a *dirham* (2.98 gr.
silver) or *dînâr* (4.25 gr. gold). (Tr.)

8. *Anwâ'*: system of computation used by the early Arabs, based on the observation of certain stars. (Tr.)

tain of these activities broadened their minds and exalted their aspirations, so that of all nations they are now the most glorious and the most given to recalling their past splendours.

It is the same with the Turks who dwell in tents in the desert and keep herds: they are the Bedouins of the non-Arabs . . . Uninterested in craftsmanship or commerce, medicine, geometry, fruit-farming, building, digging canals or collecting taxes, they care only about raiding, hunting, horsemanship, skirmishing with rival chieftains, taking booty and invading other countries. Their efforts are all directed towards these activities, and they devote all their energies to these occupations. In this way they have acquired a mastery of these skills, which for them take the place of craftsmanship and commerce and constitute their only pleasure, their glory and the subject of all their conversation. Thus have they become in the realm of warfare what the Greeks are in philosophy, the Chinese in craftsmanship, and the Arabs in the fields we have enumerated.

Jâhiz adds, however, that not all Greeks, Turks, Bedouins, etc., conform to the picture he has been painting of them. After listing the qualities required in war, he quotes a line of reasoning by which the Turks claim to be closer to the caliphate than the Arabs; he then offers some information about customary law among the Khurâsânîs and the Turks, tells some anecdotes, and concludes by apologizing for his own deficiencies.

II Jâhiz' Own Particular Type of Adab
The Taghlabî Lad and His Stick[9]

. . . When I was a young man and my purse light, I left Mosul to go privily to Raqqa;[10] and my travelling-companion was a lad from the Jazîra[11] whose like I have never seen since. He told me he was a Taghlabî and a descendant of 'Amr b. Kulthûm.[12] He carried a haversack, a water-skin and a stick. He never let go of the latter for a moment, but took it with him everywhere he

9. Taghlabî: of the tribe of Taghlib, partially Christian N. Arabian tribe. (Tr.)
10. Raqqa: town in upper Mesopotamia. (Tr.)
11. Jazîra: upper Mesopotamia. (Tr.)
12. 'Amr b. Kulthûm: pre-Islâmic poet. (Tr.)

went, which so irritated me that I almost threw it into the river. We were on foot; when we found beasts of burden we rode them, but otherwise we walked. I made some remarks to my companion about his stick; but he replied that when Moses son of 'Imrân saw a fire on Sinai and was minded to go and take a brand from it for his family, he took care to take his stick with him even that little way. When he reached the holy vale of the promised land, he heard a voice saying: "Throw away thy stick and put off thy sandals"; so he threw away his sandals, which he did not need (for God had cleansed the ground of all impurities), and God put all His miracles and signs into Moses's stick, and spoke to him from inside a bush and not from within a man or a jinn.

He continued to sing the praises of sticks, while I laughed and paid no heed to him. When we set off on our donkeys, the donkeyman remained behind; my companion's mount went well, and when it showed signs of stopping he drove it on with his stick, whereas mine would not go, well knowing that I had nothing in my hand to use on it. The boy arrived at our night's halting-place long before me, and had time to rest himself and his ass, while I had to wait for the donkeyman to come up. I said to myself: That is number one!

In the morning, when we were ready to set off again, we could find nothing to ride, and so started out on foot. When he got tired he rested on his stick; and he even ran and vaulted with it, putting one end into the ground and taking off like an arrow. When we reached the night's halting-place I was tired out, while he was still quite fresh. I said to myself: That is number two!

On the third day we passed through an area where the ground was all cracked and fissured, and came upon a terrible snake, which attacked us. All I could do was to take to my heels and abandon my companion to the reptile. But he hit it with his stick and stunned it, and when it reared up and made to strike again he felled it with another blow of his stick and killed it with a third. I said to myself: That is number three, and the most serious yet!

On the fourth day I had a great craving for meat; but I was a fugitive, and penniless. Suddenly a hare got up: my companion hit it with his stick, and before I knew what was happening he was holding it up in the air. We were able to slaughter it in the prescribed fashion.[13] I said to myself: That is number four!

Then I said to him: "If only we had a light, I would not wait for the night's halting-place to eat it." "But you have," he said, and taking a piece of wood from his haversack he rubbed it against the stick and struck a far better spark than *markh*[14] and *'afar*[15] make. He collected all the twigs and rubbish he could find, made a fire, and put the hare on to cook. When we took it off it looked unappetizing, covered with earth and ash; but the Taghlabî took it in his left hand and tapped it a few times with his stick, and everything that had stuck to it fell off. We ate, my craving for meat was assuaged, and all was well. I said to myself: That is number five!

Then we stopped at a caravanserai, and found that the rooms were full of dust and filth, for troops had been in it before us, and moreover the place was falling in ruins, and we could find no [decent] place to lie. My companion caught sight of the head of a shovel lying in a corner; he picked it up, fitted his stick into it for a handle, and began to clear out all the dirt; he cleaned the floor so thoroughly that the flagstones were exposed to view and the foul smell went away. I said to myself: That is number six!

I was not anxious to put my clothes and provisions on the floor, so he took his stick out of the shovel-head, drove it into the wall and hung my clothes up on it. I said to myself: That is number seven!

When we reached the crossroads and I was about to take leave of him, he said to me: "If you would turn aside and spend the night at my house, you would be fulfilling the obligations that devolve on a travelling-companion. The house is close at hand." So I followed him, and he took me to a house adjoining a church.

13. I.e., cutting throat with a knife.
14. *Markh*: wood used in conjunction with *'afar* (see below) for striking a light. (Tr.)
15. *'Afar*: wood used in conjunction with *markh* (q.v.) for striking a light. (Tr.)

All night long he engaged me in conversation on a variety of topics and told me interesting stories. At daybreak he took up a piece of wood and began to strike it with the famous stick, and lo! it was a prayergong without its peer in the whole world, and he seemed to me the most skilful of men in its use. "You wretch!" I said to him, "so you are no Muslim, for all you are an Arab descended from 'Amr b. Kulthûm!" "Yes, I am," he replied. "Then what are you doing beating that gong?" "Excuse me," he replied, "my father is a Christian, and the priest of this church. Since he is very old, I help him as best I can when I am at home."

I had been involved with a real devil, the cleverest, most urbane and best educated of men. I told him that I had kept count of the virtues of his stick, after having been tempted to throw it away. "Were I to start telling you about the virtues of sticks," he cried, "the night would be too short!"

Superiority of the Blacks to the Whites

Jâhiz sets out to write a disquisition on the glories of the Negro race. He quotes memorable sayings by Negroes, and goes on to enumerate the famous men who were black, quoting apposite verses by each of them.

THE ZANJ[16]

Negroes say: Everybody agrees that there is no people on earth in whom generosity is as universally well developed as the Zanj; and this is a quality found only in those of noble character. These people have a natural talent for dancing to the rhythm of the tambourine, without needing to learn it. There are no better singers anywhere in the world, no people more polished and eloquent, and no people less given to insulting language. All other peoples in the world have their stammerers, those who have difficulty in pronouncing certain sounds, and those who cannot express themselves fluently or are downright tongue-tied, except the Zanj. Sometimes some of them hold forth before their ruler

16. African Negroes, employed mainly as navvies on the extensive swampy area in the neighborhood of Basra. (Tr.)

continuously from sunrise to sunset, without needing to turn round or pause in their flow. No other nation can surpass them in bodily strength and physical thoughness. One of them will lift huge blocks and carry heavy loads that would be beyond the strength of most Bedouins or members of other races. They are courageous, energetic and generous, which are the virtues of nobility, and also good-tempered and with little propensity to evil. They are always cheerful, smiling and devoid of malice, which is a sign of a noble character. Some people say that their generosity is due to their stupidity, shortsightedness and lack of foresight, but our reply is that this is a scurvy way of commending generosity and altruism. At that rate the wisest and most intelligent man would be the most niggardly and ungenerous. But in fact the Slavs are more niggardly than the Byzantines, and the latter more intelligent and thoughtful; according to our opponents' argument, the Slavs ought to be more generous and open-handed than the Byzantines. . . .

The Zanj say to the Arabs: You are so ignorant that during the *jâhiliyya*[17] you regarded us as your equals [when it came to marrying] Arab women, but with the advent of the justice of Islam you decided this practice was bad. Yet the desert is full of Negroes married to Arab wives, and they have been princes and kings and have safeguarded your rights and sheltered you against your enemies.

Jâhiz mentions other famous Negroes, and refers to the exploits of the Abyssinians, the things their country produces, etc. He asserts that black is superior to other colours. Negroes are proud of their great numbers; also, the Arabs do not really know them, since all they see is Negro slaves. After some reflections on cross-breeding between races, and on men's taste for the female slaves commonest in their own countries, he repeats that the blacks outnumber the whites, and gives his view on the

ORIGIN OF BLACK SKIN

. . . We say that God did not make us black in order to disfigure us; rather it is our environment that has made us so. The

17. *Jâhiliyya*: period of "ignorance" before the advent of Islâm. (Tr.)

best evidence of this is that there are black tribes among the Arabs, such as the Banû Sulaim b. Mansûr,[18] and that all the peoples settled in the Harra[19] besides the Banû Sulaim are black. These tribes take slaves from among the Ashbân[20] to mind their flocks and for irrigation work, manual labour and domestic service, and their wives from among the Byzantines; and yet it takes less than three generations for the Harra to give them all the complexion of the Banû Sulaim. This Harra is such that the gazelles, ostriches, insects, wolves, foxes, sheep, asses, horses and birds that live there are all black. White and black are the results of environment, the natural properties of water and soil, distance from the sun and intensity of heat. There is no question of metamorphosis, or of punishment, disfigurement or favour meted out by God. Besides, the land of the Banû Sulaim has much in common with the land of the Turks, where the camels, beasts of burden and everything belonging to these people is similar in appearance: everything of theirs has a Turkish look. The soldiers of the frontier garrisons on this side of the 'Awâsim[21] sometimes come across Byzantine sheep mixed up with sheep belonging to the local inhabitants, but they have no difficulty in distinguishing the Byzantine flocks from the Syrian by their "Byzantinity." When one comes across the descendants of Bedouin men and women who have ended up in Khurâsân, it is immediately apparent that they are the barbarians of these parts.

III *Traditional* Adab
Misers

THE GLASS LAMP

. . . One day Abû 'Abd Allâh al-Marwazî paid a visit to a *shaikh*[22] from Khurâsân, and the latter had just lit one of those

18. Banû Sulaim b. Mansûr: tribe of the Qais confederacy of N. Arabian tribes. (Tr.)
19. Harra: basalt desert stretching from southern Syria to Medina. (Tr.)
20. Ashbân: a people regarded by Muslim writers as of Persian origin. (Tr.)
21. 'Awâsim: part of the border country between the Byzantine and Arab empires. (Tr.)
22. Shaikh: respected person, elder. (Tr.)

green pottery lamps. "Upon my soul," exclaimed Abû 'Abd Allâh, "you do nothing right. I grumbled at you for using stone lamps, and you think to please me [by replacing them] with pottery. Do you not know that stone and earthenware literally drink oil?" "Excuse me," replied the *shaikh*, "I gave this lamp to a friend of mine who is an oil merchant, and he put it in his filter for a month, so that it is super-saturated and will never absorb any more." "That is not my point. That may be a good way you have discovered of dealing with that problem. But do you not know that the flame continually burning at the end of the wick dries out the part of the lamp it is in contact with? When this place is saturated the flame soaks up the oil from it and burns it. If you were to compare the amount of oil absorbed from this place with the amount drawn up into the wick, you would find that the former is greater."

"Moreover the part of the lamp that is in contact with the wick is always running with oil. I am told that if a lighted lamp is placed inside an empty one, after one night or two at the outside the underneath one is full of oil. You can observe it also if you look at salt and bran placed underneath a lamp to level it: they are absolutely soaked in oil. All this represents loss and waste such as can be condoned only by spendthrifts. Such people are continually providing others with food and drink, but at least they occasionally reap some benefit from it, trifling though it may be; whereas all you are doing is giving food and drink to the flame. And on the Day of Resurrection God will feed the flames with those that have fed them during their lifetime!"

"Then what should one do, pray?" asked the *shaikh*.

"Get a glass lamp. Glass is better than any other material: it is non-porous and non-absorbent, and does not collect dust. As a rule the only way to remove dust is either to rub the lamp hard or else to set light to it, and either way the effect is to dry the lamp out still further. Glass, on the other hand, withstands water and wine better than pure gold; and moreover it is manufactured, whereas gold is in its natural state. If gold is to be preferred for its hardness, glass is superior by virtue of its cleanness. Finally, glass is transparent, while gold is opaque. Furthermore, since the wick in a glass lamp is situated at the centre, the edges do not get heated by the flame as they do in an ordinary lamp. When a ray of light strikes the glass, the flame and the lamp together become a single source of light, reflecting each other's rays. This effect can be observed when a ray of light strikes a mirror, the surface of water or a piece of glass: its brightness is doubled, and if it shines in someone's eye it dazzles and may even blind him. It is said in the Koran: 'God is the light of the heavens and of the earth. This light is like a niche in which is a torch set in a glass like a glittering star; the torch is lit with oil from a sacred tree, an olive neither of the East nor of the West, whose oil glows even when no fire touches it. It is light upon light. God guides to His light whom He pleases.[23] Oil in a glass lamp is "light upon light," brightness upon twofold brightness. In addition to this advantage there is the point that a glass lamp is handsomer than a stone or pottery one."

. . . .

LANDLORDS AND TENANTS

. . . Here is a story that was told me by Ma'bad[24]: While I was living in al-Kindî's[25] house, I had a cousin of mine and his son to stay. Al-Kindî at once sent me a note as follows: "If these two persons stay a day or two, I will say nothing; nevertheless, if tenants are going to take the liberty of inviting guests to stay overnight, it will not be long before they inflict them on us for long periods." "They are only staying about a month," I hastened to reply.

He[26] wrote back: "The rent of your house is thirty *dirhams*[27]; and since there are six of you, that comes to five *dirhams* a head. Now that there are two more of you, that will be another twice five *dirhams*; so from today your rent will be forty *dirhams*."

"What harm does their being here do you?" I asked; "Their weight presses only on the earth, which supports mountains, and

23. Qur'ân XXIV:35. (Tr.)
24. Ma'bad: theologian and contemporary of Jâhiz. (Tr.)
25. Al-Kindî: perhaps the celebrated philosopher and astronomer, d. after 870. (Tr.)
26. Probably Jâhiz himself. (Tr.)
27. Silver coin weighing 2.98 grams. (Tr.)

their board is entirely my responsibility. Write and let me know your reasons."

Little did I know the question I was raising or the road I was setting out on! He sent me a letter as follows:

There are several reasons that prompt me to adopt this attitude; they are well known, and do not alter. The first is that the cesspit fills up more quickly, and its costs a lot to have it emptied. Then, as the number of feet increases, there is more treading on the clay-surfaced flat roofs and the plastered floors of the bedrooms, and more wear and tear on the staircase: the clay flakes off, the plaster crumbles, and the steps get worn down —to say nothing of the fact that the ceiling joists bend and break under all the trampling about and extra weight they have to bear. When people are continually going in and out, opening and closing doors and drawing and shooting the bolt, the doors split and their fastenings get broken off. When there are more children, and twice as big a swarm of brats, the nails and hinges of the doors get torn off, and all the courtyards suffer: the children dig holes in them for their nutshell games, and crack the flagstones with their go-carts. Moreover the walls get ruined through people hammering in pegs and shelf-brackets.

When the number of members of the family, visitors, lodgers and guests goes up, there is ten times as much pouring of water and seepage from pitchers and jars as usual. Many a wall has been undermined, had its upper courses crumble and its foundations give way and threatened to collapse altogether, as the result of seepage from a pitcher or a jar, or because too much water was drawn from the well and the whole thing mishandled.

The requirements of bread, food, fuel and heating increase with the number of heads. Now fire is "no respecter of persons," and houses and their contents make ideal fuel for it. How many tenement blocks have been burnt down, resulting in ruinous expense for their owners! A disaster of this sort may coincide with a lean period and a time of financial stringency; sometimes also—and this is really criminal—the fire may spread to the neighbouring buildings, causing injury to persons and damage to property there as well.

If the property owner had only these trials and tribulations to put up with, it would perhaps be bearable; but he is regarded as a bird of ill omen, and heaped with reproaches and insults.

[To come back to tenants,] they choose to use the high rooms built on the flat roof as kitchens, even though there is ample space on the ground floor or in the courtyard—and this despite the danger to life and property that it causes. There is the further risk that in the event of fire the undamaged portions of the house are liable to be broken into by hooligans, who might unearth closely guarded secrets and hidden things: a stranger in hiding, an absconding landlord, forbidden liquor, a compromising book, treasure that there was no time to bury before the disaster—in short, all manner of situations and things that people like to keep secret.

Next, they always build their ovens and fireplaces for cooking-pots on the flat roof, where there is only a thin layer of clay —quite an inadequate protection—between them and the reeds and boards that make up the ceiling. Moreover they take very little trouble to build them properly, and do not spare a thought for the damage these ovens and fireplaces cause.

It is odd that you [tenants] should deliberately set out on an undertaking that may well be to the detriment of all of us; and it is even odder that you should neglect, indeed be quite oblivious of, your duty to our property and your own!

There are many of you that have to be begged for your rent, and procrastinate endlessly about paying. When they are several months in arrears they abscond, leaving their landlords to go hungry and rue the kindness and forbearance they lavished on them. All the thanks and reward they get is to be done an injury and made to suffer a loss.

When a tenant moves in, we will have swept and cleaned the house to make it look nice and attract custom; when he moves out, he leaves filth and dilapidations that call for heavy expenditure. Moreover he never fails to take with him the beam used for wedging the door, the ladder, sundry building materials and the water-cooler. Instead of doing his laundry on the ground floor, with the help of the copper and the paddle, he carries out this operation [upstairs,] on the beams, the joists and the balconies. If the floor of the house is plastered or paved with bricks, and the landlord thinking to save the floor, has put a stone in one corner for crushing and pounding on, the tenants, out of thoughtlessness, spite, deceitfulness or baseness, do their crushing and pounding wherever they may happen to be, without a thought for the damage they are causing. They pay no compensation, and neither apologize to the landlord nor privily ask God's forgiveness. The tenant thinks his ten *dirhams* a year [for repairs] excessive, but considers it reasonable enough that the landlord should have spent a thousand *dînârs*[28] on the purchase of the house. He keeps account of the little he gives us, but says not a word about all that we give him. And then again the passage of time will destroy anything, however well built, and will wear out new things and break down the stoutest joints. It wears away buildings as it does rocks, and attacks masonry as it does everything else, first parching and withering and then destroying. It does not take long for houses to be in ruins. The tenants who live in them have the pleasure and benefit of them: it is they who wear them out and rob them of their freshness, and their ill-treatment that ages them and brings their end nigh.

COMPREHENSIVE SCRAP-RECOVERY

. . . Abû Sa'îd used to forbid his servant-girl to throw the garbage out, and even instructed her to collect the tenants' garbage and put it with his own. Every so often he would sit down, and the servant would get a basket, tip out little heaps of rubbish in front of him and rummage through them one by one. If he found some *dirhams*, a purse of housekeeping money, a *dînâr*[29] or a piece of jewellery, it is easy to guess what he did with it. Wool was destined to be collected up and sold to the makers of pack-saddles, and similarly with pieces of cloth. Rags were sold to tray and handware merchants, pomegranate skins to dyers and tanners, bottles to glass-makers, date-stones to gazelle-breeders, peach-stones to nurserymen and nails and bits of old iron to blacksmiths. Pieces of papyrus were destined for the papermill, and sheets of paper were used as stoppers for jars. Any bits

28. Gold coin weighing 4.25 gr. (Tr.)
29. Silver and gold coins.

of wood he sold to pack-saddle makers, bones were used for
lighting the fire and pottery fragments for new kilns, and stones
were collected up for use in building. The basket was then
shaken to pack down the rubbish and put on one side to serve
as fuel for firing the oven. Pieces of pitch were sold to a pitch
merchant. If there were some clean earth left and he wanted to
make bricks, either to sell or for his own use, he would not spend
money on water, but enjoined everyone in the house to wash
and do their ablutions over this earth; then when it was well
moistened he moulded it into bricks. "Anyone," he would say,
"who knows less than I do about the principles of thrift ought
not to think of trying to save."

One of his tenants once missed an object, of the sort that get
stolen from people's houses. "Tonight," Abû Sa'îd said to them,
"throw out the sweepings: maybe the thief will be seized with
remorse and drop the object into them. He will not be conspicuous, for everyone else will come by here too." And in fact the
object was dropped into the sweepings that they put on top of
the landlord's garbage. He saw it before its owner, and charged
him for the use of his garbage for the purpose.

Love and Women

.   .   .   .

MEN AND LOVE

. . . Our observations of the state of things here below lead us
to conclude that the greatest of joys and the most perfect of
pleasures is the lover's conquest of the loved one, the possession
of the object of his wooing. The suffering and grief of the unsuccessful suitor are matched only by the joy and happiness of
the requited lover. We have noticed also that the more profound
the passion and the more smitten the lover, the deeper the pleasure and the greater the joy that result from success.

It may be argued that to triumph over a watchful enemy
gives greater satisfaction than a distraught lover's triumph over
the woman he loves. Our answer is that we have known powerful dignitaries and men in exalted positions willingly renounce
the satisfaction of venting their wrath, regarding the sacrifice

as a token of their superior nobility and rare tolerance and high-mindedness; we have known them prodigally give away their most prized possessions, even to the point of beggaring themselves, because they put good repute above wealth and luxury; but we have never known a lover give up his beloved. . . . Men only ever give other men unimportant things, compared with what they give women; and when they scent themselves, trim and dye their hair and beard, put on eye-shadow, use depilatory, shave, and are meticulous about their dress, it is only for the sake of women that they take so much trouble, and solely on their account that they go to such pains. Likewise the only purpose of high walls, stout doors, thick curtains, eunuchs, hand-maids and servants is to protect them and safeguard the pleasure they give.

. . . .

WOMEN'S SUPERIORITY TO MEN

. . . Women are superior to men in certain respects: it is they that are asked in marriage, desired, loved and courted, and they that inspire self-sacrifice and require protection. . . . An indication of the high esteem in which women are held is that if a man be asked to swear by God—there is none greater—and take his solemn oath to go on the pilgrimage to the House of God, or distribute his possessions as alms, or emancipate his slaves, all that comes easily to him and causes him no embarrassment. But let him be asked to swear to put away his wife, and he grows pale, is overcome with rage, protests, expostulates, gets angry and refuses—and this even if the oath be administered by a redoubtable ruler, if he does not love his wife or regard her highly, and if she be ugly, with but a scant dowry and precious little fortune. All this is the result of the place that God has given wives in their husbands' hearts. . . . God created a child out of a woman without the intervention of any man, but He has never created a child out of a man without a woman. Thus it is specially to woman and not to man that He vouchsafed this wonderful sign, this signal token, when He created the Messiah in Mary's bosom, without a man.

. . . .

FREE WOMEN AND SLAVES

. . . Slave-girls in general have more success with men than free women. Some people seek to explain this by saying that before acquiring a slave a man is able to examine her from every standpoint and get to know her thoroughly, albeit stopping short of the pleasure of an intimate interview with her; he buys her, then, if he thinks she suits him. In the case of a free woman, however, he is limited to consulting other women about her charms; and women know absolutely nothing about feminine beauty, men's requirements, or the qualities to look for. Men, on the other hand, are sounder judges of women: for the latter only notice their outward appearance, and neglect the characteristics that please men. A woman can only say: Her nose is like a sword-blade, she has eyes like a gazelle, her neck is a silver pitcher, he leg is like the pith of a palm-tree, her hair is bunches of grapes, etc. But there are other grounds than these for love and hate.

PORTRAIT OF A SINGING SLAVE-GIRL

The singing slave-girl is unlikely to be true and loyal in love, for both by temperament and training she is disposed to set traps and spread nets to catch lovers in their toils.

When an admirer looks at her she ogles him, smiles archly at him, flirts with him in the verses she sings, responds readily to his wishes, drinks with gusto, and shows herself anxious for him to stay, eager for his quick return and grieved at his departure. Once she feels that her charms have won him over and that the luckless man is caught in the trap, she presses her advantage home, and leads him to believe that her feelings for him are even stronger than his for her. Then she writes him notes complaining of the pain of her love, and swearing that she has filled the inkwell with her tears and wetted the paper with her saliva, that night and day he is the sole preoccupation and torment of her mind and heart, that she wants no other lover, that she prefers no other love to his, that she will never give him up, and that she wants him not for his money but for himself. Then she puts the missive into a sheet of parchment folded into six, seals it with saffron and ties it with a piece of lutestring.

She brings out her secret in front of her masters, to make the doting fellow feel still more closely bound to her. She insists on his writing back to her, and if he favours her with a reply she declares that it will be her consolation and make up for her lover's absence; then she . . . sings these lines:

My beloved's letter keeps me company: at times it converses with me, at times it is my aromatic plant.
The beginning of it made me laugh, but the rest of it brought tears to my eyes.

Next she begins to find fault with him, grows jealous of his wife, forbids him to look at the other girls, pours half her glass into his, tries to tempt him with the apple she has bitten into, offers him a sprig of her basil, and when he leaves presses on him a lock of her hair, a piece of her veil and a chip from her plectrum. On the feast of Naurûz she gives him a belt and some sweets, and at Mihrajân a ring and some apples. It is his name that she engraves on her own ring, and his name again that falls from her lips if she chances to stumble. When she sees him she sings him this line:

To look upon the object of his passion is a joy for the lover, but what terrible peril for him is the absence of the beloved!

Then she tells him that she cannot sleep for her longing for him, that her love takes away her appetite, that when he is away she never stops weeping, that she cannot think of him without getting upset or utter his name without trembling, and that she has already filled a phial with tears shed for him. . . .

It may happen, however, that she is hoist with her own petard and genuinely begins to share her lover's sufferings: in that event she betakes herself to his house, lets him have a kiss and more, and even gives herself to him if he thinks it lawful.

Sometimes she will also conceal her talents as a musician and singer in order to keep the price down for him; or she may pretend to her masters to have some sickness and buy herself out, and then fraudulently make herself out a free woman so that he may marry her without having to pay a prohibitive price. She does this when she happens on a lover who is kind, with elegant gestures, well-spoken, intelligent, sensitive and high-minded; and if he writes poetry, or recites or sings it, she thinks even more highly of him.

But for most of the time she is not straightforward, but employs treachery and wiles to suck her victim dry and then abandons him.

It sometimes happens that the visits of three or four of her lovers coincide, though they take pains to avoid such meetings and are jealous of one another when they come face to face. In that event she weeps with one eye for one of them and laughs with the other for another, or makes sheep's eyes at one behind another one's back. She whispers secrets to one of them and talks out loud to another, making each one think she is his alone and that appearances are no guide to their true intimacy. After they have gone she writes them all identical notes, telling each one how tiresome she finds the others and how eager she is to be alone with him with no one else present.

Had the devil no other fatal wiles, no other badge, and no other seductive charms, singing slave-girls would assuredly meet his purpose.

What I am saying is not censure of them: on the contrary, it is high praise. According to tradition: "The best of your women are those endowed with charm and seductiveness," and neither Hârût and Mârût,[30] nor Moses's rod, nor Pharaoh's wizardry could achieve what singing slave-girls achieve.

30. Hârût and Mârût: pair of angels believed to have taught men sorcery. (Tr.)

Law

The most important and engrossing intellectual undertaking of scholars in the first Islâmic centuries was to interpret in detail the Sacred Law, that is, precisely what God willed men to do. The Qur'ân gave some basic guidelines, but it still left many questions unanswered. At first, these efforts developed along different paths, but eventually four codified systems of law emerged, one of the most influential, noted especially for its clear, logical jurisprudence, was formulated by Shâfi'î (767-820) in a work called *Risâla* (*Treatise*).

As a devoted and serious Muslim, Shâfi'î studied the Sacred Law at all the major centers: in Mecca and Medîna, in Irâq and Syria. Toward the end of his life he composed a summary of his legal theory, excerpted below, in Cairo.

Shâfi'î was the first to describe precisely the sources of the Sacred Law. First came the Qur'ân, God's own explicit word. For matters not dealt with directly by the Qur'ân, Shâfi'î argued that the text "obey God and His prophet" showed how to find suitable answers that is, by modeling behavior on Muhammad's own divinely inspired practice (or *sunna*, in Arabic). This of course required the careful sifting and critical assessment of all reports about Muhammad's conduct in particular situations.

If no applicable instances for settling a case could be discovered from the Qur'ân or among authentic reports about Muhammad, a third source of law came into play: the consensus of the Muslim community. A passage in the Qur'ân remarked that Allâh would never mislead all the Faithful: hence the use of consensus as a source by law was argued also to be rooted in revelation. Last, if all else failed, Al-Shâfi'î admitted reasoning by analogy, but only so long as men drew parallels from the Qur'ân, *sunna* and consensus, for he was anxious to keep to truth, which could be related to divine revelation.

Looser methods of reasoning and willingness to take local consensus and traditions at face value invited the sort of human error that had corrupted Judaism and Christianity. Careless methods allowed human opinions to masquerade as God's commands, and Shâfi'î was intent on preventing Islâm from going that path. The Sacred Law as worked out by him (and thousands of other expert Muslims) was the way to guard against such a danger.

Islâm therefore came to be deeply, perhaps inextricably, identified with codes of Sacred Law, purporting to tell God's will to man. Since God's will was assumed to be unchanging, official Islâm wedded itself to a rigid and comprehensive set of laws, defining private and public behavior for all times and places. Unity and stability across time and space were guaranteed, but at the cost of inelasticity in the face of change.

SHÂFI'Î: FROM THE TREATISE

What Is al-Bayân?

12. Shâfi'î said: Al-Bayân is a collective term for a variety of meanings which have common roots but differing ramifications. The least [common denominator] of these linked but diverging meanings is that they are [all] a perspicuous declaration for those to whom they are addressed, and in whose tongue the Qur'ân was revealed;[1] they are of almost equal value for these persons, although some declarations were made emphatically clearer than others, though they differed [in clarity] to persons ignorant of the Arab tongue.

13. Shâfi'î said: The sum-total of what God has declared to His creatures in His Book, by which He invited them to worship Him in accordance with His prior decision, includes various categories.

One of these is what He has declared to His creatures by texts [in the Qur'ân], such as the aggregate of duties owing to Him: That they shall perform the prayer, pay the zakât (alms tax), perform the pilgrimage, and observe the fast. And that He has forbidden disgraceful acts—both visible and hidden—and in the textual [prohibition of] adultery, [the drinking of] wine, eating [the flesh of] dead things and of blood and pork; and He has made clear to them how to perform the duty of [the major] ablution as well as other matters stated precisely in the text [of the Qur'ân].

A second category consists of [those duties] the obligation of which He established in His Book, but the modes of which He made clear by the tongue of His Prophet. The number of prayers [each day] and the [amount of] zakât and their time [of fulfilment] are cases in point; but there are other [similar] duties which He has revealed in His Book.

A third category consists of that which the Apostle of God established by example or exhortation, but in regard to which

From *Islamic Jurisprudence: Shâfi'î's Risâla*, trans. by Majid Khadduri, Baltimore: The Johns Hopkins Press, 1961, pp. 67-70, 154-56, 158-59. Reproduced by permission.

1. I.e., the Arabs. (Tr.)

there is no precisely defined rule from God [in the Qur'ân]. For God has laid down in His Book the obligation of obedience to His Apostle and recourse to his decision. So he who accepts [a duty] on the authority of the Apostle of God accepts it by the obligation imposed by God.

A fourth category consists of what God commanded His creatures to seek through ijtihâd (personal reasoning)[2] and by it put their obedience to the test exactly as He tried their obedience by other duties which He had ordered them [to fulfil], for the Blessed and Most High said:

And We shall put you to the trial in order to know those of you who strive and endure, and We will test your accounts [Qur'ân XLVII: 33].

And He said:

And that God might try what was in your breasts and sift out what was in your hearts [Qur'ân III: 148].

And He said:

Perchance your Lord will destroy your enemy, and will make you successors in the land, that He may see how you will act [Qur'ân VII: 126].

14. Shâfi'î said: [God ordered the performance of prayer] in the direction of the Sacred Mosque[3] and said to his Prophet:

Sometimes We see thee turning thy face about toward the heaven. So We will turn thee to a direction that will satisfy thee. Turn thy face in the direction of the Sacred Mosque, and wherever you are, turn your faces in its direction [Qur'ân II: 139].

And He said:

And from whatever place thou hast gone forth, turn thy face in the direction of the Sacred Mosque; and wherever you may be, turn your faces in its direction [Qur'ân II: 145].

2. *Ijtihâd* literally means personal effort to understand the meaning implied in a certain rule of law in order to form an opinion. It implies personal legal reasoning which should be exercised by applying analogy (*qiyâs*) to an authoritative text such as the Qur'ân or tradition. (Tr.)

3. The Sacred Mosque is at Mecca. In the center of the Mosque is al-Ka'ba, the sacred shrine of Islâm. (Tr.)

Thus [God], glorified be His praise, guided [men]—should they be at a distance from the Sacred Mosque—by using the reasoning powers which he has implanted in men and which discriminate between things and their opposites and the landmarks which [He] set up for them when the Sacred Mosque, towards which He commanded them to turn their faces, is out of sight. For God said:

For it is He who has made for you the stars, that you might be guided by them in the darkness of land and sea [Qur'ân VI: 97].

And He said:

And by landmarks and by the stars they are guided [Qur'ân XVI: 16].

15. Shâfi'î said: Such landmarks may be the mountains, the nights and the days, which have winds of known names though they blow from different directions, and the sun and the moon and the stars whose risings and settings and whose places in the sky are known.

Thus [God] prescribed to men the use of personal reasoning in turning in the direction of the Sacred Mosque by means of guidance to them, which I have described, and so long as men use their personal reasoning they will not deviate from His command, glorious be His praise; but He did not permit them to pray in any direction they wished if the Sacred Mosque were out of sight. And He also instructed them about His will and providence and said: "Does man think that he will be left roaming at will?" [Qur'ân LXXV:36]. "Left roaming at will" means one who is neither commanded nor prohibited.

[Quranic] Duties Which the Sunna Specified Are Intended To Be Particular

144. God, Blessed and Most High, said:

They will ask thee for a pronouncement. Say: God pronounces to you concerning the indirect heirs. If a man perishes and has no children, but he has a sister, she shall receive a half of what he leaves and he is her heir if she has no children [Qur'ân IV: 175].

And He said:

To the men belongs a share of what parents and near relatives leave, and to the women belongs a share of what parents and near relatives leave, whether it be little or much, a share prescribed [Qur'ân IV: 8].

And He said:

And to his parents, to each one of the two belongs a sixth of what he leaves, if he has children; but if he has no children and his heirs are his parents, a third to his mother, or, if he has brothers, to his mothers a sixth, after any bequests he may bequeath or any debts [have been paid]. As to your fathers or your sons you do not know which of them is the most advantageous to you. So God apportions; verily, God is All-knowing, All-wise.

A half of what your wives leave belongs to you, if they have no children; but if they have children, a fourth of what they leave belongs to you after any bequests they may bequeath or debts [have been paid] [Qur'ân IV: 12-13].

And He said:

To them belongs a fourth of what you leave, if you have no children; but if you have children, an eighth of what you have belongs to them, after any bequest you may bequeath or debts [have been paid] [Qur'ân IV: 14].

The sunna [merely] specified what God has provided for those who are eligible to inherit: Brothers, sisters, children, and the near relatives, parents, spouses, and all those who are eligible to inherit in accordance with [the text of] the Book, provided that the legator and the legatee [either] profess the same religion [i.e. Islam] and belong to the people of the lands of Muslims[3] or are [non-Muslims] in treaty relations with Muslims [by virtue of which] their lives and property are secured. If they are polytheists, they are eligible to inherit in accordance with their [own law of] polytheism. For Sufyân [b. 'Uyayna] told us from al-Zuhrî from 'Alî b. Husayn from 'Amr b. 'Uth-

3. Dâr al-Muslimîn or Dâr al-Islâm is the territory of Islâm. It may be defined, broadly speaking, as the territory whose inhabitants observe Islâmic law, or, strictly speaking, the territory under Islâmic rule. (Tr.)

mân from Usâma b. Zayd who related that the Apostle said: "The Muslim cannot inherit from a non-Muslim, nor the non-Muslim from the Muslim."

Furthermore, the legator and the legatee must be freemen and Muslims. [For] Ibn 'Uyayna told us from Ibn Shihâb [al-Zuhrî] from Sâlim [b. 'Abd-Allâh] from his father that the Apostle said: "He who sells a slave possessing property, the property belongs to the seller unless the buyer stipulated otherwise."

145. [Shâfi'î] said: It is evident in the sunna of the Apostle that the slave cannot own property, that what he owns belongs to his master, and that ascribing to him title to property—which may be [found] in his hands—merely means that it is added to him [as an additional property], and not that he possesses it, for [the slave] cannot be an owner [so long as] he is incapable of possession, rather he himself is possessed; he may be sold, given in gift, or bequeathed [as a chattel]. For God [made lawful] the transfer of the property of the dead to the living who can own what the dead had owned. So if the slave were to inherit property whether as a father or in any other capacity his share of the inheritance would be owned by his master on his behalf, [even though] the master is neither the father of the deceased nor an heir entitled to a share in the inheritance. So if the slave were given the right of inheritance as a father, it means the master will have the right of inheritance and we would have given such a right [to a person] to whom God has not given it. For that reason, as I have pointed out, we do not favor giving [the right of] inheritance to the slave, nor to any one who is not in possession of freedom and [the faith of] Islam and who is not devoid of homicidal intent so that he is not regarded as a criminal. For Mâlik [b. Anas][4] related from Yahya b. Sa'îd from 'Amr b. Shu'ayb that the Apostle said: "He who kills [another] cannot inherit [from him]."

. . . .

4. Another early founder of a law school.

General Duties:
[Prayer]

148. God, Blessed and Most High, said:

Verily prayer has become for the believers a thing prescribed [to take place at] stipulated times [Qur'ân IV: 104].

And He said:

Observe the prayer and pay the zakât (legal alms) [Qur'ân II: 40, 77, 104 etc.]:

And He said to His Prophet:

Take of their wealth a sadaqa (free-will alms) to cleanse and purify them thereby and pray for them [Qur'ân IX: 104].

And He said:

Pilgrimage to the House is a duty to God from the people, whoever is able to make his way there [Qur'ân III: 91].

God has laid down in the Qur'ân the duties of prayer, zakât and pilgrimage and specified the modes [of their performances] through His Prophet's tongue.

So the Apostle specified that prayers [each day] shall number five; that the number of cycles[5] in the noon, 'asr[6] and the evening prayers shall number four repeated twice in the towns; and that cycles at the sunset prayer shall number three, and at the dawn prayer two.

He decreed that in all [the prayers] there should be recitals from [the Qur'ân], audible in the sunset, evening, and dawn prayers, and silent recitals in the noon and 'asr prayers.

He specified that at the beginning of every prayer there shall be the takbîr [declaration that God is great] and at the ending the taslîm [salutations on the Prophet and his house] and that each [prayer] consists of the takbîr, the recital, the bowing, and two prostrations after each inclination, but beyond these nothing is obligatory.

He decreed that prayer while one is on a journey can be

5. The rak'a (cycle) includes standing, bowing, prostration and sitting. (Tr.)
6. 'Asr is the mid-afternoon. (Tr.)

shorter—if the traveller so desires—in the three performances
that have four cycles, but he made no change in the sunset and
dawn prayers when the prayer is performed in town. However,
all prayers must be [performed] in the direction of the qibla
[facing Makka], whether one is in town or on a journey, except
in the case of prayer of fear.[7]

He decreed that supererogatory [prayers] must be performed
in the same manner; They are unlawful without the purification or the recital or any other requirements for obligatory
[prayers] such as the bowings, prostrations and the qibla
whether performed in the towns or the country or on the ground
during travel. In a supererogatory prayer, however, the rider
may pray in any direction that his animal may be moving.
[For] Ibn Abî Fudayk told us from Ibn Abî Dhi'b from 'Uthmân b. 'Abd-Allâh b. Surâqa from Jâbir b. 'Abd-Allâh that in
the campaign against the Banû Anmâr the Apostle was [seen]
praying while riding his camel toward the east. A similar tradition was transmitted by Muslim [b. Khâlid al-Zanjî] from Ibn
Jurayj from Abû Zubayr from Jâbir; but I do not know whether
the name of the Banû Anmâr was mentioned or whether the
tradition [merely] stated that [the Prophet] prayed during
travel.

.   .   .   .

7. Prayer of fear may be performed in case of a threat or an attack in war.
(Tr.)

History

Abû Ja'far Muhammad ibn Jarîr al-Tabarî (839-923) was a scholarly Muslim of Persian descent, who spent most of his adult years
in Baghdâd. He was learnèd in the law and the Qur'ân, but his most
famous work was a history. Its title, *History of Prophets and Kings*,
reflects the twin themes Tabarî regarded as important in writing of

the past: the record of prophecy, from Abraham and the Biblical prophets to Muhammad; and the record of rulers and states. His narrative, which reflects Persian and Roman political traditions, as well as those more strictly Muslim, was carried down to 915, only a few years before his death.

The excerpt that follows deals with the trial of one of Caliph Mu'tasim's generals, who bore the hereditary title Afshîn. Afshîn was the son of the ruler of a mountainous region in central Asia near Samarqand who had accepted Islâm after submitting to the Arab governor of the easternmost province of the caliphate in 822. He won great distinction in the Caliph's service by helping to put down a revolt in Azarbaijân; but later he was accused of conniving at a revolt against the caliphal authority, was arrested, tried, and starved to death in prison in 841. Tabarî's account of the trial points up the rebelliousness of the outlying provinces of the 'Abbâsid empire, and shows the degree to which pre-Islâmic religious traditions and loyalties survived among the Persians even after ostensible conversion to Islâm.

TABARÎ: FROM THE HISTORY OF
PROPHETS AND KINGS

Hârûn b.'Isâ b.al-Mansûr said, "I was a witness in the palace of al-Mu'tasim. . . . Al-Afsîn, who was not yet in the strong prison, was brought in. People of importance were present in order to rebuke him for what he had done and not a single person of high rank was left in the palace except the sons of al-Mansûr[1]—the [common] people had been dismissed. The prosecutor was Muhammad b.'Abd al-Malik al-Zayyât . . . and likewise two men ‖ from Sugd.[2]

. . . [He] summoned the two men. On them were threadbare garments and he said to them, "What happened to you?"

From *The Reign of al-Mu'tasim*, by al-Tabarî, trans. by Elma Marin, New Haven: American Oriental Society, 1951, pp. 115-23. Reprinted by permission.

1. Meaning the lineal descendants of al-Mansûr (Caliph d. 775), the actual founder of this branch of the 'Abbâsid dynasty. (Tr.)
2. Ancient Sogdiana between the Oxus and Jaxartes rivers. The two famous cities of Buhârâ and Samarqand were in Sugd. (Tr.)

They uncovered their backs which were stripped of flesh and Muhammad said to al-Afsîn, "Do you know these two?"

"Yes," he answered. "This one is a *mu'addin* and this is an *Imâm*.[3] They built a mosque in Usrûsana. I gave them each a thousand stripes because between myself and the Kings of Sugd was a pact and a stipulation that I should leave all people to their own religion and to their own beliefs. These two fell upon a house that had their idols in it (meaning the idols of the people of Usrûsana[4]) and they removed the idols and turned it into a mosque. For that I gave them a thousand stripes each because they had transgressed and kept the people from their place of worship."

"What is the book you have," Muhammad asked, "ornamented in gold, jewels and brocade which has in it blasphemies against God?"

To this al-Afsîn replied, "That is a book which I inherited from my father. In it is the choicest wisdom of the Persians. As to what you mention regarding blasphemies—I enjoyed the wisdom that was in it and ignored the rest. I found it already adorned and as there was no need for me to remove its ornaments from it I left it—like the book of Kalîla and Dimna and the Book of Mazdak[5] in your house. I did not think that this was transgressing against Islâm."

Hârûn b. 'Isâ b. al-Mansûr continued his account: "At that the Mûbad[6] came forward and said, 'Truly this man used to eat the meat of strangled animals,[7] and he urged me to eat it asserting that it was tenderer than meat that was slaughtered. Also he used to kill a black ewe every Wednesday; he would slit its middle with a sword then walk between the two halves, and after that he would eat its meat. One day he said to me, ‖ 'Truly I have given in to these people in everything I hated, even to the extent that because of them I have eaten oil and ridden

---

3. Muslim crier of prayers and Muslim prayer leader, respectively.
4. Afshîn's home province.
5. Persian books available to Muslims.
6. High priest of the Magians or Zoroastrians.
7. Muslims, like Jews, are forbidden to eat meat that has not been slaughtered with a knife. (Tr.)

camels and worn sandals. But not a hair has fallen from me!'
Meaning he had not used depilatories nor been circumcised.' "

At this al-Afsîn said, "Tell me about this man who utters
these words—is he trustworthy in his own religion?" Now the
Mûbad was a Magian who later embraced Islâm in the reign of
al-Mutawakkil,[8] one of whose boon companions he was. So perforce they said, "No."

"Then what is the meaning of your acceptance of testimony
from one you do not trust nor declare trustworthy?" al-Afsîn
asked. Then he drew near the Mûbad and said, "Was there a
door between my house and your house or a garret window rising over me through which you could obtain information about
me?"

"No," said the Mûbad.

Whereupon al-Afsîn continued, "Did I not permit you to
come to me and did I not divulge my secrets to you and talk to
you of Persia and of my sympathy for it and for its people?"

"Yes," the Mûbad replied.

Al-Afsîn went on, "Then you were neither trustworthy in
your religion nor generous in your friendship since you divulged openly the confidence I secretly told you!"

Then the Mûbad went aside and al-Marzubân b. Tarkas[9] came
forward. They said to al-Afsîn, "Do you know this man?"

"No," he replied.

Then al-Marzubân was asked, "Do you know this man?"

He replied, "Yes, he is al-Afsîn."

To al-Afsîn they said, "This is al-Marzubân."

Then al-Marzubân said to him, "O Charlatan! How long will
you fend and confuse the issues?"

"What are you talking about, O Long-Beard?"[10] al-Afsîn
asked.

"How do the people of your country write to you?" he asked
in reply.

Al-Afsîn answered, "As they used to write to my father and
grandfather."

8. Caliph (r. 847-860).
9. Ruler of district in Transoxania.
10. This is an insulting term. (Tr.)

"Explain that," said al-Marzubân.

"I will not explain it," al-Afsîn replied.

Then al-Marzubân said, "Do they not write to you thus-and-thus in the language of Usrûsana?"

"No doubt," he replied.

"Does that not mean in Arabic ‖ 'To the God of Gods from his slave So-and-So, the son of So-and-So?' "

"No doubt," he replied.

"And do Muslims allow themselves to be addresed in this way!" Muhammad b.'Abd al-Malik asked. "What do you leave for Pharaoh who said to his people, 'I am your supreme God'? "[11]

Al-Afsîn answered, "This was a custom of the people with respect to my father and grandfather and with respect to me before I embraced Islâm, and I did not want to put myself beneath them lest their obedience to me be marred."

. . . .

Then Mâziyâr, the governor of Tabaristân, came forward and they said to al-Afsîn, "Do you know this man?"

He answered, "No." So they said to al-Mâziyâr, "Do you know this man?"

He replied, "Yes. He is al-Afsîn."

Then they said to al-Afsîn, "This is al-Mâziyâr."

"Yes," responded al-Afsîn, "I recognize him now."

"Did you correspond with him?" they asked. And he replied, "No."

To al-Mâziyâr they said, "Did he write to you?"

"Yes," he answered. "His brother Hâs wrote to my brother Qûhiyâr in this way: "Truly there is no one to further this White Religion[12] except myself, you and Bâbak. But Bâbak, through his own foolishness had himself slain. I exerted myself to avert death from him but in his folly he refused any guidance but his own and so met his death. But if you rebel ‖ [the Muslim] people will have no one to send against you but me. I have cavalry and brave fearless men and if I am sent against you no one will remain to fight us except three types—Arabs, Magra-

11. Qur'ân: LXXIX:24. (Tr.)

12. Probably either the religion of Zoroaster or the doctrine of Mazdak is intended.

bîs[13] and Turks. The Arab lives like a dog—I will fling him a morsel then beat his head with a mace. And those flies (meaning the Magrabîs) they are but a handful! And as to those sons of devils (meaning the Turks) it is only a matter of time before their arrows will be spent, and then the cavalry will wheel around them once and all of them will be destroyed. After that religion will return to what it was in the days of the Persians.' "

Al-Afsîn said, "What he alleges against his brother and my brother is no responsibility of mine. But if I had written such a letter in order to win him over and to bind him firmly to me it would not have been wrong. For if I helped the Caliph with my hands it would be even more suitable to help him with my cunning and thus to take his enemy unawares and bring him to the Caliph so that I could enjoy through this the high regard of the Caliph. . . ."

. . . .

"Are you circumcised?" Ibn Abî Du'âd asked.

"No," he replied.

Then Ibn Abî Du'âd[14] said, "What kept you from that seeing that with it there comes the complete acceptance of Islâm and the purification of the unclean?"

"Is there not a place for fear in the religion of Islâm?" he answered.

"Certainly," Ibn Abî Du'âd replied.

Then al-Afsîn said, "I feared that if I permitted that member of my body to be cut ‖ I would die."

Upon hearing that Ibn Abî Du'âd said, "You may be pierced with spears and struck with swords still it will not prevent you from going to war—yet you are worried about the cut of circumcision!"

He replied, "That [war wounds] is a misfortune which may befall me and I will endure it when it comes. But this [circumcision] is a thing that I must ask to happen and I am not sure whether thereby I would not bring about my death. I did not know that leaving it undone constitutes renouncing Islâm!"[15]

13. North Africans.
14. Another man also present.
15. The *Qur'ân* has no ordinance on this subject. (Tr.)

Thereupon Ibn Abî Du'âd said, "His case is now clear to all of you. O Bugâ! (addressing Bugâ al-Kabîr Abû Mûsâ al-Turkî) take him!"[16]

Bugâ thereupon caught his hand in al-Afsîn's girdle, drawing him to him saying, "I expected this from you for a long time!" With that he drew the bottom of al-Afsîn qabâ'[17] over his head, then he caught the qabâ' firmly at his neck and made him go forth from the Bâb al-Wazîr[18] to his prison.

.   .   .   .

[Year 840/841]
It was in this year that al-Afsîn died.
Information Concerning His Death, What Was Done to Him When He Died and What Happened Afterwards

Hâmdûn b.Ismâ'îl said, "When the new fruits came al-Mu'tasim gathered some of them in a tray and said to his son, Hârûn al-Wâtiq, 'Take these fruits yourself to al-Afsîn.' So Hârûn al-Wâtiq took them and brought them to him in the building which ‖ had been built for him and in which he was imprisoned called Lu'lu'a. Al-Afsîn looked at the tray and he missed some fruit, either ijjâs or sahlûj,[19] and he said to al-Wâtiq, 'There is no God but God! How good this tray is—but there are no ijjâs or sahlûj on it for me.' Al-Wâtiq replied, 'That is true! I will go back and send the fruits to you.' Al-Afsîn had not as yet touched any of the fruit. When al-Wâtiq was about to return al-Afsîn said to him, 'Give my lord greetings and say to him: I ask you to send me a man whom you trust who will take back what I say.' "

It was then that al-Mu'tasim ordered Hâmdûn b.Ismâ'îl . . . to go to al-Afsîn's prison. Hâmdûn related the following story: "Al-Mu'tasim sent me to al-Afsîn saying to me, 'He will spin out his tale for you so do not linger.' When I came to him the tray of fruit was before him but he had not touched nor tasted a

16. Bughâ al-Kabîr: Turkish military leader who played important political role during this period.
17. Qabâ': Outer garment with full-length sleeves.
18. The Door of the Wazîrs in the Audience Hall in Sâmarrâ [the Caliphal capital at this time]. (Tr.)
19. A cold moist variety of plum and a different species of plum, respectively.

single piece. He said to me, 'Sit down' and I did and he tried to
win my sympathy as a Persian noble but I said, 'Do not spin
out this tale. The Commander of the Faithful has warned me
not to tarry with you, therefore be brief.' He replied, 'Say to the
Commander of the Faithful: You were good to me and showed
me honor but people humiliated me. Then you accepted statements about me and you did not verify them nor, with your intelligence, did you reflect on how this thing could be or how it
would be possible for me to do what was told you. You were told
that I plotted with Munkajûr to rebel and you accept this statement; and you were told that I said to the officer whom I sent
to Munkajûr, 'Do not fight him, only pretend to fight and if you
get in contact with one of us fly from him.' You ‖ are a man;
you have known war, and fought men and trained troops. Is it
possible that the head of an army would tell the troops that they
would meet certain people and so should do thus and thus? No
one would swallow this easily if he did! But if it were possible
it does not seem to me that you would believe it from an enemy
whose motives you perceive. You are always first with me, I am
naught but a slave from amongst your slaves and your creature.
But we, O Commander of the Faithful, are like a man who fos-
tered a calf until he had fattened him and he was big and his
condition beautiful. He had companions who longed to eat the
calf's meat and they proposed its slaughter to him but he did not
concur with them in that. Then they agreed to say to him one
day, 'Alas! Why did you foster this lion? This is a ferocious
beast who has grown big and when a lion is big he returns to his
kind.' The man answered them, 'Woe to you! This is a calf, not
a lion!' But they replied, 'This is a lion, ask whom you will
about it.' They had already gone to everyone who knew him and
said, 'If he asks you about the calf say to him: But this is a lion!'
So whenever the man questioned anyone about it and said, 'See
this calf—how beautiful it is!' the other would reply, 'This is a
lion! This is a lion! Alack!' Thereupon the man gave an order
concerning the calf and it was slaughtered. But I am that calf
and how can it be that I am a lion? God, O God! in my misfortune I am calling to you! You[20] have been gracious to me and

20. Meaning al-Mu'tasim. (Tr.)

honored me and you are my lord and my master. I ask God to
incline your heart to me.' "

. . . .

When Hâmdûn returned and gave al-Muʻtasim his message he
ordered that all but a little food be denied to al-Afsîn so he was
given only a loaf of bread every day until he died.

After his death he was taken to the house of Itâh, then they
brought him out ‖ and crucified him at the Public Gate so that
the populace could see him. After that he was flung down at the
Public Gate, with the wood on which he was crucified, and
burned and the ashes were carried and flung into the Tigris.

Al-Muʻtasim, at the time he ordered al-Afsîn imprisoned, sent
Sulaimân b. Wahb al-Kâtib on a certain night to inventory
everything that was in al-Afsîn's house and to write it down.
Al-Afsîn's palace was at al-Matîra.²¹ In his house was found a
tabernacle with the likeness of a man in wood in it, on him were
many ornaments and jewels and in his ears were two white
stones with gold intricately entangled on them. One of Sulaimân's men took one of the stones thinking that it was a jewel of
great value. That happened at night. But when morning came
he pulled off the gold network and found it was a stone resembling the seashell which is called *habarûn*, of the type of seashell called the Bugle Horn Shell [or: Trumpet Shell]. From his
house were taken grotesque figures and other things of that ilk
along with images and similar things. The wooden water-skin
rafts which he had prepared were there, and he also had things
in al-Wazîriya.²² Another idol was also found there and among
his books they found a book of the Magians called Zarâwah and
many other books pertaining to the religion with which he used
to worship his God. . . .

21. In Sâmarrâ.
22. Also in Sâmarrâ.

Theology

Among Muslim men of learning, speculating about the nature of God was deeply suspect. Logic-chopping led men too easily astray: the purpose of Muhammad's mission had been to correct such human error. Yet the inherent attractions of logic and the need to answer Christian theologians—who, on the strength of their inheritance of Greek philosophy, were in a position to ask their Muslim counterparts embarrassing questions about the essence and characteristics of God—constantly tempted Muslims onto the slippery ground of rational theology. Those who ventured there were called Mu'tazilites; their method of logical argument was known as '*kalâm.*'

The author of *The Elucidation of Islâm's Foundation*, Abû'l-Hasan 'Alî ibn Ismâ'îl al-Ash'arî (873-935), was of distinguished Arab descent, born in Basra. In his youth he was attracted to the Mu'tazilites, but at about the age of forty he turned his back on rational theology and espoused instead the strict school of theology founded by Ahmad ibn Hanbal (780-855). This school held that only the revelation of the Qur'ân and authenticated traditions about the Prophet could be trusted: since God would not fail to reveal through these channels everything that men needed to know about the divine, it was unnecessary to consider anything else.

Al-Ash'arî accepted this definition of theology, using the kind of logical argument familiar to Mu'tazilites to refute their conclusions and to show the futility of speculative reason as a guide to truth about God. In this paradoxical way the usefulness of reasoning as a way of showing reason's limitations came to be admitted by even the most strict and careful Muslim theologians.

ASH'ARÎ: FROM THE ELUCIDATION OF ISLÂM'S FOUNDATION
In the Name of God, the Merciful, the Compassionate.

The Sayyid and Imâm Abu 'l-Hasan 'Alî ibn Ismâ'îl al-As'arî al-Basrî (may God have mercy upon him!)[1] said:

Praise to God! the One, the Almighty, the Glorious, the only One to whom unity is ascribed, the Magnified in praise, whom the attributes of human beings do not adequately describe. He has neither adversary nor rival, and He is the Creator and the Restorer "the Doer of what He wills."[2] He is too exalted to possess consorts or children, too holy to associate with the genera of creation or things corrupt. He has not any form capable of expression, nor is a definition of Him by means of a simile possible. He has always had the attributes of primacy and power, and He will always continue to be knowing and cognizant. His knowledge embraces created things, His will is fully realized in them, and the secrets of things are not far from Him. The vicissitudes of passing time do not alter Him, nor does fatigue or weariness overtake Him in the creation of anything He creates, nor does exhaustion or loss of power touch Him. He creates things by His power, directs them by His wish, compels them by His strength, and reduces them by His might; wherefore the proud submit to His power, the lofty are subject to the strength of His lordship, doubters are cut off from a sure foundation in the knowledge of Him, to Him the necks of men submit, and the prudence of the discreet is confounded in His kingdom. By His word, the seven heavens arose, the extended earth is fixed, the firm mountains are established, the "fertilizing winds"[3] blow, the clouds pursue their journey in the celestial atmosphere, and

From *Abu-l-Hasan 'Alî-ibn Ismâ'îl al-As'arî's Al-Ibânah 'an Usûl ad-Diyânah* (*The Elucidation of Islam's Foundation*), trans. by Walter Klein, New Haven: American Oriental Society, 1940, pp. 43-55, 83-85. Reprinted by permission.

1. *Sayyid* and *imâm*: terms of honor. The devout ejaculations of the original are almost invariably omitted from the translation. (Tr.)
2. Qur'ân XI:109. (Tr.)
3. Qur'ân XV:22. (Tr.)

the seas observe their bounds. He is a compelling God, to whom
the strong do homage and the exalted bow, and the worlds
render Him their duty whether they will or no.

We praise Him as He praises Himself, and as He merits and
deserves, and as the praisers among all His creatures praise
Him. We ask His help in the manner of one who entrusts his
affairs to Him and confesses that there is no asylum or refuge
from Him, but only to Him. We ask His forgiveness in the
manner of one who confesses his wrongdoing and acknowledges
his sin. With a confession of His unity and a clear acknowledg-
ment of His lordship, we bear witness that there is no God but
Allâh alone, "who hath no associate;"[4] that He is the One who
knows what the privy thoughts shut away and the secrets en-
wrap, what souls hide, and what the seas keep out of sight, what
hearts conceal, and "how much the wombs lessen and enlarge;
with Him everything is by measure."[5] No word is concealed
from Him, no purpose is unknown to Him, "not a leaf falls but
He knoweth it, neither is there a grain in the dark places of the
earth, there is neither moisture nor dryness but it is noted in a
distinct writing,"[6] and He knows what the doers do, and that to
which the returners return. We seek guidance from Him, and
we ask Him for grace . . . to avert ruin. We bear witness that
Muhammad is His Servant, His Apostle, His Prophet, His
Trustworthy One, His Chosen One, whom He sent to His creation with the light that sheds its beams afar, with the flashing
lamp, the clear arguments, the evidences, the dazzling signs, the
compelling wonders; wherefore he delivered his message from
God, consulted His good in His creation, labored strenuously for
God with a true zeal, consulted His good in the countries of the
earth, and opposed the rebellious people, until the Word of God
was fulfilled, until he attained success, and all men obeyed the
truth with homage, and assurance of success came to him, unfa-
tigued, unwearied. Therefore, may God's grace be with him
(for he led the way to guidance and made clear the road of escape from error and blindness), and with the blessed people of

4. Qur'ân VI: 163. (Tr.)
5. *Ibid.*, XIII:9. (Tr.)
6. *Ibid.*, VI:59. (Tr.)

his house, and with his chosen Companions and his pure wives, the mothers of the faithful! By him God informed us of the religious laws . . . and the ordinances . . . of the lawful and the prohibited, and by him He made clear to us the religious law of Islâm, until by him the dark night of gloom was lifted from us, the doubts were removed from us, the screens were drawn back, the proofs were made clear to us. He brought us "a glorious Book. Vanity shall not come to it from before it, or from behind it; it is a missive sent down from the Wise and Praiseworthy,"[7] in which is comprised the knowledge of "the first and the last."[8] By him He perfected the duties and the Religion, and therefore he is the "sure road"[9] of God and His firm rope. He who holds fast to him shall escape, but he who opposes him shall err and wander. In ignorance is thy ruin, and God has urged us in His Book to hold fast to the *sunnah*[10] of His Apostle. . . .

. . . I enjoin upon you, O servants of God! the fear of God, and warn you against the world; for it is fresh and sweet, and it deceives its inhabitants and deludes those who dwell in it, and God has said, "And set before them a similitude of the present life. It is as water which We send down from heaven, and the herb of the earth is mingled with it, and on the morrow it becometh dry stubble which the winds scatter; for God hath power over all things."[11] To him who is in good circumstances in it, it brings tears later on, and upon him to whom it has imparted its joys in secret, it bestows the open sequel of its woes. Its abundant vanities are transitory, for the things it contains agree with the judgment pronounced upon it by its Lord in His words, "All on the earth shall pass away."[12] Then labor for the abiding life and for endless eternity. The world shall pass away from its inhabitants, and their works shall remain as strings upon their necks. Know that you are mortal, and then that you return to your Lord after your deaths. Assuredly He will reward those

---

7. *Ibid.*, XLI: 41, 42. (Tr.)
8. *Ibid.*, LVI: 49. (Tr.)
9. *Ibid.*, I:5 and passim. (Tr.)
10. *Sunna*: practice and example.
11. Qur'ân XVIII:43. (Tr.)
12. *Ibid.*, IV:26. (Tr.)

who have done evil with that which they have done, and He will reward those who have done good with good. Therefore, be diligent in obedience to your Lord, and refuse what He has refused you.

THE EXPOSITION OF THE BELIEF OF THE DEVIATORS
AND INNOVATORS

To begin with, there are many deviators from the truth among the Mu'tazilah[13] and the *ahl al-qadar*,[14] whose straying desires have inclined them to the acceptance of the principles (*taqlîd*)[15] of their leaders and their departed forebears; so that they interpret the Qur'ân according to their opinions with an interpretation for which God has neither revealed authority nor shown proof, and which they have not derived from the Apostle of the Lord of the Worlds or from the ancients of the past; and, as a result, they oppose the traditions of the Companions, related on the authority of the Prophet of God, concerning God's visibility to sight, although with regard to it the traditions come from various sources, and the *âtâr* upon it have been continuous, and the *ahbâr*[16] upon it have come down in steady succession. (1) They deny the intercession of the Apostle of God for sinners, and reject the traditions concerning it that are related on the authority of the ancients[17] of the past. (2) They gainsay the punishment of the grave and the doctrine that the infidels are punished in their graves, although the Companions and the Successors have agreed upon this matter unanimously. (3) They maintain the createdness of the Qur'ân; thereby approximating the belief of their brethren among the polytheists, who said, "it is merely the word of a mortal";[18] and so they think that the

13. The Mu'tazila are Ash'arî's chief adversaries. He commences with a summary of their tenets. (Tr.)

14. People who discuss predestination. (Tr.)

15. With the fixation of the law the possibility of inaugurating new schools and interpreting afresh the legal content of Islâm came to an end. There was, therefore, after this date, no alternative to *taqlîd*, by which one accepted the interpretation of a recognized authority. (Tr.)

16. *Athâr, akhbâr*: reports, stories.

17. I.e., "Fathers," or "Primitive Muslims," who were idealized and imitated.

18. Qur'ân LXXIV:25. (Tr.)

Qur'ân is like the word of a mortal. (4) They assert and are
convinced that human beings create evil; thereby approximating the belief of the Magians,[19] who assert that there are two
creators, one of them creating good and the other creating evil
(for the Qadariyyah think that God creates good and that Satan
creates evil). (5) They think that God may wish what is not,
and what He does not wish may be; in disagreement with that
upon which the Muslims have unanimously agreed, namely,
that what God wishes is, and what He does not wish is not; and
contrarily to the words of God "but ye shall not wish except
God wish"[20]—He says that we shall not wish a thing unless God
has wished that we wish it—, and to His words "If God had
wished, they would not have wrangled,"[21] and His words "Had
We wished, We had certainly given to every soul its guidance,"[22] and His words "Doer of what He wills,"[23] and His statement with reference to Su'ayb, that he said, "nor can we return
to it, except God our Lord wish; our Lord embraceth all things
in His ken."[24] Therefore the Apostle of God called them "the
Magians of this Community," because they have adopted the religion of the Magians and copied their tenets, and think that
there are two creators, the one for good and the other for evil,
just as the Magians think, and that there are evils God does not
wish, as the Magians believe. (6) They think that they, and not
God, have control over what is hurtful and what is helpful to
them, contrarily to the words of God to His Prophet, "Say: I
have no control over what may be helpful or hurtful to me, but
as God wisheth,"[25] and in opposition to the Qur'ân and to that
upon which the people of Islâm have unanimously agreed. (7)
They think that they alone, and not their Lord, have power over
their works, and assert that they are independent of God, and
attribute to themselves power over that over which they do not

19. Magians: observers of a pre-Islâmic religion of Persia, similar to that of
Zoroaster.
20. Qur'ân, LXXVI: 30. (Tr.)
21. *Ibid.*, II: 254. (Tr.)
22. *Ibid.*, XXXII: 13. (Tr.)
23. *Ibid.*, XI: 109. (Tr.)
24. *Ibid.*, VII: 87. (Tr.)
25. *Ibid.*, VII: 188. (Tr.)

attribute power to God, just as the Magians assert that Satan has power over evil that they do not assert God has. Hence they are "the Magians of this Community," since they have adopted the religion of the Magians, hold fast to their beliefs, incline to their errors, cause men to despair of God's mercy and lose their hope of His spirit, and have condemned the disobedient to Hell forever, in disagreement with God's words, "But other than this will He forgive to whom He wishes."[26] (8) They think that he who enters Hell will not come forth from it, in disagreement with the tradition, related on the authority of the Apostle of God, that God will bring forth people out of Hell after they have been burned in it and become ashes. (9) They deny that God has a face, notwithstanding His words "but the face of thy Lord shall abide resplendent with majesty and glory."[27] They deny that He has two hands, notwithstanding His words "before him whom I have created with My two hands."[28] They deny that God has an eye, notwithstanding His words "under Our eyes it floated on,"[29] and His words "that thou mightest be reared in Mine eye."[30] They deny that God has knowledge notwithstanding His words "in His knowledge He sent it down."[31] They deny that God has power, notwithstanding His words "Possessed of might, the Unshaken."[32] (10) They reject the tradition, related on the authority of the Prophet, that God descends each night to the lower heaven, and other traditions among those that the trustworthy have handed down on the authority of God's Apostle. . . .

CONCERNING THE EXPOSITION OF THE BELIEF OF THE FOLLOWERS OF THE TRUTH AND THE "SUNNAH"

If anybody says to us, ". . . now let us know the beliefs you hold and the religion you follow," the answer is:

26. *Ibid.*, IV:51. (Tr.)
27. *Ibid.*, LV:27. (Tr.)
28. *Ibid.*, XXXVIII:75. (Tr.)
29. *Ibid.*, LIV:14. (Tr.)
30. *Ibid.*, XX:40. (Tr.)
31. *Ibid.*, IV:164. (Tr.)
32. *Ibid.*, II:58. (Tr.)

The belief we hold and the religion we follow are holding fast
to the Book of our Lord, to the *sunnah* of our Prophet, and to the
traditions related on the authority of the Companions and the
Successors and the *imâms* of the *hadît*;[33]—to that we hold
firmly, professing what Abû 'Abdallâh Ahmad ibn Muhammad
ibn Hanbal[34] professed, and avoiding him who dissents from his
belief, because he is the excellent *imâm* and the perfect leader,
through whom God declared the truth, removed error, manifested the modes of action, and overcame the innovations of the
innovators, the deviation of the deviators, and the skepticism of
the skeptics. The mercy of God be upon him,—for he is an eminent *imâm* and an exalted, honored friend,— and upon all the
other *imâms* of Islâm! The substance of our belief is that we confess God, His angels, His books, His apostles, the revelation of
God, and what the trustworthy have handed down on the authority of God's Apostle, rejecting none of them. We confess
that God is one God—there is no god but He—unique, eternal,
possessing neither consort nor child; and that Muhammad is His
Servant and Apostle, whom He sent with the guidance and the
real Religion; and that Paradise is real and Hell is real; and that
there is no doubt regarding the Coming Hour; and that God will
raise up those who are in the graves; and that God is seated on
His throne (as He has said, "The Merciful is seated on the
Throne");[35] and that He has a face (as He has said, "but the
face of thy Lord shall abide resplendent with majesty and
glory");[36] and that He has two hands, *bilâ kayfa* (as He has
said, "I have created with My two hands,"[37] and as He has said,
"Nay! outstretched are both His hands");[38] and that He has an
eye, *bilâ kayfa* (as He has said, "under Our eyes it floated
on"),[39] and that anybody who thinks that the names of God are

33. The founders of the science of traditions about Muhammad.
34. 780-855. The teacher of "orthodox" theology whom Ash'arî professed to
follow.
35. Qur'ân XX:4. (Tr.)
36. *Ibid.*, LV:27. (Tr.)
37. *Ibid.*, XXXVIII:75. (Tr.) *Bilâ kayfa* means "without reference to the
'how,'" an important concept for orthodox theologians.
38. *Ibid.*, V:69. (Tr.)
39. *Ibid.*, LIV:14. (Tr.)

other than He is in error; and that God has knowledge (as He said, "in His knowledge He sent it down,"[40] and as He said, "and no female conceiveth or bringeth forth without His knowledge").[41] We also assert that God has hearing and sight, and we do not deny it as the Mu'tazilah, the Jahmiyyah, and the Hârijites deny it; and we assert that God has prowess . . . (as He has said, "Saw they not that God Who created them was mightier than they in prowess?");[42] and we believe that the Word of God is uncreated, and that He has created nothing without first saying to it, "Be!," and it is (as He has said, "Our word to a thing when We will it is but to say, 'Be!,' and it is");[43] and that there is no good or evil on earth, save what God wishes; and that things exist by God's wish; and that not a single person has the capacity to do anything until God causes him to act, and we are not independent of God, nor can we pass beyond the range of God's knowledge; and that there is no creator save God, and the works of human beings are things created and decreed by God (as He has said, "God has created you and what you make");[44] and that human beings have not the power to create anything, but are themselves created (as He has said, "Is there a creator other than God?,"[45] and as He has said, "they create nothing, but are themselves created,"[46] and as He has said, "Shall He then who creates be as he who creates not?,"[47] and as He has said, "Were they created by nothing or were they the creators?,"[48] for this is mentioned in God's Book frequently); and that God gives the faithful grace to be obedient to Him, is gracious to them, considers them, does what is salutary for them, guides them; whereas He causes the infidels to err, does not guide them, does not give them the grace to believe, as the deviators and rebels think (for, if He were gracious

40. *Ibid.*, IV:164. (Tr.)
41. *Ibid.*, XXXV:12. (Tr.)
42. *Ibid.*, XLI:14. (Tr.)
43. *Ibid.*, XVI: 42. (Tr.)
44. *Ibid.*, XXXVII:94. (Tr.)
45. *Ibid.*, XXV:3. (Tr.)
46. *Ibid.*, XVI:20. (Tr.)
47. *Ibid.*, XVI:17. (Tr.)
48. *Ibid.*, LII:35. (Tr.)

to them and did what was salutary for them, they would be sound; and if He guided them, they would be guided; as He has said, "He whom God guides is the guided, and they whom He misleads shall be the lost");[49] and that God has power to do what is salutary for the infidels and be gracious to them, that they may become believers, nevertheless He wills that they be infidels, as He knows; and that He forsakes them and seals up their hearts; and that good and evil are dependent upon the general and particular decrees of God. We believe in God's general and particular decrees, His good and His evil, His sweet and His bitter; and we know that what passes us by was not to befall us, and what befalls us was not to pass us by; and that human beings do not control for themselves what is hurtful or what is helpful, except what God wishes; and that we ought to commit our affairs to God and assert our complete need of and dependence upon Him. We believe, too, that the Qur'ân is the uncreated Word of God, and that he who believes the Qur'ân is created is an infidel. We hold that God will be seen in the next world by sight (as the moon is seen on the night it is full, so shall the faithful see Him, as we are told in the traditions that come down on the authority of God's Apostle); and we believe that the infidels will be veiled from Him when the faithful see Him in Paradise (as God has said, "Yea, they shall be shut out as by a veil from their Lord on that day");[50] and that Moses asked God for the sight of Him in this world, and "God manifested Himself to the mountain" and "turned it to dust," and taught Moses by it that he should not see Him in this world. It is our opinion that we ought not to declare a single one of the people of the *qiblah*[51] an infidel for a sin of which he is guilty, such as fornication or theft or the drinking of wine, . . . thinking that such people are infidels; but we believe that he who commits any of these mortal sins, such as fornication or theft or the like, presumptuously declaring it lawful and not acknowledging that it is forbidden, is an infidel. We believe that Islâm is more extensive than faith, and that faith is not the whole of Islâm. We

49. *Ibid.*, VII:177. (Tr.)
50. *Ibid.*, LXXXIII:15. (Tr.)
51. The direction in which one faces when praying—in the case of Muslims, towards Mecca. The people of the *qibla* are the Muslims. (Tr.)

hold that God changes men's hearts [at death], and that their
hearts are between two of God's fingers, and that God will place
the heavens on a finger and the earth on a finger [on the Last
Day], as we are told in the tradition that comes down on the authority of God's Apostle. We hold that we ought not to relegate
any of the monotheists, or those who hold fast to the faith, to
Paradise or to Hell, save him in whose favor the Apostle of God
has borne witness concerning Paradise; and we hope that sinners will attain to Paradise, but we fear that they will be punished in Hell. We believe that God, by the intercession of Muhammad, God's Apostle, will bring forth a people from Hell
after they have been burned to ashes, in accordance with what
we are told in the traditions related on the authority of God's
Apostle. We believe in the punishment of the grave, and in the
Pool, and hold that the Scales[52] are real, and the Bridge is real,
and the resurrection after death is real, and that God will line
up human beings at the Station, and settle the account with the
faithful. We believe that faith consists of words and deeds, and
is subject to increase and decrease; and we receive the authentic
traditions regarding it related on the authority of the Apostle of
God, which the trustworthy have transmitted, one just man
from another, until the tradition goes back to the Apostle of
God. We believe in affection towards our forebears in the faith,
whom God chose for the company of His Prophet, and we praise
them with the praise wherewith God praised them, and are attached to them all. We believe that the excellent *imâm*, after
the Apostle of God, is Abû Bakr the Veracious, and that God
strengthened the Religion by him and gave him success against
the backsliders, and the Muslims promoted him to the imâmate
just as the Apostle of God made him leader of prayer, and they
all named him the caliph of God's Apostle; then after him came
'Umar ibn al-Hattâb; then 'Utmân ibn 'Affân (those who
fought with him fought with him wrongfully and unright-
eously); then 'Alî ibn Abî Tâlib; wherefore these are the *imâms*
after the Apostle of God, and their caliphate is a caliphate of
prophecy.[53] We bear witness concerning Paradise in favor of

52. Qur'ân IV:6 and *passim*. (Tr.)
53. Abû Bakr, 'Umar, 'Uthmân, and 'Alî; the first four Caliphs, respectively.

the ten in whose favor the Apostle of God bore witness to it, and we are attached to all the Companions of the Prophet, and avoid what was disputed among them. We hold that the four *imâms* are orthodox, divinely guided, excellent caliphs, unmatched by others in excellence. We accept all the traditions for which the traditionists vouch: the descent into the lower heavens, and the Lord's saying, "Is there any who has a request? Is there any who asks forgiveness?," and the other things they relate and vouch for; dissenting from what the deviators and followers of error assert. We rely, in that wherein we differ, upon our Lord's Book, and the *sunnah* of our Prophet, and the unanimous consent . . . of the Muslims and what it signifies; and we do not introduce into God's religion innovations that God does not allow, nor do we believe of God what we do not know. We believe that God will come in the Day of Resurrection (as He has said, "and thy Lord shall come and the angels rank on rank");[54] and that God is near His servants, even as He wishes (as He has said, "We are nearer to him than his neck vein,"[55] and as He said, "then He came nearer and approached and was at the distance of two bows or even closer").[56] It belongs to our religion to observe the Friday Assembly, and the feasts, and the remaining prayers and public devotions under the leadship of every pious man or impious (as it is related of 'Abdallâh ibn 'Umar that he used to pray behind al-Hajjâj);[57] and we believe that the wiping of the sandals is a *sunnah* at home and in travel, contrarily to the belief of anybody who denies it; and we approve prayer for the welfare of the *imâms* of the Muslims,[58] and the confession of their imâmate; and we regard it as an error on anybody's part to approve "going out"[59] against them when

54. Qur'ân LXXXIX:23. (Tr.)

55. *Ibid.*, L:15 (Tr.)

56. *Ibid.*, LIII:8, 9. (Tr.)

57. The notorious Umayyad general, whom some of the Muslims refused to regard as a believer. (Tr.) 'Abdallâh ibn 'Umar was son of second Caliph.

58. Al-Ash'arî means the public prayer offered for the sovereign in the *khutba*. (Tr.)

59. Al-Ash'arî repudiates the practice of the Khârijites (Tr.), originally those who deserted 'Alî (fourth Caliph), when he agreed to arbitration over his right to the Caliphate.

they have clearly abandoned rectitude; and we believe in abstinence from "going out" against them with the sword, and abstinence from fighting in civil commotions. . . .[60] We confess
the going forth of Antichrist (ad-Dajjâl), as it is contained in
the tradition related on the authority of God's Apostle. We believe in the punishment of the grave, and in Munkar and Na-
kîr[61] and in their interrogation of those who are buried in their
graves. We accept the *hadît* of the Ascension, . . . and regard
as authentic many of the visions in sleep, and confess that there
are interpretations to them. We approve alms in behalf of the
Muslim dead, and prayer for their welfare; and we believe that
God helps them by it. We accept it as true that there are wizards
and witchcraft in the world, and that witchcraft exists in the
world. We believe in praying for those of the people of the
qiblah who are dead, the pious and the impious, and in the law-
fulness of being their heirs.[62] We confess that Paradise and Hell
are created,[63] and that he who dies or is slain dies or is slain at
his appointed term; and that sustenance is from God who gives
it to His creatures in the permitted and the forbidden; and that
Satan whispers to man and causes him to doubt and infects him,
. . . (as God has said, "They who swallow down usury shall
arise in the resurrection only as he ariseth whom Satan hath infected by his touch,"[64] and as He has said, "against the mischief
of the stealthily withdrawing whisperer, who whispereth in
man's breast—against *jinn* and men").[65] We believe that God
can design particularly for the just the signs He manifests to
them. Our belief regarding the children of the polytheists is that
God will kindle a fire for them in the next world, and then will

60. No matter how great the provocation, the Sunnites discountenanced
resistance of the ruling power. (Tr.)
61. The angels of the grave. (Tr.)
62. Only those of the same religion may inherit from each other. Naturally,
if one Muslim considered another Muslim an infidel, he could not consist-
ently inherit from him. It was the Khârijites particularly who felt such
scruples. (Tr.)
63. The vital question regarding Paradise and Hell was really whether or
not they would disappear. (Tr.) The Sunnites held that they would.
64. Qur'ân II:276. (Tr.)
65. *Ibid.*, CXIV:4-6. (Tr.) *Jinn: spirits.*

say to them, "Rush into it!," as the tradition tells us concerning it. We hold that God knows what human beings are doing, and what they are going to do, what has been, what is, and how what is not would have been if it had been. We believe in obedience to the *imâms* and in the sincere counsel of the Muslims. We approve separation from every innovating tendency, and the avoidance of the people of straying impulses. We will give arguments for the beliefs of ours we have mentioned, and the remaining ones we have not mentioned, chapter by chapter, and matter by matter, God willing.

THE DISCUSSION CONCERNING GOD'S BEING
SEATED ON THE THRONE

If anybody says, "What do you say regarding God's being seated on the Throne?," the answer is: We say that God is seated on His Throne, as He has said, "The Merciful is seated on the Throne."[66] God has also said, "The good word riseth up to Him;"[67] and, "but God took him up to Himself;"[68] and, "From the heaven to the earth He governeth all things; hereafter shall they come up to Him."[69] He has also said, quoting Pharaoh: "O, Haman! build for me a tower that I may reach the avenues, the avenues of the heavens, and may mount to the God of Moses, for I verily deem Him a liar;"[70] and so Pharaoh gave the lie to Moses, the prophet of God, for saying that God was above the heavens. God has also said, "What! are you sure that He who is in heaven will not cleave the earth beneath you?"[71] Now the Throne is above the heavens; wherefore, since the Throne is above the heavens, He said, "What! are you sure that He who is in heaven . . . ?," because He is seated on the Throne, which is above the heavens, for all that which is on high is heaven, and, therefore, the Throne is the highest thing in the heavens. Also, when He says, "What! are you sure that He who is in heaven . . . ?," He does not mean all the heavens,

66. *Ibid.*, XX:4. (Tr.)
67. *Ibid.*, XXXV:11. (Tr.)
68. *Ibid.*, IV:156. (Tr.)
69. *Ibid.*, XXXII:4. (Tr.)
70. *Ibid.*, XL:38, 39. (Tr.)
71. *Ibid.*, LXVII:16. (Tr.)

but has in mind only the Throne, which is the highest thing in the heavens. Do you not agree that God is speaking of the heavens when He says, "and He appointed . . . the moon," in them, "for light,"[72] yet He does not mean that the moon fills them entirely, and that it is in them entirely? Then, too, see the Muslims all raising their hands, when they pray, towards heaven, because God is seated on the Throne, which is above the heavens; but, if God were not upon the Throne, they would not raise their hands towards the Throne, just as they do not lower them, when they pray, to the earth.

Question. Some of the Mu'tazilah and the Jahmiyyah and the Harûriyyah have said that God's words "The Merciful is seated on the Throne"[73] mean that He has the mastery and reigns and exercises power, and that God is in every place, and they deny that God is on His Throne, as the true believers say, and hold the opinion, regarding God's being seated, that it is God's power. But, if this were as they put it, there would be no difference between the Throne and the earth; for God has power over the earth and over gardens and over everything in the world; and, therefore, if God were seated on the Throne in the sense of having the mastery, since He has the mastery over all things, He would certainly be seated on the Throne and on the earth and on heaven and on gardens and on each separate thing, because He has power over created things, possessing the mastery over them. But, since He has power over all things, and no Muslim regards it as right to say that God is seated on the gardens and on the waste, God's being seated on the Throne cannot mean His having the mastery that is common to all things; and it is necessarily true that its meaning is a being seated that belongs particularly to the Throne and not to all things. But the Mu'tazilah and the Harûriyyah and the Jahmiyyah think that God is in every place; and so they are compelled to admit that He is in the womb of Mary and in gardens and the waste; and this is contrary to the Religion. May God be exalted above their belief!

Answer. It may be said to them: If He is not seated on the Throne (in the sense of the Throne particularly, and not any-

72. *Ibid.*, X:5. (Tr.)
73. *Ibid.*, XX:4.

thing else, as the scholars and the *âtâr* traditionists and those who relate the *ahbâr* say), but is in every place, then He is under the earth, over which the heaven is; and if He is under the earth and the earth above Him and the heaven above the earth, then this compels you to believe that God is under the depth, and created things are above Him, and that He is above the height, and created things are below Him; and if this is true He must be under that above which He is and above that under which He is, and this is impossible and self-contradictory. May God be very far above your calumny against Him!

Philosophy

Muslim study of philosophy began with the translation of Greek texts, especially of Plato and Aristotle, into Arabic. Unlike theologians, including the Mu'tazilites, Muslim students of philosophy did not start by assuming the truth of the revealed text of the Qur'ân. Instead they boldly set out, like their Greek predecessors, to pursue reason and logic wherever it might carry them.

This raised a critical question about the relation between truth as revealed to the Prophet Muhammad and truth attained by philosophical reasoning. Were they the same? Or if they differed, which was to be preferred? For public consumption, Muslim philosophers argued that the two avenues to truth could not contradict one another; in private, however, some of them thought revelation was a vulgar popularization and distortion of truth.

Muhammad ibn Muhammad ibn Tarkham Abû Nasr Al-Farâbî (*ca.* 870-950) was among the earliest Muslim students of philosophy. He was of Turkish origin, born in the city of Farâb in Turkestân—hence the name by which he is commonly known. His father was a soldier, perhaps a member of the caliph's bodyguard. Farâbî lived in Baghdâd for a while, but in 942 accepted an invitation to Aleppo in Syria, where a local ruler named Saif al-Dawla held court. He remained there until his death.

On the key question of the relation between reason and revelation, Farâbî took a middle position. Attributing to the ancients the view that revelation imitated philosophic truth, Farâbî himself argued that the true knower, like Plato's Philosopher King, must do as the prophets had done, that is, explain truth to the crowd in ways they could appreciate—through myth, allegory, and symbols. Thus he assigned to philosophers a function ordinarily associated with prophets. Such a view, needless to say, shocked some pious Muslims, for it ranked the Prophet Muhammad below the ideal Philosopher, whose knowledge came from his own effort rather than from God.

FARÂBÎ: FROM THE ATTAINMENT
OF HAPPINESS

55 Every instruction is composed of two things: (a) making what is being studied comprehensible and causing its idea to be established in the soul and (b) causing others to assent to what is comprehended and established in the soul. There are two ways of making a thing comprehensible: first, by causing its essence to be perceived by the intellect, and second, by causing it to be imagined through the similitude that imitates it. Assent, too, is brought about by one of two methods, either the method of certain demonstration or the method of persuasion. Now when one acquires knowledge of the beings or receives instruction in them, if he perceives their ideas themselves with his intellect, and his assent to them is by means of certain demonstration, then the science that comprises these cognitions is *philosophy*. But if they are known by imagining them through similitudes that imitate them, and assent to what is imagined of them is caused by persuasive methods, then the ancients call what comprises these cognitions *religion*. And if those intelligibles themselves are adopted, and *persuasive* methods are used, then the religion comprising them is called *popular, generally accepted*, and *external* philosophy. Therefore, according to the ancients, religion is an imitation of philosophy. Both comprise the same

From *Alfarabi's Philosophy of Plato and Aristotle*, trans. by Muhsin Mahdi, © 1962 by The Free Press, A Division of The Macmillan Company, pp. 44-47. Reprinted by permission of the Macmillan Company.

subjects and both give an account of the ultimate principles of the beings. For both supply knowledge about the first principle and cause of the beings, and both give an account of the ultimate end for the sake of which man is made—that is, supreme happiness—and the ultimate end of every one of the other beings. In everything of which philosophy gives an account based on intellectual perception or conception, religion gives an account based on imagination. In everything demonstrated by philosophy, religion employs persuasion. Philosophy gives an account of the ultimate principles (that is, the essence of the first principle and the essences of the incorporeal second principles), as they are perceived by the intellect. Religion sets forth their images by means of similitudes of them taken from corporeal principles and imitates them by their likenesses among political offices. It imitates the divine acts by means of the functions of political offices. It imitates the actions of natural powers and principles by their likenesses among the faculties, states, and arts that have to do with the will, just as Plato does in the *Timaeus*. It imitates the intelligibles by their likenesses among the sensibles: for instance, some imitate *matter* by *abyss* or *darkness* or *water*, and *nothingness* by *darkness*. It imitates the classes of supreme happiness—that is, the ends of the acts of the human virtues—by their likenesses among the goods that are believed to be the ends. It imitates the classes of true happiness by means of the ones that are believed to be happiness. It imitates the ranks of the beings by their likenesses among spatial and temporal ranks. And it attempts to bring the similitudes of these things as close as possible to their essences. Also, in everything of which philosophy gives an account that is demonstrative and certain, religion gives an account based on persuasive arguments. Finally, philosophy is prior to religion in time.

56 Again, it is evident that when one seeks to bring into actual existence the intelligibles of the things depending on the will supplied by practical philosophy, he ought to prescribe the conditions that render possible their actual existence. Once the conditions that render their actual existence possible are prescribed, the voluntary intelligibles are embodied in laws. Therefore the legislator is he who, by the excellence of his delibera-

tion, has the capacity to find the conditions required for the actual existence of voluntary intelligibles in such a way as to lead to the achievement of supreme happiness. It is also evident that only after perceiving them by his intellect should the legislator seek to discover their conditions, and he cannot find their conditions that enable him to guide others toward supreme happiness without having perceived supreme happiness with his intellect. Nor can these things become intelligible (and the legislative craft thereby hold the supreme office) without his having beforehand acquired philosophy. Therefore, if he intends to possess a craft that is authoritative rather than subservient, the legislator must be a philosopher. Similarly, if the philosopher who has acquired the theoretical virtues does not have the capacity for bringing them about in all others according to their capacities, then what he has acquired from them has no validity. Yet he cannot find the states and the conditions by which the voluntary intelligibles assume actual existence, if he does not possess the deliberative virtue; and the deliberative virtue cannot exist in him without the practical virtue. Moreover, he cannot bring them about in all others according to their capacities except by a faculty that enables him to excel in persuasion and in representing things through images.

57 It follows, then, that the idea of *Imam*,[1] Philosopher, and Legislator is a single idea. However, the name *philosopher* signifies primarily theoretical virtue. But if it be determined that the theoretical virtue reach its ultimate perfection in every respect, it follows necessarily that he must possess all the other faculties as well. *Legislator* signifies excellence of knowledge concerning the conditions of practical intelligibles, the faculty for finding them, and the faculty for bringing them about in nations and cities. When it is determined that they be brought into existence on the basis of knowledge, it will follow that the theoretical virtue must precede the others—the existence of the inferior presupposes the existence of the higher. The name *prince* signifies sovereignty and ability. To be completely able, one has to possess the power of the greatest ability. His ability to do a thing must not result only from external things; he himself must pos-

---

1. Religious leader, originally the Prophet himself.

sess great ability because his art, skill, and virtue are of exceedingly great power. This is not possible except by great power of knowledge, great power of deliberation, and great power of [moral] virtue and art. Otherwise he is not truly able nor sovereign. For if his ability stops short of this, it is still imperfect. Similarly, if his ability is restricted to goods inferior to supreme happiness, his ability is incomplete and he is not perfect. Therefore the true prince is the same as the philosopher-legislator. As to the idea of *Imam* in the Arabic language, it signifies merely the one whose example is followed and who is well received: that is, either his perfection is well received or his purpose is well received. If he is not well received in all the infinite activities, virtues, and arts, then he is not truly well received. Only when all other arts, virtues, and activities seek to realize *his* purpose and no other, will his art be the most powerful art, his [moral] virtue the most powerful virtue, his deliberation the most powerful deliberation, and his science the most powerful science. For with all of these powers he will be exploiting the powers of others so as to accomplish his own purpose. This is not possible without the theoretical sciences, without the greatest of all deliberative virtues, and without the rest of those things that are in the philosopher.

58 So let it be clear to you that the idea of the Philosopher, Supreme Ruler, Prince, Legislator, and *Imam* is but a single idea. No matter which one of these words you take, if you proceed to look at what each of them signifies among the majority of those who speak our language, you will find that they all finally agree by signifying one and the same idea.

59 Once the images representing the theoretical things demonstrated in the theoretical sciences are produced in the souls of the multitude and they are made to assent to their images, and once the practical things (together with the conditions of the possibility of their existence) take hold of their souls and dominate them so that they are unable to resolve to do anything else, then the theoretical and practical things are realized. Now these things are *philosophy* when they are in the soul of the legislator. They [are] the *religion* when they are in the souls of the multitude. For when the legislator knows these things, they are

evident to him by sure insight, whereas what is established in the souls of the multitude is through an image and a persuasive argument. Although it is the legislator who also represents these things through images, neither the images nor the persuasive arguments are intended for himself. As far as he is concerned, they are certain. He is the one who invents the images and the persuasive arguments, but not for the sake of establishing these things in his own soul as a religion for himself. No, the images and the persuasive arguments are intended for others, whereas, so far as he is concerned, these things are certain. They are a religion for others, whereas, so far as he is concerned, they are philosophy. Such, then, is true philosophy and the true philosopher.

Poetry

Poetry had been prized above all other forms of literature among the Arabs from pre-Islâmic days. Language and verse forms changed after the great Islâmic conquests, but the high esteem in which rulers and chieftains held accomplished poets did not diminish. Praise of a generous, brave, and noble patron became a stock in trade for successful poets; a niggardly ruler, on the other hand, had to fear poetic ridicule and insult, which, if catchy enough, might even embarrass him among his subjects. In a limited way poets were equivalent to modern journalists and public relations men.

Abû'l-Tayyib Ahmad ibn al-Husayn al-Dju'fî al-Mutanabbî (915-955) led an adventurous life. Born in Irâq, son of a humble water carrier, he spent part of his boyhood among Bedouin Arabs, from whom he learned old-fashioned desert language and ideals. He felt himself to be an Arab among Arabs and despised other peoples whom he felt to be responsible for the political decline of the caliphate, which was clearly apparent in his day.

In matters of religion Mutanabbî was attracted to Shî'î doctrines, and in 928, at age 13, even declared himself to be a Prophet with a

new Qur'ân. A few years later he led an uprising; he was imprisoned when it failed. Despite this turbulent start in life, in 939 Mutanabbî became court poet to the governor of Damascus. In 948 he
shifted to the court of Saif al-Dawla at Aleppo, where he wrote his
greatest poems. (Farâbî also was at this court when the poet arrived.)

In 957 Mutanabbî left Aleppo for reasons unknown, gravitating to
Egypt and the court of the slave king Kâfûr. Three years later the
poet fled the country in anger, taking revenge on his erstwhile patron by writing bitter satires against him. Mutanabbî next set out
for Baghdâd but was killed resisting thieves before he reached the
city.

The selections that follow include samples of Mutanabbî's praise
for Saif al-Dawla and of his attack on Kâfûr. As in all efforts at
translating poetry, much of the power of the original evaporates in
English. Suffice it to say that most experts count Mutanabbî as the
best of the classical Arabic poets.

MUTANABBÎ: FOUR POEMS

Panegyric to Saif al-Daula on his departure from Antioch

Whither do you intend, great prince? We are the herbs of the
hills, and you are the clouds;
we are the ones time has been miserly towards respecting you,
and the days cheated of your presence.
Whether at war or at peace, you aim at the heights, whether
you tarry or hasten.
Would that we were your steeds when you ride forth, and your
tents when you alight!
Every day you load up afresh, and journey to glory, there to
dwell;
and when souls are mighty, the bodies are wearied in their
quest.
Even so the moons rise over us, and even so the great seas are
unquiet;
and our wont is comely patience, were it with anything but
your absence that we were tried.

From *Poems of al-Mutanabbi*, trans. by Arthur J. Arberry, London: Cambridge University Press, 1967, pp. 54, 56, 76, 110, 112, 114, 116. Reprinted
by permission.

Every life you do not grace is death; every sun that you are not
is darkness.

End the desolation that we suffer, you in whom the numerous
army finds joy,

you who are present in the war quiet of heart, as though the
battling were a compact,[1]

you who smite the squadrons until the neck-bones and the feet
meet each other;

and when you halt for a space in any place, to injure it is prohibited to time,[2]

and the herbs produced by the lands is joy, and the rains shed
by the clouds is wine.

Whenever it is said, "He has reached the end", he shows us
such bounty as the bountiful have never been guided to,

and battling before which the foemen cower, and brisk beneficence at which men are amazed.

The awe inspired in the hearts by Saif al-Daula the king, the
object of our hopes, is itself a sword;[3]

so it is much for the brave to shun him, and it is much for the
eloquent to speak a greeting.[4]

To Saif al-Daula on his recovery from an illness

Glory and nobility were preserved when you were preserved,
and the pain passed from you to your enemies;[5]

the raids were healed with your healing, and noble exploits
therewith rejoiced, and the steady showers cascaded,[6]

and light which had left the sun, as though the loss of light were
a sickness in its body, returned to it,

---

1. "A compact": *sc.* not to lead to your death or danger. (Tr.)

2. "To injure it": by drought or the like. (Tr.)

3. "A sword" punning on the name Saif al-Daula ("Sword of the State").
(Tr.)

4. The awe inspired by Saif al-Daula is enough to silence even the ready
tongue, and merely to be allowed to greet him thus simply is a great mercy.
(Tr.)

5. The enemies were pained because the prince could now resume his campaign against them. (Tr.)

6. The "showers" of bounty were resumed as abundant as ever. (Tr.)

and your lightning shone forth for me from the cheeks of a king
such that the rain never falls, save when he smiles.[7]
He is named the Sword, but not because of any resemblance, for
how should master and servant resemble each other?
The Arabs are unique in the world in being of his race, and the
non-Arabs share with the Arabs in enjoying his beneficence.
Allah has reserved His succour exclusively for Islam, even
though all nations partake of His blessings.
I do not single out you alone for felicitation on recovery; when
you are safe and sound, all men are safe and sound.

*Satire on Kâfûr composed on 9 Dhu'l-Hijja 350 (19 January
962), one day before the poet's departure from Egypt*

Festival day—with what circumstance have you returned, day
of festival? With what has happened in the past, or with some
matter quite new that is to occur in you?[8]
As for my dear ones, the desert stretches between me and them;
would that there stretched between me and you a desert, beyond
which were a desert.
But for my questing the heights, lean, powerful she-camel had
never travelled with me where I have ridden her, neither long-
bodied, short-haired mare,
and more agreeable as bed-fellow than my sword would have
been the slender, delicate maidens matching its lustre.
Time has left not of my heart nor of my liver anything to be
enslaved by eye or neck.
My two wine-bearers, is this wine in your cups, or is there in
your cups anxiety and sleeplessness?
Am I a rock? What is it with me, that I am not stirred by this
liquor and these songs?

7. The "lightning" is the white flash of the prince's teeth revealed in a
smile; the "rain" is again his bounty. (Tr.)
8. This famous satire composed on quitting the court of Kâfûr opens with
the erotic prelude; the conventional two companions, here in the role of cup-
bearers, are addressed (verse 6) before the poet launches upon his complaint
and ferocious satire. The "day of 'Arafa" (9 Dhu'l-Hijja) on which the pilgrims to Mecca and Medina halt at the hill of 'Arafât was observed as a
festival. (Tr.)

When I desired pure red wine, I found it when the beloved of my soul was missing.

What have I encountered of the world? and the most astonishing part of it is that I am envied for that over which I weep.[9]

I am become the most ample of the wealthy as to treasurer and hand; I am the rich one, and my properties are promises.[10]

Indeed I have alighted amongst liars whose guest is denied alike hospitality and departure;

men's generosity is with their hands, and their generosity is with their tongues—would that neither they existed nor their generosity!

Death seizes not a soul of their souls, without death has in his hand a stick because of its stench,[11]

every one of them flaccid as to the leather strap of his belly, swollen in the flanks, not to be counted amongst either men or women.[12]

Whenever a wicked slave assassinates his master or betrays him, has he to get his training in Egypt?

There, the eunuch has become the chieftain of the runaway slaves, the free man is enslaved, and the slave is obeyed.

The gardeners of Egypt are asleep to the tricks of its foxes which have gotten indigestion, and yet the grape-clusters are not at an end.[13]

The slave is no brother to the godly free man, even though he be born in the clothes of the free.

Do not buy a slave without buying a stick with him, for slaves are filthy and of scant good.

I never thought I should live to see the day when a dog would do me evil and be praised into the bargain,[14]

nor did I imagine that true men would have ceased to exist, and

9. "Envied": *sc.* by other poets. (Tr.)

10. Kâfûr is the poet's treasurer and "hand" of bounties, but his gifts are only promises. (Tr.)

11. "A stick" for poking at, to avoid handling, their stinking corpses. (Tr.)

12. "Leather straps" as for binding up a water-skin, an elegant way of saying that they fart. (Tr.)

13. The "gardeners" are the aristocrats, heedless of the deprivations of the slaves ("foxes"). (Tr.)

14. "Praised" in the expected panegyrics. (Tr.)

that the like of the father of bounty would still be here[15]

and that that negro with his pierced camel's lip would be obeyed by those cowardly hirelings.

Hungry, he eats of my provisions, and detains me, that he may be called, "Mighty of worth, much sought after".

A man who is controlled by a pregnant slave-woman is indeed oppressed, hot-eyed, faint-hearted.[16]

What a predicament! alas for one accepting it—for the like of it were created the long-necked Mahrî camels;[17]

in such a situation, he who drinks of death enjoys its taste; doom is honey-sweet when one is humiliated.

Who ever taught the eunuch negro nobility? His "white" people, or his royal ancestors?

or his ear bleeding in the hand of the slave-broker? or his worth, seeing that for two farthings he would be rejected?

Wretched Kâfûr is the most deserving of the base to be excused in regard to every baseness—and sometimes excusing is a reproach—

and that is because white stallions are incapable of gentility, so how about black eunuchs?[18]

A satire against Kâfûr

From which road, pray, does nobility approach you? Where are the cupping-jars, Kâfûr, and the clippers?[19]

Those whom your hands controlled had exceeded themselves, so that through you they have been made aware that a dog is over them.

Nothing is fouler than a stallion with a membrum virile being led along by a slave girl without a womb.[20]

15. The "father of bounty" is ironically applied to Kâfûr; the word meaning "bounty" has the root-meaning of "white," and can also imply "misfortune." (Tr.)

16. Kâfûr is called "a pregnant slave-women" because of his fat belly. "Hot-eyed" because of the scalding tears. (Tr.)

17. The camels were created for making a rapid departure. (Tr.)

18. The "white stallions" are the other princes, who have already failed the poet. (Tr.)

19. Kâfûr is only fit to be a barber. (Tr.)

20. Explained as a reference to Kâfûr's tutelage of the Prince, or to his commanding the army. The eunuch is compared to a woman, and a slave-woman at that. (Tr.)

The nobles of every sort of men are of their own selves, but the
nobles of the Muslims are vile slaves.

Is it the goal of religion that you should pluck out your beards,
O community whose ignorance is a laughing-stock to other
nations?

Is there no brave lad who will bring down the Indian sword on
his skull, so that the doubts and suspicions of men may cease?

For he is a proof whereby the materialist, the agnostic and the
atheist torment the hearts.[21]

How all-powerful God is to put to shame His creatures, and not
to prove true a people in what they have alleged![22]

21. Kâfûr is a living support for the arguments of those who deny the omnipotence of God. (Tr.)
22. God intends to punish the Egyptians by putting Kâfûr in power over
them; this is the reason for the situation, and not God's impotence as the
atheists assert. (Tr.)

'Abbâsid Decline

Muslim political theory held that the entire community of the faithful ought to follow one leader, successor to the Prophet (Arabic:
khalîfa). In the first Muslim centuries reality more or less corre-
sponded to this principle, although individual caliphs may have
fallen short of the role pious Muslims required of them. By the tenth
century, however, Turkish military officers had usurped power in
Baghdâd and had reduced the caliph to a figurehead. In the provinces a variety of upstarts, must of them inspired in some degree by
heterodox Shî'î religious doctrines, came to power. The following
selection from The Experiences of the Nations, a history of the Islâmic empire to 980, describes how the Caliph Muqtadir came to
office in 908 and shows that the supreme office of Islâm had become
hollow. Its author, Abû 'Alî Ahmad ibn Muhammad ibn Miskawaih
(d. 1030), a high court official of Persian descent, also wrote on
questions of ethics as well as history.

IBN MISKAWAIH: FROM THE EXPERIENCES OF THE NATIONS

The Caliphate of al-Muqtadir Billah[1]

Account of the procedure at the proclamation of JA'FAR *son of* MU'TADID,[2] *whose kunyah[3] was* ABU'L-FADL, *and who was thirteen years of age at the time.*

When Muktafi's[4] illness grew serious, his vizier[5] 'Abbas b. *Ha*san began to consider whom he should appoint Caliph; and his choice wavered. On his way from his own palace to that of the Sultan he used to be accompanied by one of the four persons who had charge of the bureaux. . . . When the first of these was his companion, and was consulted by him on the matter, he nominated Abu'l-'Abbas 'Abdallah son of Mu'tazz,[6] eulogizing his character. The next day his companion was the third of these . . . [above-mentioned men, Ibn al-Furat], who, when consulted, replied that this was a matter to which he was unaccustomed; he begged therefore to be excused; he was accustomed to being consulted only about officials. 'Abbas displayed annoyance, and said: This is hedging; you know well what is wise. When he insisted, Ibn al-Furat said: If the vizier's choice is fixed upon an individual, let him ask God's blessing and proceed with the execution of his plan. He understood (said Ibn al-Furat) that I referred to Ibn al-Mu'tazz, about whom rumour was rife. But he said to me: All I want of you is your candid advice. I replied: If that is what the vizier requires, then what

---

From *The Eclipse of the 'Abbasid Caliphate; Original Chronicles of the Fourth Islamic Century (The Concluding Portion of the Experiences of Nations by Miskawaihi)*, trans. & ed. by D. S. Margoliouth, London; Basil Blackwell, 1921, Vol. 4, pp. 1-3. Reprinted by permission of Basil Blackwell & Mott Ltd.

1. Caliph (r. 908-832).
2. Caliph (r. 892-902), father of Muqtadir, whose given name was Ja'far.
3. Kunya: honorific name.
4. Caliph (r. 902-908).
5. Correctly, *wazîr*: chief officer of Caliph.
6. Caliph (r. 866-869).

I say is: *For God's sake do not appoint to the post a man who knows the house of one, the fortune of another, the gardens of a third, the slave-girl of a fourth, the estate of a fifth, and the horse of a sixth; not one who has mixed with people, has had experience of affairs, has gone through his apprenticeship, and made calculations of people's fortunes.* The vizier requested me to repeat those words several times, and said at last: Then whom do you nominate? I replied: Ja'far son of Mu'tadid![7] What, he said, Ja'far is a child! True, I said, only he is Mu'tadid's son. Why should you introduce a man who will govern, and knows our resources, who will administer affairs himself, and regard himself as independent? Why not deliver the empire to a man who will leave *you* to administer it?

On the third day 'Abbas asked the advice of . . . 'Ali b. 'Isa,[8] and tried hard to make him nominate someone. He declined, saying: I shall nominate no-one; only let God be feared, and religion be considered.

'Abbas b. *H*asan inclined to Ibn al-Furat's view, and with this there coincided the testament of Muktafi, which assigned to his brother Ja'far the sucession to the Caliphate. So when Muktafi died, late in the day on Saturday . . . Aug. 13, 908, the vizier 'Abbas appointed Ja'far to the Caliphate, albeit unwillingly, owing to Ja'far's tender years. *S*afi the *H*urami (attendant of the women's apartments) went to bring him down the river from Ibn *T*ahir's palace[9]; when the *harraqah*[10] in which he was brought came on its way to the palace of 'Abbas b. *H*asan, the retainers of 'Abbas called out to the boatman to come inside. It occurred to *S*afi the *H*urami that 'Abbas only desired Ja'far to enter his palace because he had changed his mind with regard to the prince; fearing then that the vizier might transfer his choice to some one else, *S*afi told the boatman not to go in, and drawing his sword said to the boatman: If you go inside, I will

7. Caliph (r. 892-902); he had restored the might and independence of the Caliphate. (Tr.)

8. One of the four men mentioned above.

9. The princes who were not actually of the reigning family were confined here at this time. (Tr.)

10. Some form of rivercraft. (Tr.)

slash off your head. So the boatman proceeded without stopping
to the Sultan's Palace.

Ja'far's appointment was then effected, and he took the title
al-Muqtadir Billah ("the powerful through God"). The new
Sultan gave 'Abbas a free hand, and the latter gave out the ac-
cession money.[11]

11. The gratuity given to the troops on the occasion of a sovereign's acces-
sion. (Tr.)

III

Political Fragmentation
and Cultural Florescence
(1000-1400)

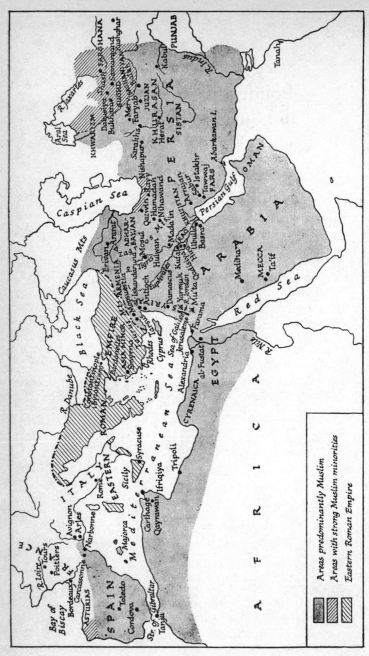

From *The Social Structure of Islam* by Reuben Levy (1971) by permission of Cambridge University Press.

Areas predominantly Muslim
Areas with strong Muslim minorities
Eastern Roman Empire

Introduction

After 945, the real power of the Caliph in Baghdâd dissolved. Provincial governors usurped authority, Shî'î sectarian religious leaders challenged the legitimacy of the Caliph's rule, and Turkish military officers made the person of the Caliph a puppet for their own advantage. After about a century of confusion, Turkish nomads (later known as Seljûqs) fresh from the steppes of central Asia took power in Irân, later extending their government westward into Asia Minor as well. The helpless Caliph came to terms with the Seljûqs willingly enough. They had military power and a modicum of social cohesion conspicuously lacking in the rest of Muslim society; and they did not challenge the 'Abbâsids' right to call themselves Caliph. Instead, Seljûq sultâns supported the 'Abbâsids as symbols of the unity of Islâm, while keeping government in their own hands.

There were, however, many other successor states to the caliphate, and the Seljûq sultânate itself soon broke up into quarreling fragments. Despite political confusion, the centuries from about 1000 to 1400 were a time of far-reaching cultural innovation among Islâmic peoples. The reconciliation of mystical Sûfism with official Islâm was a central achievement, associated especially with the brilliant scholar Abû Hamîd Muhammad al-Ghazâlî. There also ensued a brilliant flowering of Persian literature, suffused with Sûfî piety. Jalaluddin Rûmî was among the most influential of the Persian poets, as much for his role in founding a widespread dervish order, as on the strength of his poetry itself.

Despite the caliphate's decline in power, new leadership emerged that repelled the Christian crusade (1097-1291). Yet the crusade and Muslim counter-attack also led to cultural intermingling, as may be seen from the passage by Usâma ibn Munqidh. A far greater disaster for Islâm was the Mongol conquest of Irân and Mesopotamia; when the Mongols captured Baghdâd in 1258 they destroyed the caliphate, depriving Islâm of even a symbolic single leadership. Excerpts from historical writers Juvainî and Ibn al-Athîr describe the conquest.

But the vitality of the Faith was soon apparent even in the face of disaster. Within less than a century the heirs of the Mongol conquerors became Muslim; a widespread missionary expansion followed which carried Islâm into a broad region of Africa, into Asia Minor and to the lands and islands of the Indian Ocean. The last reading of this section, from Ibn Batûta, shows how this process went forward even in remote and little-known places.

Crusades

Christian warriors from France and adjacent parts of western Europe (known to Muslims as "Franks") set out in 1097 to free the Holy Land from Muslim rule. By 1099, when a band of Crusaders captured Jerusalem, they had met with success, largely because of local rivalries among the Muslim rulers of Syria and Palestine who failed to unite against the invaders. But the Christians were divided too and, before long, trade and war across the Christian-Muslim frontier resulted in mutual acquaintance and, within limits, mutual respect.

Yet the Franks seemed strange and barbarous to a Muslim warrior and gentleman like Usâma ibn Munqidh (1095-1188), whose reminiscences, unusually personal for a Muslim of his day, reveal the limited interpenetration of Muslim and Christian chivalrous traditions that took place during his long lifetime. Usâma's life coincided almost exactly with the period of Christian sovereignty over the Holy Land. In the year before he died, Saladin, having united Syria and Egypt under his government, directed the united Muslim strength against the Crusaders and captured Jerusalem for Islâm once again (1187). Another century elapsed before the last Christian stronghold, the city of Acre, surrendered to another Muslim conqueror (1291), thus terminating the Frankish political presence in Palestine after nearly 200 years.

USÂMA: FROM MEMOIRS

An Appreciation of the Frankish Character

Their lack of sense.—Mysterious are the works of the Creator, the author of all things! When one comes to recount cases regarding the Franks, he cannot but glorify Allah (exalted is he!) and sanctify him, for he sees them as animals possessing the virtues of courage and fighting, but nothing else; just as animals have only the virtues of strength and carrying loads. I shall now give some instances of their doings and their curious mentality.

In the army of King Fulk, son of Fulk, was a Frankish reverend knight who had just arrived from their land in order to make the holy pilgrimage and then return home. He was of my intimate fellowship and kept such constant company with me that he began to call me "my brother." Between us were mutual bonds of amity and friendship. When he resolved to return by sea to his homeland, he said to me:

My brother, I am leaving for my country and I want thee to send with me thy son (my son, who was then fourteen years old, was at that time in my company) to our country, where he can see the knights and learn wisdom and chivalry. When he returns, he will be like a wise man.

Thus there fell upon my ears words which would never come out of the head of a sensible man; for even if my son were to be taken captive, his captivity could not bring him a worse misfortune than carrying him into the lands of the Franks. However, I said to the man:

By thy life, this has exactly been my idea. But the only thing that prevented me from carrying it out was the fact that his grandmother, my mother, is so fond of him and did not this time let him come out with me until she exacted an oath from me to the effect that I would return him to her.

From *Memoirs of an Arab-Syrian Gentleman or an Arab Knight in the Crusades; Memoirs of Usâmah Ibn-Munqidh*, trans. by Philip K. Hitti, Columbia University Press, 1929 (Reprinted by Khayats, Beirut, 1964), pp. 161-70, 67-70, 79-80, 93-96, 133-34, 144-46, 154, 159-60. Reprinted by permission Philip K. Hitti.

Thereupon he asked, "Is thy mother still alive?" "Yes," I re-plied. "Well," said he, "disobey her not."

Their curious medication.—A case illustrating their curious medicine is the following:

The lord of al-Munaytirah[1] wrote to my uncle asking him to dispatch a physician to treat certain sick persons among his people. My uncle sent him a Christian physician named Thâbit. Thâbit was absent but ten days when he returned. So we said to him, "How quickly hast thou healed thy patients!" He said:

They brought before me a knight in whose leg an abscess had grown; and a woman afflicted with imbecility.[2] To the knight I applied a small poultice until the abscess opened and became well; and the woman I put on diet and made her humor wet. Then a Frankish physician came to them and said, "This man knows nothing about treating them." He then said to the knight, "Which wouldst thou prefer, living with one leg or dying with two?" The latter replied, "Living with one leg." The physician said, "Bring me a strong knight and a sharp ax." A knight came with the ax. And I was standing by. Then the physician laid the leg of the patient on a block of wood and bade the knight strike his leg with the ax and chop it off at one blow. Accordingly he struck it—while I was looking on—one blow, but the leg was not severed. He dealt another blow, upon which the marrow of the leg flowed out and the patient died on the spot. He then examined the woman and said, "This is a woman in whose head there is a devil which has possessed her. Shave off her hair." Accordingly they shaved it off and the woman began once more to eat their ordinary diet—garlic and mustard. Her imbecility took a turn for the worse. The physician then said, "The devil has penetrated through her head." He therefore took a razor, made a deep cruciform incision on it, peeled off the skin at the middle of the incision until the bone of the skull was exposed and rubbed it with salt. The woman also expired instantly. Thereupon I asked them whether my services were needed any longer, and when they replied in the negative I turned home, having learned of their medicine what I knew not before.

1. In Lebanon near Afqa, . . . i.e., ancient Adonis. (Tr.)
2. Ar. *nashâf*, "dryness," is not used as a name of a disease. I take the word therefore to be Persian *nishâf* = "imbecility." (Tr.)

I have, however, witnessed a case of their medicine which was quite different from that.

The king of the Franks[3] had for treasurer a knight named Bernard [*barnâd*], who (may Allah's curse be upon him!) was one of the most accursed and wicked among the Franks. A horse kicked him in the leg, which was subsequently infected and which opened in fourteen different places. Every time one of these cuts would close in one place, another would open in another place. All this happened while I was praying for his perdition. Then came to him a Frankish physician and removed from the leg all the ointments which were on it and began to wash it with very strong vinegar. By this treatment all the cuts were healed and the man became well again. He was up again like a devil.

Another case illustrating their curious medicine is the following:

In Shayzar we had an artisan named abu-al-Fath, who had a boy whose neck was afflicted with scrofula. Every time a part of it would close, another part would open. This man happened to go to Antioch on business of his, accompanied by his son. A Frank noticed the boy and asked his father about him. Abu-al-Fath replied, "This is my son." The Frank said to him, "Wilt thou swear by thy religion that if I prescribe to thee a medicine which will cure thy boy, thou wilt charge nobody fees for prescribing it thyself? In that case, I shall prescribe to thee a medicine which will cure the boy." The man took the oath and the Frank said:

Take uncrushed leaves of glasswort, burn them, then soak the ashes in olive oil and sharp vinegar. Treat the scrofula with them until the spot on which it is growing is eaten up. Then take burnt lead, soak it in ghee butter [*samn*] and treat him with it. That will cure him.

The father treated the boy accordingly, and the boy was cured. The sores closed and the boy returned to his normal condition of health.

I have myself treated with this medicine many who were af-

3. Fulk of Anjou, king of Jerusalem. (Tr.)

flicted with such disease, and the treatment was successful in removing the cause of the complaint.

Newly arrived Franks are especially rough: One insists that Usâmah should pray eastward.—Everyone who is a fresh emigrant from the Frankish lands is ruder in character than those who have become acclimatized and have held long association with the Moslems. Here is an illustration of their rude character.

Whenever I visited Jerusalem I always entered the Aqsa Mosque, beside which stood a small mosque which the Franks had converted into a church. When I used to enter the Aqsa Mosque, which was occupied by the Templars [*al-dâwiyyah*], who were my friends, the Templars would evacuate the little adjoining mosque so that I might pray in it. One day[4] I entered this mosque, repeated the first formula, "Allah is great," and stood up in the act of praying, upon which one of the Franks rushed on me, got hold of me and turned my face eastward saying, "This is the way thou shouldst pray!" A group of Templars hastened to him, seized him and repelled him from me. I resumed my prayer. The same man, while the others were otherwise busy, rushed once more on me and turned my face eastward, saying, "This is the way thou shouldst pray!" The Templars again came in to him and expelled him. They apologized to me, saying, "This is a stranger who has only recently arrived from the land of the Franks and he has never before seen anyone praying except eastward." Thereupon I said to myself, "I have had enough prayer." So I went out and have ever been surprised at the conduct of this devil of a man, at the change in the color of his face, his trembling and his sentiment at the sight of one praying towards the *qiblah*.[5]

Another wants to show to a Moslem God as a child.—I saw one of the Franks come to al-Amîr Mu'în-al-Dîn (may Allah's mercy rest upon his soul!) when he was in the Dome of the Rock[6] and say to him, "Dost thou want to see God as a child?" Mu'în-al-Dîn said, "Yes." The Frank walked ahead of us until

4. About 1140. (Tr.)
5. The direction of the Ka'ba in the holy city, Mecca. (Tr.)
6. *al-sakhra*, the mosque standing near al-Aqsa in Jerusalem. (Tr.) Mu'în al-Dîn Anâr was at that time the ruler of Damascus.

he showed us the picture of Mary with Christ (may peace be upon him!) as an infant in her lap. He then said, "This is God as a child." But Allah is exalted far above what the infidels say about him!

Franks lack jealousy in sex affairs.—The Franks are void of all zeal and jealousy. One of them may be walking along with his wife. He meets another man who takes the wife by the hand and steps aside to converse with her while the husband is standing on one side waiting for his wife to conclude the conversation. If she lingers too long for him, he leaves her alone with the conversant and goes away.

Here is an illustration which I myself witnessed:

When I used to visit Nâblus,[7] I always took lodging with a man named Mu'izz, whose home was a lodging house for the Moslems. The house had windows which opened to the road, and there stood opposite to it on the other side of the road a house belonging to a Frank who sold wine for the merchants. He would take some wine in a bottle and go around announcing it by shouting, "So and so, the merchant, has just opened a cask full of this wine. He who wants to buy some of it will find it in such and such a place." The Frank's pay for the announcement made would be the wine in that bottle. One day this Frank went home and found a man with his wife in the same bed. He asked him, "What could have made thee enter into my wife's room?" The man replied, "I was tired, so I went in to rest." "But how," asked he, "didst thou get into my bed?" The other replied, "I found a bed that was spread, so I slept in it." "But," said he, "my wife was sleeping together with thee!" The other replied, "Well, the bed is hers. How could I therefore have prevented her from using her own bed?" "By the truth of my religion," said the husband, "if thou shouldst do it again, thou and I would have a quarrel." Such was for the Frank the entire expression of his disapproval and the limit of his jealousy.

Another illustration:

We had with us a bath-keeper named Sâlim, originally an inhabitant of al-Ma'arrah,[8] who had charge of the bath of my

7. Neapolis, ancient Shechem. (Tr.)
8. Ma'arra al-Nu'mân, between Hamâ and Aleppo. (Tr.)

father (may Allah's mercy rest upon his soul!). This man related the following story:

I once opened a bath in al-Ma'arrah in order to earn my living. To
this bath there came a Frankish knight. The Franks disapprove of
girding a cover around one's waist while in the bath. So this Frank
stretched out his arm and pulled off my cover from my waist and
threw it away. He looked and saw that I had recently shaved off my
pubes. So he shouted, "Sâlim!" As I drew near him he stretched his
hand over my pubes and said, "Sâlim, good! By the truth of my religion, do the same for me." Saying this, he lay on his back and I
found that in that place the hair was like his beard. So I shaved it
off. Then he passed his hand over the place and, finding it smooth,
he said, "Sâlim, by the truth of my religion, do the same to madame
[al-dâma]" (al-dâma in their language means the lady), referring
to his wife. He then said to a servant of his, "Tell madame to come
here." Accordingly the servant went and brought her and made her
enter the bath. She also lay on her back. The knight repeated, "Do
what thou hast done to me." So I shaved all that hair while her husband was sitting looking at me. At last he thanked me and handed
me the pay for my service.

Consider now this great contradiction! They have neither
jealousy nor zeal but they have great courage, although courage
is nothing but the product of zeal and of ambition to be above
ill repute.

Here is a story analogous to the one related above:

I entered the public bath in Sûr [Tyre] and took my place in
a secluded part. One of my servants thereupon said to me,
"There is with us in the bath a woman." When I went out, I sat
on one of the stone benches and behold! the woman who was in
the bath had come out all dressed and was standing with her
father just opposite me. But I could not be sure that she was a
woman. So I said to one of my companions, "By Allah, see if
this is a woman," by which I meant that he should ask about
her. But he went, as I was looking at him, lifted the end of her
robe and looked carefully at her. Thereupon her father turned
toward me and said, "This is my daughter. Her mother is dead
and she has nobody to wash her hair. So I took her in with me
to the bath and washed her head." I replied, "Thou hast well

done! This is something for which thou shalt be rewarded [by Allah]!"

Another curious case of medication.—A curious case relating to their medicine is the following, which was related to me by William of Bures [*kilyâm dabûr*], the lord of Tabarayyah [Tiberias], who was one of the principal chiefs among the Franks. It happened that William had accompanied al-Amîr Mu'în-al-Dîn (may Allah's mercy rest upon his soul!) from 'Akka to Tabarayyah when I was in his company too. On the way William related to us the following story in these words:

We had in our country a highly esteemed knight who was taken ill and was on the point of death. We thereupon came to one of our great priests and said to him, "Come with us and examine so and so, the knight." "I will," he replied, and walked along with us while we were assured in ourselves that if he would only lay his hand on him the patient would recover. When the priest saw the patient, he said, "Bring me some wax." We fetched him a little wax, which he softened and shaped like the knuckles of fingers, and he stuck one in each nostril. The knight died on the spot. We said to him, "He is dead." "Yes," he replied, "he was suffering great pain, so I closed up his nose that he might die and get relief."

. . . .

A funny race between two aged women.—We shall now leave the discusion of their treatment of the orifices of the body to something else.

I found myself in Tabarayyah at the time the Franks were celebrating one of their feasts. The cavaliers went out to exercise with lances. With them went out two decrepit, aged women whom they stationed at one end of the race course. At the other end of the field they left a pig which they had scalded and laid on a rock. They then made the two aged women run a race while each one of them was accompanied by a detachment of horsemen urging her on. At every step they took, the women would fall down and rise again, while the spectators would laugh. Finally one of them got ahead of the other and won that pig for a prize.

Their judicial trials: A duel.—I attended one day a duel in Nâblus between two Franks. The reason for this was that certain

Moslem thieves took by surprise one of the villages of Nâblus. One of the peasants of that village was charged with having acted as guide for the thieves when they fell upon the village. So he fled away. The king[9] sent and arrested his children. The peasant thereupon came back to the king and said, "Let justice be done in my case. I challenge to a duel the man who claimed that I guided the thieves to the village." The king then said to the tenant who held the village in fief, "Bring forth someone to fight the duel with him." The tenant went to his village, where a blacksmith lived, took hold of him and ordered him to fight the duel. The tenant became thus sure of the safety of his own peasants, none of whom would be killed and his estate ruined.

I saw this blacksmith. He was a physically strong young man, but his heart failed him. He would walk a few steps and then sit down and ask for a drink. The one who had made the challenge was an old man, but he was strong in spirit and he would rub the nail of his thumb against that of the forefinger in defiance, as if he was not worrying over the duel. Then came the viscount [al-biskund], i.e., the seignior of the town, and gave each one of the two contestants a cudgel and a shield and arranged the people in a circle around them.

The two met. The old man would press the blacksmith backward until he would get him as far as the circle, then he would come back to the middle of the arena. They went on exchanging blows until they looked like pillars smeared with blood. The contest was prolonged and the viscount began to urge them to hurry, saying, "Hurry on." The fact that the smith was given to the use of the hammer proved now of great advantage to him. The old man was worn out and the smith gave him a blow which made him fall. His cudgel fell under his back. The smith knelt down over him and tried to stick his fingers into the eyes of his adversary, but could not do it because of the great quantity of blood flowing out. Then he rose up and hit his head with the cudgel until he killed him. They then fastened a rope around the neck of the dead person, dragged him away and hanged him. The lord who brought the smith now came, gave the smith his own mantle, made him mount the horse behind him and

9. Fulk of Anjou, king of Jerusalem (1131-42). (Tr.)

rode off with him. This case illustrates the kind of jurisprudence and legal decisions the Franks have—may Allah's curse be upon them!

Ordeal by water.—I once went in the company of al-Amîr Mu'în-al-Dîn (may Allah's mercy rest upon his soul!) to Jerusalem. We stopped at Nâblus. There a blind man, a Moslem, who was still young and was well dressed, presented himself before al-amîr carrying fruits for him and asked permission to be admitted into his service in Damascus. The amîr consented. I inquired about this man and was informed that his mother had been married to a Frank whom she had killed. Her son used to practice ruses against the Frankish pilgrims and coöperate with his mother in assassinating them. They finally brought charges against him and tried his case according to the Frankish way of procedure.

They installed a huge cask and filled it with water. Across it they set a board of wood. They then bound the arms of the man charged with the act, tied a rope around his shoulders and dropped him into the cask, their idea being that in case he was innocent, he would sink in the water and they would then lift him up with the rope so that he might not die in the water; and in case he was guilty, he would not sink in the water. This man did his best to sink when they dropped him into the water, but he could not do it. So he had to submit to their sentence against him—may Allah's curse be upon them! They pierced his eyeballs with red-hot awls.

. . . .

A Frank domesticated in Syria abstains from eating pork.— Among the Franks are those who have become acclimatized and have associated long with the Moslems. These are much better than the recent comers from the Frankish lands. But they constitute the exception and cannot be treated as a rule.

Here is an illustration. I dispatched one of my men to Antioch on business. There was in Antioch at that time al-Ra'îs Theodoros Sophianos [*tâdrus ibn-al-saffi*], to whom I was bound by mutual ties of amity. His influence in Antioch was supreme. One day he said to my man, "I am invited by a friend of mine who is a Frank. Thou shouldst come with me so that thou mayest see their fashions." My man related the story in the following words:

    I went along with him and we came to the home of a knight who belonged to the old category of knights who came with the early expeditions of the Franks. He had been by that time stricken off the register and exempted from service, and possessed in Antioch an estate on the income of which he lived. The knight presented an excellent table, with food extraordinarily clean and delicious. Seeing me abstaining from food, he said, "Eat, be of good cheer! I never eat Frankish dishes, but I have Egyptian women cooks and never eat except their cooking. Besides, pork never enters my home." I ate, but guardedly, and after that we departed.

    As I was passing in the market place, a Frankish woman all of a sudden hung to my clothes and began to mutter words in their language, and I could not understand what she was saying. This made me immediately the center of a big crowd of Franks. I was convinced that death was at hand. But all of a sudden that same knight approached. On seeing me, he came and said to that woman, "What is the matter between thee and this Moslem?" She replied, "This is he who has killed my brother Hurso ['urs]." This Hurso was a knight in Afâmiyah who was killed by someone of the army of Hamâh. The Christian knight shouted at her, saying, "This is a bourgeois [burjâsi] (i.e., a merchant) who neither fights nor attends a fight." He also yelled at the people who had assembled, and they all dispersed. Then he took me by the hand and went away. Thus the effect of that meal was my deliverance from certain death.[10]

  •   •   •   •   •   •   •

    Usâmah's experiences in an attack on Afâmiyah, 1119.—A few days after the departure of my uncle, the public announcer called us to arms, and I started at the head of a small band, hardly amounting to twenty horsemen, with full conviction that Afâmiyah[11] had no cavalry in it. Accompanying me was a great body of pillagers and Bedouins. As soon as we arrived in the Valley of Bohemond, and while the pillagers and the Arabs were scattered all over the planted fields, a large army of the Franks set out against us. They had been reinforced that very

10. This passage suggests the reciprocity of acculturation which occurred between Frank and Muslim.

11. Apamea, a town in northern Syria, north of Shayzar, Usâma's home.

night by sixty horsemen and sixty footmen. They repulsed us from the valley, and we retreated before them until we joined those of our number who were already in the fields, pillaging them. Seeing us, the Franks raised a violent uproar. Death seemed an easy thing to me in comparison with the loss of that crowd in my charge. So I turned against a horseman in their vanguard, who had taken off his coat of mail in order to be light enough to pass before us, and thrust my lance into his chest. He instantly flew off his saddle, dead. I then faced their horsemen as they followed, and they all took to flight. Though a tyro in warfare, and having never before that day taken part in a battle, I, with a mare under me as swift as a bird, went on, now pursuing them and plying them with my lance, now taking cover from them.

In the rear guard of the Franks was a cavalier on a black horse, large as a camel, wearing a coat of mail and the full armor of war. I was afraid of this horseman, lest he should be drawing me further ahead in order to get an opportunity to turn back and attack me. All of a sudden I saw him spur his horse, and as the horse began to wave its tail, I knew that it was already exhausted. So I rushed on the horseman and smote him with my lance, which pierced him through and projected about a cubit in front of him. The lightness of my body, the force of the thrust and the swiftness of my horse made me lose my seat on the saddle. Moving backward a little, I pulled out my lance, fully assuming that I had killed him. I then assembled my comrades and found them all safe and sound.

In my company was a young mameluke[12] holding the halter of an extra black mare which belonged to me. Under him was a good female riding mule with a saddle the tassels of which were silver. The mameluke dismounted from the mule, left it by itself and jumped on the back of the mare, which flew with him towards Shayzar.

On my return to my comrades, who had caught the mule, I asked about that boy. They said, "He's gone." I immediately knew that he would reach Shayzar and cause anxiety to my father (may Allah's mercy rest upon his soul!). I therefore

12. Slave.

called one of the soldiers and said to him, "Hasten to Shayzar and inform my father of what has happened."

In the meantime the boy had arrived and my father had him brought before him and asked, "What things have ye met?" The boy said, "O my lord, the Franks have set out against us with a thousand men, and I doubt if any of our men would escape with the exception of my master. "But how would thy master," asked my father, "of all the men, escape?" "Well," replied the slave, "I have seen him covered with full armor riding on a green mare." Here he was interrupted in his conversation by the arrival of the horseman whom I had sent. The horseman related to my father the facts. I arrived right after him, and my father (may Allah's mercy rest upon his soul!) questioned me. So I said to him:

O my lord, that was the first fight in which I took part. But the moment I saw that the Franks were in contact with our men, then I felt that death would be an easy matter for me. So I turned back to the Franks, either to be killed or to protect that crowd.

My father (may Allah's mercy rest upon his soul!) quoted the following verse as illustrating my case:

The coward among men flees precipitately before danger facing his
    own mother,
But the brave one protects even him whom it is not his duty to
    shelter.

My uncle (may Allah's mercy rest upon his soul!) returned a few days later from his visit to Najm-al-Dîn Îlghâzi[13] (may Allah's mercy rest upon his soul!). A messenger came to summon me to present myself before my uncle at a time in which it was not his custom to call me. So I hurried to him, and, behold, a Frank was in his company. My uncle said to me:

Here is a knight who has come from Afâmiyah in order to see the horseman who struck Philip the knight, for verily the Franks have all been astounded on account of that blow which pierced two layers of links in the knight's coat of mail and yet did not kill him.

"How," said I, "could he have survived?" The Frankish night replied, "The thrust fell upon the skin of his side." "Fate is an

13. Amîr of Mâridîn.

impregnable stronghold," I exclaimed. But I never thought that the knight would survive that blow.

My comment is that he who is on the point of striking with his lance should hold his lance as tightly as possible with his hand and under his arm, close to his side, and should let his horse run and effect the required thrust; for if he should move his hand while holding the lance or stretch out his arm with the lance, then his thrust would have no effect whatsoever and would result in no harm.

. . . .

Usâmah's father: A warrior.—My father (may Allah's mercy rest upon his soul!) was greatly addicted to warfare. His body bore scars of terrible wounds. And withal he died on his own bed. One day he took part in a battle in full armor, wearing on his head a Moslem helmet with a nasal. Someone (in that period their combats were generally with the Arabs) launched a javelin at him, which struck the nasal of the helmet. The nasal bent and made my father's nose bleed, but it caused him no harm. But if Allah (praise be to his name!) had decreed that the javelin should deviate from the helmet's nasal, then it would have killed him.

On another occasion he was hit with an arrow in his leg. In his slipper he had a dagger. The arrow struck the dagger and was broken on it, without even wounding him—thanks to the excellent protection of Allah (exalted is he!).

. . . .

The high position enjoyed by the Frankish knights.—The Franks (may Allah render them helpless!) possess none of the virtues of men except courage, consider no precedence or high rank except that of the knights, and have nobody that counts except the knights. These are the men on whose counsel they rely, and the ones who make legal decisions and judgments. I once[14] brought a case before them, relative to certain flocks of sheep which the lord of Bâniyâs[15] had taken from the forest in the course of a period of truce between them and us. At that time,

14. In 1140. (Tr.)
15. Caesarea Philippi, Paneas, whose lord at this time was Renier, surnamed Brus. (Tr.)

I was in Damascus. So I said to King Fulk, son of Fulk,[16] "This man has trespassed upon our rights and taken away our flocks at the lambing time. The sheep gave birth and the lambkins died. Then he returned the sheep, after having lost so many of them." The king said to six, seven knights, "Arise and judge this case for him." The knights went out from his audience chamber, retired by themselves and consulted together until they all agreed upon one thing. Then they returned to the audience chamber of the king and said, "We have passed judgment to the effect that the lord of Bâniyâs should be fined the amount of the damage he wrought among their sheep." The king accordingly ordered him to pay that fine. He pleaded with me, urged and implored me until I finally accepted from him four hundred dînârs. Such a judgment, after having been pronounced by the knights, not even the king nor any of the chieftains of the Franks can alter or revoke. Thus the knight is something great in their esteem.

The king said to me, "By the truth of my religion, I rejoiced yesterday very much indeed." I replied, "May Allah always make the king rejoice! What made thee rejoice?" He said, "I was told that thou wert a great knight, but I did not believe previous to that that thou wert a knight." "O my lord," I replied, "I am a knight according to the manner of my race and my people." If the knight is thin and tall the Franks admire him more.

Tancred's guarantee of safety proves worthless.—Tancred,[17] who was the first lord of Antioch after Bohemond, had previous to this pitched his camp against us.[18] After the fight, we had a reconciliation, and he sent a message requesting that a horse belonging to an attendant of my uncle, 'Izz-al-Dîn (may Allah's mercy rest upon his soul!), be given him. That was a noble steed. My uncle dispatched it to him mounted by one of our men, a Kurd named Hasanûn, one of our valiant cavaliers, young, good-looking and thin, in order to hold races with other

16. Fulk V, count of Anjou, who was installed on the death of his father-in-law, Baldwin II, fourth king of Jerusalem, in 1131. (Tr.)

17. Arabic *dankari*, who succeeded Bohemond I, in 1104. (Tr.)

18. November 27, 1108. (Tr.)

horses in the presence of Tancred. Hasanûn ran a race and his
horse out-ran all the horses which were in the course. He was
brought before Tancred, and the knights began to inspect his
arms and wonder at his thin physique and his youth, recognizing in him a valiant cavalier. Tancred bestowed a robe of
honor on him. But Hasanûn said to him, "O my lord, I wish that
thou wouldst give me thy guarantee of safety to the effect that if
I should fall into thy hands at war time thou wouldst favor me
and set me free." Tancred gave him his guarantee of safety—as
Hasanûn imagined, for these people speak nothing but Frankish; we do not understand what they say.

A year or more passed.[19] The period of truce having expired,
Tancred advanced anew at the head of the army of Antioch. A
battle ensued near the wall of our lower town. Our horsemen
had met their vanguard, and one of our men, a Kurd, named
Kâmil al-Mashtûb, had used his lance on them to great effect.
Kâmil and Hasanûn were peers in valor. This took place while
Hasanûn on his mare was standing near my father (may Allah's mercy rest upon his soul!) and awaiting his charger, which
his attendant was bringing to him from the veterinary, and his
quilted jerkin. The attendant was late and Hasanûn was getting
impatient, seeing the lance blows of Kâmil al-Mashtûb. So he
said to my father, "O my lord, put at my disposal light equipment." My father replied, "Here are the mules laden with arms
and standing still. Whatever suits thee, put on." I was at that
time standing behind my father. I was a mere lad,[20] and that
was the first day in which I saw actual fighting. Hasanûn examined the jerkins, in their cases on the backs of the mules, but
none of them suited him. In the meantime, he was boiling in his
desire to proceed and do what Kâmil al-Mashtûb was doing. So
he charged on horseback, void of arms. A Frankish knight intercepted his way and struck the mare in its croup. The mare, getting the bit in its teeth, rushed with its rider on its back until it
threw him off amidst the lines of the Franks. They took him
prisoner and inflicted on him all varieties of torture. They even
wanted to put out his left eye. But Tancred (may Allah's curse

19. Spring of 1110. (Tr.)
20. Fifteen years old. (Tr.)

be upon him!) said to them, "Rather put out his right eye, so
that when he carries his shield his left eye will be covered, and
he will be no more able to see anything." So they put out his
right eye in accordance with the orders of Tancred and demanded as a ransom from him one thousand dînârs and a black
horse, which belonged to my father, of Khafâjah breed[21] and one
of the most magnificent horses. My father (may Allah's mercy
rest upon his soul!) ransomed him for that horse.

Adventures with Lions and Other Wild Animals

A glimpse into Usâmah's breeding.—I never saw my father
(may Allah's mercy rest upon his soul!) forbid my taking part
in a combat or facing a danger, in spite of all the sympathy and
preference he cherished towards me and of which I was cognizant. This is what I noticed in regard to him on a certain day.[22]
We had with us in Shayzar certain hostages, consisting of
Frankish and Armenian knights, whom Baldwin,[23] the king of
the Franks, had offered as security for a financial obligation
which he owed to Husâm-al-Dîn Timurtâsh ibn-Îlghâzi[24] (may
Allah's mercy rest upon his soul!). When the amount due was
paid and the hostages were waiting to go back home, Khîrkhân,
the lord of Hims, dispatched some horsemen who lay in ambush
for them in the suburbs of Shayzar. As the hostages were on
their way home, the men in ambush came out and captured
them. When the cry for help reached us, my uncle and my father (may Allah's mercy rest upon their souls!) mounted their
horses and stood in a certain spot, sending to the release of the
hostages everyone who came. I then arrived. My father said to
me, "Pursue the marauders with thy men, hurl yourselves on
them and deliver your hostages." Accordingly I pursued them,
overtook them after a race covering most of the day and delivered those of the hostages who had fallen into their hands, in
addition to capturing some of the Hims' horsemen. But the thing

21. The Khafâja horses, so called after an Arab tribe, were one of the noblest
breeds. (Tr.)
22. In 1124. (Tr.)
23. Baldwin II of Jerusalem. (Tr.)
24. The lord of Mâridîn. (Tr.)

that surprised me was my father's word: "Hurl yourselves on them."

Once I was with him (may Allah's mercy rest upon his soul!) while he was standing in the interior court of his house, when a big serpent stuck its head out on the frieze of the arches of the portico over the court. My father stood in his place watching it as I carried a ladder which was on one side of the court and put it in a position below the serpent. Climbing to the serpent, under the very eyes of my father, who was watching me but not forbidding me, I pulled out a little knife from my belt, applied it to the neck of the serpent, while it was sleeping, with less than a cubit between my face and itself, and began to saw the neck. The serpent pulled its body out and wound itself around my lower arm, where it remained until I cut its head off and threw its body down to the floor of the house lifeless.

On one occasion only I saw my father (may Allah's mercy rest upon his soul!) act differently. One day we set out to kill a lion which had made its appearance at al-Jisr.[25] When we reached the place, the lion jumped on us from a thicket in which it lay hidden. It turned itself on our horses; then it stopped while my brother, Bahâ'-al-Dawlah Munqidh (may Allah's mercy rest upon his soul!), and I stood between the lion and the procession headed by my father and my uncle (may Allah's mercy rest upon their souls!) and including a small body of troops. The lion then crouched on the very edge of the river, beating its chest against the ground and roaring. Presently I made an onset on it, but my father (may Allah's mercy rest upon his soul!) yelled at me, saying, "Face it not, thou crazy one! It will get thee!" But I smote it with the lance and, by Allah, it stirred not from its place, and died on the spot. I never saw my father forbid me a fight except on that day.

The unlucky march of the Franks against Damascus.—Another illustration of the execution of divine will in the fates and ages of men.

The Franks (may Allah render them helpless!) unanimously

25. The bridge of Shayzar spanning the Orontes. (Tr.)

agreed to direct their forces against Damascus and capture it. Accordingly they concentrated a considerable army,[26] which was joined by the lord of al-Ruha[27] and Tell-Bâshir[28] and the lord of Antioch.[29] On his way to Damascus, the lord of Antioch stopped in front of Shayzar. The princes were so sure of the conquest and possession of Damascus that they had already bargained amongst themselves for the houses of Damascus, its baths and its bazaars, and in turn sold them to the bourgeois [al-burjâsiyyah], who paid the prices in cash.

Kafartâb at that time belonged to the lord of Antioch. He now detached from his troops a hundred picked horsemen, whom he ordered to stay in Kafartâb as a check against us and against Hamâh. When he marched against Damascus, the Moslems of Syria assembled to attack Kafartâb. They dispatched one of our men, named Qunayb ibn-Mâlik, to spy for them on Kafartâb during the night. Arriving in the city, he made a tour around it and returned, saying, "Rejoice at the booty and safety [awaiting you]!" The Moslems marched against the troops in it, had an encounter with them at an ambush,[30] and Allah (worthy of admiration is he!) gave victory to the Moslems, who killed all the Franks.

. . . .

When the lord of Antioch, who was then fighting against Damascus, was told "The Moslems have killed thy men," he replied, "This is not true. I have left in Kafartâb a hundred knights who can meet all the Moslems put together."

By the decree of Allah (worthy of admiration is he!) the Moslems in Damascus, too, won the victory over the Franks and slaughtered of them a great number, capturing all their animals. So they departed from Damascus in the most miserable and humiliating manner—praise be to Allah the lord of the worlds!

26. This was the army of Baldwin I of Jerusalem in the year 1113. (Tr.)
27. Edessa, modern Urfa. (Tr.)
28. Tell-Bâshir, the "Turbessel" of the Franks, lay between Aleppo and al-Ruha. The lord was Joscelin I. . . . (Tr.)
29. Roger. (Tr.)
30. *mutakamman*, orthography not clear. The word may be the name of a place, *Milkin*, *Btikkîn*, or something like it. (Tr.)

A Kurd carries his brother's head as a trophy.—One of the amazing things that happened in connection with the Franks in the course of that combat was the following: In the army of Hamâh were two Kurdish brothers, one named Badr and the other 'Annâz. The latter, 'Annâz, was feeble of sight. When the Franks were overpowered and massacred, their heads were cut off and tied to the sides of the horses. 'Annâz cut off one head and tied it to the back of his horse. Seeing him, the army of Hamâh said to him, "O 'Annâz, what is this head with thee?" He replied, "Worthy of admiration is Allah because of what happened between me and him which resulted in my killing him!" They said to him, "Man, this is the head of thy brother, Badr!" 'Annâz looked at the head and investigated, it, and behold! it was the head of his brother. He was so ashamed of himself before the men that he left Hamâh and we do not know where he went. In fact, we never heard a word about him since. It was, however, the Franks who killed his brother, Badr, in that battle.

Usâmah's mother as a warrior.—On that day my mother (may Allah have mercy upon her soul!) distributed my swords and quilted jerkins. She came to a sister of mine who was well advanced in years and said, "Put on thy shoes and thy wrapper."[31] This she did. My mother then led her to the balcony in my house overlooking the valley from the east. She made her take a seat there, and my mother herself sat at the entrance to the balcony. Allah (praise be to him!) gave us victory over the enemy [the Ismâ'ilites].[32] I then came to my house seeking some of my weapons, but found nothing except the scabbards of the swords and the leather bags of the jerkins. I said, "O mother, where are my arms?" She replied, "My dear son, I have given the arms to those who would fight in our behalf, not believing that thou wert still alive." I said, "And my sister, what is she

31. *izâr*, a thin cover for the body, worn by Moslem women over their clothes and veiling their faces.
32. Ismâ'ilites: a radical Shî'ite movement attempting to gain political power in Syria. This reminds the reader that the Crusaders were not the only source of political turmoil. Equals Bâtinites below.

doing here?" She replied, "O my dear son, I have given her a seat at the balcony and sat behind her so that in case I found that the Bâtinites had reached us, I could push her and throw her into the valley, preferring to see her dead rather than to see her captive in the hands of the peasants and ravishers." I thanked my mother for her deed, and so did my sister, who prayed that mother be rewarded [by Allah] in her behalf. Such solicitude for honor is indeed stronger than the solicitude of men.

.   .   .   .

Usâmah's grandmother gives him wise advice.—No one can deny magnanimity, enthusiasm and sound judgment in the case of noble women. One day I went out with my father (may Allah's mercy rest upon his soul!) to the hunt. My father was especially fond of hunting and had a collection of falcons, sha-hins,[33] sakers, cheetahs and braches such as hardly anybody else possessed. He used to ride at the head of forty cavaliers from among his children and mamelukes, each one of whom was an expert hunter knowing all and took as booty all the women, children, silver and beasts of burden they had.

At that time there was in Shayzar a woman named Nadrah, daughter of Bûzarmât, who was the wife of one of our men. This woman went out with our men, captured a Frank and introduced him into her house. She went out again, captured another Frank and brought him in. Again she went out and captured still another. Thus she had three Franks in her house. After taking as booty what they had and what suited her of their possessions, she went out and called some of her neighbors, who killed them.

During the same night my two uncles, with the army, arrived. Some of the Franks had taken to flight and were pursued by certain men from Shayzar, who killed them in the environs of the town. The horses of my uncles' army, on entering the town in the nighttime, began to stumble over corpses without knowing what they were stumbling over, until one of the cavaliers dismounted and saw the corpses in the darkness. This terrified our men, for they thought the town had been raided by

33. Arabic *shâhîn*, from Hindi *shâhîn*, is a falcon of the peregrine type, as is also the saker. The braches, mentioned below, were hounds. (Tr.)

surprise. In fact, it was booty which Allah (exalted and majestic is he!) had delivered into the hands of our people.

Prefers to be a Frankish shoemaker's wife to life in a Moslem castle.—A number of maids taken captive from the Franks were brought into the home of my father (may Allah's mercy rest upon his soul!). The Franks (may Allah's curse be upon them!) are an accursed race, the members of which do not assimilate except with their own kin. My father saw among them a pretty maid who was in the prime of youth, and said to his housekeeper, "Introduce this woman into the bath, repair her clothing and prepare her for a journey." This she did. He then delivered the maid to a servant of his and sent her to al-Amîr Shihâb-al-Dîn Mâlik ibn-Sâlim, the lord of the Castle of Ja'bar, who was a friend of his. He also wrote him a letter, saying, "We have won some booty from the Franks, from which I am sending thee a share." The maid suited Shihâb-al-Dîn, and he was pleased with her. He took her to himself and she bore him a boy, whom he called Badrân. Badrân's father named him his heir apparent, and he became of age. On his father's death, Badrân became the governor of the town and its people, his mother being the real power. She entered into conspiracy with a band of men and let herself down from the castle by a rope. The band took her to Sarûj,[34] which belonged at that time to the Franks. There she married a Frankish shoemaker, while her son was the lord of the Castle of Ja'bar.

A Frank and his children revert to Christianity.—Among the Frankish captives who were carried into my father's home was an aged woman accompanied by her daughter—a young woman of great beauty—and a robust[35] son. The son accepted Islam, and his conversion was genuine, judging by what he showed in the practice of prayer and fasting. He learned the art of working marble from a stonecutter who had paved the home of my father. After staying for a long time with us my father gave him as wife a woman who belonged to a pious family, and paid all necessary expenses for his wedding and home. His wife bore him two sons. The boys grew up. When they were five or six

34. In Mesopotamia, southwest of Edessa. (Tr.)
35. Meaning maybe "who was of age."

years old, their father, young Râ'ûl, who was very happy at having them, took them with their mother and everything that his house contained and on the second morning joined the Franks in Afâmiyah, where he and his children became Christians, after having practiced Islam with its prayers and faith. May Allah, therefore, purify the world from such people!

The New Mysticism: Theology

The Seljûq sultâns established official schools, called *madrasa*s, for training experts in the official learning of Islâm. Abû Hamîd Muhammad al-Ghazâlî (1058-1111), a brilliant young scholar, taught at such a school in Baghdâd. His academic success, however, coincided with a spiritual and intellectual crisis, for he began to have doubts about the truths of religion he was supposed to teach.

Ghazâlî's problem remained private for several years. He lectured to large audiences while privately seeking escape from his dilemma through the study of philosophy. But his studies proved ineffectual, and eventually he became ill and unable to lecture. Leaving Baghdâd he retreated to his home town in eastern Irân and for eleven years lived the life the life of a poor mystic, or Sûfî.

A popular Muslim belief held that a reviver of true religion came once every century; and in 1106 a new Muslim century began. (See Note on Chronology.) Ghazâlî allowed himself to think that he might be the man chosen by God for this role in the new century, and in 1106 he began to teach again, attracting an enthusiastic and influential following. Ghazâlî, more than any other single man, fused the official learning of Islâm with the previously heterodox but increasingly popular mystical path to God. Through his work, Islâm attained a new emotional vibrancy and power that carried it to fresh misionary successes in the following centuries.

The following selection is part of *That Which Delivers from Error*, an autobiography written just before Ghazâlî resumed active teaching. In this account of his path to faith and salvation, Ghazâlî first explains his skepticism and search for truth; then refutes the claims of alternative teachings; and concludes by showing how the mystic path of the Sûfî may be combined with the ordinary rules and routines of Muslim piety to create a new, truly satisfactory life style.

This work is probably not an accurate historical account of Ghazâlî's experience; it conforms to a literary model already popular before his time. It does, however, schematize the dilemma of official Islâm, caught up too closely in applying cut and dried laws to particular cases to be able to tap the wellsprings of feeling; a dilemma from which Ghazâlî's own example, supported by the lives and teachings of thousands upon thousands of other Sûfî seekers after God, effectually rescued the faith while still retaining obedience to the legal system which the first generations of learnèd Muslims had so conscientiously created.

GHAZÂLÎ: FROM THAT WHICH DELIVERS FROM ERROR

Deliverance from Error
and Attachment to the Lord of Might and Majesty
In the name of God, the Merciful and Compassionate

INTRODUCTION

Praise be to Him with Whose praise every message and every discourse commences. And blessings be upon Muhammad the Chosen, the Prophet and Messenger, and on his house and his Companions, who guide men away from error.

You have asked me, my brother in religion, to show you the aims and inmost nature of the sciences and the perplexing depths of the religious systems. You have begged me to relate to you the difficulties I encountered in my attempt to extricate the truth from the confusion of contending sects and to distinguish the different ways and methods, and the venture I made in climbing from the plain of naive and second-hand belief (*taqlîd*) to the peak of direct vision. You want me to describe, firstly

From *The Faith and Practice of al-Ghazâlî*, trans. by W. Montgomery Watt, London: George Allen & Unwin Ltd., 1953, pp. 19-30, 52-63, 68-85. Reprinted by permission of the publishers and Humanities Press, Inc., New York.

what profit I derived from the science of theology (*kalâm*), secondly, what I disapprove of in the methods of the party of *ta'lîm*
(authoritative instruction), who restrict the apprehension of
truth to the blind following (*taqlîd*) of the Imam,[1] thirdly, what
I rejected of the methods of philosophy, and lastly, what I approved in the Sufi way of life. You would know, too, what essential truths became clear to me in my manifold investigations into
the doctrines held by men, why I gave up teaching in Baghdad
although I had many students, and why I returned to it at
Naysâbûr (Nîshâpûr) after a long interval. I am proceeding to
answer your request, for I recognise that your desire is genuine.
In this I seek the help of God and trust in Him; I ask His succour and take refuge with Him.

You must know—and may God most high perfect you in the
right way and soften your hearts to receive the truth—that
the different religious observances and religious communities
of the human race and likewise the different theological systems
of the religious leaders, with all the multiplicity of sects and variety of practices, constitute ocean depths in which the majority
drown and only a minority reach safety. Each separate group
thinks that it alone is saved, and "each party is rejoicing in what
they have" (Qur'an 23, 55; 30, 31). This is what was foretold
by the prince of the Messengers[2] (God bless him), who is true
and trustworthy, when he said, "My community will be split up
into seventy-three sects, and but one of them is saved"; and what
he foretold has indeed almost come about.

From my early youth, since I attained the age of puberty before I was twenty, until the present time when I am over fifty,
I have ever recklessly launched out into the midst of these ocean
depths, I have ever bravely embarked on this open sea, throwing
aside all craven caution; I have poked into every dark recess, I
have made an assault on every problem, I have plunged into
every abyss, I have scrutinized the creed of every sect, I have
tried to lay bare the inmost doctrines of every community. All
this I have done that I might distinguish between true and false,

---

1. *Imâm* literally means prayer leader; here it refers to the Imâms of the
Shî'îs, i.e., religious authorities descended from 'Alî, the fourth Caliph.
2. Muhammad.

between sound tradition and heretical innovation. Whenever I
meet one of the Bâtinîyah,[3] I like to study his creed; whenever
I meet one of the Zâhirîyah,[4] I want to know the essentials of his
belief. If it is a philosopher, I try to become acquainted with the
essence of his philosophy; if a scholastic theologian I busy myself in examining his theological reasoning; if a Sufi, I yearn to
fathom the secret of his mysticism; if an ascetic (*muta'abbid*),
I investigate the basis of his ascetic practices; if one of the
Zanâdiqah or Mu'attilah,[5] I look beneath the surface to discover
the reasons for his bold adoption of such a creed.

To thirst after a comprehension of things as they really are
was my habit and custom from a very early age. It was instinc-
tive with me, a part of my God-given nature, a matter of temperament and not of my choice or contriving. Consequently as I
drew near the age of adolescence the bonds of mere authority
(*taqlîd*) ceased to hold me and inherited beliefs lost their grip
upon me, for I saw that Christian youths always grew up to be
Christians, Jewish youths to be Jews and Muslim youths to be
Muslims. I heard, too, the Tradition related of the Prophet of
God according to which he said: "Everyone who is born is born
with a sound nature; it is his parents who make him a Jew or a
Christian or a Magian." My inmost being was moved to discover
what this original nature really was and what the beliefs derived from the authority of parents and teachers really were.
The attempt to distinguish between these authority-based opinions and their principles developed the mind, for in distinguishing the true in them from the false differences appeared.

I therefore said within myself: "To begin with, what I am
looking for is knowledge of what things really are, so I must undoubtedly try to find what knowledge really is." It was plain to
me that sure and certain knowledge is that knowledge in which
the object is disclosed in such a fashion that no doubt remains
along with it, that no possibility of error or illusion accompanies

3. Those who look for a hidden or deeper meaning in religious externals,
such as Shî'îs or Sûfîs.
4. The opposite of Bâtiniyya, those who study the externals, such as
theologians.
5. Extremists. Zanâdiqa was the general term for free-thinkers of all sorts.

it, and that the mind cannot even entertain such a supposition. Certain knowledge must also be infallible; and this infallibility or security from error is such that no attempt to show the falsity of the knowledge can occasion doubt or denial, even though the attempt is made by someone who turns stones into gold or a rod into a serpent. Thus, I know that ten is more than three. Let us suppose that someone says to me: "No, three is more than ten, and in proof of that I shall change this rod into a serpent"; and let us suppose that he actually changes the rod into a serpent and that I witness him doing so. No doubts about what I know are raised in me because of this. The only result is that I wonder precisely how he is able to produce this change. Of doubt about my knowledge there is no trace.

After these reflections I knew that whatever I do not know in this fashion and with this mode of certainty is not reliable and infallible knowledge; and knowledge that is not infallible is not certain knowledge.

PRELIMINARIES: SCEPTICISM AND THE DENIAL OF ALL KNOWLEDGE

Thereupon I investigated the various kinds of knowledge I had, and found myself destitute of all knowledge with this characteristic of infallibility except in the case of sense-perception and necessary truths. So I said: "Now that despair has come over me, there is no point in studying any problems except on the basis of what is self-evident, namely, necessary truths and the affirmations of the senses. I must first bring these to be judged in order that I may be certain on this matter. Is my reliance on sense-perception and my trust in the soundness of necessary truths of the same kind as my previous trust in the beliefs I had merely taken over from others and as the trust most men have in the results of thinking? Or is it a justified trust that is in no danger of being betrayed or destroyed"?

I proceeded therefore with extreme earnestness to reflect on sense-perception and on necessary truths, to see whether I could make myself doubt them. The outcome of this protracted effort to induce doubt was that I could no longer trust sense-perception either. Doubt began to spread here and say: "From where does this reliance on sense-perception come? The most powerful sense is that of sight. Yet when it looks at the shadow (*sc.* of a stick or the gnomon of a sundial), it sees it standing still, and judges that there is no motion. Then by experiment and observation after an hour it knows that the shadow is moving and, moreover, that it is moving not by fits and starts but gradually and steadily by infinitely small distances in such a way that it is never in a state of rest. Again, it looks at the heavenly body (*sc.* the sun) and sees it small, the size of a shilling;[6] yet geometrical computations show that it is greater than the earth in size."

In this and similar cases of sense-perception the sense as judge forms his judgements, but another judge, the intellect, shows him repeatedly to be wrong; and the charge of falsity cannot be rebutted.

To this I said: "My reliance on sense-perception also has been destroyed. Perhaps only those intellectual truths which are first principles (or derived from first principles) are to be relied upon, such as the assertion than ten are more than three, that the same thing cannot be both affirmed and denied at one time, that one thing is not both generated in time and eternal, nor both existent and non-existent, nor both necessary and impossible."

Sense-perception replied: "Do you not expect that your reliance on intellectual truths will fare like your reliance on sense-perception? You used to trust in me; then along came the intellect-judge and proved me wrong; if it were not for the intellect-judge you would have continued to regard me as true. Perhaps behind intellectual apprehension there is another judge who, if he manifests himself, will show the falsity of intellect in its judging, just as, when intellect manifested itself, it showed the falsity of sense in its judging. The fact that such a supra-intellectual apprehension has not manifested itself is no proof that it is impossible."

My ego hesitated a little about the reply to that, and sense-perception heightened the difficulty by referring to dreams. "Do you not see," it said, "how, when you are asleep, you believe things and imagine circumstances, holding them to be stable and enduring, and, so long as you are in that dream-condition, have

6. Literally *dînâr*, an Islâmic gold coin, weighing about 4.25 grams.

no doubts about them? And is it not the case that when you awake you know that all you have imagined and believed is unfounded and ineffectual? Why then are you confident that all your waking beliefs, whether from sense or intellect, are genuine? They are true in respect of your present state; but it is possible that a state will come upon you whose relation to your waking consciousness is analogous to the relation of the latter to dreaming. In comparison with this state your waking consciousness would be like dreaming! When you have entered into this state, you will be certain that all the suppositions of your intellect are empty imaginings. It may be that that state is what the Sufis claim as their special 'state' (sc. mystic union or ecstasy), for they consider that in their 'states' (or ecstasies), which occur when they have withdrawn into themselves and are absent from their senses, they witness states (or circumstances) which do not tally with these principles of the intellect. Perhaps that 'state' is death; for the Messenger of God[7] (God bless and preserve him) says: 'The people are dreaming; when they die, they become awake.' So perhaps life in this world is a dream by comparison with the world to come; and when a man dies, things come to appear differently to him from what he now beholds, and at the same time the words are addressed to him: 'We have taken off thee thy covering, and thy sight today is sharp' " (Qur'an 50, 21).

When these thoughts had occurred to me and penetrated my being, I tried to find some way of treating my unhealthy condition; but it was not easy. Such ideas can only be repelled by demonstration; but a demonstration requires a knowledge of first principles; since this is not admitted, however, it is impossible to make the demonstration. The disease was baffling, and lasted almost two months, during which I was a sceptic in fact though not in theory nor in outward expression. At length God cured me of my malady; my being was restored to health and an even balance; the necessary truths of the intellect became once more accepted, as I regained confidence in their certain and trustworthy character.

This did not come about by systematic demonstration or mar-

7. Muhammad.

shalled argument, but by a light which God most high cast into
my breast. That light is the key to the greater part of knowledge. Whoever thinks that the understanding of things Divine
rests upon strict proofs has in his thought narrowed down the
wideness of God's mercy. When the Messenger of God (peace
be upon him) was asked about "enlarging" and its meaning in
the verse, "Whenever God wills to guide a man, He enlarges his
breast for *islâm* (i.e. surrender to God)" (Qur'an 6, 125), he
said, "It is a light which God most high casts into the heart."
When asked, "What is the sign of it?" he said, "Withdrawal
from the mansion of deception and return to the mansion of
eternity." It was about this light that Muhammad (peace be
upon him) said, "God created the creatures in darkness, and
then sprinkled upon them some of His light." From that light
must be sought an intuitive understanding of things Divine.
That light at certain times gushes from the spring of Divine
generosity, and for it one must watch and wait—as Muhammad
(peace be upon him) said: "In the days of your age your Lord
has gusts of favour; then place yourselves in the way of them."

The point of these accounts is that the task is perfectly fulfilled when the quest is prosecuted up to the stage of seeking
what is not sought (but stops short of that). For first principles
are not sought, since they are present and to hand; and if what
is present is sought for, it becomes hidden and lost. When, however, a man seeks what is sought (and that only), he is not accused of falling short in the seeking of what is sought.

THE CLASSES OF SEEKERS

When God by His grace and abundant generosity cured me
of this disease, I came to regard the various seekers (*sc.* after
truth) as comprising four groups:—

(1) the *Theologians* (*mutakallimûn*), who claim that they
are the exponents of thought and intellectual speculation;

(2) the *Bâtinîyah*, who consider that they, as the party of
"authoritative instruction" (*ta'lîm*), alone derive truth from the
infallible *imam*;

(3) the *Philosophers*, who regard themselves as the exponents
of logic and demonstration;

(4) the *Sufis or Mystics*, who claim that they alone enter into the "presence" (*sc.* of God), and possess vision and intuitive understanding.

I said within myself: "The truth cannot lie outside these four classes. These are the people who tread the paths of the quest for truth. If the truth is not with them, no point remains in trying to apprehend the truth. There is certainly no point in trying to return to the level of naïve and derivative belief (*taqlîd*) once it has been left, since a condition of being at such a level is that one should not know one is there; when a man comes to know that, the glass of his naïve beliefs is broken. This is a breakage which cannot be mended, a breakage not to be repaired by patching or by assembling of fragments. The glass must be melted once again in the furnace for a new start, and out of it another fresh vessel formed."

I now hastened to follow out these four ways and investigate what these groups had achieved, commencing with the science of theology and then taking the way of philosophy, the "authoritative instruction" of the Bâtinîyah, and the way of mysticism, in that order.

The Science of Theology: Its Aims and Achievements. I commenced, then, with the science of Theology (*'ilm al-kalâm*), and obtained a thorough grasp of it. I read the books of sound theologians and myself wrote some books on the subject. But it was a science, I found, which, though attaining its own aim, did not attain mine. Its aim was merely to preserve the creed of orthodoxy and to defend it against the deviations of heretics.

Now God sent to His servants by the mouth of His messenger, in the Qur'an and Traditions, a creed which is the truth and whose contents are the basis of man's welfare in both religious and secular affairs. But Satan too sent, in the suggestions of heretics, things contrary to orthodoxy; men tended to accept his suggestions and almost corrupted the true creed for its adherents. So God brought into being the class of theologians, and moved them to support traditional orthodoxy with the weapon of systematic argument by laying bare the confused doctrines invented by the heretics at variance with traditional orthodoxy. This is the origin of theology and theologians.

In due course a group of theologians performed the task to which God invited them; they successfully preserved orthodoxy, defended the creed received from the prophetic source and rectified heretical innovations. Nevertheless in so doing they based their arguments on premises which they took from their opponents and which they were compelled to admit by naîve belief (*taqlîd*), or the consensus of the community, or bare acceptance of Qur'an and Traditions. For the most part their efforts were devoted to making explicit the contradictions of their opponents and criticizing them in respect of the logical consequences of what they admitted.

This was of little use in the case of one who admitted nothing at all save logically necessary truths. Theology was not adequate to my case and was unable to cure the malady of which I complained. It is true that, when theology appeared as a recognized discipline and much effort had been expended in it over a considerable period of time, the theologians, becoming very earnest in their endeavours to defend orthodoxy by the study of what things really are, embarked on a study of substances and accidents with their nature and properties. But, since that was not the aim of their science, they did not deal with the question thoroughly in their thinking and consequently did not arrive at results sufficient to dispel universally the darkness of confusion due to the different views of men. I do not exclude the possibility that for others than myself these results have been sufficient; indeed, I do not doubt that this has been so for quite a number. But these results were mingled with naïve belief in certain matters which are not included among first principles.

My purpose here, however, is to describe my own case, not to disparage those who sought a remedy thereby, for the healing drugs vary with the disease. How often one sick man's medicine proves to be another's poison!

Philosophy. After I had done with theology I started on philosophy. I was convinced that a man cannot grasp what is defective in any of the sciences unless he has so complete a grasp of the science in question that he equals its most learned exponents in the· appreciation of its fundamental principles, and even goes beyond and surpasses them, probing into some of the tangles and profundities which the very professors of the science have neglected. Then and only then is it possible that what he has to assert about its defects is true.

So far as I could see none of the doctors of Islam had devoted thought and attention to philosophy. In their writings none of the theologians engaged in polemic against the philosophers, apart from obscure and scattered utterances so plainly erroneous and inconsistent that no person of ordinary intelligence would be likely to be deceived, far less one versed in the sciences.

I realized that to refute a system before understanding it and becoming acquainted with its depths is to act blindly. I therefore set out in all earnestness to acquire a knowledge of philosophy from books, by private study without the help of an instructor. I made progress towards this aim during my hours of free time after teaching in the religious sciences and writing, for at this period I was burdened with the teaching and instruction of three hundred students in Baghdad. By my solitary reading during the hours thus snatched God brought me in less than two years to a complete understanding of the sciences of the philosophers. Thereafter I continued to reflect assiduously for nearly a year on what I had assimilated, going over it in my mind again and again and probing its tangled depths, until I comprehended surely and certainly how far it was deceitful and confusing and how far true and a representation of reality.

Hear now an account of this discipline and of the achievement of the sciences it comprises. There are various schools of philosophers, I perceived, and their sciences are divided into various branches; but throughout their numerous schools they suffer from the defect of being infidels and irreligious men, even although of the different groups of philosophers—older and most ancient, earlier and more recent—some are much closer to the truth than others.

[Ghazâlî goes on to divide philosophers into Materialists, Naturalists, and Theists, and asserts that they are all affected by unbelief. The Materialists claim that the world has existed everlastingly without need of a Creator. Naturalists are led to believe in the Creator through their study of nature but, also because of this study, they deny the possibility of resurrection and the Last Day. The Theists include Socrates, Plato, and Aristotle and their Muslim interpreters (largely Ibn Sîna and Farâbî); this group attacks the other two groups but also argues against the truth of religion. Thus students of the philosophers all fall into heresy and unbelief by taking as the highest authorities those who deny or overlook religion.

Ghazâlî next attacks the Ta'lîmiyya (i.e., Ghazâlî's term for groups like and including Shî'ites and especially the Ismâ'îlites whom he had studied closely), who accept their *imâm*, or religious leader, as an infallible instructor in charge of the Truth. Ghazâlî states that the proper response to the Ta'lîmiyya is to accept the need for an infallible instructor, but to insist that Muhammad and not some other *imām* was that instructor. His conclusion about the Ta'lîmiyya, or Bâtiniyya as he also calls them here, follows.]

My present aim is rather to show that the Bâtinîyah have nothing to cure them or save them from the darkness of mere opinions. Their inability to demonstrate that a specific person is Imam is not their only weakness. We went a long way in agreeing with them; we accepted their assertion that "instruction" is needed and an infallible "instructor"; we conceded that he is the one they specified. Yet when we asked them what knowledge they had gained from this infallible person, and raised objections against them, they did not understand these, far less answer them, and in their perplexity had recourse to the "hidden Imam" and said one must journey to see him. The astonishing thing is that they squander their lives in searching for the "instructor" and in boasting that they have found him, yet without learning anything at all from him. They are like a man smeared with filth, who so wearies himself with the search for water that when he comes upon it he does not use it but remains smeared with dirt.

There are indeed certain of them who lay claim to have some special knowledge. But this knowledge, as they describe it, amounts to some trifling details of the philosophy of Pythagoras. The latter was one of the earliest of the ancients and his philosophical system is the weakest of all; Aristotle not only criticized him but showed the weakness and corruption of his thought. Yet

he is the person followed in the *Book of the Brethren of Purity*,[8]
which is really but the dregs of philosophy.

It is truly amazing that men should toil all their life long
searching for knowledge and in the end be content with such
feeble and emaciated knowledge, while imagining that they
have attained the utmost aims of the sciences! These claimants to
knowledge also we have examined, probing into both external
and internal features of their views. All they amounted to was a
deception of the ordinary man and the weak intellect by proving
the need for an "instructor," Their further arguments to show
that there is no need for instruction by theological reasoning are
strong and unanswerable until one tries to help them to prove
the need for an "instructor" by saying, "Give us some examples
of his knowledge and of his 'instruction.' " Then the exponent
is at a loss. "Now that you have submitted this difficulty to me,"
he says, "I shall search for a solution; my present object, however, is limited to what I have already said." He knows that, if
he were to attempt to proceed further, his shameful condition
would be revealed and he would be unable to resolve the least of
the problems—that he would be unable even to understand
them, far less to answer them.

This is the real condition in which they are. As it is said, "Try
them and you will hate them!"—after we had tried them we
left them also severely alone.

The Ways of Mysticism. When I had finished with these sciences, I next turned with set purpose to the method of mysticism
(or Sufism). I knew that the complete mystic "way" includes
both intellectual belief and practical activity; the latter consists
in getting rid of the obstacles in the self and in stripping off its
base characteristics and vicious morals, so that the heart may
attain to freedom from what is not God and to constant recollection of Him.

The intellectual belief was easier to me than the practical activity. I began to acquaint myself with their belief by reading
their books, such as *The Food of the Hearts* by Abû Tâlib al-

8. Group of tenth-century encyclopedists, who uncritically included such
sciences as the study of dreams, magic, and alchemy in their investigations.
Their ideas were similar to the Ismâ'îlîs.

Makkî (God have mercy upon him), the works of al-Hârith al-Muhâsibî, the various anecdotes about al-Junayd, ash-Shiblî and Abû Yazîd al-Bistâmî (may God sanctify their spirits), and other discourses of their leading men.[9] I thus comprehended their fundamental teachings on the intellectual side, and progressed, as far as is possible by study and oral instruction, in the knowledge of mysticism. It became clear to me, however, that what is most distinctive of mysticism is something which cannot be apprehended by study, but only by immediate experience (*dhawq*—literally "tasting"), by ecstasy and by a moral change. What a difference there is between *knowing* the definition of health and satiety, together with their causes and presuppositions, and *being* healthy and satisfied! What a difference between being acquainted with the definition of drunkenness— namely, that it designates a state arising from the domination of the seat of the intellect by vapours arising from the stomach— and being drunk! Indeed, the drunken man while in that condition does not know the definition of drunkenness nor the scientific account of it; he has not the very least scientific knowledge of it. The sober man, on the other hand, knows the definition of drunkenness and its basis, yet he is not drunk in the very least. Again the doctor, when he is himself ill, knows the definition and causes of health and the remedies which restore it, and yet is lacking in health. Similarly there is a difference between knowing the true nature and causes and conditions of the ascetic life and actually leading such a life and forsaking the world.

I apprehended clearly that the mystics were men who had real experiences, not men of words, and that I had already progressed as far as was possible by way of intellectual apprehension. What remained for me was not to be attained by oral instruction and study but only by immediate experience and by walking in the mystic way.

9. Abû Tâlib al-Makkî, d. 966, wrote on the practical requirements of piety; Muhâsibî, *ca.* 781-857, early mystic and an important influence on Ghazâlî's ideas on piety; Shiblî, d. 773, early mystic; Junaîd, d. 910, ninth-century proponent of love mysticism, along with Muhâsibî, the greatest orthodox exponent of a sober type of mysticism; Abû Yazîd al-Bistâmî, one of the most celebrated mystics, d. between 874 and 877.

Now from the sciences I had laboured at and the paths I had traversed in my investigation of the revelational and rational sciences (that is, presumably, theology and philosophy), there had come to me a sure faith in God most high, in prophethood (or revelation), and in the Last Day. These three credal principles were firmly rooted in my being, not through any carefully argued proofs, but by reason of various causes, coincidences and experiences which are not capable of being stated in detail.

It had already become clear to me that I had no hope of the bliss of the world to come save through a God-fearing life and the withdrawal of myself from vain desire. It was clear to me too that the key to all this was to sever the attachment of the heart to worldly things by leaving the mansion of deception and returning to that of eternity, and to advance towards God most high with all earnestness. It was also clear that this was only to be achieved by turning away from wealth and position and fleeing from all time-consuming entanglements.

Next I considered the circumstances of my life, and realized that I was caught in a veritable thicket of attachments. I also considered my activities, of which the best was my teaching and lecturing, and realized that in them I was dealing with sciences that were unimportant and contributed nothing to the attainment of eternal life.

After that I examined my motive in my work of teaching, and realized that it was not a pure desire for the things of God, but that the impulse moving me was the desire for an influential position and public recognition. I saw for certain that I was on the brink of a crumbling bank of sand and in imminent danger of hell-fire unless I set about to mend my ways.

I reflected on this continuously for a time, while the choice still remained open to me. One day I would form the resolution to quit Baghdad and get rid of these adverse circumstances; the next day I would abandon my resolution. I put one foot forward and drew the other back. If in the morning I had a genuine longing to seek eternal life, by the evening the attack of a whole host of desires had reduced it to impotence. Worldly desires were striving to keep me by their chains just where I was, while the voice of faith was calling, "To the road! to the road! What is left of life is but little and the journey before you is long. All that keeps you busy, both intellectually and practically, is but hypocrisy and delusion. If you do not prepare *now* for eternal life, when will you prepare? If you do not now sever these attachments, when will you sever them?" On hearing that, the impulse would be stirred and the resolution made to take to flight.

Soon, however, Satan would return. "This is a passing mood," he would say; "do not yield to it, for it will quickly disappear; if you comply with it and leave this influential position, these comfortable and dignified circumstances where you are free from troubles and disturbances, this state of safety and security where you are untouched by the contentions of your adversaries, then you will probably come to yourself again and will not find it easy to return to all this."

For nearly six months beginning with Rajab 488 A.H. (= July 1095 A.D.), I was continuously tossed about between the attractions of worldly desires and the impulses towards eternal life. In that month the matter ceased to be one of choice and became one of compulsion. God caused my tongue to dry up so that I was prevented from lecturing. One particular day I would make an effort to lecture in order to gratify the hearts of my following, but my tongue would not utter a single word nor could I accomplish anything at all.

This impediment in my speech produced grief in my heart, and at the same time my power to digest and assimilate food and drink was impaired; I could hardly swallow or digest a single mouthful of food. My powers became so weakened that the doctors gave up all hope of successful treatment. "This trouble arises from the heart," they said, "and from there it has spread through the constitution; the only method of treatment is that the anxiety which has come over the heart should be allayed."

Thereupon, perceiving my impotence and having altogether lost my power of choice, I sought refuge with God most high as one who is driven to Him, because he is without further resources of his own. He answered me, He who "answers him who is driven (to Him by affliction) when he calls upon Him" (Qur'an 27, 63). He made it easy for my heart to turn away from position and wealth, from children and friends. I openly professed that I had resolved to set out for Mecca, while privately I made arrangements to travel to Syria. I took this precaution in case the Caliph and all my friends should oppose my resolve to make my residence in Syria. This stratagem for my departure from Baghdad I gracefully executed, and had it in mind never to return there. There was much talk about me among all the religious leaders of 'Iraq, since none of them would allow that withdrawal from such a state of life as I was in could have a religious cause, for they looked upon that as the culmination of a religious career; that was the sum of their knowledge.

Much confusion now came into people's minds as they tried to account for my conduct. Those at a distance from 'Iraq supposed that it was due to some apprehension I had of action by the government. On the other hand those who were close to the governing circles and had witnessed how eagerly and assiduously they sought me and how I withdrew from them and showed no great regard for what they said, would say, "This is a supernatural affair; it must be an evil influence which has befallen the people of Islam and especially the circle of the learned."

I left Baghdad, then. I distributed what wealth I had, retaining only as much as would suffice myself and provide sustenance for my children. This I could easily manage, as the wealth of 'Iraq was available for good works, since it constitutes a trust fund for the benefit of the Muslims. Nowhere in the world have I seen better financial arrangements to assist a scholar to provide for his children.

In due course I entered Damascus, and there I remained for nearly two years with no other occupation than the cultivation of retirement and solitude, together with religious and ascetic exercises, as I busied myself purifying my soul, improving my character and cleansing my heart for the constant recollection of God most high, as I had learnt from my study of mysticism. I used to go into retreat for a period in the mosque of Damascus, going up the minaret of the mosque for the whole day and shutting myself in so as to be alone.

At length I made my way from Damascus to the Holy House

(that is, Jerusalem). There I used to enter into the precinct of the Rock every day and shut myself in.

Next there arose in me a prompting to fulfil the duty of the Pilgrimage, gain the blessings of Mecca and Medina, and perform the visitation of the Messenger of God most high (peace be upon him), after first performing the visitation of al-Khalîl, the Friend of God (God bless him).[10] I therefore made the journey to the Hijaz. Before long, however, various concerns, together with the entreaties of my children, drew me back to my home (country); and so I came to it again, though at one time no one had seemed less likely than myself to return to it. Here, too, I sought retirement, still longing for solitude and the purification of the heart for the recollection (of God). The events of the interval, the anxieties about my family, and the necessities of my livelihood altered the aspect of my purpose and impaired the quality of my solitude, for I experienced pure ecstasy only occasionally, although I did not cease to hope for that; obstacles would hold me back, yet I always returned to it.

I continued at this stage for the space of ten years, and during these periods of solitude there were revealed to me things innumerable and unfathomable. This much I shall say about that in order that others may be helped: I learnt with certainty that it is above all the mystics who walk on the road of God; their life is the best life, their method the soundest method, their character the purest character; indeed, were the intellect of the intellectuals and the learning of the learned and the scholarship of the scholars, who are versed in the profundities of revealed truth, brought together in the attempt to improve the life and character of the mystics, they would find no way of doing so; for to the mystics all movement and all rest, whether external or internal, brings illumination from the light of the lamp of prophetic revelation; and behind the light of prophetic revelation there is no other light on the face of the earth from which illumination may be received.

In general, then, how is a mystic "way" (*tarîqah*) described?

10. That is, Abraham, who is buried in the cave of Machpelah under the mosque at Hebron, which is called "al-Khalîl" in Arabic; similarly the visitation of the Messenger is the formal visit to his tomb at Medina. (Tr.)

The purity which is the first condition of it (*sc.* as bodily purity is the prior condition of formal Worship for Muslims) is the purification of the heart completely from what is other than God most high; the key to it, which corresponds to the opening act of adoration in prayer, is the sinking of the heart completely in the recollection of God; and the end of it is complete absorption (*fanâ'*) in God. At least this is its end relatively to those first steps which almost come within the sphere of choice and personal responsibility; but in reality in the actual mystic "way" it is the first step, what comes before it being, as it were, the antechamber for those who are journeying towards it.

With this first stage of the "way" there begin the revelations and visions. The mystics in their waking state now behold angels and the spirits of the prophets; they hear these speaking to them and are instructed by them. Later, a higher state is reached; instead of beholding forms and figures, they come to stages in the "way" which it is hard to describe in language; if a man attempts to express these, his words inevitably contain what is clearly erroneous.

In general what they manage to achieve is nearness to God; some, however, would conceive of this as "inherence" (*hulûl*), some as "union" (*ittihâd*) and some as "connection" (*wusûl*). All that is erroneous. In my book, *The Noblest Aim*, I have explained the nature of the error here. Yet he who has attained the mystic "state" need do no more than say:

Of the things I do not remember, what was, was;

Think it good; do not ask an account of it.

(Ibn al-Muʻtazz).[11]

In general the man to whom He has granted no immediate experience at all, apprehends no more of what prophetic revelation really is than the name. The miraculous graces given to the saints are in truth the beginnings of the prophets; and that was the first "state" of the Messenger of God (peace be unto him) when he went out to Mount Hirâ', and was given up entirely to his Lord, and worshipped, so that the bedouin said, "Muhammad loves his Lord passionately."

Now this is a mystical "state" which is realized in immediate

11. A mystic who died 908.

experience by those who walk in the way leading to it. Those to whom it is not granted to have immediate experience can become assured of it by trial (*se.* contact with mystics or observation of them) and by hearsay, if they have sufficiently numerous opportunities of associating with mystics to understand that (*sc.* ecstasy) with certainty by means of what accompanies the "states." Whoever sits in their company derives from them this faith; and none who sits in their company is pained.

Those to whom it is not even granted to have contacts with mystics may know with certainty the possibility of ecstasy by the evidence of demonstration, as I have remarked in the section entitled *The Wonders of the Heart* of my *Revival of the Religious Sciences* [ca. 1106].

Certainty reached by demonstration is *knowledge* (*'ilm*); actual acquaintance with that "state" is *immediate experience* (*dhawq*); the acceptance of it as probable from hearsay and trial (or observation) is *faith* (*îmân*). These are three degrees. "God will raise those of you who have faith and those who have been given knowledge in degrees (*sc.* of honour)" (Qur'an 58, 12).

Behind the mystics, however, there is a crowd of ignorant people. They deny this fundamentally, they are astonished at this line of thought, they listen and mock. "Amazing," they say. "What nonsense they talk!" About such people God most high has said: "Some of them listen to you, until, upon going out from you, they say to those to whom knowledge has been given, 'What did he say just now?' These are the people on whose hearts God sets a seal and they follow their passions." (Qur'an 47, 18) He makes them deaf, and blinds their sight.

Among the things that necessarily became clear to me from my practice of the mystic "way" was the true nature and special characteristics of prophetic revelation). . . .

. . . .

THE REASON FOR TEACHING AFTER MY
WITHDRAWAL FROM IT

I had persevered thus for nearly ten years in retirement and solitude. I had come of necessity—from reasons which I do not

226 POLITICAL FRAGMENTATION

enumerate, partly immediate experience, partly demonstrative knowledge, partly acceptance in faith—to a realization of various truths. I saw that man was constituted of body and heart; by "heart" I mean the real nature of his spirit which is the seat of his knowledge of God, and not the flesh and blood which he shares with the corpse and the brute beast. I saw that just as there is health and disease in the body, respectively causing it to prosper and to perish, so also there is in the heart, on the one hand, health and soundness—and "only he who comes to God with a sound heart" (Qur'an 26, 89) is saved—and, on the other hand, disease, in which is eternal and other worldly destruction —as God most high says, "in their hearts is disease" (Qur'an 2, 9). I saw that to be ignorant of God is destructive poison, and to disobey Him by following desire is the thing that produces the disease, while to know God most high is the life-giving antidote and to obey Him by opposing desire is the healing medicine. I saw, too, that the only way to treat the heart, to end its disease and procure its health, is by medicines, just as that is the only way of treating the body.

Moreover, the medicines of the body are effective in producing health through some property in them which the intellectuals do not apprehend with their intellectual apparatus, but in respect of which one must accept the statement of the doctors; and these in turn are dependent on the prophets who by the property of phophethood have grasped the properties of things. Similarly I came of necessity to realize that in the case of the medicines of formal worship, which have been fixed and determined by the prophets, the manner of their effectiveness is not apprehended by the intellectual explanations of the intellectuals; one must rather accept the statements (taqlîd) of the prophets who apprehended those properties by the light of prophecy, not by intellectual explanation.

Again, medicines are composed of ingredients differing in kind and quantity—one, for instance, is twice another in weight and amount; and this quantitative difference involves secret lore of the same type as knowledge of the properties. Similarly, formal worship, which is the medicine for the disease of the hearts is compounded of acts differing in kind and amount; the prostration (*sujûd*) is the double of the bowing (*rukû'*) in amount, and the morning worship half of the afternoon worship; and such arrangements are not without a mystery of the same type as the properties which are grasped by the light of prophecy. Indeed a man is very foolish and very ignorant if he tries to show by intellectual means that these arrangements are wise, or if he fancies that they are specified accidentally and not from a Divine mystery in them which fixes them by way of the property.

Yet again, medicines have bases, which are the principal active ingredients, and "additions" (auxiliaries or correctives), which are complementary, each of them having its specific influence on the action of the bases. Similarly, the supererogatory practices and the 'customs' are complements which perfect the efficacy of the basic elements of formal worship.

In general, the prophets are the physicians of the diseases of hearts. The only advantage of the intellect is that it informed us of that, bearing witness to prophetic revelation by believing (*sc.* the trustworthiness of the prophets) and to itself by being unable to apprehend what is apprehended by the eye of prophecy; then it took us by the hand and entrusted us to prophetic revelation, as the blind are entrusted to their guides and anxious patients to sympathetic doctors. Thus far may the intellect proceed. In what lies beyond it has no part, save in the understanding of what the physician communicates to it.

These, then, are matters which we learnt by a necessity like that of direct vision in the period of solitude and retirement.

We next observed the laxity of men's belief in the principle of prophecy and in its actuality and in conduct according to the norms elucidated by prophecy; we ascertained that this was widespread among the people. When I considered the reasons for people's laxity and weakness of faith, I found there were four:

a reason connected with those who engage in philosophy;

a reason connected with those who engage in the mystic way;

a reason connected with those who profess the doctrine of *ta'lîm*;[12]

12. Ta'lîm, the doctrine that Truth or Knowledge comes only from an infallible *imâm*. Professed by Shî'îs or Ismâ'îlîs.

a reason based on the practice of those who are popularly described as having knowledge.

For a time I went after individual men, questioning those who fell short in observing the Law. I would question one about his doubts and investigate his inmost beliefs. "Why is it," I said, "that you fall short in that? If you believe in the future life and, instead of preparing for it, sell it in order to buy this world, then that is folly! You do not normally sell two things for one; how can you give up an endless life for a limited number of days? If, on the other hand, you do not believe in it, then you are an infidel! Dispose yourself to faith. Observe what is the cause of your hidden unbelief, for that is the doctrinal system you inwardly adopt and the cause of your outward daring, even though you do not give expression to it out of respect towards the faith and reverence for the mention of the law!"

(1) One would say: "If it were obligatory to observe this matter, then those learned in religious questions would be foremost in doing so; but, among persons of distinction, A does not perform the Worship, B drinks wine, C devours the property of trusts and orphans, D accepts the munificence of the sovereign and does not refrain from forbidden things, E accepts bribes for giving judgement or bearing witness; and so on."

A second man claims to have knowledge of mysticism and considers that he has made such progress that he is above the need for formal worship.

A third man is taken up with another of the doubts of the "Latitudinarians."[13] These are those who stray from the path of mysticism.

(2) A fourth man, having met the party of ta'lim would say: "Truth is difficult, the way to it blocked, and the disputes over it numerous. No one system of doctrine is preferable to any other. Rational proofs contradict one another, and no confidence can be placed in the speculations of the speculative thinkers (ashâb al-ra'y). He who summons to ta'lim makes assertions without proof. How then through doubt can I keep certainty?"

13. Latitudinarians: antinomians among Sûfîs or Shî'îs who allowed their belief either in the "hidden" meaning or the "hidden" imâm to reduce their literal religious obligations to insignificance.

(3) A fifth man says: "I do not perform these acts out of obedience to authority (*taqlîdan*). I have studied philosophy and I know that prophecy actually exists and that its achievement is wise and beneficial. I see that the acts of worship it prescribes aim at keeping order among the common people and restraining them from fighting and quarreling with one another and from giving rein to their desires. But I am not one of the ignorant common people that I should enter within the narrow confines of duty. On the contrary I am one of the wise, I follow wisdom, and thereby see clearly (for myself) so that I do not require to follow authority."

This is the final word of the faith of those who study the system of the theistic philosophers, as you may learn from the works of Ibn Sînâ and Abû Nasr al-Fârâbî.[14]

These are the people who show politeness to Islam. Often you see one of them reading the Qur'an, attending the Friday assembly and public Worship and praising the sacred Law. Nevertheless he does not refrain from drinking wine and from various wicked and immoral practices! If someone says to him, "If the prophetic revelation is not genuine, why do you join in the prayers?" perhaps he will reply, "To exercise my body, and because it is a custom in the place, and to keep my wealth and family." Or perhaps he says, "The sacred Law is genuine; the prophetic revelation is true"; then he is asked, "And why then do you drink wine?" and he replies, "Wine is forbidden only because it leads to enmity and hatred; I am sufficiently wise to guard against that, and so I take wine to make my mind more lively." Ibn Sînâ actually writes in his *Testament* that he swore to God that he would do various things, and in particular that he would praise what the sacred Law prescribed, that he would not be lax in taking part in the public worship of God, and that he would not drink for pleasure but only as a tonic or medicine. Thus the net result of his purity of faith and observance of the obligations of worship was that he made an exception of drinking wine for medical purposes!

Such is the faith of those philosophers who profess religious faith. Many have been deceived by them; and the deceit has

14. Ibn Sîna, d. 1037, and Farâbî, d. 950, Muslim neo-Platonic philosophers.

been the greater because of the ineffectiveness of the criticism levelled against the philosophers, since that consisted, as we have shown above, in denying geometry and logic and others of their sciences which possess necessary truth.

I observed, then, to what an extent and for what reasons faith was weak among the various classes of men; and I observed how I myself was occupied with the resolving of this doubt, indeed I had devoted so much time and energy to the study of their sciences and methods—I mean those of the mystics, the philosophers, the "authoritarian instructionists" . . . and the outstanding scholars . . . —that to show up their errors was easier for me than drinking water. As I observed all this, the impression was formed in me: "That is a fixed and determinate character of this time; what benefit to you, then, are solitude and retirement, since the sickness has become general, the doctors have fallen ill, and mankind has reached the verge of destruction?" I said to myself, however: "When will you busy yourself in resolving these difficulties and attacking these obscurities, seeing it is an age of slackness, an era of futility? Even if you were to labour at summoning men from their worthless ways to the truth, the people of this age would be united in showing hostility to you. How will you stand up to them? How will you live among them, seeing that such a project is only to be executed with the aid of time and through a pious sovereign who is all-powerful?"

I believed that it was permissible for me in the sight of God to continue in retirement on the ground of my inability to demonstrate the truth by argument. But God most high determined Himself to stir up the impulse of the sovereign of the time, though not by any external means; the latter[15] gave me strict orders to hasten to Naysâbûr (Nîshâpûr) to tackle the problem of this lukewarmness in religious matters. So strict was the injunction that, had I persisted in disobeying it, I should at length have been cut off! I came to realize, too, that the grounds which had made retirement permissible had lost their force. "It is not right that your motive for clinging to retirement should be lazi-

15. The Seljûq sultân Muhammad.

ness and love of ease, the quest for spiritual power and preservation from worldly contamination. It was not because of the
difficulty of restoring men to health that you gave yourself this
permission."

Now God most high says: "In the name of God, the Merciful,
the Compassionate. Alif, Lâm, Mîm.[16] Do the people think that
they will be left in the position that they say, 'We have believed,'
without their being tried? We tried those who were before them"
(Qur'an 29, 1), and what follows. He (may He be exalted!) says
to His messenger, who is the noblest of His creatures: "Messengers have been counted false before thee, but they patiently endured the falsehood laid to their charge and the insults done
them, until Our help came to them; no one can change the words
of God, and surely there has come to thee some information
about those who were sent (as messengers)." (Qur'an 6, 34).
He (may He be exalted) says too: "In the name of God, the
Merciful, the Compassionate. Yâ', Sîn. By the Qur'an that de-
cides . . . Thou wilt only warn him who follows the Reminder"
(Qur'an 36, 1 and 11).

On this matter I consulted a number of men skilled in the
science of the heart and with experience of contemplation. They
unanimously advised me to abandon my retirement and leave
the *zâwiyah*.[17] My resolution was further strengthened by numerous visions of good men in all of which alike I was given
the assurance that this impulse was a source of good, was genuine guidance, and had been determined by God most high for
the beginning of this century; for God most high has promised
to revive His religion at the beginning of each century.[18] My
hope became strong, and all these considerations caused the fa-
vourable view of the project to prevail.

16. Three letters of the Arabic alphabet which begin Sûra XXIX. Their
meaning is undetermined.
17. *Zâwiya*: Arabic for a monastery-like retreat for Sûfîs. Ghazâlî had
founded one at Tûs during his retirement, to train young disciples in Sûfism.
18. There was a well-known Tradition to the effect that at the beginning of
each century God would send a man to revive religion. The events in question took place a few months before the beginning of the sixth century of the
Muslim era.

God most high facilitated my move to Naysâbûr to deal with this serious problem in Dhu'l-Qa'dah, the eleventh month of 499 (=July, 1106 A.D.). I had originally left Baghdad in Dhu'l-Qa'dah, 488, (=November, 1095), so that my period of retirement had extended to eleven years. It was God most high who determined this move, and it is an example of the wonderful way in which He determines events, since there was not a whisper of it in my heart while I was living in retirement. In the same way my departure from Baghdad and withdrawal from my position there had not even occurred to my mind as a possibility. But God is the upsetter of hearts and positions. As the Tradition has it, "The heart of the believer is between two of the fingers of the Merciful."

In myself I know that, even if I went back to the work of disseminating knowledge, yet I did not go back. To go back is to return to the previous state of things. Previously, however, I had been disseminating the knowledge by which worldly success is attained; by word and deed I had called men to it; and that had been my aim and intention. But now I am calling men to the knowledge whereby worldly success is given up and its low position in the scale of real worth is recognized. This is now my intention, my aim, my desire; God knows that this is so. It is my earnest longing that I may make myself and others better. I do not know whether I shall reach my goal or whether I shall be taken away while short of my object. I believe, however, both by certain faith and by intuition that there is no power and no might save with God, the high, the mighty, and that I do not move of myself but am moved by Him, I do not work of myself but am used by Him. I ask Him first of all to reform me and then to reform through me, to guide me and then to guide through me, to show me the truth of what is true and to grant of His bounty that I may follow it, and to show me the falsity of what is false and to grant of His bounty that I may turn away from it.

We now return to the earlier topic of the causes for the weakness of faith, and consider how to guide men aright and deliver them from the perils they face.

For those who profess perplexity as a result of what they have heard from the party of *ta'lîm*, the treatment is that prescribed in our book, *The Just Balance*, and we shall not lengthen this essay by repeating it.

As for the fanciful assertions of the Latitudinarians (*Ahl-al-Ibâhah*), we have collected their doubts under seven heads, and resolved them, in our book, *The Chemistry of Happiness*.

In reply to those who through philosophy have corrupted their faith to the extent of denying prophecy in principle, we have discussed the reality of prophecy and how it exists of necessity, by showing that there exists a knowledge of the properties of medicines, stars, and so forth. We introduced this preliminary study precisely for this purpose; we based the demonstration on medical and astronomical properties precisely because these are included in the science of the Philosophers. To every one who is expert in some branch of science, be it astronomy (? astrology) or medicine, physics, magic or charm-making, we offer proof of prophecy based on his own branch of science.

The man who verbally professes belief in prophecy, but equates the prescriptions of the revealed scriptures with (philosophic) wisdom, really disbelieves in prophecy, and believes only in a certain judge (*v.l.* philosopher) the ascendancy of whose star is such that it determines men to follow him. This is not prophecy at all. On the contrary, faith in prophecy is to acknowledge the existence of a sphere beyond reason; into this sphere an eye penetrates whereby man apprehends special objects-of-apprehension. From these reason is excluded in the same way as the hearing is excluded from apprehending colours and sight from apprehending sounds and all the senses from apprehending the objects-of-reason.

If our opponent does not admit this, well, we have given a demonstration that a suprarational sphere is possible, indeed that it actually exists. If, however, he admits our contention, he has affirmed the existence of things called properties with which the operations of reason are not concerned at all; indeed, reason almost denies them and judges them absurd. For instance, the weight of a *dâniq* (about eight grains) of opium is a deadly poison, freezing the blood in the veins through its excess of cold. The man who claims a knowledge of physics considers that when a composite substance becomes cold it always does so through the two elements of water and earth, since these are the cold elements. It is well-known, however, that many pounds of water and earth are not productive of cold in the interior of the body to the same extent as this weight of opium. If a physicist were informed of this fact, and had not discovered it by experiment, he would say, "This is impossible; the proof of its impossibility is that the opium contains the elements of fire and air, and these elements do not increase cold; even supposing it was entirely composed of water and earth, that would not necessitate this extreme freezing action, much less does it do so when the two hot elements are joined with them." He supposes that this is a proof!

Most of the philosophers' proofs in natural science and theology are constructed in this fashion. They conceive of things according to the measure of their observations and reasonings. What they are unfamiliar with they suppose impossible. If it were not that veridical vision in sleep is familiar, then, when someone claimed to gain knowledge of the unseen while his senses were at rest, men with such intellects would deny it. If you said to one, "Is it possible for there to be in the world a thing, the size of a grain, which, if placed in a town, will consume that town in its entirety and then consume itself, so that nothing is left of the town and what it contained nor of the thing itself?"; he would say, "This is absurd; it is an old wives' tale." Yet this is the case with fire, although, when he heard it, someone who had no acquaintance with fire would reject it. The rejection of the strange features of the world to come usually belongs to this class. To the physicist we reply: "You are compelled to admit that in opium there is a property which leads to freezing, although this is not consonant with nature as rationally conceived; why then is it not possible that there should be in the positive precepts of the Divine law properties leading to the healing and purifying of hearts, which are not apprehended by intellectual wisdom but are perceived only by the eye of prophecy?" Indeed in various pronouncements in their writings they have actually recognized properties more surprising than these, such as the wonderful properties observed when the fol-

lowing figure was employed in treating cases of childbirth where
delivery was difficult:—

4	9	2
3	5	7
8	1	6

IV	IX	II
III	V	VII
VIII	I	VI

The figure is inscribed on two pieces of cloth untouched by
water. The woman looks at them with her eye and places them
under her feet, and at once the child quickly emerges. The phys-
icists acknowledge the possibility of that, and describe it in the
book entitled *The Marvels of Properties*.

The figure consists of nine squares with a number in each,
such that the sum of each row or line, vertically, horizontally
and diagonally, is fifteen.

How on earth is it possible for anyone to believe that, and
then not to have sufficient breadth of mind to believe that the
arrangement of the formal prayers—two *rak'ahs*[19] in the morning, four at midday and three at sunset—is so made on account
of properties not apprehended by philosophical reflection? The
grounds of these arrangements are the difference of the times
of day, but these properties are perceived only by the light of
prophecy.

It is curious, however, that, if we replace the above expressions by expressions from astrology, they admit the difference of
times as reasonable. We may say, for example: "Is it not the
case that the horoscope varies according as the sun is in the
ascendant, in the ecliptic or in declension? And in their horo-
scopes do they make this variation the basis of the difference of
treatment and of length of life and hour of death? Is there not a
distinction between declension and the sun's being in the ecliptic, and likewise between sunset and the sun's being towards
setting? Is there any way to believe this?" If it were not that he
hears it in astrological terminology, he would probably have

19. *Rak'a*: Unit of prayer consisting of three postures.

experimentally observed its falsity a hundred times. Yet he goes on habitually believing in it, so that if an astrologer says to him, "If the sun is in the ecliptic, and star A confronts, while the ascendant is constellation B, then, should you put on a new garment at that time, you will be killed in that garment"; he will not put on the garment at that time, even though he may suffer from extreme cold and even though he hears this from an astrologer whose falsity he has acknowledged a hundred times.

How on earth when a man's mind is capable of accepting such strange statements and is compelled to acknowledge that these are properties—the knowledge of which is a miracle for some of the prophets—how does he come to reject a similar fact in respect of what he hears of the teaching of a prophet, especially when that prophet speaks truth, is accredited by miracles, and is never known to have been in error?

If the philosopher denies the possibility of there being such properties in the number of *rak'ahs*, the casting of stones (in the valley of Mina during the Pilgrimage), the number of the elements of the Pilgrimage and the other ceremonies of worship of the sacred law, he will not find, in principle, any difference between these and the properties of drugs and stars. He may say, "I have some experience in medical and astronomical (or astrological) matters, and have found some points in the science true; as a result belief in it has become firmly settled in me and my heart has lost all inclination to shun it and look askance at it; prophecy, however, I have no experience of; how shall I know that it actually exists, even if I admit its possibility?"

I reply: "You do not confine yourself to believing what you have experience of, but, where you have received information about the experience of others, you accept them as authorities. Listen then to the words of the prophets, for they have had experience, they have had direct vision of the truth in respect of all that is dealt with in revelation. Walk in their way and you too will come to know something of that by direct vision."

Moreover I say: "Even if you have not experienced it, yet your mind judges it an absolute obligation to believe in it and follow it. Let us suppose that a man of full age and sound mind, who has never experienced illness, now falls ill; and let us suppose that he has a father who is a good man and a competent physician, of whose reputation in medicine he has been hearing as long as he can remember. His father compounds a drug for him, saying, 'This will make you better from your illness and cure your symptoms.' What judgment does his intellect make here, even if the drug is bitter and disagreeable to the taste? Does he take it? Or does he disbelieve and say, 'I do not understand the connection of this drug with the achieving of a cure; I have had no experience of it.' You would certainly think him a fool if he did that! Similarly people of vision think you a fool when you hesitate and remain undecided."

You may say: "How am I to know the good will of the Prophet (peace be upon him) and his knowledge of this medical art?" I reply: "How do you know the good will of your father, seeing this is not something perceived by the senses? The fact is that you have come to know it necessarily and indubitably by comparing his attitude at different times and observing his actions in various circumstances."

If one considers the sayings of the Messenger of God (peace be upon him) and what is related in Tradition about his concern for showing to people the true way and about his graciousness in leading men by various acts of sympathy and kindness to improve their character and conduct and to better their mutual relations—leading them, in fine, to what is the indispensable basis of all betterment, religious and secular alike—if one considers this, one comes to the necessary knowledge that his good will towards his people is greater than that of a father towards his child.

Again, if one considers the marvellous acts mainfested in his case and the wonderful mysteries declared by his mouth in the Qur'an and in the Traditions, and his predictions of events in the distant future, together with the fulfilment of these predictions, then one will know necessarily that he attained to the sphere which is beyond reason, where an eye opened in him by which the mysteries were laid bare which only the elect apprehend, the mysteries which are not apprehended by the intellect.

This is the method of reaching necessary knowledge that the Prophet (peace be upon him) is to be believed. Make the experiment, reflect on the Qur'an, read the Traditions; then you will know that by seeing for yourself.

We have now dealt with the students of philosophy in sufficient detail, discussing the question at some length in view of the great need for such criticism at the present time.

(4) As for the fourth cause of weakness of faith, namely, the evil lives of the religious leaders ('ulamâ,' singular 'âlim) this disease is cured by three things.

(a) The first is that you should say to yourself that the 'âlim whom you consider to eat what is prohibited has a knowledge that wine and pork and usury are prohibited and also that lying and backbiting and slander are prohibited. You yourself also know that and yet you do these latter things, not because you do not believe they are sins, but because your desire overcomes you. Now the other man's desire is like your desire; it has overcome him, just as yours has overcome you. His knowledge of other matters beyond this (such as theological arguments and the application of legal principles) distinguishes him from you but does not imply any greater abstinence from specific forbidden things. Many a believer in medical science does not hold back from fruit and from cold water even though the doctor has told him to abstain from them! That does not show that they are not harmful, or that his faith in medicine is not genuine. Such a line of thought helps one to put up with the faults of the 'ulamâ.'

(b) The second thing is to say to the ordinary man: "You must believe that the 'âlim has regarded his knowledge as a treasure laid up for himself in the future life, imagining that it will deliver him and make intercession for him, so that consequently he is somewhat remiss in his conduct in view of the excellence of his knowledge. Now although that might be an additional point against him, yet it may also be an additional degree of honour for him, and it is certainly possible that, even if he leaves duties undone, he will be brought to safety by his knowledge. But if you, who are an ordinary man, observing him, leave duty undone, then, since you are destitute of knowledge, you will perish through your evil conduct and will have no intercessor!"

(c) The third point is the fact that the genuine *'âlim* does not commit a sin except by a slip, and the sins are not part of his intention at all. Genuine knowledge is that which informs us that sin is a deadly poison and that the world to come is better than this; and the man who knows that does not give up the good for what is lower than it.

This knowledge is not attained by means of the various special branches of knowledge to which most people devote their attention. As a result, most people's knowledge only makes them bolder in disobeying God most high. Genuine knowledge, however, increases a man's reverence and fear and hope; and these come between him and sins (in the strict sense) as distinct from the unintentional faults which are inseparable from man in his times of weakness. This proneness to lesser sins does not argue any weakness of faith, however. The believer, when he goes astray, repents. He is far from sinning intentionally and deliberately.

These are the points I wanted to discuss in criticism of the faults of the philosophers and the party of *ta'lîm* and the faults of those who oppose them without using their methods.

We pray God Almighty that He will number us among those whom He has chosen and elected, whom He has led to the truth and guided, whom He has inspired to recollect Him and not to forget Him, whom He has preserved from the evil in themselves so that they do not prefer ought to Him, and whom He has made His own so that they serve only Him.

The New Mysticism: Poetry

Sûfî mysticism combined with older legalism to give Islâm a new character after about 1100. In addition Sûfism inspired important new forms of religious association, the darvîsh orders (*tarîqa*s). These religious communities were built around a master and his disciples; the most enduring and influential of them developed their own rituals and distinctive patterns of dress.

The rise of Sûfism and of the darvîsh orders coincided with a remarkable revival of the Persian language as a vehicle for poetry and religious expression. The principal pioneer of this development was Jalâluddîn Rûmî (1207-1273). Rûmî was born in eastern Irân, and while still a boy, he accompanied his father—himself a famous man of religion—on wanderings that carried them to the court of the Seljûq sultan of Konya in Asia Minor. When his father died in 1230, Rûmî succeeded him as teacher in the local *madrasa,* but soon gave up that post in order to devote himself to mystical exercises.

Rûmî's master in Sûfî ways was a wandering darvîsh named Shams-i Dîn who came originally from Tabrîz in Irân. In due season Rûmî attracted a following of fellow seekers after mystical union with God. Music, dance, and recitation of Rûmî's poems (themselves composed in an ecstatic mood induced by music and dance) gave the Mevlevi darvîshes (as Rûmî's followers are known) a distinctive and very powerful style of piety. Westerners commonly call them dancing, or whirling, darvîshes (or dervishes). The order still exists and is influential in several Muslim lands.

A selection from Rûmî's short lyrical poems inspired by Shams-i Dîn is translated here. Some of the themes of Sûfî piety that find expression here may be unfamiliar: the notion that man is a microcosm of the universe, for instance, which was capable of extreme elaboration. The central metaphor, however, was the comparison of the Sûfî relation with God to the relation between human lovers; and this, too, was capable of indefinite elaboration. Finally, drunkenness was treated as a symbol; and the bodily equivalent of the mystical bliss that came when the yearning Sûfî finally encountered God.

These metaphors hovered on the verge of sacrilege. Wine-drinking, for instance, was prohibited in the Qur'ân, so that praise of drunkenness was shocking indeed to pious Muslims, unless understood metaphorically. Even today, when endless repetition has reduced Rûmî's figures of speech to clichés, his words retain extraordinary emotional residue for Muslims because of persistent ambiguity between spiritual and bodily, moral and immoral meanings.

FROM RÛMÎ: DÎVÂN-I SHAMS-I TABRÎZ

I

The man of God[1] is drunken without wine,
The man of God is full without meat.

The man of God is distraught and bewildered,
The man of God has no food or sleep.

The man of God is a king[2] 'neath darvish-cloak,
The man of God is a treasure in a ruin.[3]

The man of God is not of air and earth,
The man of God is not of fire and water.[4]

The man of God is a boundless sea,
The man of God rains pearls without a cloud.[5]

The man of God hath hundred moons and skies,
The man of God hath hundred suns.

The man of God is made wise by the Truth,
The man of God is not learned from book.

The man of God is beyond infidelity and religion,
To the man of God right and wrong are alike.[6]

From *Selected Poems from the Dîvâni Shamsi Tabrîz* (by Rûmî), trans. by Reynold A. Nicholson, London: Cambridge University Press, 1898, pp. 15, 17, 125, 127, 129, 131, 81, 83, 85, 15, 17, 121, 123, 95, 97. Reprinted by permission.

1. I.e., the perfect Sûfî.

2. A king in the spiritual world.

3. It is a well-known Oriental fancy that treasures guarded by inviolable talismans lie buried in the ruins and remains of ancient splendour, e.g. the site of Persepolis. (Tr.)

4. Bodies are composed of the four elements, earth, water, fire, and air. The "man of God," casting off this phenomenal vesture, which does not belong to his true essence and which only veils the divine principle within him, "breaks through to the Oneness." (Tr.)

5. He can perform miracles, because his will is identical with the divine Will. The metaphor is drawn from the notion, found in Pliny, that the oyster is impregnated by rain-drops, which in due course become pearls. (Tr.)

6. The Truth is independent of outward forms: it shines as brightly in the tavern as in the mosque or the church; moreover, the religion of the heart, which alone has value, is not the monopoly of any particular creed. In reality all creeds are one . . . the Sûfî adept is above law. Whatever he does proceeds directly from God, just as a flute produces harmonies or discords at the will of the musician. (Tr.)

The man of God has ridden away from Not-being,
The man of God is gloriously attended.
The man of God is concealed, Shamsi Dîn;[7]
The man of God do thou seek and find!

II

What is to be done, O Moslems? for I do not recognise myself.[8]
I am neither Christian, nor Jew, nor Gabr,[9] nor Moslem.
I am not of the East, nor of the West, nor of the land, nor of the
sea;
I am not of Nature's mint, nor of the circling heavens.
I am not of earth, nor of water, nor of air, nor of fire;
I am not of the empyrean, nor of the dust, nor of existence, nor
of entity.
I am not of India, nor of China, nor of Bulgaria, nor of Saqsîn;[10]
I am not of the kingdom of 'Irâqain, nor of the country of Khor-
âsân.[11]
I am not of this world, nor of the next, nor of Paradise, nor of
Hell;
I am not of Adam, nor of Eve, nor of Eden and Rizwân.[12]
My place is the Placeless, my trace is the Traceless;
'Tis neither body nor soul, for I belong to the soul of the Beloved.
I have put duality away, I have seen that the two worlds are
one;
One I seek, One I know, One I see, One I call.

7. Refers to the tradition, common to Judaism, too, that there are a certain
number of saintly men on earth but that they are unknown to one another.
Shams-i Dîn was Rûmî's *darvîsh* acquaintance who became his spiritual
master and inspired these poems.

8. The purpose of negation of self is to clear the way for the apprehension
of the fact that there is no existence but the One. . . . (Tr.)

9. Gabr: a Magian or Zoroastrian, counted as "People of the Book" in the
Qur'ân.

10. For Bulgaria, read Bulghar, a town on the Volga, one hundred miles
south of Kazan. Saqsîn, apparently in territory of Khazars, between Crimea
and Caspian Sea.

11. 'Irâqain: "The Two Irâqs," 'Irâq 'Ajamî, the great central province of
western Persia; 'Irâq, 'Arabî, between the Tigris and Euphrates. Khurâsân:
important province of eastern Persia.

12. Rizwân, the angel who has the keys of Paradise.

*He is the first, He is the last, He is the outward, He is the in-
    ward;*
I know none other except "Yâ Hû" and "Yâ man Hû."[13]
I am intoxicated with Love's cup, the two worlds have passed out
    of my ken;
I have no business save carouse and revelry.[14]
If once in my life I spent a moment without thee,
From that time and from that hour I repent of my life.
If once in this world I win a moment with thee,
I will trample on both worlds, I will dance in triumph for ever.
O Shamsi Tabrîz,[15] I am so drunken in this world,
That except of drunkenness and revelry I have no tale to tell.

III

No joy have I found in the two worlds apart from thee, Beloved.
Many wonders I have seen: I have not seen a wonder like thee.
They say that blazing fire is the infidel's portion:
I have seen none, save Abû Lahab, excluded from thy fire.[16]
Often have I laid the spiritual ear at the window of the heart:[17]
I heard much discourse, but the lips I did not see.
Of a sudden thou didst lavish grace upon thy servant:
I saw no cause for it but thy infinite kindness.
O chosen Cup-bearer, O apple of mine eyes, the like of thee
Ne'er appeared in Persia, nor in Arabia have I found it.
Pour out wine till I become a wanderer from myself;
For in selfhood and existence I have felt only fatigue.
O thou who art milk and sugar, O thou who art sun and moon,
O thou who art mother and father, I have known no kin but thee.

13. Yâ Hû: "O He" (Jahve, Jehovah), one of the most familiar darvîsh-cries. (Tr.) Yâ man Hû: "O He who is." (Tr.)
14. Meaning spiritual rapture and ecstasy. The two worlds: finite and infinite.
15. See note 7 above.
16. The celestial fire of love. 'Abdu 'l Uzzâ, surnamed Abû Lahab (father of flame), was the uncle and bitter enemy of Muhammad, who denounced him as follows: "The hands of Abû Lahab shall perish and he shall perish. Neither his wealth shall profit him, nor what he hath gained. He shall enter into the flaming fire" (Sûra CXI). (Tr.)
17. The window which reflects God's light.

O indestructible Love, O divine Minstrel,
Thou art both stay and refuge: a name equal to thee I have not
    found.
We are pieces of steel, and thy love is the magnet:
Thou art the source of all aspiration, in myself I have seen none.
Silence, O brother! put learning and culture away:
Till Thou namedst culture, I knew no culture but Thee.

IV

Grasp the skirt of his favour, for on a sudden he will flee;
But draw him not, as an arrow, for he will flee from the bow.[18]
What delusive forms does he take, what tricks does he invent!
If he is present in form, he will flee by the way of spirit.
Seek him in the sky, he shines in water, like the moon;
When you come into the water, he will flee to the sky.
Seek him in the placeless, he will sign you to place;
When you seek him in place, he will flee to the placeless.
As the arrow speeds from the bow, like the bird of your imagina-
    tion,
Know that the Absolute will certainly flee from the Imaginary.
I will flee from this and that, not for weariness, but for fear
That my gracious Beauty will flee from this and that.
As the wind I am fleet of foot, from love of the rose I am like the
    zephyr;
The rose in dread of autumn will flee from the garden.
His name will flee, when it sees an attempt at speech,
So that you cannot even say, "Such an one will flee."
He will flee from you, so that if you limn his picture,
The picture will fly from the tablet, the impression will flee
from the soul.

V

A beauty that all night long teaches love-tricks to Venus and the
    moon,
Whose two eyes by their witchery seal up the two eyes of
    heaven.

18. . . . He who seeks God must not rely on his own exertions, but rather
allow himself, wisely passive, to be swept along by the unseen current of
divine energy in which all finite existences are flowing backwards to their
original source. (Tr.)

Look to your hearts! I, whate'er betide, O Moslems,
Am so mingled with him that no heart is mingled with me.
I was born of his love at the first, I gave him my heart at the
    last;
When the fruit springs from the bough, on that bough it hangs.
The tip of his curl is saying, "Ho! betake thee to rope-dancing."[19]
The cheek of his candle is saying, "Where is a moth that it may
    burn?"
For the sake of dancing on that rope, O heart, make haste, be-
    come a hoop;
Cast thyself on the flame, when his candle is lit.
Thou wilt never more endure without the flame, when thou hast
    known the rapture of burning;
If the water of life should come to thee, it would not stir thee
    from the flame.

VI

David said: "O Lord, since thou hast no need of us,
Say, then, what wisdom was there in creating the two worlds?"
God said to him: "O temporal man, I was a hidden treasure;
I sought that that treasure of loving kindness and bounty should
    be revealed.
I displayed a mirror—its face the heart, its back the world—
Its back is better than its face—if the face is unknown to thee."[20]
When straw is mixed with clay, how should the mirror be suc-
    cessful?
When you part the straw from the clay, the mirror becomes
    clear.[21]
Grape-juice does not turn to wine, unless it ferment awhile in
    the jar;

19. . . . The heart entangled in the Beloved's tresses typifies (1) Man bewildered and held captive by worldly illusions, and (2) as here, the lover
spell-bound in contemplation of the mysterious beauty of God. (Tr.)
20. Every object reflects one or more of the divine attributes, but Man, as
the microcosm, reflects them all. . . . the earthly part of Man is compared
to the back, his eternal attributes to the face of a mirror. He is "blackened
on one side with the darkness of Not-being in order to reflect Real Being."
(Tr.)
21. Straw is mixed with clay to form a kind of stucco or mortar. . . . Unless
you are pure clay, i.e. entirely purged of self, the divine image reflected in
your heart will be blurred and incomplete. (Tr.)

Would you have your heart grow bright, you must take a little
    trouble.
The soul which issued forth from the body—my king saith to it:
"Thou art come even as thou wentest: where are the traces of
    my benefactions?"
'Tis notorious that copper by alchemy becomes gold:
Our copper has been transmuted by this rare alchemy.
From God's grace this sun[22] wants no crown or robe:
He is cap to a hundred bald men and cloak to ten naked.
Child, Jesus sate on an ass for humility's sake:
How else should the zephyr ride on the back of an ass?[23]
O spirit, make thy head in search and seeking like the water of
    a stream,
And O reason, to gain eternal life[24] tread everlastingly the way
    of death.
Keep God in remembrance till self is forgotten,
That you may be lost in the Called, without distraction of caller
    and call.

VII

Thee I choose, of all the world, alone;
Wilt thou suffer me to sit in grief?
My heart is as a pen in thy hand,
Thou art the cause if I am glad or melancholy.
Save what thou willest, what will have I?
Save what thou showest, what do I see?
Thou mak'st grow out of me now a thorn and now a rose;
Now I smell roses and now pull thorns.
If thou keep'st me that, that I am;
If thou woulds't have me this, I am this.
In the vessel where thou givest colour to the soul
Who am I, what is my love and hate?
Thou wert first, and last thou shalt be;

22. I.e., Shams-i Dîn, Rûmî's spiritual mentor.
23. St. Matthew, chapter XXI. Zephyr is an allusion to the quickening
breath of Jesus, which Muslims call the breath of God. (Tr.)
24. . . . eternal life in God, only to be gained through annihilation of self.
(Tr.)

Make my last better than my first.
When thou art hidden, I am of the infidels;
When thou art manifest, I am of the faithful.[25]
I have nothing, except thou hast bestowed it;
What dost thou seek from my bosom and sleeve?[26]

VIII

When my bier moveth on the day of death,
Think not my heart is in this world.
Do not weep for me and cry "Woe, woe!"
Thou wilt fall in the devil's snare: that is woe.
When thou seest my hearse, cry not "Parted, parted!"
Union and meeting are mine in that hour.
If thou commit me to the grave, say not "Farewell, farewell!"
For the grave is a curtain hiding the communion of Paradise.
After beholding descent, consider resurrection;
Why should setting be injurious to the sun and moon?
To thee it seems a setting, but 'tis a rising;
Tho' the vault seems a prison, 'tis the release of the soul.
What seed went down into the earth but it grew?
Why this doubt of thine as regards the seed of man?
What bucket was lowered but it came out brimful?
Why should the Joseph[27] of the spirit complain of the well?
Shut thy mouth on this side and open it beyond,
For in placeless air will be thy triumphal song.

25. The mystic is alternately rapt to the shining heights of vision and plunged in the dark abyss of separation: these opposite states, resulting from the conflict of Being and Not-being, are to him what faith and infidelity are to common men. (Tr.)
26. The bosom of the shirt serves as a pocket, and loose money is often carried in the sleeve. (Tr.)
27. Referring to the Old Testament Joseph, whose earthly tribulations, e.g., being thrown on the well by his brothers, should seem insignificant compared to his knowledge of salvation at death.

Mongols

The Mongols, whose culture and political organization combined Chinese and nomadic pagan elements, burst upon Islâm like a destructive storm. By the time of Chîngîz Khân's death (1227), Irân had been overrun; but the final disasters were the capture of Baghdâd (1258) and the coup de grâce both to the caliphate and to the irrigation that had made Irâq fertile for centuries. The Mongols were savage in slaughtering those who opposed them; but once the initial shock of conquest had passed, contacts with China opened new cultural vistas to Islâm. Art flourished and the new rulers of Irân, the Îl-khâns, became Muslim in 1295 and patronized a growing Persian literature. Nevertheless, the fall of the caliphate represented a break with earlier Muslim political-religious ideas, and subsequent efforts to develop a new form of political legitimacy for Muslim states and rulers did not find secure basis in religious principles.

The dazed response of Muslim writers to initial defeat is suggested by the brief passage from the history of Ibn al-Athîr (d. 1233), who witnessed the first Mongol onslaught. The ways in which Mongol rulers were assimilated by Muslim society is suggested by the second author, 'Alâ' al-Dîn 'Atâ-Mâlik Juvainî (1226-1283). Juvainî came from a distinguished family of office-holders —his father served the Mongols in various capacities. While Juvainî was still a young man he went to Karakorum, the seat of the Great Khân. There he began to write his *History of the World Conqueror*. In 1259 the founder of the Îl-Khân dynasty appointed him governor of Baghdâd. He worked at his book in his spare time.

As a high servant of the Mongols, Juvainî both knew them well and admired their military virtues. As a Muslim he had to explain how God could allow pagan horsemen to rule over Muslims. His work reflects the ambiguity of his position and reveals vividly the variety of peoples, religions, and cultures at the Mongol court.

IBN AL-ATHÎR: FROM GREAT HISTORY

Account of the Outbreak of the Tartars into the Lands of Islâm Under the year A.H. *617 (*A.D. *1220-1221)*

For some years I continued averse from mentioning this event, deeming it so horrible that I shrank from recording it, and ever withdrawing one foot as I advanced the other. To whom, indeed, can it be easy to write the announcement of the death-blow of Islâm and the Muslims, or who is he on whom the remembrance thereof can weigh lightly? O would that my mother had not born me, or that I had died and become a forgotten thing ere this befell! Yet withal a number of my friends urged me to set it down in writing, and I hesitated long; but at last came to the conclusion that to omit this matter [from my history] could serve no useful purpose.

I say, therefore, that this thing involves the description of the greatest catastrophe and the most dire calamity (of the like of which days and nights are innocent) which befell all men generally, and the Muslims in particular; so that, should one say that the world, since God Almighty created Adam until now, hath not been afflicted with the like thereof, he would but speak the truth. For indeed history doth not contain aught which approaches or comes nigh unto it. For of the most grievous calamities recorded was what Nebuchadnezzar inflicted on the children of Israel by his slaughter of them and his destruction of Jerusalem; and what was Jerusalem in comparison to the countries which these accursed miscreants destroyed, each city of which was double the size of Jerusalem? Or what were the children of Israel compared to those whom these slew? For verily those whom they massacred in a single city exceeded all the children of Israel. Nay, it is unlikely that mankind will see the like of this calamity, until the world comes to an end and perishes, except the final outbreak of Gog and Magog. For even Antichrist will spare such as follow him, though he destroy those who op-

From *A Literary History of Persia* by Edward G. Browne, Cambridge: Cambridge University Press, 1902, Vol. 2, pp. 427-431. Reprinted by permission.

pose him; but these [Tartars]¹ spared none, slaying women and
men and children, ripping open pregnant women and killing
unborn babes. Verily to God do we belong, and unto Him do we
return, and there is no strength and no power save in God, the
High, the Almighty, in face of this catastrophe, whereof the
sparks flew far and wide, and the hurt was universal; and which
passed over the lands like clouds driven by the wind. For these
were a people who emerged from the confines of China, and
attacked the cities of Turkistân, like Kâshghar and Balâsâghûn,
and thence advanced on the cities of Transoxiana, such as Samarqand, Bukhârâ and the like, taking possession of them, and
treating their inhabitants in such wise as we shall mention; and
of them one division then passed on into Khurâsân, until they
had made an end of taking possession, and destroying, and slaying, and plundering, and thence passing on to Ray, Hamadân
and the Highlands, and the cities contained therein, even to the
limits of 'Irâq,² whence they marched on the towns of Adhar-
bayjân and Arrâniyya, destroying them and slaying most of
their inhabitants, of whom none escaped save a small remnant;
and all this in less than a year; this is a thing whereof the like
hath not been heard. And when they had finished with Adhar-
bayjân and Arrâniyya, they passed on to Darband-i-Shirwân,
and occupied its cities, none of which escaped save the fortress
wherein was their King; wherefore they passed by it to the countries of the Lân and the Lakiz and the various nationalities
which dwell in that region, and plundered, slew, and destroyed
them to the full. And thence they made their way to the lands
of Qipchâq, who are the most numerous of the Turks, and slew
all such as withstood them, while the survivors fled to the fords
and mountain-tops, and abandoned their country, which these
Tartars overran. All this they did in the briefest space of time,

1. They are properly called *Tatar* (by the Arabs), or *Tâtâr* (by the
Persians). The European form was dictated by a desire to connect them
with Tartarus, on account of their hellish deeds and infernal cruelty. (Tr.)

2. I.e., Mesopotamia, or *'Irâq-i-'Arab* as it is now called to distinguish it
from *'Irâq-i-'Ajam*. (Tr.) All the place-names which precede and follow
simply describe the rapid westward progress of the Mongols from northern
China to western Irân.

remaining only for so long as their march required and no more.

Another division, distinct from that mentioned above, marched on Ghazna and its dependencies, and those parts of India, Sîstân and Kirmân which border thereon, and wrought therein deeds like unto the other, nay, yet more grievous. Now this is a thing the like of which ear hath not heard; for Alexander, concerning whom historians agree that he conquered the world, did not do so with such swiftness, but only in the space of about ten years; neither did he slay, but was satisfied that men should be subject to him. But these Tartars conquered most of the habitable globe, and the best, the most flourishing and most populous part thereof, and that whereof the inhabitants were the most advanced in character and conduct, in about a year; nor did any country escape their devastations which did not fearfully expect them and dread their arrival.

Moreover they need no commissariat, nor the conveyance of supplies, for they have with them sheep, cows, horses, and the like quadrupeds, the flesh of which they eat, [needing] naught else. As for their beasts which they ride, these dig into the earth with their hoofs and eat the roots of plants, knowing naught of barley. And so, when they alight anywhere, they have need of nothing from without. As for their religion, they worship the sun when it arises, and regard nothing as unlawful, for they eat all beasts, even dogs, pigs, and the like; nor do they recognise the marriage-tie, for several men are in marital relations with one woman, and if a child is born, it knows not who is its father.

Therefore Islâm and the Muslims have been afflicted during this period with calamities wherewith no people hath been visited. These Tartars (may God confound them!) came from the East, and wrought deeds which horrify all who hear of them, and which thou shalt, please God, see set forth in full detail in their proper connection. And of these [calamities] was the invasion of Syria by the Franks (may God curse them!) out of the West, and their attack on Egypt, and occupation of the port of Damietta therein, so that Egypt and Syria were like to be conquered by them, but for the grace of God and the help which He vouchsafed us against them, as we have mentioned under the year 614 (A.D. 1217-18). Of these [calamities], moreover, was

that the sword was drawn between those [of the Muslims] who
escaped from these two foes, and strife was rampant [amongst
them], as we have also mentioned: and verily unto God do we
belong and unto Him do we return! We ask God to vouchsafe
victory to Islâm and the Muslims, for there is none other to aid,
help, or defend the True Faith. But if God intends evil to any
people, naught can avert it, nor have they any ruler save Him.
As for these Tartars, their achievements were only rendered
possible by the absence of any effective obstacle; and the cause
of this absence was that Muhammad Khwârazmshâh[3] had overrun the [Muslim] lands, slaying and destroying their Kings, so
that he remained alone ruling over all these countries; wherefore, when he was defeated by the Tartars, none was left in the
lands to check those or protect these, that so God might accomplish a thing which was to be done.

It is now time for us to describe how they first burst forth into
the [Muslim] lands.[4]

"Stories have been related to me," he says, "which the hearer
can scarcely credit, as to the terror of them [i.e., the Mongols]
which God Almighty cast into men's hearts; so that it is said that
a single one of them would enter a village or a quarter wherein
were many people, and would continue to slay them one after
another, none daring to stretch forth his hand against this horseman. And I have heard that one of them took a man captive,
but had not with him any weapon wherewith to kill him; and
he said to his prisoner, 'Lay your head on the ground and do not
move'; and he did so, and the Tartar went and fetched his sword
and slew him therewith. Another man related to me as follows:
—'I was going,' said he, 'with seventeen others along a road, and

3. The last Muslim defender in Irân against the Mongols. At the beginning
of the thirteenth century, the empire of the Khwarazmshah included nearly
the whole of Persia.

4. This was written nearly thirty years before the crowning catastrophe,
to wit, the sack of Baghdâd and the extinction of the Caliphate, took place;
for this happened in February, 1258, while Ibn al-Athîr concludes his
chronicle with the year . . . 1230-31, and died two years later. Nor did he
witness the horrors of which he writes, but only heard them from terrified
fugitives, of whose personal narratives he records several under the year
with which his chronicle closes. (Tr.)

there met us a Tartar horseman, and bade us bind one another's arms. My companions began to do as he bade them, but I said to them, "He is but one man; wherefore, then, should we not kill him and flee?" They replied, "We are afraid." I said, "This man intends to kill you immediately; let us therefore rather kill him, that perhaps God may deliver us." But I swear by God that not one of them dared to do this, so I took a knife and slew him, and we fled and escaped.' And such occurrences were many."

JUVAINÎ: FROM THE HISTORY OF
THE WORLD CONQUEROR

OF THE LAWS WHICH CHINGIZ-KHAN FRAMED AND THE YASAS
WHICH HE PROMULGATED AFTER HIS RISE TO POWER

God Almighty in wisdom and intelligence distinguished Chingiz-Khan from all his coevals and in alertness of mind and absoluteness of power exalted him above all the kings of the world; so that all that has been recorded touching the practice of the mighty Chosroes[1] of old and all that has been written concerning the customs and usages of the Pharaohs and Caesars was by Chingiz-Khan invented from the page of his own mind without the toil of perusing records or the trouble of conforming with tradition; while all that pertains to the method of subjugating countries and relates to the crushing of the power of enemies and the raising of the station of followers was the product of his own understanding and the compilation of his own intellect. And indeed, Alexander, who was so addicted to the devising of talismans and the solving of enigmas, had he lived in the age of Chingiz-Khan, would have been his pupil in craft and cunning, and of all the talismans for the taking of strongholds he would have found none better than blindly to follow in his footsteps: whereof there can be no clearer proof nor more certain

From *The History of the World Conqueror* by 'Ala-ad-Din 'Ata-Malik *Juvaini Translated from the text of Mirza Muhammad Qazvini*, trans. by John Andrew Boyle, Manchester: Manchester University Press, 1958, vol. I, pp. 23-34, 153, 159-64, 201-7. Reprinted by permission.

1. Chosroes (Cyrus) Nushirwân (531-579), Persian king of Sassanian dynasty.

evidence than that having such numerous and powerful foes and
such mighty and well-accoutred enemies, whereof each was the
faghfur[2] of the time and the Chosroes of the age, he sallied forth,
a single man, with few troops and no accoutrement, and reduced
and subjugated the lords of the horizons from the East unto the
West; and whoever presumed to oppose and resist him, that
man, in enforcement of the *yasas* and ordinances which he imposed, he utterly destroyed, together with all his followers, children, partisans, armies, lands and territories. There has been
transmitted to us a tradition of the traditions of God which says:
*"Those are my horsemen; through them shall I avenge me on
those that rebelled against me,"* nor is there a shadow of doubt
but that these words are a reference to the horsemen of Chingiz-
Khan and to his people. And so it was that when the world by
reason of the variety of its creatures was become a raging sea,
and the kings and nobles of every country by reason of the
arrogance of pride and the insolence of vainglory had reached
the very zenith of *"Vainglory is my tunic, and pride my cloak,"*
then did God, in accordance with the above-mentioned promise,
endow Chingiz-Khan with the strength of might and the victory
of dominion—*"Verily, the might of the Lord is great indeed"*;[3]
and when through pride of wealth, and power, and station the
greater part of the cities and countries of the world encountered
him with rebellion and hatred and refused to yield allegiance
(and especially the countries of Islam, from the frontiers of
Turkestan to uttermost Syria), then wherever there was a king,
or a ruler, or the governor of a city that offered him resistance,
him he annihilated together with his family and followers, kinsmen and strangers; so that where there had been a hundred
thousand people there remained, without exaggeration, not a
hundred souls alive; as a proof of which statement may be cited
the fate of the various cities, whereof mention has been made in
the proper place.

　　In accordance and agreement with his own mind he estab-

　　2. The Facfur of Marco Polo, the Persian translation (lit. "son of God") of
one of the titles of the Emperor of China (Tr.), usually rendered in English
as "Son of Heaven."

　　3. Qur'ân LXX:12. (Tr.)

lished a rule for every occasion and a regulation for every circumstance; while for every crime he fixed a penalty. And since
the Tartar peoples had no script of their own, he gave orders
that Mongol children should learn writing from the Uighur[4];
and that these *yasas* and ordinances should be written down on
rolls. These rolls are called the *Great Book of Yasas* and are kept
in the treasury of the chief princes. Wherever a khan ascends
the throne, or a great army is mobilized, or the princes assemble
and begin [to consult together] concerning affairs of state and
the administration thereof, they produce these rolls and model
their actions thereon; and proceed with the disposition of armies
or the destruction of provinces and cities in the manner therein
prescribed.

At the time of the first beginnings of his dominion, when the
Mongol tribes were united to him, he abolished reprehensible
customs which had been practised by those peoples and had enjoyed recognition amongst them; and established such usages
as were praiseworthy from the point of view of reason. There
are many of these ordinances that are in conformity with the
Shari'at.[5]

In the messages which he sent in all directions calling on the
peoples to yield him allegiance, he never had recourse to intimi-
dation or violent threats, as was the custom with the tyrant kings
of old, who used to menace their enemies with the size of their
territory and the magnitude of their equipment and supplies;
the Mongols, on the contrary, as their uttermost warning, would
write thus: "If ye submit not, nor surrender, what know we
thereof? The Ancient God, He knoweth." If one reflects upon
their signification, [one sees that] these are the words of them
that put their trust in God—*God Almighty hath said "And for
him that putteth his trust in Him God will be all-sufficient"*[6]—
so that of necessity such a one obtains whatever he has borne in
his heart and yearned after, and attains his every wish.

4. The Uighur: a Turkish people of what is today western China—Sinki-
ang, sometimes called Chinese Turkestan.

5. I.e., Muslim law. Juvainî is at pains to show pagan Mongols as suitable
rulers over Muslims.

6. Qur'ân LXV:3. (Tr.)

Being the adherent of no religion and the follower of no creed, he eschewed bigotry, and the preference of one faith to another, and the placing of some above others; rather he honoured and respected the learned and pious of every sect, recognizing such conduct as the way to the Court of God. And as he viewed the Moslems with the eye of respect, so also did he hold the Christians and idolaters in high esteem. As for his children and grandchildren, several of them have chosen a religion according to their inclination, some adopting Islam, others embracing Christianity, others selecting idoltary and others again cleaving to the ancient canon of their fathers and forefathers and inclining in no direction; but these are now a minority. But though they have adopted some religion they still for the most part avoid all show of fanaticism and do not swerve from the *yasa* of Chingiz-Khan, namely, to consider all sects as one and not to distinguish them from one another.

It is one of their laudable cutsoms that they have closed the doors of ceremony, and preoccupation with titles, and excessive aloofness and inaccessibility; which things are customary with the fortunate and the mighty. When one of them ascends the throne of the Khanate, he receives one additional name, that of Khan or Qa'an, than which nothing more is written [in official documents]; while the other sons and his brothers are addressed by the name they were given at birth, both in their presence and in their absence; and this applies both to commoners and to the nobility. And likewise in directing their correspondence they write only the simple name, making no difference between Sultan and commoner; and write only the gist of the matter in hand, avoiding all superfluous titles and formulas.

He paid great attention to the chase and used to say that the hunting of wild beasts was a proper occupation for the commanders of armies; and that instruction and training therein was incumbent on warriors and men-at-arms, [who should learn] how the huntsmen come up with the quarry, how they hunt it, in what manner they array themselves and after what fashion they surround it according as the party is great or small. For when the Mongols wish to go a-hunting, they first send out scouts to ascertain what kinds of game are available and whether it is scarce or abundant. And when they are not engaged in warfare, they are ever eager for the chase and encourage their armies thus to occupy themselves; not for the sake of the game alone, but also in order that they may become accustomed and inured to hunting and familiarized with the handling of the bow and the endurance of hardships. Whenever the Khan sets out on the great hunt (which takes place at the beginning of the winter season), he issues orders that the troops stationed around his headquarters and in the neighbourhood of the *ordus*[7] shall make preparations for the chase, mounting several men from each company of ten in accordance with instructions and distributing such equipment in the way of arms and other matters as are suitable for the locality where it is desired to hunt. The right wing, left wing and centre of the army are drawn up and entrusted to the great emirs; and they set out together with the Royal Ladies and the concubines, as well as provisions of food and drink. For a month, or two, or three they form a hunting ring and drive the game slowly and gradually before them, taking care lest any escape from the ring. And if, unexpectedly, any game should break through, a minute inquiry is made into the cause and reason, and the commanders of thousands, hundreds and tens are clubbed therefor, and often even put to death. And if (for example) a man does not keep to the line (which they call *nerge*) but takes a step forwards or backwards, severe punishment is dealt out to him and is never remitted. For two or three months, by day and by night, they drive the game in this manner, like a flock of sheep, and dispatch messages to the Khan to inform him of the condition of the quarry, its scarcity or plenty, whither it has come and from whence it has been started. Finally, when the ring has been contracted to a diameter of two or three parasangs, they bind ropes together and cast felts over them; while the troops come to a halt all around the ring, standing shoulder to shoulder. The ring is now filled with the cries and commotion of every manner of game and the roaring and tumult of every kind of ferocious beast; all thinking that the appointed hour of "*And when the wild beasts shall be gathered*

7. *Ordus*: the largest unit of the Mongol army, sometimes translated as "horde."

together"[8] is come; lions becoming familiar with wild asses, hyaenas friendly with foxes, wolves intimate with hares. When the ring has been so much contracted that the wild beasts are unable to stir, first the Khan rides in together with some of his retinue; then, after he has wearied of the sport, they dismount upon high ground in the centre of the *nerge* to watch the princes likewise entering the ring, and after them, in due order, the *noyans*,[9] the commanders and the troops. Several days pass in this manner; then, when nothing is left of the game but a few wounded and emaciated stragglers, old men and greybeards humbly approach the Khan, offer up prayers for his well-being and intercede for the lives of the remaining animals asking that they be suffered to depart to some place nearer to grass and water. Thereupon they collect together all the game that they have bagged; and if the enumeration of every species of animal proves impracticable they count only the beasts of prey and the wild asses.

A friend has related how during the reign of Qa'an[10] they were hunting one winter in this fashion and Qa'an, in order to view the scene, had seated himself upon a hilltop; whereupon beasts of every kind set their faces towards his throne and from the foot of the hill set up a wailing and lamentation like that of petitioners for justice. Qa'an commanded that they should be set free and the hand of injury withheld from them.

It was Qa'an that commanded that between the land of Khitai[11] and his winter quarters a wall should be built of wood and clay, and gates set into it; so that much game might enter it from a great distance and they might hunt it after the manner described. In the region of Almaligh and Quyas[12] Chaghatai constructed a hunting ground in the very same manner.

Now war—with its killing, counting of the slain and sparing of the survivors—is after the same fashion, and indeed analogous

8. Qur'ân, LXXXI, 5. (Tr.)

9. *Noyans*: Generals.

10. I.e., Ogedei (Ogetei), the second son and first successor of Chîngîz-Khân. (Tr.)

11. I.e., China.

12. Almalîgh or Almalîq, the "Apple-Orchard," was situated . . . in the valley of the Ili [River]. . . . Quyas lay beyond Barskhan and two rivers, the Greater and the Lesser Keiken, flowed from it to the Ili. (Tr.)

in every detail, because all that is left in the neighbourhood of the battlefield are a few broken-down wretches.

With regard to the organization of their army, from the time of Adam down to the present day, when the greater part of the climes are at the disposition and command of the seed of Chingiz-Khan, it can be read in no history and is recorded in no book that any of the kings that were lords of the nations ever attained an army like the army of the Tartars, so patient of hardship, so grateful for comforts, so obedient to its commanders both in prosperity and adversity; and this not in hope of wages and fiefs nor in expectation of income or promotion. This is, indeed, the best way to organize an army; for lions, so long as they are not hungry, will not hunt or attack any animal. There is a Persian proverb: "An overfed dog catches no game," and it has also been said: "*Starve thy dog that it may follow thee.*"

What army in the whole world can equal the Mongol army? In time of action, when attacking and assaulting, they are like trained wild beasts out after game, and in the days of peace and security they are like sheep, yielding milk, and wool, and many other useful things. In misfortune and adversity they are free from dissension and opposition. It is an army after the fashion of a peasantry, being liable to all manner of contributions . . . and rendering without complaint whatever is enjoined upon it, whether *qupchur*,[13] occasional taxes, . . . the maintenance . . . of travellers or the upkeep of post stations . . . with the provision of mounts . . . and food . . . therefor. It is also a peasantry in the guise of an army, all of them, great and small, noble and base, in time of battle becoming swordsmen, archers and lancers and advancing in whatever manner the occasion requires. Whenever the slaying of foes and the attacking of rebels is purposed, they specify all that will be of service for that business, from the various arms and implements down to banners, needles, ropes, mounts and pack animals such as donkeys and camels; and every man must provide his share according to his ten or hundred. On the day of review, also, they display their equipment, and if only a little be missing, those responsible are

13. Originally equivalent to the Arabic *marâ'î* "pasturage levy" this term was afterwards applied to irregular levies in general. (Tr.)

severely punished. Even when they are actually engaged in fighting, there is exacted from them as much of the various taxes as in expedient, while any service which they used to perform when present devolves upon their wives and those of them that remain behind. Thus if work be afoot in which a man has his share of forced labour . . . , and if the man himself be absent, his wife goes forth in person and performs that duty in his stead.

The reviewing and mustering of the army has been so arranged that they have abolished the registry of inspection . . . and dismissed the officials and clerks. For they have divided all the people into companies of ten, appointing one of the ten to be the commander of the nine others; while from among each ten commanders one has been given the title of "commander of the hundred," all the hundred having been placed under his command. And so it is with each thousand men and so also with each ten thousand, over whom they have appointed a commander whom they call "commander of the *tümen*."[14] In accordance with this arrangement, if in an emergency any man or thing be required, they apply to the commanders of *tümen*; who in turn apply to the commanders of thousands, and so on down to the commanders of tens. There is a true equality in this; each man toils as much as the next, and no difference is made between them, no attention being paid to wealth or power. If there is a sudden call for soldiers an order is issued that so many thousand men must present themselves in such and such a place at such and such an hour of that day or night. *"They shall not retard it* (their appointed time) *an hour; and they shall not advance it."*[15] And they arrive not a twinkling of an eye before or after the appointed hour. Their obedience and submissiveness is such that if there be a commander of a hundred thousand between whom and the Khan there is a distance of sunrise and sunset, and if he but commit some fault, the Khan dispatches a single horseman to punish him after the manner prescribed: if his head has been demanded, he cuts it off, and if gold be required, he takes it from him.

14. In Turkish "ten thousand." This pattern of organization was taken over by other dynasties, particularly the Mamlûks in Egypt.
15. Qur'ân VII:32. (Tr.)

Another *yasa* is that no man may depart to another unit than the hundred, thousand or ten to which he has been assigned, nor may he seek refuge elsewhere. And if this order be transgressed the man who transferred is executed in the presence of the troops, while he that received him is severely punished. For this reason no man can give refuge to another; if (for example) the commander be a prince, he does not permit the meanest person to take refuge in his company and so avoids a breach of the *yasa*. Therefore no man can take liberties with his commander or leader, nor can another commander entice him away.

Furthermore, when moonlike damsels are found in the army they are gathered together and dispatched from the tens to the hundreds, and each man makes a different choice up to the commander of the *tümen*, who makes his choice also and takes the maidens so chosen to the Khan or the princes. These too make their selection, and upon those that are deemed worthy and are fair to look upon they recite the words "*Keep them honourably*," and upon the other, "*Put them away with kindness*."[16] And they cause them to attend on the Royal Ladies until such time as it pleases them to bestow them on others or to lie with them themselves.

Again, when the extent of their territories became broad and vast and important events fell out, it became essential to ascertain the activities of their enemies, and it was also necessary to transport goods from the West to the East and from the Far East to the West. Therefore throughout the length and breadth of the land they established *yams*,[17] and made arrangements for the upkeep and expenses of each *yam*, assigning thereto a fixed number of men and beasts as well as food, drink and other necessities. All this they shared out amongst the *tümen*, each two *tümen* having to supply one *yam*. Thus, in accordance with the census, they so distribute and exact the charge, that messengers need make no long detour in order to obtain fresh mounts while at the same time the peasantry and the army are not placed in constant inconvenience. Moreover strict orders were issued to

16. Qur'ân II:229. (Tr.)
17. Post stations.

the messengers with regard to the sparing of the mounts, etc., to recount all of which would delay us too long. Every year the *yams* are inspected, and whatever is missing or lost has to be replaced by the peasantry.

Since all countries and peoples have come under their domination, they have established a census after their accustomed fashion and classified everyone into tens, hundreds and thousands; and required military service and the equipment of *yams* together with the expenses entailed and the provision of fodder —this is addition to ordinary taxes; and over and above all this they have fixed the *qupchur*[18] charges also.

They have a custom that if an official or a peasant die, they do not interfere with the estate he leaves, be it much or little, nor may anyone else tamper with it. And if he have no heir, it is given to his apprentice or his slave. On no account is the property of a dead man admitted to the treasury, for they regard such a procedure as inauspicious.

When Hûlegû appointed me to [the governorship of] Baghdad, the inheritance taxes were in force in all that region; I swept away that system and abolished the imposts that had been levied in the countries of Tustar and Bayat.[19]

There are many other *yasas*, to record each of which would delay us too long; we have therefore limited ourselves to the mention of the above.

OF MERV AND THE FATE THEREOF

Merv was the residence of Sultan Sanjar[20] and the rendezvous of great and small. In extent of territory it excelled among the lands of Khorasan, and the bird of peace and security flew over its confines. The number of its chief men rivalled the drops of April rain, and its earth contended with the heavens; its *dihqans*, from the greatness of their riches, breathed the breath of equal-

18. Qupchur: originally equivalent to the Arabic pasturage levy, this term was afterward applied to irregular levies in general.
19. I.e. Shustar in Khuzistan; [Bayat], the westernmost district of Khuzistan (north of the Kerkha). (Tr.)
20. Sanjar, Seljûq *sultân* defeated by Kara-Khitay in 1141. Merv is in Khurâsân in central Irân.

ity with the monarchs and emirs of the age and set down the
foot of parity with the mighty and haughty ones of the world.

. . . Chingiz-Khan dispatched Toli to conquer the countries of
Khorasan with men of action and lions of battle; and raising
levies from the subject territories which lay across their path
such as Abivard, Sarakhs, etc., they assembled an army of seven
thousand men. Drawing near to Merv they sent four hundred
horsemen across the ford by way of vanguard. These came by
night to the bank where the Turcomans[21] were encamped and
watched their activities. Twelve thousand Turcoman horsemen
were assembled there and used at every dawn to go to the gates
in order to attack the town.

> Upon a jet-black night whose face was washed with pitch,
> when neither Mars was visible, nor Saturn, nor Mercury

the Mongols laid an ambush in their pathway and waited in
silence. The Turcomans were unable to recognize one another
[in the dark] and as they arrived in small groups the Mongols
cast them into the water and on to the wind of annihilation.
Having thus broken their strength the Mongols came like the
wind to their encampment and left the trace of the wolf upon
the herd. And thus the Turcomans, whose numbers exceeded
seventy thousand, were defeated by a mere handful of men.
Most of them flung themselves into the water and were drowned,
while the remainder took to flight. For since the Mongols were
aided by Fortune and assisted by Fate, none was able to contend
with them and he whose time was not yet come fled away casting down his arms.

The Mongols proceeded in this manner till nightfall and collected on the plain a herd of sixty thousand cattle (including
sheep) which the Turcomans had driven from the gates, as well
as other possessions, the amount of which was beyond computation. On the next day, which was the first of Muharram, 618
[25th of February, 1221], and the last of the lives of most of the

21. By Turcomans Juvainî means the nomadic Turkish tribes (specifically
the Ghuzz from whom the Seljûqs and later Ottomans were descended) who
lived in the area and who might fight either for the Mongols or for the
Muslims.

inhabitants of Merv, Toli, that furious lion, arrived with an army like unto a dark night and a raging sea and in multitude exceeding the sands of the desert, "all warriors of great renown."

He advanced in person to the Gate of Victory together with some five hundred horse and rode right round the town; and for six days they inspected the outworks, walls, moat and minaret [sic][22] and reached the conclusion that the townspeople's supplies would suffice to defend them and that the walls were a stout bastion that would withstand their attack.

On the seventh day,

> When the shining sun sought to cast his glittering lasso
>   from the lofty citadel,

the armies gathered together and halted before the Shahristan Gate. They joined battle, some two hundred men issuing from the gate and attacking. Toli dismounted in person—

> He uttered a roar like a furious elephant, raised his
>   shield above his head and showed his hand

—and advanced upon them. And the Mongols attacked in his company driving them back into the town. Others issued forth from another gate but the Mongols stationed there repelled the attack. And so the townspeople were nowhere able to achieve any result and could not even put their heads out of the gates. Finally the world donned garments of mourning, and the Mongols took up positions in several rings around the fortifications and kept watch throughout the night, so that none had any means of egress.

Mujir-al-Mulk[23] saw no way out save surrender and submission. In the morning, therefore, when the sun had raised the black veil from his moonlike face, he dispatched Jamal-ad-Din, one of the chief *imams*[24] of Merv, as his ambassador and sued for quarter. Being reassured by fair words and promises, he got together presents from the quadrupeds in the town—horses, camels and mules—and went to Toli [in person]. Toli ques-

22. *manâra*: perhaps the turrets on the wall are meant. (Tr.)
23. Governor left by the Khwarazmshah.
24. Religious leaders.

tioned him about the town and asked for details regarding the wealthy and notable. Mujir-al-Mulk gave him a list of two hundred persons, and Toli ordered them to be brought into his presence. Of the questioning of these persons one might have said that *"the Earth quaked with her quaking"* and of the digging up of their buried possessions, both money and goods, that *"the Earth cast forth her burdens."*[25]

The Mongels now entered the town and drove all the inhabitants, nobles and commoners, out on to the plain. For four days and nights the people continued to come out of the town; the Mongols detained them all, separating the women from the men. Alas! how many peri-like[26] ones did they drag from the bosoms of their husbands! How many sisters did they separate from their brothers! How many parents were distraught at the ravishment of their virgin daughters!

The Mongols ordered that, apart from four hundred artisans whom they specified and selected from amongst the men and some children, girls and boys, whom they bore off into captivity, the whole population, including the women and children, should be killed, and no one, whether woman or man, be spared. The people of Merv were then distributed among the soldiers and levies, and, in short, to each man was allotted the execution of three or four hundred persons. The people . . . of Sarakhs[27] in avenging their cadi exceeded [the ferocity of] such as had no knowledge of Islam or religion and passed all bounds in the abasement and humiliation [of their fellow Moslems]. So many had been killed by nightfall that the mountains became hillocks,[28] and the plain was soaked with the blood of the mighty.

We have grown old in a land in whose expanses one treads on nought but the cheeks of maidens and the breasts of striplings.

Then, at Toli's command, the outworks were destroyed, the citadel levelled with the ground and the *maqsura* of the mosque

25. Quotations from Qur'ân XLIX: 1 and 2.
26. Fairy-faced.
27. Sarakhs: a town not far southeast of Merv.
28. I.e. the mountains seemed no more than hillocks when surounded by the huge piles of dead. (Tr.)

belonging to the sect of the greatest *imam* Abu-Hanifa[29] (*God have mercy on him!*) set on fire. One might have said that this was in vengeance for what befell in the time of the righteous rule of Shams-ad-Din Mas'ud of Herat, the vizier of the kingdom of Sultan Tekish,[30] who caused a Friday mosque to be built for the followers of the *imam* Shafi'i,[31] which fanatics set fire to by night.

When the Mongols had finished plundering and leading captive and massacring, Ziya-ad-Din 'Ali, one of the notables of Merv, who had been spared by reason of his retirement, received orders to enter the town and be emir and governor of those that reassembled out of nooks and crannies. The Mongols also left Barmas as *shahna*.[32]

When the army departed, those that had sought refuge in holes and cavities came out again, and there were gathered together some five thousand persons. A party of Mongols belonging to the rearguard then arrived and wished to have their share of slaughter. They commanded therefore that each person should bring a skirtful of grain out on to the plain for the Mongols; and in this way they cast into the well of annihilation most of those that had previously escaped. Then they proceeded along the road to Nishapur and slew all they found of those who had turned back from the plain and fled from the Mongols when half way out to meet them. In this manner many persons lost their lives, and hereafter Taisi, who had turned back from Yeme Noyan's army, arrived in Merv; he too laid balm on their wounds, and all that the Mongols found there were drawn out of the noose of life and caused to drink the draught of annihilation.

> *By God, we live in violent times: if we saw them in a*
> *dream we should be terrified.*

29. Abû-Hanîfa al-Nu'mân was the founder of the Hânifî sect, one of the four orthodox sects of the Sunnîs. (Tr.) *Maqsûra*: a box or stall in the mosque near the *mihrâb* (the niche indicating the direction of prayer) reserved for the ruler.

30. Sultân Tekish, the father of Muhammad Khwarazm-Shah. (Tr.)

31. Muhammad b. Idrîs al-Shâfi'î, was the founder of the Shâfi'î sect of Sunnî Islâm. (Tr.)

32. The representative of the conqueror in conquered territory responsible in particular for the collection of tribute.

The people are in such an evil plight that he that has
died deserves to rejoice.

Now the *sayyid* 'Izz-ad-Din Nassaba was one of the great
sayyids[33] and renowned for his piety and virtue. He now together with other other persons passed thirteen days and nights
in counting the people slain within the town. Taking into account only those that were plain to see and leaving aside those
that had been killed in holes and cavities and in the villages and
deserts, they arrived at a figure of more than one million three
hundred thousand. 'Izz-ad-Din quoted a quartain of 'Umar-i-
Khayyam[34] which was *à propos* of the occasion:

The form of a cup in which it has been moulded together
Even the drunkard does not hold it lawful to shatter.
So many lovely heads and feet—by his art
Who has joined them in love and who has broken them in hate?

OF THE DEEDS AND ACTIONS OF QA'AN[35]

When the hand of the creation of power had placed the signet
of the Empire upon the finger of his fortune, as has already been
set forth, he dispatched armies to all sides and every land, and
most of the climes were purged of his adversaries. The fame of
justice and beneficence became an ear-ring in all ears and his
favours and kindnesses like bracelets on the hands and forearms
of all. His Court became an asylum to all the world and his presence a refuge and shelter to the whole earth. As the lights of the
dawn of his equity were without the dust of the darkness of evening . . . , so the extent of his empire reached from farthest
Chin and Machin to the utmost districts of Syria. . . . His
bounty was general to all mankind, and waited not for month
or year.[36] His being and generosity were two courses running
neck and neck, and his nature and constancy twin sucklings
at one breast. . . . During his reign the reeling world came to

---

33. *Sayyid*: the title given to descendants of 'Alî in the line of his son
Husain.
34. Famous Persian mathematician and poet (d. *ca.* 1132).
35. Ogetei, Chîngîz' successor.
36. I.e. he was generous at all times, not merely on festive occasions. (Tr.)

rest and the cruelties of the implacable heavens were tempered. In the time of his Khanate

> Heaven, that swift steed that had never been tamed, ambled
>   gently under the saddle of obedience to him.

And in the prospect of his mercy and compassion hope revived in every breast. And such as had survived the sword remained in the noose of life and the bed of security. The banners of the Mohammedan faith were unfurled in the farthest lands of infidelity and the remotest countries of polytheism, whose nostrils the scent of Islam had not yet reached. And opposite the temples of idols were reared up the shrines of God the Merciful. The fame of his justice caused the chaining of strays, and the report of his bounty occasioned the capture of wild beasts. Because of the awe he inspired the froward were enslaved, and by reason of the severity of his punishment the haughty were humbled. His *yarligh*[37] did the work of the sword, and the pages of his letters stole the lustre from the sabres of cavalry.

> *He routed them with fear before he pursued them and put*
>   *them to flight with letters, without squadrons.*

The generals of his Court and the servants of his fortune led armies to the East and the West, while Qa'an was able to dispense with being present in person, and in accordance with the verses,

> The world is half for rejoicing and half for acquiring
>   fame.
> When thou loosenest thine own bonds are loosened, and when
>   thou bindest thou thyself art bound,

and in opposition to the words of advisers and censurers, rejecting this saying of theirs:

> *When the king spends his mornings engaged in amusement,*
>   *condemn his kingdom to woe and destruction,*

he was ever spreading the carpet of merrymaking and treading the path of excess in constant application to wine and the company of peri-faced ones of beautiful form.

37. *Yarligh*: Royal proclamation or decree.

In the distribution of gifts he bore the palm from all his predecessors. Being by nature extravagantly bountiful and liberal he
gave away everything that came in from the farthest and nearest parts of the Empire without its being registered by account-
ant . . . or inspector. . . . No mortal returned from his presence without his lot or share and no petitioner heard from his
tongue the words *No* and *Nay*.[38]

> *No in answering cuts the wings of desires and on that*
> *account resembles the scissors.*

Those in need that came to him from every side speedily returned with their wishes unexpectedly fulfilled, and office-seek-
ers and petitioners straightway went home with whatever each
of them had desired.

> *For the voice of the petitioner was sweeter and more*
> *desirable to his ear than the melodies of music.*

Upon those that came from distant and rebellious . . . lands he
bestowed presents in the same way as upon those that were from
near and subject countries. And no one went away from his
presence disappointed or frustrated. From time to time the pillars of the Empire and the Court would object to his extravagance, saying that if there was no escape from his conferring of
gifts and favours it was incumbent upon him to bestow them on
his servants and subjects. Qa'an would reply: "The censorious
are devoid of the jewel of wit and understanding, and their
words are idle in two ways. Firstly, because when the fame of
our manners and customs has reached the rebellious, their hearts
will necessarily incline towards us, for *'Man is the slave of
kindness'*; and by reason of that beneficence the army and the
people will be saved the trouble of encountering and fighting
them and spared much toil and hardship. And secondly, it is even
clearer—since this world has notoriously been faithful to none
but in the end has turned the back of cruelty—that it beseems a
wide-awake man, who is adorned with the light of understanding, to keep himself alive by the perpetuation of a good name."

38. A reference to the shape of the letter *lâm-alif* used to write *lâ* "no."

> Come, let us not tread the world in evil; let us by
>   striving take every opportunity of doing good.
> If I die with a good name, it is well; I need a name
>   since for the body there is death.

And whenever the kings of olden time were mentioned together with their customs and usages, and reference was made to their storing up and hoarding of gold and silver, he would say that those who deposited valuable treasures beneath the earth were devoid of their share of intellect and strong understanding, for no distinction could be made between that treasure and the dust, seeing that it could be neither the cause of warding off harm nor the occasion of a source of advantage. When the day of doom arrived, of what assistance would be the treasures they had laid by and of what avail to them?

> *Where are the Khusraus, the first mighty ones? They*
>   *stored up treasures, and the treasures endured not,*
>   *neither did they endure.*

"As for us, for the sake of our good name we shall store up our treasures in the corners of men's hearts and shall leave nothing over for the morrow.

> Even in their sleep the Sultans of the age do not see
>   as much wealth as is the tenth part of what we bestow
>   as presents from what is ready at hand.
> We have given the silver and gold of the whole world to
>   mankind because they are the acts of generosity of
>   our riskless hand."

The above is but a brief account of his actions. It may be that those who hear and read this history will regard these statements as belonging to the category of *"The fairest poetry is the falsest."* In order to prove their truth we shall in a succinct manner free from the contingencies of detraction or hyperbole recount some few anecdotes wherefrom these statements may be fully confirmed, though indeed they are but little out of much and as one out of a thousand.

(i) It is laid down in the *yasa* and custom of the Mongols that in the season of spring and summer no one may sit in water by day, nor wash his hands in a stream, nor draw water in gold or silver vessels, nor lay out washed garments upon the plain; it being their belief that such actions increase the thunder and lightning. For in the country where they live it rains most of the time from the beginning of spring until the end of summer, and the clashing of the thunder is such that when it roars *"they thrust their fingers into their ears because of the thunder-clap, for fear of death,"* and the flashing of the lightning is such that *"the lightning almost snatcheth away their eyes"*;[39] and it has been observed that when it lightnings and thunders they become *"as mute as fishes."* Every year that one of them is struck by lightning they drive his tribe and household out from amongst the tribes for a period of three years, during which time they may not enter the *ordu*[40] of the princes. Similarly if an animal in their herds and flocks is so struck, they proceed in the same manner for several months. And when such a happening occurs they eat no food for the remainder of the month, and as in the case of their periods of mourning, they hold a celebration . . . at the end of that month.

One day Qa'an was returning from his hunting ground together with Chaghatai when at noon they beheld a Moslem sitting in midstream washing himself. Now Chaghatai was extremely zealous in enforcing the *yasa* and spared no one who had deviated even slightly from it. When he caught sight of this man in the water, from the flame of the fire of his anger he wished to commit the earth of his being to the wind of annihilation and to cut off the source of his life. But Qa'an said: "To-day it is late and we are tired. This man shall be held in custody until to-morrow, when we can inquire into his case and ascertain the reason for his violating our *yasa*." And he ordered Danishmand Hajib to take charge of the man till the morning, when his innocence or guilt might be discovered; he also told Danishmand, in secret, to have a *balish*[41] of silver thrown in the water where the man had been sitting and to instruct the

39. Qur'ân II:18. (Tr.)
40. Camp.
41. Originally an ingot of metal weighing about 4½ pounds. The *balish* was the currency of the steppes at the beginning of the thirteenth century.

man, when he was examined, to say that he was a poor man with many obligations, that this *balish* was his whole capital and that it was for this reason that he had acted so rashly. On the next day the guilty man was examined in Qa'an's presence. Qa'an listened to the excuse with the ear of acceptance, but by way of precaution someone went to the spot and the *balish* was taken out of the water. Then Qa'an said: "To whom could it occur to meditate breaking our *yasa* and commandment or swerving a single hair's-breadth therefrom? But it seems to be that this man is a person of poor estate and little property and so has sacrificed himself for a single *balish*." He commanded that the man should be given ten more *balish* in addition to the one; and a written statement was taken from him that he would not commit a similar action again. And so he not only escaped with his life but acquired property. And on this account free-men became the slaves of this act, which was better than immense treasures.

> *And from his fair sword there came blades wherewith the freeman was enslaved and the careworn liberated.*

(ii) When they first rose to power they made a *yasa* that no one should slaughter animals by cutting their throats but should slit open their breasts after the Mongols' own fashion.

A Moslem bought a sheep in the market, took it home, closed the gates securely and slaughtered the animal after the Moslem fashion in [the lane between] two or three houses, not knowing that he was being watched by a Qifchaq, who, awaiting his opportunity, had followed him from the market. When he drew the knife across the sheep's throat, the Qifchaq leapt down from the roof, bound him tight and bore him off to the Court of the World-Emperor. Qa'an examined the case and sent out scribes to investigate. When the circumstances were made known to his clear intellect, he spoke as follows: "This poor man has observed the commandment of our *yasa* and this Turk has infringed it." The Moslem's life was spared and he was treated with favour . . . , while the ill-natured Qifchaq was handed over to the executioners of Fate.

> If one zephyr of thy favour passes through the forest, the
> musk deer carries off its navel from the jaws of the lion.

Expansion of Islâm

The patchwork of Muslim states and societies that had emerged by the fourteenth century was held together by common religious traditions, by a knowledge of Arabic among the learnèd, and by a reverence for the Sacred Law. Travelers moved to and fro freely, for one of the duties laid upon pious Muslims was to make a pilgrimage to Mecca at least once in a lifetime. As more and more distant regions came within the realm of Islâm, the flow of pilgrims was constant.

Men expert in Arabic and the sacred sciences could fit in almost anywhere, and in outlying regions, where learning was hard to come by, a master of the Qur'ân and of the Sacred Law was often especially welcome. Such persons were able to instruct people not only in matters of religion but in matters of law and everyday manners, thus easing the transition from local folkways to participation in the great world of Islâm.

Muhammad ibn-'Abdallâh ibn Batûta (1304-1377) was a young man of learning who made a pilgrimage to Mecca and kept on traveling for some twenty-five years before returning to his birthplace in Tangiers. He traversed Persia, Asia Minor, and the Crimea, visited Constantinople, then went overland across the Volga to India, where he set out for China. The following account of his travels deals with his experiences in the Maldive Islands, where he served as judge of the Sacred Law, more or less against his will, and with his visit to China. He returned via Sumatra, Arabia, and North Africa. In Tangiers someone else edited his voluminous recollections.

Ibn Batûta's picture of how Islâm made converts in the Maldive Islands and of the role of traders, religious experts, and local rulers in propagating the faith of Muhammad, offers vivid insight into a process which continued to operate wherever Islâm has abutted upon primitive societies. Vast regions of Africa and southeast Asia have been brought within the realm of Islâm and conversion continues even today.

IBN BATÛTA: FROM TRAVELS

. . . I decided to travel to Dhîbat-al-Mahal [Maldive is-
lands], about which I had heard a number of tales. Ten days
after embarking at Câlicût we reached these islands, which are
one of the wonders of the world and number about two thousand
in all. Each hundred or less of them form a circular cluster resembling a ring, this ring having one entrance like a gateway,
and only through this entrance can ships reach the islands.
When a vessel arrives at any one of them it must needs take one
of the inhabitants to pilot it to the other islands. They are so
close-set that on leaving one island the tops of the palms on another are visible. If a ship loses its course it is unable to enter
and is carried by the wind to the Coromandel coast or Ceylon.

The inhabitants of the Maldives are all Muslims, pious and
upright. The islands are divided into twelve districts, each under
a governor whom they call the *Kardûi*. The district of Mahal,
which has given its name to the whole archipelago, is the residence of their sultans. There is no agriculture at all on any of
the islands, except that a cereal resembling millet is grown in
one district and carried thence to Mahal. The inhabitants live on
a fish called *qulb-al-mâs*,[1] which has red flesh and no grease and
smells like mutton. On catching it they cut it in four, cook it
lightly, then smoke it in palm leaf baskets. When it is quite dry,
they eat it. Some of these fish are exported to India, China, and
Yemen. Most of the trees on those islands are coco-palms, which
with the fish mentioned above provide food for the inhabitants.
The coco-palm is an extraordinary tree; it bears twelve bunches
a year, one in each month. Some are small, some large, some
dry and some green, never changing. They make milk, oil, and
honey from it, as we have already related.

The people of the Maldive Islands are upright and pious,

From *Travels in Asia and Africa: 1325-1354, by Ibn Battûta*, trans. by
H. A. R. Gibb, New York, 1929, pp. 241-60, 282-300. Reprinted by permission
of Routledge & Kegan Paul, Ltd.

1. Maldive *kalu-bili-mas*, black bonito fish, from its black appearance after
smoking. (Tr.)

sound in belief and sincere in thought; their bodies are weak, they are unused to fighting, and their armour is prayer. Once when I ordered a thief's hand to be cut off, a number of those in the room fainted. The Indian pirates do not raid or molest them, as they have learned from experience that anyone who seizes anything from them speedily meets misfortune. In each island of theirs there are beautiful mosques, and most of their buildings are made of wood. They are very cleanly and avoid filth; most of them bathe twice a day to cleanse themselves, because of the extreme heat there and their profuse perspiration. They make plentiful use of perfumed oils, such as oil of sandalwood. Their garments are simply aprons; one they tie round their waists in place of trousers, and on their backs they place other cloths resembling the pilgrim garments. Some wear a turban, others a small kerchief instead. When any of them meets the qâdî[2] or preacher, he removes his cloth from his shoulders, uncovering his back, and accompanies him thus to his house. All, high or low, are bare-footed; their lanes are kept swept and clean and are shaded by trees, so that to walk in them is like walking in an orchard. In spite of that every person entering a house must wash his feet with water from a jar kept in a chamber in the vestibule, and wipe them with a rough towel of palm matting which he finds there. The same practice is followed on entering a mosque.

From these islands there are exported the fish we have mentioned, coconuts, cloths, and cotton turbans, as well as brass utensils, of which they have a great many, cowrie shells, and *qanbar*. This is the hairy integument of the coconut, which they tan in pits on the shore, and afterwards beat out with bars; the women then spin it and it is made into cords for sewing [the planks of] ships together. These cords are exported to India, China, and Yemen, and are better than hemp. The Indian and Yemenite ships are sewn together with them, for the Indian Ocean is full of reefs, and if a ship is nailed with iron nails it breaks up on striking the rocks, whereas if it is sewn together with cords, it is given a certain resilience and does not fall to pieces. The inhabitants of these islands use cowrie shells as

2. Qâdî: judge.

money. This is an animal which they gather in the sea and place in pits, where its flesh disappears, leaving its white shell. They are used for buying and selling at the rate of four hundred thousand shells for a gold dinar,[3] but they often fall in value to twelve hundred thousand for a dinar. They sell them in exchange for rice to the people of Bengal, who also use them as money, as well as to the Yemenites, who use them instead of sand [as ballast] in their ships. These shells are used also by the negroes in their lands; I saw them being sold at Mâllî and Gawgaw[4] at the rate of 1,150 for a gold dinar.

Their womenfolk do not cover their hands, not even their queen does so, and they comb their hair and gather it at one side. Most of them wear only an apron from their waists to the ground, the rest of their bodies being uncovered. When I held the qâdîship there, I tried to put an end to this practice and ordered them to wear clothes, but I met with no success. No woman was admitted to my presence in a lawsuit unless her body was covered, but apart from that I was unable to effect anything. I had some slave-girls who wore garments like those worn at Delhi and who covered their heads, but it was more of a disfigurement than an ornament in their case, since they were not accustomed to it. A singular custom amongst them is to hire themselves out as servants in houses at a fixed wage of five dinars or less, their employer being responsible for their upkeep; they do not look upon this as dishonourable, and most of their girls do so. You will find ten or twenty of them in a rich man's house. Every utensil that a girl breaks is charged up against her. When she wishes to transfer from one house to another, her new employers give her the sum which she owes to her former employers; she pays this to the latter and remains so much in debt to her new employers. The chief occupation of these hired women is spinning qanbar. It is easy to get married in these islands on account of the smallness of the dowries and the pleasures of their women's society. When ships arrive, the crew marry wives, and when they are about to sail they divorce

3. Dînâr: The gold unit of the Arab monetary system, weighing about 4.25 grams.
4. In the West African Sahara.

them. It is really a sort of temporary marriage. The women never leave their country.*

The cause of these islands becoming Mohammedan was, as it is generally received among them, and as some learned and respectable persons among them informed me, as follows. When they were in a state of infidelity, there appeared to them every month a spectre from among the genii. This came from the sea. Its appearance was that of a ship filled with candles. When they saw him, it was their custom to take and dress up a young woman who was a virgin, and place her in the idol-temple which stood on the sea-shore, and had windows looking towards him. Here they left her for the night. When they came in the morning, they found her vitiated and dead. This they continued doing month after month, casting lots among themselves, and each, to whom the lot fell, giving up and dressing out his daughter for the spectre. After this there came to them a western Arab, named Abu'l Barakât the Berber. This was a holy man, and one who had committed the Korân to memory. He happened to lodge in the house of an old woman in the island of Mohl.⁵ One day, when he entered the house, he saw her with a company of her female inmates weeping and lamenting, and asked them what was the matter. A person who acted as interpreter between him and them said, that the lot had fallen upon this old woman, who was now adorning her daughter for the spectre: for this it was she was crying: this too was her only child. The Mogrebine,⁶ who was a beardless man, said to her: I will go to the spectre to-night instead of thy daughter. If he takes me, then I shall redeem her: but if I come off safe, then that will be to the praise of God. They carried him accordingly to the idol-house that night, as if he had been the daughter of the old woman, the magistrate knowing nothing whatever of the matter. The Mogrebine entered, and sitting down in the window, began to read

* The following paragraph on the Islâmization of the Maldives is from *The Travels of Ibn Batuta*, trans. by Samuel Lee, London: The Oriental Translation Committee, 1829, pp. 179-80.

5. The principal island of the group, Mahal.

6. Referring to Abû al-Barakât.

the Korân. By and bye the spectre came, with eyes flaming like fire; but when he had got near enough to hear the Korân, he plunged into the sea. In this manner the Mogrebine remained till morning, reading his Korân, when the old woman came with her household, and the great personages of the district, in order to fetch out the young woman and burn her, as it was their custom. But when they saw the old man reading the Korân, just as they had left him, they were greatly astonished. The old woman then told them what she had done, and why she had desired him to do this. They then carried the Mogrebine to their King, whose name was Shanwân, and told him the whole of the affair; and he was much astonished at the Arab. Upon this the Mogrebine presented the doctrine of Islamism to the King, and pressed him to receive it; who replied: Stay with us another month, and then, if you will do as you now have done, and escape from the spectre with safety, I will become a Mohammedan. So God opened the heart of the King for the reception of Islamism before the completion of the month,—of himself, of his household, his children, and his nobles. When, however, the second month came, they went with the Mogrebine to the idol-house, according to former custom, the King himself being also present; and when the following morning had arrived, they found the Mogrebine sitting and reading his Koran; having had the same rencontre with the spectre that he had on the former occasion. They then broke the images, rased the idol-house to the ground, and all became Mohammedans. The sect into which they entered was that of the Mogrebine; namely, that of Ibn Mâlik.[7] Till this very day they make much of the Mogrebines, on account of this man. I was residing for some time in these islands, without having any knowledge of this circumstance; upon a certain night, however, when I saw them exulting and praising God, as they were proceeding towards the sea, with Korâns on their heads, I asked them what they were about; when they told me of the spectre. They then said: Look towards the sea, and you will see him. I looked, and behold, he resembled a ship filled with candles and torches. This, said they, is the spectre; which,

7. The predominant rite of West Africa.

when we do as you have seen us doing, goes away and does us
no injury.†

It is a strange thing about these islands that their ruler is a
woman, Khadîja. The sovereignty belonged to her grandfather,
then to her father, and after his death to her brother Shihâb ad-
Dîn, who was a minor. When he was deposed and put to death
some years later, none of the royal house remained but Khadîja
and her two younger sisters, so they raised Khadîja to the throne.
She was married to their preacher, Jamâl ad-Dîn, who became
Wazîr[8] and the real holder of authority, but orders are issued in
her name only. They write the orders on palm leaves with a
curved iron instrument resembling a knife; they write nothing
on paper but copies of the Koran and works on theology. When
a stranger comes to the islands and visits the audience-hall custom demands that he take two pieces of cloth with him. He
makes obeisance towards the Sultana[9] and throws down one of
these cloths, then to her Wazîr, who is her husband Jamâl ad-
Dîn, and throws down the other. Her army comprises about a
thousand men, recruited from abroad, though some are natives.
They come to the palace every day, make obeisance, and retire,
and they are paid in rice monthly. At the end of each month
they come to the palace, make obeisance, and say to the Wazîr
"Transmit our homage and make it known that we have come
for our pay," whereupon orders are given for it to be issued to
them. The qâdî and the officials, whom they call wazîrs, also
present their homage daily at the palace and after the eunuchs
have transmitted it they withdraw. The qâdî is held in greater
respect among the people than all the other functionaries; his
orders are obeyed as implicitly as those of the ruler or even more
so. He sits on a carpet in the palace, and enjoys the entire revenue of three islands, according to ancient custom. There is no
prison in these islands; criminals are confined in wooden chambers intended for merchandise. Each of them is secured by a

† The Lee material ends here.
8. Prime Minister.
9. Khadîja.

piece of wood, as is done amongst us [in Morocco] with Christian prisoners.

When I arrived at these islands I disembarked on one of them called Kannalûs, a fine island containing many mosques, and I put up at the house of one of the pious persons there. On this island I met a man called Muhammad, belonging to Dhafâr, who told me that if I entered the island of Mahal the Wazîr would detain me there, because they had no qâdî. Now my design was to sail from there to Ma'bar [Coromandel], Ceylon, and Bengal, and thence on to China. When I had spent a fortnight at Kannalûs, I set sail again with my companions, and having visited on our way several other islands, at which we were received with honour and hospitably entertained, arrived on the tenth day at the island of Mahal, the seat of the Sultana and her husband, and anchored in its harbour. The custom of the country is that no one may go ashore without permission. When permission was given to us I wished to repair to one of the mosques, but the attendants on shore prevented me, saying that it was imperative that I should visit the Wazîr. I had previously enjoined the captain of the ship to say, if he were asked about me, "I do not know him," fearing that I should be detained by them, and ignorant of the fact that some busybody had written to them telling them about me and that I had been qâdî at Delhi. On reaching the palace we halted in some porticoes by the third gateway. The qâdî 'Isâ of Yemen came up and greeted me and I greeted the Wazîr. The captain brought ten pieces of cloth and made obeisance towards the Sultana, throwing down one piece, then to the Wazîr, throwing down another in the same way. When he had thrown them all down he was asked about me and answered "I do not know him." Afterwards they brought out betel and rose-water to us, this being their mark of honour, and lodged us in a house, where they sent us food, consisting of a large platter of rice surrounded by plates containing salted meat, chickens, ghee, and fish. Two days later the Wazîr sent me a robe, with a hospitality-gift of food and a hundred thousand cowries for my expenses.

When ten days had passed a ship arrived from Ceylon bringing some darwîshes, Arabs and Persians, who recognized me and

told the Wazîr's attendants who I was. This made him still more
delighted to have me, and at the beginning of Ramadân[10] he
sent for me to join in a banquet attended by the amîrs and ministers. Later on I asked his permission to give a banquet to the
darwîshes who had come from visiting the Foot [of Adam, in
Ceylon]. He gave permission, and sent me five sheep, which are
rarities among them because they are imported from Ma'bar,
Mulaybâr, and Maqdashaw, together with rice, chickens, ghee,
and spices. I sent all this to the house of the wazîr Sulaymân,
who had it excellently cooked for me, and added to it besides
sending carpets and brass utensils. I asked the Wazîr's permission for some of the ministers to attend my banquet, and he said
to me "And I shall come too." So I thanked him and on returning home to my house found him already there with the ministers and high officials. The Wazîr sat in an elevated wooden
pavilion, and all the amîrs and ministers who came greeted him
and threw down an unsewn cloth, so that there were collected
about a hundred cloths, which were taken by the darwîshes. The
food was then served, and when the guests had eaten, the Koran-
readers chanted in beautiful voices. The darwîshes then began
their ritual chants and dances. I had made ready a fire and they
went into it, treading it with their feet, and some of them ate
it as one eats sweetmeats, until it was extinguished. When the
night came to an end, the Wazîr withdrew and I went with him.
As we passed by an orchard belonging to the treasury he said to
me "This orchard is yours, and I shall build a house in it for
you to live in." I thanked him and prayed for his happiness.
Afterwards he sent me two slave-girls, some pieces of silk, and
a casket of jewels.

The attitude of the Wazîr afterwards became hostile to me for
the following reason. The wazîr Sulaymân had sent to me pro-
posing that I should marry his daughter, and I sent to the Wazîr
Jamâl ad-Dîn to ask his permission for my acceptance. The messenger returned to me and said "The proposal does not find
favour with him, for he wishes to marry you to his own daughter
when her period of widowhood comes to an end." But I for my
part refused that, in fear of the ill luck attached to her, for she

10. The month of fasting from sunrise to sunset as prescribed in the Qur'ân.

had already had two husbands who had died before consummating the marriage. Meanwhile I was seriously attacked by fever, for every person who comes to this island inevitably contracts fever. I determined therefore to leave it, sold some of the jewels for cowries, and hired a vessel to take me to Bengal. When I went to take leave of the Wazîr, the qâdî came out to me and said "The Wazîr says 'If you wish to go, give us back what we have given you and go.'" I replied "I have bought cowries with some of the jewels, so do what you like with those." He came back to me and said "He says 'We gave you gold, not cowries.'" I said "I shall sell them and give you back the gold." So I went to the merchants, asking them to buy back the cowries from me, but the Wazîr forbade them to do so, his purpose in all this being to prevent my leaving him. Afterwards he sent one of his courtiers to me to say "The Wazîr says 'Stay with us, and you shall have what you will.'" So reasoning with myself that I was in their power and that if I did not stay of my own free will I should be kept by main force, and that it was better to stay of my own choice, I said to his messenger "Very well, I shall stay with him." When the messenger returned to him he was overjoyed, and summoned me. As I entered he rose and embraced me saying "We wish you to stay near us and you wish to go away from us!" I made my excuses, which he accepted, and said to him "If you wish me to stay I have some conditions to make." He replied "Granted. Name them." I said "I cannot walk on foot." (Now it is their custom that no one rides there except the Wazîr, and when I had been given a horse and rode out on it, the population, men and boys, used to follow me in amazement. At length I complained to him, so he had the *dunqura* beaten and a public proclamation made that no one was to follow me. The *dunqura* is a sort of brass basin which is beaten with an iron rod and can be heard at a great distance; after beating it any proclamation which it is desired to make is publicly announced.) The Wazîr said "If you wish to ride in a palanquin, do so; if not we have a horse and a mare—choose which of them you wish." So I chose the mare and it was brought to me on the spot, along with a robe. Then I said "What shall I do with the cowries I bought?" He replied "Send one of your companies to sell them for you in Bengal." I said "I shall, on condition that you too send someone to help him in the transaction." He agreed to that, so I sent off my companion Abû Muhammad and they sent a man named al-Hâjj 'Alî.

Immediately after the Ramadân fast I made an agreement with the wazîr Sulaymân to marry his daughter, so I sent to the Wazîr Jamâl ad-Dîn requesting that the ceremony might be held in his presence at the palace. He gave his consent, and sent the customary betel and sandalwood. The guests arrived but the wazîr Sulaymân delayed. He was sent for but still did not come, and on being summoned a second time excused himself on the ground of his daughter's illness. The Wazîr then said to me privily "His daughter has refused, and she is her own mistress. The people have assembled, so what do you say to marrying the Sultana's mother-in-law?" (It was her daughter to whom the Wazîr's son was married.) I said "Very well," so the qâdî and notaries were summoned, and the profession of faith recited. The Wazîr paid her dowry, and she was conducted to me a few days later. She was one of the best of women.

After this marriage the Wazîr forced me to take the office of qâdî. The reason for this was that I had reproached the qâdî for his practice of taking a tenth of all estates when he divided them amongst the heirs, saying to him "You should have nothing but a fee agreed upon between you and the heirs." Besides he never did anything properly. When I was appointed, I strove my utmost to establish the prescriptions of the Sacred Law. There are no lawsuits there like those in our land. The first bad custom I changed was the practice of divorced wives of staying in the houses of their former husbands, for they all do so till they marry another husband. I soon put that to rights. About twenty-five men who had acted thus were brought before me; I had them beaten and paraded in the bazaars, and the women put away from them. Afterwards I gave strict injunctions that the prayers were to be observed, and ordered men to go swiftly to the streets and bazaars after the Friday service; anyone whom they found not having prayed I had beaten and paraded. I compelled the salaried prayer-leaders and muezzins to be assiduous in their duties and sent letters to all the islands to the same effect.

I tried also to make the women wear clothes, but I could not manage that.

Meanwhile I had married three other wives, one the daughter of a wazîr whom they held in high esteem and whose grandfather had been sultan, another the former wife of Shihâb ad-Dîn. After these marriages the islanders came to fear me, because of their weakness, and they exerted themselves to turn the Wazîr against me by slanders, until our relations became strained. Now it happened that a slave belonging to the sultan Shihâb ad-Dîn was brought before me on a charge of adultery, and I had him beaten and put in prison. The Wazîr sent some of his principal attendants to me to ask me to set him at liberty. I said to them "Are you going to intercede for a negro slave who has violated his master's honour, when you yourselves but yesterday deposed Shihâb ad-Dîn and put him to death because he had entered the house of one of his slaves?" Thereupon I sent for the slave and had him beaten with bamboo rods, which give heavier blows than whips, and paraded through the island with a rope round his neck. When the Wazîr heard of this he fell into a violent rage, assembled the ministers and army commanders and sent for me. I came to him, and though I usually made obeisance to him, I did not make obeisance but simply said *Salâm 'alaykum.*[11] Then I said to those present "Be my witnesses that I resign the office of qâdî because of my inability to carry out its duties." The Wazîr addressed me, whereupon I mounted [to the dais], sat down in a place facing him, and answered him in the most uncompromising manner. At this point the muezzin chanted the call to the sunset prayer and he went into his palace saying "They say that I am sultan, but I sent for this fellow to vent my wrath on him and he vented his wrath on me." The respect in which I was held amongst them was due solely to the sultan of India, for they were aware of the regard in which he held me, and even though they are far distant from him yet the fear of him is in their hearts.

When the Wazîr entered his palace he sent for the former qâdî who had been removed from office. This man had an arrogant tongue, and said to me "Our master asks you why you vio-

11. Standard greeting, "Peace be upon you."

lated his dignity in the presence of witnesses, and did not make obeisance to him." I answered "I used to make obeisance to him only because I was on good terms with him, but when his attitude changed I gave that up. The greeting of Muslims is *Salâm* and nothing more, and I said *Salâm*." He sent him to me a second time to say "You are aiming only at leaving us; give back your wives' dowries and pay your debts and go, if you will." On hearing this I made obeisance to him, went to my house, and acquitted all the debts I had contracted. On learning that I had done so and was bent upon going, the Wazîr repented of what he had said and withheld his permission for my departure. So I swore with the most solemn oaths that I had no alternative but to leave, and removed all my possessions to a mosque on the coast. I made a compact with two of the ministers that I should go to the land of Ma'bar [Coromandel], the king of which was the husband of my wife's sister, and fetch troops from there to bring the islands under his authority, and that I should be his representative in them. I arranged that the signal between us should be the hoisting of white flags on the ships; when they saw these they were to rise in revolt on the shore. I had never suggested this to myself until the Wazîr became estranged from me. He was afraid of me and used to say "This man will without doubt seize the wazîrate, either in my lifetime or after my death." He was constantly making enquiries about me and saying "I have heard that the king of India has sent him money to aid him to revolt against me." He feared my departure, lest I should fetch troops from Ma'bar, and sent to me asking me to stay until he could fit out a vessel for me, but I refused. The ministers and chief men came to me at the mosque and begged me to return. I said to them "If I had not sworn I should return." They suggested that I should go to one of the islands to avoid breaking my oath and then return, so I said "Very well," in order to satisfy them. When the night fixed for my departure came I went to take leave of the Wazîr, and he embraced me and wept so copiously that his tears dropped on my feet. He passed the following night guarding the island in person, for fear that my relatives by marriage and my friends would rise in revolt against him.

I set sail and reached the island of the wazîr 'Alî. Here my wife was attacked by severe pains and wished to go back, so I divorced her and left her there, sending word to that effect to the Wazîr, because she was the mother of his son's wife. We continued to travel through the islands from one district to another and came to a tiny island in which there was but one house, occupied by a weaver. He had a wife and family, a few coco-palms and a small boat, with which he used to fish and to cross over to any of the islands he wished to visit. His island contained also a few banana trees, but we saw no land birds on it except two ravens, which came out to us on our arrival and circled above our vessel. And I swear I envied that man, and wished that the island had been mine, that I might have made it my retreat until the inevitable hour should befall me. We then came to the island of Mulûk where the ship belonging to the captain Ibrâhîm was lying. This was the ship in which I had decided to travel to Ma'bar. Ibrâhîm and his companions met me and showed me great hospitality. The Wazîr had sent instructions that I was to receive in this island thirty dinars' worth of cowries, together with a quantity of coconut, honey, betel, areca-nuts, and fish every day. I stayed seventy days at Mulûk and married two wives there. The islanders were afraid that Ibrâhîm would plunder them at the moment of sailing, so they proposed to seize all the weapons on his ship and keep them until the day of his departure. A dispute arose over this, and we returned to Mahal but did not enter the harbour. I wrote to the Wazîr to tell him what had occurred, whereupon he wrote to say that there was no cause for seizing the weapons. We returned to Mulûk and set sail from there in the middle of Rabî' II., 745 (22nd August 1344). Four months later the Wazîr Jamâl ad-Dîn died—may God have mercy upon him.

We set sail without an experienced pilot on board, the distance between the island and Ma'bar being a three days' journey, and travelled for nine days, emerging on the ninth day at the island of Saylân [Ceylon]. We saw the mountain of Sarandîb there, rising into the heavens like a column of smoke.[12]

12. Adam's Peak. (Tr.)

When we came to the island, the sailors said "This port is not in the territory of the sultan whose country can safely be visited by merchants. It is in the territory of Sultan Ayrî Shakarwatî, who is an evil tyrant and keeps pirate vessels."[13] We were afraid to put into this harbour, but as a gale arose thereafter and we dreaded the sinking of the ship, I said to the captain "Put me ashore and I shall get you a safe-conduct from this sultan." He did as I asked and put me ashore, whereupon the infidels came to us and said "What are you?" I told them that I was the brother-in-law and friend of the sultan of Ma'bar, that I had come to visit him, and that the contents of the ship were a present for him. They went to their sultan and informed him of this. Thereupon he summoned me, and I visited him in the town of Battâla [Puttelam], which is his capital. It is a small and pretty town, surrounded by a wooden wall with wooden towers. The whole of its coasts are covered with cinnamon trees brought down by torrents and heaped up like hills on the shore. They are taken without payment by the people of Ma'bar and Mulaybâr, but in return for this they give presents of woven stuffs and similar articles to the sultan. It is a day and a night's journey from this island to the land of Ma'bar.

When I entered the presence of the infidel Sultan Ayrî Shakarwatî, he rose to meet me, seated me beside him, and spoke most kindly to me. He said "Your companions may land in safety and will be my guests until they sail, for the sultan of Ma'bar and I are friends." He then ordered me to be lodged and I stayed with him three days, enjoying great consideration which increased every day. He understood Persian and was delighted with the tales I told him of kings and countries. One day, after presenting me with some valuable pearls, he said "Do not be shy, but ask me for anything that you want." I replied "Since reaching this island I have had but one desire, to visit the blessed

13. The old Sinhalese kingdom of Ceylon was invaded about 1314 by the Pandyas, whose own kingdom at Madura in Ma'bar, which had existed since at least the third century B.C.E., was now in the hands of Muslims. The leader of the invaders was Arya Chakravarti, but Ibn Batûta's patron was more probably a later general of the same name, who in 1371 erected forts at Colombo and elsewhere. (Tr.)

Foot of Adam." (They call Adam Bâbâ, and Eve they call Mâmâ.) "That is simple," he answered, "We shall send an escort with you to take you to it." "That is what I want," said I, then I added "And this ship that I came in can set out in safety for Ma'bar, and when I return you will send me in your own vessels." "Certainly" he replied. When I related this to the captain, however, he said to me "I shall not sail until you return, even if I wait a year on your account," so I told the sultan of this, and he said "He will remain as my guest until you come back."

The sultan then gave me a palanquin, which was carried by his slaves, and sent with me four Yogis, whose custom it is to make an annual pilgrimage to the Foot, three Brahmans,[14] ten other persons from his entourage, and fifteen men to carry provisions. Water is plentiful along that road. On the first day we encamped beside a river, which we crossed on a raft, made of bamboo canes. Thence we journeyed to Manâr Mandalî [Minneri-Mandel], a fine town situated at the extremity of the sultan's territories. The inhabitants entertained us with a fine banquet, the chief dish at which was buffalo calves, which they hunt in a forest there and bring in alive. After passing the small town of Bandar Salâwât [Chilaw] our way lay through rugged country intersected with streams. In this part there are many elephants, but they do no harm to pilgrims and strangers, through the blessed favour of the Shaykh Abû 'Abdallâh, who was the first to open up this road for the pilgrimage to the Foot. These infidels used formerly to prevent Muslims from making this pilgrimage and would maltreat them, and neither eat nor trade with them, but since the adventure that happened to the Shaykh, as we have related above, they honour the Muslims, allow them to enter their houses, eat with them, and have no suspicions regarding their dealings with their wives and children. To this day they continue to pay the greatest veneration to this Shaykh, and call him "the Great Shaykh."

After this we came to the town of Kunakâr, which is the capi-

14. The hollow on the summit of Adam's Peak, venerated by the Muslims as the imprint of Adam's foot, was equally venerated by the Brahmans and Buddhists, as the mark of Siva's and Buddha's foot respectively. (Tr.)

tal of the principal sultan in this land.[15] It lies in a narrow valley between two hills, near a great lake called the Lake of Rubies, because rubies are found in it. Outside the town is the mosque of Shaykh 'Othmân of Shîrâz, known as the Shâwush; the sultan and inhabitants visit his tomb and venerate him. He was the guide to the Foot, and when his hand and foot were cut off, his sons and slaves took his place as guides. The reason for his mutilation was that he killed a cow. The Hindu infidels have a law that anyone who kills a cow is slaughtered in the same fashion or else put in its skin and burned. As Shaykh 'Othmân was so highly revered by them, they cut off his hand and foot instead, and assigned to him the revenues of one of the bazaars. The sultan of Kunakâr is called the Kunar, and possesses a white elephant, the only white elephant I have seen in the whole world. He rides on it at festivals and puts great rubies on its forehead. The marvellous rubies called *bahramân* [carbuncles] are found only in this town. Some are taken from the lake and these are regarded by them as the most valuable, and some are obtained by digging. In the island of Ceylon rubies are found in all parts. The land is private property, and a man buys a parcel of it and digs for rubies. Some of them are red, some yellow [topazes], and some blue [sapphires]. Their custom is that all rubies of the value of a hundred *fanams* belong to the sultan, who pays their price and takes them; those of less value belong to the finders. A hundred *fanams* equal in value six gold dinars.

We went on from Kunakâr and halted at a cave called after Ustâ Mahmûd the Lûrî, a pious man who dug out this cave at the foot of a hill beside a small lake. Thence we travelled to the Lake of Monkeys. There are in these mountains vast numbers of monkeys. They are black and have long tails, and their males are bearded like men. Shaykh 'Othmân and his sons and others as well told me that these monkeys have a chief, whom they obey as if he were a king. He fastens on his head a fillet of leaves and leans upon a staff. On his right and his left are four monkeys carrying staves in their hands. When the chief monkey sits down the four monkeys stand behind him, and his female and

15. Kunakâr is certainly Kornegalle (Kurunagala), the residence of the old dynasty of Sinhalese kings at this period. (Tr.)

young come and sit in front of him every day. The other monkeys come and sit at a distance from him, then one of the four monkeys addresses them and all the monkeys withdraw. After this each one brings a banana or a lemon or some such fruit, and the monkey chief with his young and the four monkeys eat. One of the Yogis told me that he had seen the four monkeys in the presence of their chief beating a monkey with sticks and after the beating pulling out its hair. We continued our journey to a place called "The Old Woman's Hut," which is the end of the inhabited part, and marched thence by a number of grottoes. In this place we saw the flying leech, which sits on trees and in the vegetation near water. When a man approaches it jumps out at him, and wheresoever it alights on his body the blood flows freely. The inhabitants keep a lemon in readiness for it; they squeeze this over it and it falls off them, then they scrape the place on which it alighted with a wooden knife which they have for the purpose.

The mountain of Sarandîb [Adam's Peak] is one of the highest in the world. We saw it from the sea when we were nine days' journey away, and when we climbed it we saw the clouds below us, shutting out our view of its base. On it there are many evergreen trees and flowers of various colours, including a red rose as big as the palm of a hand. There are two tracks on the mountain leading to the Foot, one called Bâbâ track and the other Mâmâ track, meaning Adam and Eve. The Mâmâ track is easy and is the route by which the pilgrims return, but anyone who goes by that way is not considered by them to have made the pilgrimage at all. The Bâbâ track is difficult and stiff climbing. Former generations cut a sort of stairway on the mountain, and fixed iron stanchions on it, to which they attached chains for climbers to hold on by.[16] There are ten such chains, two at the foot of the hill by the "threshold," seven successive chains farther on, and the tenth is the "Chain of the Profession of Faith," so called because when one reaches it and looks down to the foot of the hill, he is seized by apprehensions and recites the profession of faith for fear of falling. When you climb past this chain you find a rough track. From the tenth chain to the

16. These chains are still in existence.

grotto of Khidr is seven miles; this grotto lies in a wide plateau, and near by it is a spring full of fish, but no one catches them. Close to this there are two tanks cut in the rock on either side of the path. At the grotto of Khidr the pilgrims leave their belongings and ascend thence for two miles to the summit of the mountain where the Foot is.

The blessed Footprint, the Foot of our father Adam, is on a lofty black rock in a wide plateau. The blessed Foot sank into the rock far enough to leave its impression hollowed out. It is eleven spans long. In ancient days the Chinese came here and cut out of the rock the mark of the great toe and the adjoining parts. They put this in a temple at Zaytûn, where it is visited by men from the farthest parts of the land. In the rock where the Foot is there are nine holes cut out, in which the infidel pilgrims place offerings of gold, precious stones, and jewels. You can see the darwîshes, after they reach the grotto of Khidr, racing one another to take what there is in these holes. We, for our part, found nothing in them but a few stones and a little gold, which we gave to the guide. It is customary for the pilgrims to stay at the grotto of Khidr for three days, visiting the Foot every morning and evening, and we followed this practice. When the three days were over we returned by the Mâmâ track, halting at a number of villages on the mountain. At the foot of the mountain there is an ancient tree whose leaves never fall, situated in a place that cannot be got at. I have never met anyone who has seen its leaves. I saw there a number of Yogis who never quit the base of the mountain waiting for its leaves to fall. They tell lying tales about it, one being that whosoever eats of it regains his youth, even if he be an old man, but that is false. Beneath the mountain is the great lake from which the rubies are taken; its water is a bright blue to the sight.

We travelled thence to Dînawar, a large town on the coast, inhabited by merchants. In this town there is an idol, known as Dînawar, in a vast temple,[17] in which there are about a thousand Brahmans and Yogis, and about five hundred women, daughters of the infidels, who sing and dance every night in front of the

17. Dînawar here stands for Dewandera, the site of a famous temple of Vishnu near Dondra Head, the southernmost point of Ceylon. (Tr.)

idol. The city and all its revenues form an endowment belonging to the idol, from which all who live in the temple and who visit it are supplied with food. The idol itself is of gold, about a man's height, and in the place of its eyes it has two great rubies, which, as I am told, shine at night like lamps. We went on to the town of Qâlî [Point de Galle], a small place eighteen miles from Dînawar, and journeyed thence to the town of Kalanbû [Colombo], which is one of the finest and largest towns in Ceylon. In it resides the wazîr and ruler of the sea Jâlasti, who has with him about five hundred Abyssinians. Three days after leaving Kalanbû we reached Battâla again and visited the sultan of whom we have spoken above. I found the captain Ibrâhîm awaiting me and we set sail for the land of Ma'bar.

The land of China is of vast extent, and abounding in produce, fruits, grain, gold and silver. In this respect there is no country in the world that can rival it. It is traversed by the river called the "Water of Life," which rises in some mountains, called the "Mountain of Apes," near the city of Khân-Bâliq [Peking] and flows through the centre of China for the space of six months' journey, until finally it reaches Sîn as-Sîn [Canton].[18] It is bordered by villages, fields, fruit gardens, and bazaars, just like the Egyptian Nile, only that [the country through which runs] this river is even more richly cultivated and populous, and there are many waterwheels on it. In the land of China there is abundant sugar-cane, equal, nay superior, in quality to that of Egypt, as well as grapes and plums. I used to think that the 'Othmânî plums of Damascus had no equal, until I saw the plums in China. It has wonderful melons too, like those of Khwârizm and Isfahân. All the fruits which we have in our country are to be found there, either much the same or of better quality. Wheat is very abundant in China, indeed better wheat I have never seen, and the

18. The description of this great river, traversing China from north to south and flowing into the sea at Canton, has sometimes been taken to prove that Ibn Batûta's journey to China, or at least in China, is a pure fiction. It must, however, be borne in mind that he knew no more of China than the fringe which he himself visited, supplemented by what he could gather from various (and doubtless not always reliable) informants, and in this passage he is merely reproducing the common view of his time. (Tr.)

same may be said of their lentils and chick-peas.

The Chinese pottery [porcelain] is manufactured only in the towns of Zaytûn and Sîn-kalân. It is made of the soil of some mountains in that district, which takes fire like charcoal, as we shall relate subsequently. They mix this with some stones which they have, burn the whole for three days, then pour water over it. This gives a kind of clay which they cause to ferment. The best quality of [porcelain is made from] clay that has fermented for a complete month, but no more, the poorer quality [from clay] that has fermented for ten days. The price of this porcelain there is the same as, or even less than, that of ordinary pottery in our country. It is exported to India and other countries, even reaching as far as our own lands in the West, and it is the finest of all makes of pottery.

The hens and cocks in China are very big indeed, bigger than geese in our country, and hens' eggs there are bigger than our goose eggs. On the other hand their geese are not at all large. We bought a hen once and set about cooking it, but it was too big for one pot, so we put it in two. Cocks over there are about the size of ostriches; often a cock will shed its feathers and [nothing but] a great red body remains. The first time I saw a Chinese cock was in the city of Kawlam. I took it for an ostrich and was amazed at it, but its owner told me that in China there were some even bigger than that, and when I got to China I saw for myself the truth of what he had told me about them.

The Chinese themselves are infidels, who worship idols and burn their dead like the Hindus. The king of China is a Tatar, one of the descendants of Tinkiz [Chingiz] Khân. In every Chinese city there is a quarter for Muslims in which they live by themselves, and in which they have mosques both for the Friday services and for other reliigous purposes. The Muslims are honoured and respected. The Chinese infidels eat the flesh of swine and dogs, and sell it in their markets. They are wealthy folk and well-to-do, but they make no display either in their food or their clothes. You will see one of their principal merchants, a man so rich that his wealth cannot be counted, wearing a coarse cotton tunic. But there is one thing that the Chinese take a pride in, that is, gold and silver plate. Every one of them carries a stick, on which they lean in walking, and which they call "the third leg." Silk is very plentiful among them, because the silk-worm attaches itself to fruits and feeds on them without requiring much care. For that reason it is so common to be worn by even the very poorest there. Were it not for the merchants it would have no value at all, for a single piece of cotton cloth is sold in their country for the price of many pieces of silk. It is customary amongst them for a merchant to cast what gold and silver he has into ingots, each weighing a hundredweight or more or less, and to put those ingots above the door of his house.

The Chinese use neither [gold] dinars nor [silver] dirhams[19] in their commerce. All the gold and silver that comes into their country is cast by them into ingots, as we have described. Their buying and selling is carried on exclusively by means of pieces of paper, each of the size of the palm of the hand, and stamped with the sultan's seal. Twenty-five of these pieces of paper are called a *bâlisht*, which takes the place of the dinar with us [as the unit of currency].[20] When these notes become torn by handling, one takes them to an office corresponding to our mint, and receives their equivalent in new notes on delivering up the old ones. This transaction is made without charge and involves no expense, for those who have the duty of making the notes receive regular salaries from the sultan. Indeed the direction of that office is given to one of their principal amîrs. If anyone goes to the bazaar with a silver dirham or a dinar, intending to buy something, no one will accept it from him or pay any attention to him until he changes it for *bâlisht*, and with that he may buy what he will.

All the inhabitants of China and of Cathay[21] use in place of

19. *Dînâr*, the gold unit of the Muslim monetary system, weighing about 4.25 grams; *dirham*, the silver unit, about 3 grams.
20. *Bâlisht*, originally an ingot of metal weighing about 4.5 pounds, was the currency of the steppes at the beginning of the thirteenth century.
21. Cathay (*Khitây*), a term employed first by the Muslims and from them by European travelers and missionaries from the thirteenth to the sixteenth century, denoted the northern part of China, in contrast to *Sîn* or China proper in the south. The name was certainly derived from the Khitây Turks, who founded a dynasty which reigned at Peking during the tenth and eleventh centuries. (Tr.)

charcoal a kind of lumpy earth found in their country. It resembles our fuller's earth, and its colour too is the colour of fuller's earth. Elephants [are used to] carry loads of it. They break it up into pieces about the size of pieces of charcoal with us, and set it on fire and it burns like charcoal, only giving out more heat than a charcoal fire. When it is reduced to cinders, they knead it with water, dry it, and use it again for cooking, and so on over and over again until it is entirely consumed. It is from this clay that they make the Chinese porcelain ware, after adding to it some other stones, as we have related.[22]

The Chinese are of all peoples the most skilful in the arts and possessed of the greatest mastery of them. This characteristic of theirs is well known, and has frequently been described at length in the works of various writers. In regard to portraiture there is none, whether Greek or any other, who can match them in precision, for in this art they show a marvellous talent. I myself saw an extraordinary example of this gift of theirs. I never returned to any of their cities after I had visited it a first time without finding my portrait and the portraits of my companions drawn on the walls and on sheets of paper exhibited in the bazaars. When I visited the sultan's city I passed with my companions through the painters' bazaar on my way to the sultan's palace. We were dressed after the 'Irâqî fashion. On returning from the palace in the evening, I passed through the same bazaar, and saw my portrait and those of my companions drawn on a sheet of paper which they had affixed to the wall. Each of us set to examining the other's portrait [and found that] the likeness was perfect in every respect. I was told that the sultan had ordered them to do this, and that they had come to the palace while we were there and had been observing us and drawing our portraits without our noticing it. This is a custom of theirs, I mean making portraits of all who pass through their country. In fact they have brought this to such perfection that if a stranger commits any offence that obliges him to flee from

22. In this passage Ibn Batûta obviously confuses coal and porcelain clay, possibly owing to a custom followed in China of powdering the coal and mixing it with clay to form "patent fuel." (Tr.)

China, they send his portrait far and wide. A search is then made for him and wheresoever the [person bearing a] resemblance to that portrait is found he is arrested.

When a Muhammadan merchant enters any town in China, he is given the choice between staying with some specified merchant among the Muslims domiciled there, or going to a hostelry. If he chooses to stay with the merchant, his money is taken into custody and put under the charge of the resident merchant. The latter then pays from it all his expenses with honesty and charity. When the visitor wishes to depart, his money is examined, and if any of it is found to be missing, the resident merchant who was put in charge of it is obliged to make good the deficit. If the visitor chooses to go to the hostelry, his property is deposited under the charge of the keeper of the hostelry. The keeper buys for him whatever he desires and presents him with an account. If he desires to take a concubine, the keeper purchases a slave-girl for him and lodges him in an apartment opening out of the hostelry, and purveys for them both. Slave-girls fetch a low price; yet all the Chinese sell their sons and daughters, and consider it no disgrace. They are not compelled, however, to travel with those who buy them, nor on the other hand, are they hindered from going if they choose to do so. In the same way, if a stranger desires to marry, marry he may; but as for spending his money in debauchery, no, that he may not do. They say "We will not have it noised about amongst Muslims that their people waste their substance in our country, because it is a land of riotous living and [women of] surpassing beauty."

China is the safest and best regulated of countries for a traveller. A man may go by himself a nine months' journey, carrying with him large sums of money, without any fear on that account. The system by which they ensure his safety is as follows. At every post-station in their country they have a hostelry controlled by an officer, who is stationed there with a company of horsemen and footsoldiers. After sunset or later in the evening the officer visits the hostelry with his clerk, registers the names of all travellers staying there for the night, seals up the list, and locks them into the hostelry. After sunrise he returns with his clerk, calls each person by name, and writes a detailed description of them on the list. He then sends a man with them to conduct them to the next post-station and bring back a clearance certificate from the controller there to the effect that all these persons have arrived at that station. If the guide does not produce this document, he is held responsible for them. This is the practice at every station in their country from Sîn as-Sîn to Khân-Bâliq. In these hostelries there is everything that the traveller requires in the way of provisions, especially fowls and geese. Sheep on the other hand, are scarce with them.

To return to the account of our journey. The first city which we reached after our sea voyage was the city of Zaytûn. [Now although *zaytûn* means "olives"] there are no olives in this city, nor indeed in all the lands of the Chinese nor in India; it is simply a name which has been given to the place. Zaytûn is an immense city. In it are woven the damask silk and satin fabrics which go by its name, and which are superior to the fabrics of Khansâ and Khân-Bâliq. The port of Zaytûn is one of the largest in the world, or perhaps the very largest. I saw in it about a hundred large junks; as for small junks, they could not be counted for multitude. It is formed by a large inlet of the sea which penetrates the land to the point where it unites with the great river. In this city, as in all Chinese towns, a man will have a fruit-garden and a field with his house set in the middle of it, just as in the town of Sijilmâsa in our own country.[23] For this reason their towns are extensive. The Muslims live in a town apart from the others.

On the day that I reached Zaytûn I saw there the amîr who had come to India as an envoy with the present [to the sultan], and who afterwards travelled with our party and was shipwrecked on the junk. He greeted me, and introduced me to the controller of the *douane* and saw that I was given good apartments [there]. I received visits from the qâdî of the Muslims, the shaykh al-Islâm, and the principal merchants. Amongst the latter was Sharaf ad-Dîn of Tabrîz, one of the merchants from

23. Sijilmâsa was in the neighborhood of Tafilelt, in Southern Morocco. (Tr.)

whom I had borrowed at the time of my arrival in India, and
the one who had treated me most fairly. He knew the Koran by
heart and used to recite it constantly. These merchants, living
as they do in a land of infidels, are overjoyed when a Muslim
comes to them. They say "He has come from the land of Islâm,"
and they make *him* the recipient of the tithes on their properties,
so that he becomes as rich as themselves.[24] There was living at
Zaytûn, amongst other eminent shaykhs, Burhân ad-Dîn of
Kâzarûn, who has a hermitage outside the town, and it is to him
that the merchants pay the sums they vow to Shaykh Abû Ishâq
of Kâzarûn.

When the controller of the *douane* learned my story he wrote
to the Qân,[25] who is their Emperor, to inform him of my arrival
on a mission from the king of India. I asked him to send with
me someone to conduct me to the district of Sîn [Sîn as-Sîn],
which they call Sîn-kalân,[26] so that I might see that district,
which is in his province, in the interval before the arrival of
the Qân's reply. He granted my request, and sent one of his
officers to conduct me. I sailed up the river on a vessel resembling the war galleys in our country, except that in this the
rowers plied their oars standing upright, their place being in
the centre of the vessel, while the passengers were at the fore-
part and the stern. They spread over the ship awnings made
from a plant which grows in their country, resembling but different from flax, and finer than hemp [perhaps grass-cloth].
We sailed up this river for twenty-seven days. Every day we
used to tie up about noon by a village where we could buy what
we needed and pray the noon prayers, then in the evenings we
went ashore at another village and so on, until we reached the
city of Sîn-kalân or Sîn as-Sîn. Porcelain is manufactured there

24. The sense of this passage is quite clear. According to the Qur'ân, the
legal alms area to be given to "parents, kindred, orphans, the poor, and the
wayfarer." The Muslim community at Zaytûn was so wealthy that the only
one of these five classes to which the alms were of any value was the last.
(Tr.)
25. The Arabic and Persian writers (like Marco Polo) conventionally use
the term Qân or Qa'ân for the "Great Khân" of the Mongols. (Tr.)
26. Great China. (Tr.)

as well as at Zaytûn, and hereabouts the river of the "Water of Life" flows into the sea, so they call the place "The Meeting of the Waters." Sîn-kalân is a city of the first rank, in regard to size and the quality of its bazaars. One of the largest of these is the porcelain bazaar, from which porcelain is exported to all parts of China, to India, and to Yemen. In the centre of this city there is an enormous temple with nine portals; inside each of which there is a portico with benches where the inmates of the temple sit. Between the second and third portals there is a place containing chambers, which are occupied by the blind and crippled. Each of the occupants receives subsistence and clothing from the endowment of the temple. There are similar establishments between all the portals. In the interior there is a hospital for the sick and a kitchen for cooking food, and it has a staff of doctors and servitors. I was told that aged persons who are incapacitated from gaining their livelihood receive subsistence and clothing at this temple, likewise orphans and destitute widows. This temple was built by one of their kings, who moreover endowed it with [the revenues of] this city and the villages and fruit gardens belonging to it. The portrait of this king is painted in the temple we have described, and they worship it.

In one of the quarters of this city is the Muhammadan town, where the Muslims have their cathedral mosque, hospice and bazaar. They have also a qâdî and a shaykh, for in every one of the cities of China there must always be a Shaykh al-Islâm, to whom all matters concerning the Muslims are referred [*i.e.* who acts as intermediary between the government and the Muslim community], and a qâdî to decide legal cases between them. My quarters were in the house of Awhad ad-Dîn of Sinjâr, one of their principal men, of excellent character and immensely wealthy. I stayed with him for fourteen days, during which gifts were poured upon me one after the other from the qâdî and other Muslims. Every day they made a new entertainment, to which they came in beautifully-appointed boats, bringing musicians with them. Beyond the city of Sîn-kalân there is no other city, either infidel or Muslim. It is sixty days' journey, so I was told, from there to the Rampart of Gog and Magog, the intervening territory being occupied by nomadic infidels, who eat men when they get hold of them.[27] On that account no one ever crosses their country or visits it, and I did not find in Sîn-kalân anyone who had himself seen the Rampart or even seen anyone who had seen it.

A few days after my return to Zaytûn, the Qân's order arrived with instructions to convey me to his capital with all honour and dignity, by water if I preferred, otherwise by land. I chose to sail up the river, so they made ready for me a fine vessel of the sort that is designed for the use of governors. The governor sent his staff with us, and he, and likewise the qâdî and the Muslim merchants, sent us large quantities of provisions. We travelled as state-guests, eating our midday meal at one village, and our evening meal at another. After ten days' journey we reached Qanjanfû, a large and beautiful city set in a broad plain and surrounded by fruit-gardens, which gave the place the look of the Ghûta at Damascus.[28] On our arrival, we were met outside the town by the qâdî, the Shaykh al-Islâm, and the merchants, with standards, drums, trumpets, and bugles, and musicians. They brought horses for us, so we rode in on horseback while they walked on foot before us. No one rode along with us but the qâdî and the Shaykh al-Islâm. The governor of the city with his staff also came out [to meet us], for the sultan's guest is held in very high honour by them, and so we entered the city. It has four walls; between the first and second live the sultan's slaves, who are some of them day-guards and others night-guards of the city; between the second and third are the quarters of the mounted troops and the general who governs the city; within the third wall live the Muslims (it was here that we lodged at the house of their shaykh), and within the fourth is the Chinese quarter, which is the largest of these four cities

27. The site of the Rampart of Gog and Magog, the building of which is described in the Qur'ân and attributed to Alexander the Great, was a standing problem to the Arabic geographers. It was generally regarded as lying at the northeastern end of the habitable world, and was vaguely confused with the Great Wall of China. But Ibn Batûta could have had no idea that China was *within* the Wall, and his question appears to have been put at random, perhaps on hearing some chance reference to the Great Wall. (Tr.)
28. The Ghûta is the name given to the wide plain covered with fruit trees around Damascus. (Tr.)

[in one]. The distance separating each gate in this city from the next is three or four miles, and every inhabitant, as we have said, has his own orchard, house, and grounds.

One day as I was staying at Qanjanfû, a very large vessel came in, belonging to one of their most respected doctors. I was asked if he might see me, and he was announced as "Mawlânâ [Our master *i.e.* The reverend] Qiwâm ad-Dîn of Ceuta." His name roused my interest, and when he came in and we fell to conversation after the usual greetings, it struck me that I knew him. I kept looking at him intently, and at last he said "I see you are looking at me as if you knew me." So I said to him "Where do you come from?" He replied "From Ceuta." "And I" said I "from Tangier." Whereupon he broke into fresh greetings to me, and wept until I wept in sympathy with him. I then said to him "Did you go to India?" He replied "Yes, I went to the capital, Delhi." Then when he told me that, I remembered him and said "Are you al-Bushrî?" and he replied "Yes." I remembered he had come to Delhi with his mother's brother, Abu-'l-Qâsim of Murcia, as a beardless youth and a very clever student. I had spoken of him to the sultan of India, who gave him three thousand dinars and invited him to stay at his court, but he refused, as he was set on going to China, where he prospered exceedingly, and acquired enormous wealth. He told me that he had about fifty white slaves and as many slave-girls, and presented me with two of each, along with many other gifts. I met his brother in after years in the Negrolands—what a distance lies between them!

I stayed at Qanjanfû for fifteen days and then continued my journey. The land of China, in spite of all that is agreeable in it, did not attract me. On the contrary I was sorely grieved that heathendom had so strong a hold over it. Whenever I went out of my house I used to see any number of revolting things, and that distressed me so much that I used to keep indoors and go out only in case of necessity. When I met Muslims in China I always felt just as though I were meeting my own faith and kin. So great was the kindness of this doctor al-Bushrî that when I left Qanjanfû he accompanied me for four days, until I reached the town of Baywam Qutlû. This is a small town, inhabited by

Chinese, a proportion of them being troops, the rest common people. The Muslim community there consists of four houses only, the inhabitants of which are agents of my learned friend. We put up at the house of one of them, and stayed with him for three days, after which I bade the doctor adieu and set out again.

I sailed up the river with the usual routine, stopping for dinner at one village, and for supper at another. After seventeen days of this, we reached the city of Khansâ [Hang-chow], which is the biggest city I have ever seen on the face of the earth.[29] It is so long that it takes three days to traverse in the ordinary routine of marches and halts. It is built after the Chinese fashion already described, each person, that is, having his own house and garden. It is divided into six cities, as we shall describe later. On our arrival a party came out to meet us, consisting of the qâdî and the Shaykh al-Islâm of the city, and the family of 'Othmân ibn Affân of Egypt, who are the principal Muslim residents there, accompanied by a white flag, drums, bugles, and trumpets. The governor of the city also came out [to meet us] with his escort, and so we entered the town.

Khansâ consists of six cities, each with its own wall, and an outer wall surrounding the whole. In the first city are the quarters of the city guards and their commander; I was told by the qâdî and others that they mustered twelve thousand men on the register of troops. We passed the first night after our entry in the house of their commander. On the second day we entered the second city through a gate called the Jews' Gate. In this city live the Jews, Christians, and sun-worshipping Turks, a large number in all; its governor is a Chinese and we passed the second night in his house. On the third day we entered the third city, and this is inhabited by the Muslims. Theirs is a fine city, and their bazaars are arranged just as they are in Islamic countries; they have mosques in it and muezzins—we heard them calling to the noon prayers as we entered. We stayed here in the mansion of the family of 'Othmân ibn 'Affân of Egypt. He was a

29. It is agreed by all travelers, both Christian and Muslim, that what Marco Polo calls "the most noble city of Kinsay . . . beyond dispute the finest and noblest in the world" was indeed the largest city in the world in the fourteenth century. (Tr.)

wealthy merchant, who conceived a liking for this city and made his home in it, so that it came to be called 'Othmânîya after him, and he transmitted to his posterity the influence and respect which he enjoyed there. It was he who built the cathedral mosque of Khansâ, and endowed it with large benefactions. The number of Muslims in this city is very large, and our stay with them lasted fifteen days. Every day and night we were the guests at a new entertainment, and they continuously provided the most sumptuous meats, and went out with us every day on pleasure rides into different quarters of the city.

One day they rode out with me and we entered the fourth city, which is the seat of government, and in which the chief governor Qurtay resides. When we entered the gate leading to it, my companions were separated from me, and I was found by the wazîr, who conducted me to the palace of the chief governor Qurtay. It was on this occasion that he took from me the mantle which the saint Jalâl ad-Dîn of Shîrâz had given me, as I have already related. No one resides in this city, which is the most beautiful of the six, except the sultan's slaves and servants. It is traversed by three streams, one of them being a canal taken off from the great river, which is used by small boats bringing provisions and coal to the town, and there are pleasure boats on it as well. The citadel[30] lies in the centre of this city. It is of enormous size, and the government house stands in the middle of it, surrounded by [the court of] the citadel on all sides. Within it there are arcades, in which sit workmen making rich garments and weapons. The amîr Qurtay told me that there were sixteen hundred master-workmen there, each with three or four apprentices working under him. They are all without exception the slaves of the Qân; they have chains on their feet, and they live outside the fortress. They are permitted to go out to the bazaars in the city, but may not go beyond its gate. They are passed in review before the governor every day, a hundred at a time, and if any one of them is missing, his commander is held responsible for him. Their custom is that when one of them has served for

30. The word translated *citadel* means "inner city occupied by the ruler or governor." The viceroy's palace was not in the center of Hang-chow, however, but at the southern end. (Tr.)

ten years, he is freed from his chains and given the choice between staying in service, without chains, or going wherever he
will within the Qân's dominions, but not outside them. When
he reaches the age of fifty he is exempted from work and maintained [by the state]. In the same way anyone else who has
attained this age or thereabouts is maintained. Anyone who
reaches the age of sixty is regarded by them as a child, and legal
penalties cease to be applicable to him. Old men in China are
greatly respected, and each one of them is called Atâ, which
means "Father."

The amîr Qurtay is the principal amîr in China.[31] He entertained us in his palace, and prepared a banquet, . . . which was
attended by the principal men of the city. He had Muslim cooks
brought, who slaughtered the animals [in accordance with Muslim ritual, so that the food should be ceremonially clean] and
cooked the food. This amîr, in spite of his exalted rank, presented the dishes to us with his own hand, and with his own
hand carved the meat. We stayed with him as his guests for
three days. He sent his son with us to the canal, where we went
on board a ship resembling a fire-ship, and the amîr's son went
on another along with musicians and singers. They sang in
Chinese, Arabic, and Persian. The amîr's son was a great admirer of Persian melody, and when they sang a certain Persian
poem he commanded them to repeat it over and over again, until
I learned it from them by heart. It has a pleasant lilt. . . . On
[the] canal there was assembled a large crowd in ships with
brightly-coloured sails and silk awnings, and their ships too were
admirably painted. They began a mimic battle and bombarded
each other with oranges and lemons. We returned in the evening to the amîr's palace, and spent the night there. The musicians were there, and sang all kinds of pleasing melodies.

That same night a certain juggler, one of the Qân's slaves,
was there. The amîr said to him "Show us some of your feats."

31. Qurtay appears to be a contraction of Qarâtây, a common Turkish title,
but no governor of this name is mentioned in Chinese works, so far as is
known. It is probable that it was the title given to the commander by the
Turkish troops. (Tr.)

So he took a wooden ball with holes in which there were long leather thongs, and threw it into the air. It rose right out of our sight, for we were sitting in the middle of the palace court, during the season of intense heat. When nothing, but a short piece of the cord remained in his hand, he ordered one of his apprentices to go up the rope, which he did until he too disappeared from our sight. The juggler called him three times without receiving any reply, so he took a knife in his hand, as if he were enraged, and climbed up the rope until he disappeared as well. The next thing was that he threw the boy's hand to the ground, and then threw down his foot, followed by his other hand, then his other foot, then his trunk, and finally his head. After that he came down himself puffing and blowing, with his clothes all smeared with blood, and kissed the ground in front of the amîr, saying something to him in Chinese. The amîr gave him some order, and thereupon he took the boy's limbs, placed them each touching the other, and gave him a kick, and up he rose as sound as ever. I was amazed and took palpitation of the heart, just as had happened to me when I saw something similar at the court of the king of India, so they administered some potion to me which removed my distress. The qâdî Afkhar ad-Dîn was sitting beside me, and he said to me: "By God, there was no climbing or coming down or cutting up of limbs at all; the whole thing is just hocus-pocus."

On the following day we entered the fifth and largest city, which is inhabited by the common folk. Its bazaars are good and contain very skilful artificers; it is there that the fabrics which take their name from this town are woven. We passed a night in this city as the guests of its governor, and on the morrow entered the sixth city through a gate called Boatmen's gate. This sixth city, which lies on the banks of the great river, is inhabited by seamen, fishermen, caulkers, and carpenters, along with archers and footsoldiers, all of them being slaves of the sultan. No other persons live [in this town] with them, and their numbers are very great. We spent a night there as the guests of its governor. The amîr Qurtay equipped a vessel for us with all that was needed in the way of provisions, etc., and sent his suite with us

to arrange for our hospitable reception [on the journey]. So
we left this city, which is the last of the provinces of China
[proper], and entered the land of Khitâ [Cathay].

Cathay is the best cultivated country in the world. There is
not a spot in the whole extent of it that is not brought under
cultivation. The reason is that if any part is left uncultivated its
inhabitants or their neighbours are assessed for the land-tax due
thereon. Fruit-gardens, villages, and fields extend along both
banks of this river without interruption from the city of Khansâ
to the city of Khân-Bâliq [Peking], which is a space of sixty-
four days' journey. There are no Muslims to be found in these
districts, except casual travellers, since the country is not suitable for [their] permanent residence, and there is no large city
in it, only villages and wide spaces, covered with corn, fruit-
trees, and sugarcane. I have never seen anything in the world
like it, except a space of four days' journey between Anbâr and
'Âna [in 'Irâq]. We used to disembark every night and stay in
the villages in order to receive our provisions as guests of the
sultan.

Thus we completed our journey to the city of Khân-Bâliq,
also called Khâniqû,[32] the capital of the Qân—he being their
emperor, whose dominion extends over the countries of China
and Cathay. When we arrived there we moored at a distance of
ten miles from the city, as is their custom, and a written report
of our arrival was sent to the admirals, who gave us permission
to enter the port of the city. Having done so, we disembarked
and entered the town, which is one of the largest towns in the
world. It is not laid out, however, after the Chinese fashion, with
gardens inside the city, but is just like the cities in other countries with gardens outside the walls. The sultan's city lies in the
centre, like a citadel, as we shall relate. I stayed with Shaykh
Burhân ad-Dîn of Sâgharj—the same man to whom the king of
India sent 40,000 dinars with an invitation to him [to come to
India], and who took the money and paid his debts with them,
but refused to go to the king and set out [instead] for China.
The Qân set him at the head of all the Muslims who live in his
territories, and gave him the title of *Sadr al-Jihân*. The word

32. Peking. (Tr.)

qân is a term applied by them to every person who exercises the sovereignty over [all] the provinces, just as every ruler of the country of Lûr is called *atâbeg*. His name is Pâshây, and there is no infidel on the face of the earth who owns an empire greater than his. His palace lies in the centre of the [inner] city, which is appropriated to his residence. The greater part of it is constructed of carved wood, and it is excellently planned.

When we reached the capital Khân-Bâliq, we found that the Qân was absent from it at that time, as he had gone out to fight his cousin Fîrûz, who had rebelled against him in the district of Qarâqorum and Bish-Bâligh in Cathay. The distance between these places and the capital is a three months' journey through cultivated districts. After his departure the majority of his amîrs threw off their allegiance to him and agreed to depose him because he had departed from the precepts of the *Yasâq*, that is, the precepts which were laid down by their ancestor Tinkîz [Chingiz] Khân, who laid waste the lands of Islâm. They went over to his rebel nephew and wrote to the Qân to the effect that he should abdicate and retain the city of Khansâ as an appanage. He refused to do so, fought them, and was defeated and killed.

It was a few days after our arrival at his capital that the news of this was received. The city was decorated; trumpets, bugles and drums were played, and games and entertainments held for the space of a month. Thereafter the slain Qân was brought, with about a hundred other slain, his cousins, relatives, and intimates. A great *nâ'ûs*, that is, a subterranean chamber, was dug for him and richly furnished. The Qân was laid in it with his weapons, and all the gold and silver plate from his palace was deposited in it with him. With him also were put four slavegirls and six of the principal mamlûks,[33] who carried drinking vessels, then the door of the chamber was built up and the whole thing covered over with earth until it reached the size of a large mound. After that they brought four horses and drove them about the Qân's grave until they stopped [from exhaustion], then they set up a wooden erection over the grave and suspended the horses on it, having first driven a piece of wood through each horse from tail to mouth. The above-mentioned relatives of the

33. Male slaves.

Qân were also placed in subterranean chambers along with their weapons and house utensils, and they impaled over the tombs of the principal members, of whom there were ten, three horses each, and over the tombs of the rest one horse each.

This day was observed as a solemn holiday, and not one person was absent from the ceremony, men or women, Muslim or heathen. They were all dressed in mourning robes, which are white capes in the case of the infidels and [long] white garments in the case of the Muslims. The Qân's khâtûns and courtiers lived in tents near his grave for forty days, some even more than that, up to a year; and a bazaar was established there to supply the food and other things which they required. Such practices as these are observed, so far as I can record, by no other people in these days. The heathen Indians and Chinese, on the other hand, burn their dead; other people do indeed bury the dead man, but they do not put anyone in with him. However, I have been told by trustworthy persons in the Negrolands that the heathen there, when their king died, used to make a *nâ'ûs* for him and put in with him some of his courtiers and servants, along with thirty of the sons and daughters of their principal families, first breaking their hands and feet, and they put in drinking vessels along with them.

When the Qân was slain, as we have related, and his nephew Fîrûz obtained the sovereign power, he chose to make his capital at the city of Qarâqorum, on account of its proximity to the territories of his cousins, the kings of Turkistân and Transoxania. Afterwards several of the amîrs who were not present when the Qân was killed revolted against him and intercepted communications and the disorders grew to serious proportions.

IV

The Era of the Three Empires
(1400-1800)

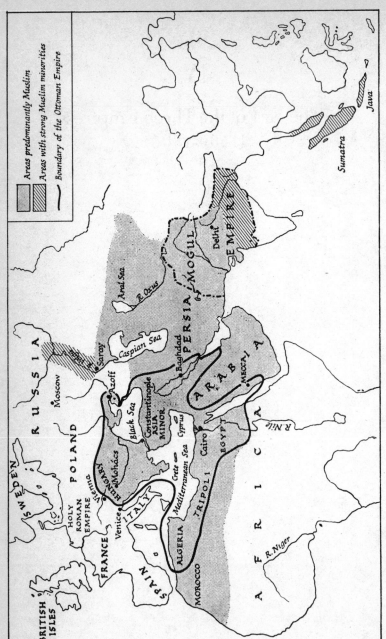

Areas predominantly Muslim
Areas with strong Muslim minorities
Boundary of the Ottoman Empire

BRITISH
ISLES

SWEDEN

RUSSIA

POLAND

HOLY
ROMAN
EMPIRE

FRANCE

Vienna

Venice

ITALY

SPAIN

MOROCCO

ALGERIA

TRIPOLI

AFRICA

R. Niger

Mediterranean Sea

HUNGARY

Mohács

Black Sea

Azoff

Moscow

Saray

R. Volga

Aral Sea

R. Oxus

Caspian Sea

Constantinople

ASIA MINOR

Crete

Cyprus

Cairo

EGYPT

R. Nile

ARABIA

MECCA

Baghdad

PERSIA

MOGUL

EMPIRE

Delhi

Sumatra

Java

From *The Social Structure of Islam* by Reuben Levy (1971) by permission of Cambridge University Press.

Introduction

By 1550, three vast empires—Ottoman, Safavid, Mughal—divided the heartlands of Islâm. In each of these states the monarch's central power rested on his control of cannon and other gunpowder weapons. No wall could stand for long against a besieger with enough of the right gunpowder weapons. Each ruler's reach was defined, in large part, by the time required to transport siege guns to distant parts: because he could usually not afford to be away from his capital for an entire year, lest someone usurp power during his absence, three to four months' travel time from the capital fairly well defined the limits of these states.

The three empires reached their apex in the sixteenth century. The Ottoman Sultân, Sulaymân the Lawgiver (r. 1520-1566), the Safavid Shâh 'Abbâs (r. 1586-1628), the Mughal Shâh Akbar (r. 1556-1605), emperor of India, were the most famous monarchs. Each inherited a religious propaganda. Each depended mainly on a careful counterpoise between a standing army paid in cash and a "feudal" force, supported by land grants. Professionalization and bureaucratization complemented military centralization, and the empire began to accommodate religious pluralism, ethnic diversity, and cultural divergences.

Patronage of art and learning characterized each court, but beneath the splendor we can detect a common fragility. The rulers and their servants were psychologically distant from the rank and file of the subject populations, and they were more interested in collecting taxes than in serving the interests or forwarding the prosperity of the peasants and townsmen who supported them. In addition, the smooth functioning of the administrative and military machine depended on the personality of the ruler. It was hard to train an heir to the throne without giving him means to rebel; the alternative of confining potential heirs to the harem brought individuals to power who were not prepared for the difficult role of reigning monarch. This dilemma, inherent in a polygamous family system which did not recognize any clear rule of succession, was never solved.

Ottoman Conquest of Constantinople

From as early as 717 Constantinople, the seat of the Byzantine emperors and bulwark of Christendom, had beckoned Muslim ambitions, but it was only in 1453 that the Ottoman Sultân, Mehmed the Conqueror, captured the city and made it his capital. The Ottoman state grew up around a core of hardy frontier fighters, located initially in Asia Minor across the Sea of Marmara from Constantinople. Osmân, founder of the dynasty, began to lead a band of warriors against the Christians about 1291; a hundred years later Ottoman power extended from the Danube to the upper Euphrates. In 1402 the Sultân Bayezid was defeated and captured by the Mongol conqueror, Tamerlane. This shook the Ottoman state to its foundations, but when Sultân Mehmed came to power in 1451, the unity and strength of the state had been restored, and a series of Christian crusades had been turned back. Constantinople lay within the young ruler's grasp, and he seized it despite heroic resistance.

The account of Mehmed's famous victory which follows is from the hand of a Greek, known as Kritovoulos. He was not present at the seige himself, but entered Mehmed's service and became governor of the island of Imbros, which may have been his home. Nothing else is known about him. Kritovoulos wrote in Greek and as a Greek, saddened by the conquest of Constantinople. But he also admired Mehmed and seems to have had accurate knowledge about what happened on both sides of the struggle.

KRITOVOULOS: FROM HISTORY OF
MEHMED THE CONQUEROR

To the Supreme Emperor, King of Kings, Mehmed, the fortunate, the victor, the winner of trophies, the triumphant, the in-

From *History of Mehmed the Conqueror*, by Kritovoulos, trans. by Charles T. Riggs, copyright 1954 by Princeton University Press, pp. 3, 5-6, 12-16, 22-27, 33, 55-58, 66-74, 76-77, 82-83. Reprinted by permission of Princeton University Press.

vincible, Lord of land and sea, by the will of God, Kritovoulos the Islander, servant of thy servants.

Seeing that you are the author of many great deeds, O most mighty Emperor, and in the belief that the many great achievements of generals and kings of old, nor merely of Persians and Greeks, are not worthy to be compared in glory and bravery and martial valor with yours, I do not think it just that they and their deeds and accomplishments, as set forth in the Greek historians and their writings from contemporary times and up to the present, should be celebrated and admired by all, and that these should enjoy everlasting remembrance, while you, so great and powerful a man, possessing almost all the lands under the sun, and glorious in your great and brilliant exploits, should have no witness, for the future, of your valor and the greatest and best of your deeds, like one of the unknown and inglorious ones who are till now unworthy of any memorial or record in Greek; or that the deeds of others, petty as they are in comparison to yours, should be better known and more famed before men because done by Greeks and in Greek history, while your accomplishments, vast as they are, and in no way inferior to those of Alexander the Macedonian, or of the generals and kings of his rank, should not be set forth in Greek to the Greeks, nor passed on to posterity for the undying praise and glory of your deeds.

Indeed, you are the only one of kings, or at any rate one of a very few, who have united deeds with words and wisdom and majesty; for you are both a good king and a mighty warrior. So I have deemed it fitting and right, trusting in your favor, to undertake the present effort and commit to writing in Greek, as best I may, your merits and accomplishments, which far exceed in number and greatness those of any other.

. . . .

So, having written all these things and related them in this book, I now send it to your Royal attention and wisdom, to be examined and judged. And if the bravery recorded in it be in accord with the fact, and comparable to your acts, and it be attested by the Royal approval, I shall acknowledge my gratitude to God, and to you, O Sultan, for providing such material for me by the best of deeds for description by my words. And so I shall be encouraged to prepare for the coming effort, and joyfully give myself to the remaining part of the work which, under God, I shall undertake for you, simply trying to ascertain many of the imperatively needed facts now unknown to me—which is the reason for the delay until now of this whole manuscript.

And if my words seem far inferior to your deeds, so that they do not attain to the greatness of those acts—as indeed must be the case—let the book be condemned as useless, while I myself, reverencing you at a distance in silent awe, yield in the matter of historical record to others who in such things are more competent than I.

. . . .

BEGINNING OF THE HISTORY

§16. It was the year 6959 from the beginning [A.D. 1451] when the Sultan Murad came to the end of his life,[1] having lived a total of fifty-two years and having reigned thirty-one, a very good man in every way, high-minded, and also a very great general who had exhibited throughout his life many brave and wonderful deeds, as indeed these exploits show. He was the sixth of the brilliant line of the Ottomans, a nobleman of noblemen.

§17. These men are of the very oldest people, that of Achaemenes and Perses, and springing from them, all the kings of the Persians are descended. There were indeed Persians of other lines, as Herodotus relates, but they were common and ordinary while these were alone the illustrious line of kings—those who had their primitive origin from Achaemenes and Perses.

§18. So too the Greeks are descended from Danaus and Linges, who were in origin Egyptians, from the town of Chemis, situated in the marsh land. They migrated into Greece. Ages afterwards, the descendants of these people, who were called Achaemenidae and Persidae, crossed over into Asia and settled

1. Kritovoulos uses Byzantine chronology, reckoning 5,508 years from Creation to the birth of Christ. Murad II reigned 1421-1451.

at first in Persia. And when they died, they left their race and name to that place.

§19. So when this Murad, of whom I spoke, died, his son Mehmed succeeded to the sultanate, he being the seventh Sultan and now in the twentieth year of his life. He was sent for from Asia, for it was there that he had his province which had been assigned him by his father.[2]

§20. Just at that period the Divine power sent many unusual, unexpected, and prodigious signs. These occurred both at the birth of this man and also at his entering on his rule as Sultan. For strange and exceptional earthquakes took place, and subterranean rumblings, also severe thunder and lightning from heaven, and whirlwinds and terrible storms, and an unusual light appeared in the sky, and many similar signs which the Divine power is accustomed to exhibit at the time of the greatest events and changes in the customary order.

§21. The soothsayers, sages and prophets and inspired persons foretold and foresaw many things that were to happen, and announced that the new Sultan would have every sort of good fortune and virtue, that his dominion would be very large in every way, and that he would surpass all the sultans before him in the very great abundance of his glory and wealth and power and accomplishments.

§22. When he became heir to a great realm and master of many soldiers and enlisted men, and had under his power already the largest and best parts of both Asia and Europe, he did not believe that these were enough for him nor was he content with what he had: instead he immediately overran the whole world in his calculations and resolved to rule it in emulation of the Alexanders and Pompeys and Caesars and kings and generals of their sort.

HOW THE SULTAN WAS ALSO A PHILOSOPHER

§23. His physical powers helped him well. His energies were keen for everything, and the power of his spirit gave him ability

2. This refers to the practice of most Turkish rulers of sending their sons to govern a province under the care of an *atâbeg*, as preparation for future rule.

to rule and to be kingly. To this end also his wisdom aided, as well as his fine knowledge of all the doings of the ancients. For he studied all the writings of the Arabs and Persians [Ottomans], and whatever works of the Greeks had been translated into the language of the Arabs and Persians—I refer particularly to the works of the Peripatetics and Stoics. So he used the most important philosophies of the teachers of the Arabs and Persians.[3]

TREATIES OF THE SULTAN WITH CONSTANTINE, KING OF THE ROMANS [BYZANTINES], AND KARAMAN

§24. He did not postpone anything or put off any action, but immediately carried everything through. First he made a treaty with the Romans and the Emperor Constantine [XIII];[4] and after that, with Karaman,[5] the ruler of Upper Phrygia and Cilicia, believing that for the present this move was beneficial to his affairs.

SCRUTINY OF THE LISTS OF THE ARMY, ETC.

§25. Then he gave himself to an examination of his whole realm. Using his judgment about the governorships of the nations under him, he deposed some of the governors and substituted others who he deemed to be superior to the former in strategy and knowledge and justice. It was his aim, above all, to have every province under him ruled as well and as justly as possible.

§26. He also went over the registers and battle order of the troops, cavalry and infantry, which are paid from the royal treasuries. He especially made the royal palace subject of considerable thought and increased the pay of its troops. I refer to the "new recruits," his personal guard of foot-soldiers, customarily called in their own language Yenitsari [Janissaries], a term meaning "new levy." He realized how important these

3. Apparently Mehmed II did not know Greek. The Ottomans are referred to as Arabs and Persians because Kritovoulos tries to avoid use of "Turks." By Mehmed II's time the "Turkish" element was being downplayed for the "Islâmic."

4. Constantine XIII Palaeologus, 1448-1453.

5. The most important of the Anatolian Seljûqs' successor-states, and the Ottomans' principal Anatolian Muslim rival.

were for himself, for the protection of his person and of the whole realm.

§27. In addition to this, he collected a supply of arms and arrows and other things needful and useful in preparation for war. Then he examined his family treasury, looking especially closely into its overseers. He carefully questioned the officials in charge of the annual taxes and obliged them to render accounts.

EXAMINATION OF THE PUBLIC FUNDS, AND OF THEIR TREASURERS

§28. And he discovered that much of the public and royal revenue was being badly spent and wasted to no good purpose, about one-third of the yearly revenues which were recoverd for the royal treasury. So he set the keeping of this in good order. He greatly increased the annual revenue. He brought many of the tax officials to reason through fear, and for them substituted trustworthy and wise men to collect and safekeep the funds. His father had dealt with such matters in a much more hit-or-miss manner, but he made short work of them.

§29. So, with the arrangement of these affairs in this fashion, the ordering of the reign in the best possible manner, there passed the year 6959 from the beginning [A.D. 1451], the first year of the reign of the Sultan. Thus he prepared for greater things; and so everything contributed to the plan he had before him.

§30. And this plan was: he meant to build a strong fortress on the Bosporus on the European side, opposite to the Asiatic fortress on the other side, at the point where it is narrowest and swiftest, and so to control the straits by uniting both continents, Asia and Europe; and to cross there whenever he should choose, quite independently of any other individuals and with no least question that it was the Sultan himself who controlled the passage.

.   .   .   .

RETURN OF THE SULTAN TO ADRIANOPLE AND THE
BUILDING OF THE NEW PALACE

§53. During the same period he also built a splendid palace near Adrianople, on the banks of the Hebrus River beyond the city. It was adorned with splendid stones and transparent marbles, and was resplendent with much gold and silver within and without and embellished with sculptures and paintings and with many other costly things carefully designed and wrought. Around it he planted gardens decked with all sorts of shrubs and domestic trees bearing beautiful fruit. In these gardens he put various kinds of domestic and wild animals and flocks of birds, and made the place attractive with many other beautiful things which he knew would bring enjoyment and beauty and pleasure. And in his zeal he constructed a royal courtyard very near this, and made ample barracks for the new cavalry and infantry troops, in it and around it, guarding the palace on all sides.

§54. He also resolved to carry into execution immediately the plan which he had long since studied out and elaborated in his mind and toward which he had bent every purpose from the start, and to wait no longer nor delay. This plan was to make war against the Romans [Byzantines] and their Emperor Constantine and to besiege the city. For he thought, as was true, that if he could succeed in capturing it and becoming master of it, there was nothing to hinder him from sallying forth from it in a short time, as from a stronghold for all the environs, and overrunning all and subduing them to himself. For this reason he could no longer be restrained at all. He did not think he ought to stay quiet in his own parts any longer and maintain peace, but believed he should speedily make war and capture the city.

§55. There were also certain supernatural signs that urged him to this, together with some oracles, auguries, soothsayings, and other such things, to which he gave great weight, and on which men rely to tell them the future. All these pointed to the same conclusion, and gave him strong hopes that he could capture the city. So, calling together all those in authority, that is, the governors, the generals, the captains of cavalry, the majors

of battalions, and the chiefs of the soldiery, he made them the
following address.

Speech of the Sultan Inciting His Followers To Battle
Against the City. Also a Recital of Previous Deeds
of His Forefathers, and a Brief Survey of the Entire Rule

§56. "My friends and men of my empire! You all know very
well that our forefathers secured this kingdom that we now hold
at the cost of many struggles and very great dangers and that,
having passed it along in succession from their fathers, from
father to son, they handed it down to me. For some of the oldest
of you were sharers in many of the exploits carried through by
them—those at least of you who are of maturer years—and the
younger of you have heard of these deeds from your fathers.
They are not such very ancient events nor of such a sort as to
be forgotten through the lapse of time. Still the eyewitness of
those who have seen testifies better than does the hearing of
deeds that happened but yesterday or the day before.

OF THE COURAGE OF THE HEROES

§57. "It is perfectly possible to see even now, all over our
land, signs of those deeds clearly shown—the walls of castles
and towns torn down but yesterday or the day before, the
ground, so to speak, still red and damp with their blood, and
many other such clearly-read monuments of their herosim and
valor stand as ever-memorable proofs of their courage in danger.
And they exhibited in it all such heroism of spirit and firmness
of purpose, and greatness of mind that, from the very beginning,
from their very small kingdom and power, they set their minds
on the destruction of the rule of the Romans [Byzantines], and
hoped to secure complete power over Asia and Europe.

OF THE CONQUEST OF ASIA

§58. "And indeed, they did not belie themselves. Sallying
forth at the start from the mountains of Cilicia and Taurus, with
a small force, as I said, but with the greatest forethought and
prudence, they quickly overran Lycia, Pamplylia, and upper
Phrygia. They destroyed the Lydians, Carians, Mysians, and

lower Phrygians and the Ionians, all of the Greek seacoast. Then they subdued the Galatians, Cappadocians, Pamphlagonians, Chalybians, Bithynians, Hellespontians—in a word, all the land which the Taurus encloses from Cilicia clear to Sinope on the Euxine Sea, which territory they call Lower Asia, they captured within a short time and made it secure for themselves.

THE BEGINNING OF THE CROSSING INTO EUROPE

§59. "They made themselves masters of all this region and of its coasts, and gained a firm control over the cities in it. And having established their capital in Brusa, they crossed the Hellespont in fairly great numbers, it is true, but not for open warfare, rather for plundering and quick surprise raids as opportunity offered. At the same time they were held in check by the sea, because the Romans [Byzantines] had control of it. But they captured the peak of the mountain in front of the monument of Helle, opposite the ishthmus of Chersonesus, and having taken the castle there, by assault or by stratagem, they at first made raids from there and used the methods of banditry and of unforeseen attack and plunder, despoiling those who were near by.

THE CONQUEST OF EUROPE

§60. "But when they had advanced a short distance and were constantly becoming numerically stronger, they also captured some of the near-by fortresses, some by force of assault and others through stratagems. Thus they came down into the plain, and there nothing was any obstacle to them any more. They occupied the level country, sacked the villages and captured the cities, overthrew castles, defeated armies, and subdued many peoples. In a word, they overran without much delay the whole of Thrace and Macedonia. So they destroyed the Mysians [Bulgarians], who lived in the interior and along the Ister [Danube] River; also the Illyrians [Albanians], the Triballians [Serbs], the Hellenes, and many other races, and they subdued mighty castles and many large cities, some of them inland and others lying along the coasts.

§61. "But why should I waste time enumerating cities and nations? All the land that the Danube bounds, from its mouths

at the Euxine Sea[6] up to the junction with the Save, and going
thence inland between the Bistres [Bosnians] and the Dalma-
tians between the Save and the Albanians, toward the south and
west as far as the Ionian Gulf [the Adriatic Sea]—all this they
conquered and overthrew, subjecting to taxation all who were
in it. In addition, they conquered the Getae [Wallachians] beyond the Danube, and not only that, but all the coastlands except the Peloponnesus, a territory with a circumference of more
than a thousand stadia.

§62. "All this was not done without toil, nor as if one did it
by simply speaking the word, nor without opposition and resistance by those who were strong enough to resist. Nor did they
get the mastery without bloodshed and without dangers. And
they have not kept it till now without these. It cost them much
blood, many wounds, and much sweat and pain.

§63. "For many great nations in both Asia and Europe took
up arms against them, and struggled bravely, even to death, in
behalf of liberty, and with valor. And many large cities among
these peoples, fortified by walls and the bodies and arms and
wealth and valor of their inhabitants, and many other things,
rose up to resist. And fortified castles that were hard to capture,
and places hard to cross, and many difficulties, and numerous
rivers not easily crossed, and many such obstacles delayed them.

IN PRAISE OF THOSE MEN AND THEIR KINGS

§64. "But the greatest obstacle of all was the forces of the
Romans [Byzantines], both on land and on sea, always opposing
them and fighting them and giving them much resistance and
many struggles. Still, none of these things checked their forward
progress, or curbed their impetuosity and valor until, having
overthrown and completely demolished all, they firmly held the
rule. They showed everyone their great strength, being valorous
men to the very end and never yielding anything, from the very
start, of their plans and ideals. Whenever they conquered their
enemies, they went forward against them a great distance. And
when they were beaten, they did not fall back or give up their

6. Ancient name for Black Sea. Kritovoulos treats his theme in a self-
consciously traditional style, requiring use of old geographical terms.

good hope, but because of their confidence in themselves and their hope for the future, they endured everything, even when it was unknown to the Fates; moreover they bore up valiantly under events, daring even beyond their powers, taking unbelievable risks, and keeping good hope even in the worst circumstances.

§65. "They were also unyielding in distress, indefatigable in whatever they thought was advantageous to them, and eager for none of the pleasant things. They were quick to recognize duty, and swift to put into execution what they conceived as such. They always took delight in long absences from home in order to get possession of something they did not have. They were never content with what they had, nor did they allow others to be. They did not consider what was present as of any value, for they always went after the things they did not have, and they considered what they had not yet attained but which they had in mind, as if they already had it. They got very little encouragement out of what they already had, because of their desire for greater things, even though they toiled hard to gain and enjoy what they did not have. Their bodies they used as though they belonged to other persons as far as pain or danger was concerned. They did not in the least spare them, often even for mistaken purposes, and they kept their spirits unconquered. Thus, laboring all through their epoch, they chose for themselves a life full of struggles and pains. So they brought the realm to such a point of glory and strength, by their numbers and wealth and by the arms and ships and all that they had, and handed it down to us very great in appearance and most capable for either war or peace. Let us not seem to betray the trust!

§66. "Our part, then, is not to destroy the achievements of our ancestors, not detract from our own glory which we have secured through a long period. We are famed among all peoples for our courage and strategy and valor, and until now have been considered, and rightly so, as unconquerable. But now we are defeated by one city, and that one no longer daring to trust to itself but almost emptied of all its inhabitants and entirely cut off from and deprived of all the good things it previously enjoyed by the long-continued and repeated attacks and sieges of our forces, so that it is no longer a city but survives only in name. As for the rest, it is only farm land and an enclosure of plants and vineyards, as you see, and worthless houses and empty walls, most of them in ruins. And you see how it is located in the midst of our realm, finely situated by land and sea, how many great difficulties it has given us from the beginning, and still gives us now—always fighting against us, lying in wait for our goods and battening on our misfortunes and injuring us as much as possible.

THE PLAN OF THE CASTLE

. . . .

§86. "Let us not then delay any longer, but let us attack the City swiftly with all our powers and with this conviction: that we shall either capture it with one blow or shall never withdraw from it, even if we must die, until we become masters of it.

§87. "And I myself will first of all be with you and gladly share your travails, and will direct everything in the best way. I will reward the brave with appropriate gifts, each after his worth and valor, according as each is conspicuous in danger or distinguished for some special exploit."

VOTING FOR WAR BY THE SULTAN AND BY ALL

§88. So, when he had said this, he cast his vote for war. And practically all of those present applauded what was said by the Sultan, praising him for his good will and knowledge, bravery and valor, and agreeing with him, and still further inciting each other to war—some of them because of their own ambition and hope of gain, hoping from that time on to make something out of it and secure more riches for themselves, others to please the Sultan and at the same time wishing to make some gain themselves out of such affairs, and still others, with no knowledge of war—those who were young and inexperienced in such things.

§89. But those whose ideas were against the step for various reasons and especially because of the misfortunes they had had in war and the difficulties usually attendant on it, wanted to advise against making war. However, seeing the insistence and zeal of the Sultan, they were afraid, as it seems to me, and unwillingly yielded and were carried along with the majority. So the war was sanctioned by all.

A SURPRISING PLAN AND DECISION[7]

§172. Sultan Mehmed considered it necessary in preparation for his next move to get possession of the harbor and open the Horn for his own ships to sail in. So, since every effort and device of his had failed to force the entrance, he made a wise decision, and one worthy of his intellect and power. It succeeded in accomplishing his purpose and in putting an end to all uncertainties.

§173. He ordered the commanders of the vessels to construct as quickly as possible glideways leading from the outer sea to the inner sea, that is, from the harbor to the Horn, near the place called Diplokion, and to cover them with beams. This road, measured from sea to sea, is just about eight stadia. It is very steep for more than half the way, until you reach the summit of the hill, and from there again it descends to the inner sea of the Horn. And as the glideways were completed sooner than expected, because of the large number of workers, he brought up the ships and placed large cradles under them, with stays against each of their sides to hold them up. And having under-girded them well with ropes, he fastened long cables to the corners and gave them to the soldiers to drag, some of them by hand, and others by certain machines and capstans.

§174. So the ships were dragged along very swiftly. And their crews, as they followed them, rejoiced at the event and boasted of it. Then they manned the ships on the land as if they were on the sea. Some of them hoisted the sails with a shout, as if they were setting sail, and the breeze caught the sails and bellied them out. Others seated themselves on the benches, holding the oars in their hands and moving them as if rowing. And the commanders, running along by the sockets of the masts with whistlings and shouting, and with their whips beating the oars-

7. Mehmed had personally assigned various divisions to their stations surrounding the land side of the city. He first had the gates attacked with battering ram, then had his engineers build a very large cannon on the spot, and then resorted to the plan whose description follows.

men on the benches, ordered them to row. The ships, borne along over the land as if on the sea, were some of them being pulled up the ascent to the top of the hill while others were being hauled down the slope into the harbor, lowering the sails with shouting and great noise.

§175. It was a strange spectacle, and unbelievable in the telling except to those who actually did see it—the sight of ships borne along on the mainland as if sailing on the sea, with their crews and their sails and all their equipment. I believe this was a much greater feat than the cutting of a canal across at Athos by Xerxes, and much stranger to see and to hear about. Furthermore, this event of but yesterday, before our very eyes, makes it easier to believe that the other also actually happened, for without this one, the other would have seemed a myth and sounded like idle talk.

§176. Thus, then, there assembled in the bay called Cold Waters, a little beyond Galata, a respectable fleet of some sixty-seven vessels. They were moored there.

§177. The Romans, when they saw such an unheard-of thing actually happen, and warships lying at anchor in the Horn— which they never would have suspected—were astounded at the impossibility of the spectacle, and were overcome by the greatest consternation and perplexity. They did not know what to do now, but were in despair. In fact they had left unguarded the walls along the Horn for a distance of about thirty stadia, and even so they did not have enough men for the rest of the walls, either for defense or for attack, whether citizens or men from elsewhere. Instead, two or even three battlements had but a single defender.

§178. And now, when this sea-wall also became open to attack and had to be guarded, they were compelled to strip the other battlements and bring men there. This constituted a manifest danger, since the defenders were taken away from the rest of the wall while those remaining were not enough to guard it, being so few.

§179. Not only was there this difficulty, but, the bridge being completed, heavy infantry and bowmen could cross against the wall. Hence that part also had to be guarded. And the ships near the mouth of the harbor and at the chain, galleons and triremes alike, as well as the other ships in the harbor had the greater need to be on guard since now they were subject to attack from within as well as from outside. Therefore in many directions they appeared to have, and actually had, difficulties. Still, they did not neglect anything that could be done.

§180. Giustinianni[8] removed one of his galleons from the mouth of the harbor plus three of the Italian triremes, and took them against the end of the gulf where the Sultan's ships were anchored. There he anchored so as to fight from them and prevent the [Ottoman] warships from going out anywhere in the gulf or being able to do any harm to the harbor or its shipping. This he thought was the best plan as a counter-measure. But it was only a temporary expedient.

§181. For Sultan Mehmed, seeing this, made the following counter-moves: He ordered the cannon-makers to transfer the cannon secretly by night and place them near the shore, opposite to where the ships and the galleon were moored, and fire stones at them. This they did with great speed, and they hit one of the triremes in the middle and sank it with all on board, excepting a very few who swam to the other triremes. Then the crews quickly moved the ships away a good distance, and anchored there. If this had not been done quickly, the other triremes also would have been sunk, with their crews, as well as the galleon, for they seemed to have had no sense at all of their danger. They were thus very near to destruction, for the cannon were ready to fire the stone balls at them.

§182. But when this failed, the Romans had nothing else they could do. They simply fired at the ships from the walls with catapults and javelins and prevented them from moving about. And from the triremes at the mouth of the harbor some attacked them every day and chased them back and prevented their injuring anything in the harbor. And they often pursued them till near the land, toward their own men. Then these ships would again turn and attack the triremes, and men would follow on foot, firing and being fired on, and so they had long-range exchanges daily.

8. Commander of the Genoese fleet aiding the Byzantines.

POSITION AND ORDERS GIVEN THE GENERALS

. . . .

§215. Then the Sultan mounted his horse and went around to all the other divisions, reviewing them and giving his orders to all in general and each in particular. He encouraged them and stirred them up for the battle, especially the officers of the troops, calling each one by name. Then, having passed along the entire army, along the wall from sea to sea, and having given the necessary orders and encouraged and incited all for the fight, and having urged them to play the man, he ordered them to have their food and rest until the battle-cry should be given and they should see the signal. And after doing all this, he went back to his tent, had his meal, and rested.

§216. Now the Romans, seeing the army so quiet and more tranquil than usual, marveled at the fact and ventured on various explanations and guesses. Some—not judging it aright—thought this was a preparation for withdrawal. Others—and this proved correct—believed that it was a preparation for battle and an alert, things which they had been expecting in the near future. So they passed the word along and then went in silence to their own divisions and made all sorts of preparations.

§217. The hour was already advanced, the day was declining and near evening, and the sun was at the Ottomans' backs but shining in the faces of their enemies. This was just as the Sultan had wished; accordingly he gave the order first for the trumpets to sound the battle-signal, and the other instruments, the pipes and flutes and cymbals too, as loud as they could. All the trumpets of the other divisions, with the other instruments in turn, sounded all together, a great and fearsome sound. Everything shook and quivered at the noise. After that, the standards were displayed.

§218. To begin, the archers and slingers and those in charge of the cannon and the muskets, in accord with the commands given them, advanced against the wall slowly and gradually. When they got within bowshot, they halted to fight. And first they exchanged fire with the heavier weapons, with arrows from the archers, stones from the slingers, and iron and leaden balls from the cannon and muskets. Then, as they closed with battleaxes and javelins and spears, hurling them at each other and being hurled at pitilessly in rage and fierce anger. On both sides there was loud shouting and blasphemy and cursing. Many on each side were wounded, and not a few died. This kept up till sunset, a space of about two or three hours.

§219. Then, with fine insight, the Sultan summoned the shield-bearers, heavy infantry and other troops and said: "Go to it, friends and children mine! It is time now to show yourselves good fighters!" They immediately crossed the moat, with shouts and fearful yells, and attacked the outer wall. All of it, however, had been demolished by the cannon. There were only stockades of great beams instead of a wall, and bundles of vine-branches, and jars full of earth. At that point a fierce battle ensued close in and with the weapons of hand-to-hand fighting. The heavy infantry and shield-bearers fought to overcome the defenders and get over the stockade, while the Romans and Italians tried to fight these off and to guard the stockade. At times the infantry did get over the wall and the stockade, pressing forward bravely and unhesitatingly. And at times they were stoutly forced back and driven off.

§220. The Sultan followed them up, as they struggled bravely, and encouraged them. He ordered those in charge of the cannon to put the match to the cannon. And these, being set off, fired their stone balls against the defenders and worked no little destruction on both sides, among those in the near vicinity.

§221. So, then, the two sides struggled and fought bravely and vigorously. Most of the night passed, and the Romans were successful and prevailed not a little. Also, Giustinianni and his men kept their positions stubbornly, and guarded the stockade and defended themselves bravely against the aggressors.

.   .   .   .

§226. Sultan Mehmed saw that the attacking divisions were very much worn out by the battle and had not made any progress worth mentioning, and that the Romans and Italians were not only fighting stoutly but were prevailing in the battle. He was very indignant at this, considering that it ought not to be endured any longer. Immediately he brought up the divisions which he had been reserving for later on, men who were ex-

tremely well armed, daring and brave, and far in advance of
the rest in experience and valor. They were the elite of the
army: heavy infantry, bowmen, and lancers, and his own bodyguard, and along with them those of the division called Yenitsari
[Janissaries].

§227. Calling to them and urging them to prove themselves
now as heroes, he led the attack against the wall, himself at the
head until they reached the moat. There he ordered the bowmen, slingers, and musketeers to stand at a distance and fire to
the right, against the defenders on the palisade and on the bat-
tered wall. They were to keep up so heavy a fire that those
defenders would be unable to fight, or to expose themselves because of the cloud of arrows and other projectiles falling like
snowflakes.

§228. To all the rest, the heavy infantry and the shield-
bearers, the Sultan gave orders to cross the moat swiftly and
attack the palisade. With a loud and terrifying war-cry and
with fierce impetuosity and wrath, they advanced as if mad.
Being young and strong and full of daring, and especially because they were fighting in the Sultan's presence, their valor
exceeded every expectation. They attacked the palisade and
fought bravely without any hesitation. Needing no further orders, they knocked down the turrets which had been built out
in front, broke the yardarms, scattered the materials that had
been gathered, and forced the defenders back inside the palisade.

§229. Giustinianni with his men, and the Romans in that section fought bravely with lances, axes, pikes, javelins, and other
weapons of offense. It was a hand-to-hand encounter, and they
stopped the attackers and prevented them from getting inside
the palisade. There was much shouting on both sides—the
mingled sounds of blasphemy, insults, threats, attackers, defenders, shooters, those shot at, killers and dying, of those who in
anger and wrath did all sorts of terrible things. And it was a
sight to see there: a hard fight going on hand-to-hand with
great determination and for the greatest rewards, heroes fighting valiantly, the one party struggling with all their might to
force back the defenders, get possession of the wall, enter the
City, and fall upon the children and women and the treasures,

the other party bravely agonizing to drive them off and guard
their possessions, even if they were not to succeed in prevailing
and in keeping them.

§230. Instead, the hapless Romans were destined finally to be
brought under the yoke of servitude and to suffer its horrors. For
although they battled bravely, and though they lacked nothing
of willingness and daring in the contest, Giustinianni received
a mortal wound in the breast from an arrow fired by a crossbow.
It passed clear through his breastplate, and he fell where he was
and was carried to his tent in a hopeless condition. All who were
with him were scattered, being upset by their loss. They abandoned the palisade and wall where they had been fighting, and
thought of only one thing—how they could carry him on to the
galleons and get away safe themselves.

§231. But the Emperor Constantine besought them earnestly,
and made promises to them if they would wait a little while,
till the fighting should subside. They would not consent, however, but taking up their leader and all their armor, they
boarded the galleons in haste and with all speed, giving no
consideration to the other defenders.

§232. The Emperor Constantine forbade the others to follow.
Then, though he had no idea what to do next—for he had no
other reserves to fill the places thus left vacant, the ranks of
those who had so suddenly deserted, and meantime the battle
raged fiercely and all had to see to their own ranks and places
and fight there—still, with his remaining Romans and his bodyguard, which was so few as to be easily counted, he took his
stand in front of the palisade and fought bravely.

§233. Sultan Mehmed, who happened to be fighting quite
near by, saw that the palisade and the other part of the wall
that had been destroyed were now empty of men and deserted
by the defenders. He noted that men were slipping away secretly and that those who remained were fighting feebly because they were so few. Realizing from this that the defenders
had fled and that the wall was deserted, he shouted out:
"Friends, we have the City! We have it! They are already fleeing from us! They can't stand it any longer! The wall is bare of
defenders! It needs just a little more effort and the City is taken!

Don't weaken, but on with the work with all your might, and be men and I am with you!"

CAPTURE OF THE CITY

§234. So saying, he led them himself. And they, with a shout on the run and with a fearsome yell, went on ahead of the Sultan, pressing on up to the palisade. After a long and bitter struggle they hurled back the Romans from there and climbed by force up the palisade. They dashed some of their foe down into the ditch between the great wall and the palisade, which was deep and hard to get out of, and they killed them there. The rest they drove back to the gate.

DEATH OF EMPEROR CONSTANTINE

§235. He had opened this gate in the great wall, so as to go easily over to the palisade. Now there was a great struggle there and great slaughter among those stationed there, for they were attacked by the heavy infantry and not a few others in irregular formation, who had been attracted from many points by the shouting. There the Emperor Constantine, with all who were with him, fell in gallant combat.

§236. The heavy infantry were already streaming through the little gate into the City, and others had rushed in through the breach in the great wall. Then all the rest of the army, with a rush and a roar, poured in brilliantly and scattered all over the City. And the Sultan stood before the great wall, where the standard also was and the ensigns, and watched the proceedings. The day was already breaking.

GREAT RUSH, AND MANY KILLED

§237. Then a great slaughter occurred of those who happened to be there: some of them were on the streets, for they had already left the houses and were running toward the tumult when they fell unexpectedly on the swords of the soldiers; others were in their own homes and fell victims to the violence of the Janissaries and other soldiers, without any rhyme or reason; others were resisting, relying on their own courage; still others were fleeing to the churches and making supplication—men, women, and children, everyone, for there was no quarter given.

§238. The soldiers fell on them with anger and great wrath. For one thing, they were actuated by the hardships of the siege. For another, some foolish people had hurled taunts and curses at them from the battlements all through the siege. Now, in general they killed so as to frighten all the City, and to terrorize and enslave all by the slaughter.

PLUNDER OF THE CITY

§239. When they had had enough of murder, and the City was reduced to slavery, some of the troops turned to the mansions of the mighty, by bands and companies and divisions, for plunder and spoil. Others went to the robbing of churches, and others dispersed to the simple homes of the common people, stealing, robbing, plundering, killing, insulting, taking and enslaving men, women, and children, old and young, priests, monks—in short, every age and class.

HERE, TOO, A SAD TRAGEDY

§240. There was a further sight, terrible and pitiful beyond all tragedies: young and chaste women of noble birth and well to do, accustomed to remain at home and who had hardly ever left their own premises, and handsome and lovely maidens of splendid and renowned families, till then unsullied by male eyes —some of these were dragged by force from their chambers and hauled off pitilessly and dishonorably.

§241. Other women, sleeping in their beds, had to endure nightmares. Men with swords, their hands bloodstained with murder, breathing out rage, speaking out murder indiscriminate, flushed with all the worst things—this crowd, made up of men from every race and nation, brought together by chance, like wild and ferocious beasts, leaped into the houses, driving them out mercilessly, dragging, rending, forcing, hauling them disgracefully into the public highways, insulting them and doing every evil thing.

§242. They say that many of the maidens, even at the mere unaccustomed sight and sound of these men, were terror-stricken and came near losing their very lives. And there were also honorable old men who were dragged by their white hair, and some of them beaten unmercifully. And well-born and beautiful young boys were carried off.

§243. There were priests who were driven along, and consecrated virgins who were honorable and wholly unsullied, devoted to God alone and living for Him to whom they had consecrated themselves. Some of these were forced out of their cells and driven off, and others dragged out of the churches where they had taken refuge and driven off with insult and dishonor, their cheeks scratched, amid wailing and lamentation and bitter tears. Tender children were snatched pitilessly from their mothers, young brides separated ruthlessly from their newly-married husbands. And ten thousand other terrible deeds were done.

PLUNDERING AND ROBBING OF THE CHURCHES

§244. And the desecrating and plundering and robbing of the churches—how can one describe it in words? Some things they threw in dishonor on the ground—ikons and reliquaries and other objects from the churches. The crowd snatched some of these, and some were given over to the fire while others were torn to shreds and scattered at the crossroads. The last resting-places of the blessed men of old were opened, and their remains were taken out and disgracefully torn to pieces, even to shreds, and made the sport of the wind while others were thrown on the streets.

§245. Chalices and goblets and vessels to hold the holy sacrifice, some of them were used for drinking and carousing, and others were broken up or melted down and sold. Holy vessels and costly robes richly embroidered with much gold or brilliant with precious stones and pearls were some of them given to the most wicked men for no good use, while others were consigned to the fire and melted down for gold.

§246. And holy and divine books, and others mainly of profane literature and philosophy, were either given to the flames or dishonorably trampled under foot. Many of them were sold for two or three pieces of money, and sometimes for pennies only, not for gain so much as in contempt. Holy altars were torn from their foundations and overthrown. The walls of sanctuaries and cloisters were explored, and the holy places of the shrines were dug into and overthrown in the search for gold. Many other such things they dared to do.

§247. Those unfortunate Romans who had been assigned to other parts of the wall and were fighting there, on land and by the sea, supposed that the City was still safe and had not suffered reverses, and that their women and children were free— for they had no knowledge at all of what had happened. They kept on fighting lustily, powerfully resisting the attackers and brilliantly driving off those who were trying to scale the walls. But when they saw the enemy in their rear, attacking them from inside the City, and saw women and children being led away captives and shamefully treated, some were overwhelmed with hopelessness and threw themselves with their weapons over the wall and were killed, while others in utter despair dropped their weapons from hands already paralyzed, and surrendered to the enemy without a struggle, to be treated as the enemy chose.

NUMBER OF ROMANS WHO DIED IN THE STRUGGLE, AND OF THE PRISONERS TAKEN

§255. There died, of Romans and of foreigners, as was reported, in all the fighting and in the capture itself, all told, men, women and children, well-nigh four thousand, and a little more than fifty thousand were taken prisoners, including about five hundred from the whole army.

ENTRY OF THE SULTAN INTO THE CITY, AND HIS SEEING OF IT ALL, AND HIS GRIEF

§256. After this the Sultan entered the City and looked about to see its great size, its situation, its grandeur and beauty, its teeming population, its loveliness, and the costliness of its churches and public buildings and of the private houses and community houses and of those of the officials. He also saw the setting of the harbor and of the arsenals, and how skilfully and ingeniously they had everything arranged in the City—in a word, all the construction and adornment of it. When he saw what a large number had been killed, and the ruin of the buildings, and the wholesale ruin and destruction of the City, he was filled with compassion and repented not a little at the destruction and plundering. Tears fell from his eyes as he groaned deeply and passionately: "What a city we have given over to plunder and destruction!"

SYMPATHY

§257. Thus he suffered in spirit. And indeed this was a great blow to us, in this one city, a disaster the like of which had occurred in no one of the great renowned cities of history, whether one speaks of the size of the captured City or of the bitterness and harshness of the deed. And no less did it astound all others than it did those who went through it and suffered, through the unreasonable and unusual character of the event and through the overwhelming and unheard-of horror of it.

EPILOGUE

§276. As for the great City of Constantine, raised to a great height of glory and dominion and wealth in its own times, overshadowing to an infinite degree all the cities around it, renowned for its glory, wealth, authority, power, and greatness, and all its other qualities, it thus came to its end.

§277. The Sultan Mehmed, when he had carefully viewed the City and all its contents, went back to the camp and divided the spoils. First he took the customary toll of the spoils for himself. Then also, as prizes from all the rest, he chose out beautiful virgins and those of the best families, and the handsomest boys, some of whom he even bought from the soldiers. He also chose some of the distinguished men who, he was informed, were above the rest in family and intelligence and valor. . . .

§278. For the Sultan was overcome with pity for the men and their misfortune, as he saw from what good circumstances they had fallen into such great predicaments. And he had good intentions towards them, even though his ill will soon overcame these plans.

§279. After arranging these affairs and all that concerned with the soldiers, suitably in accordance with his intentions, he honored some of them with government positions and offices, and others with money, and still others with stipends and many other sorts of gifts. He also did kindnesses to and personally received those whom he knew to have fought well. And after making an address to them and telling them many things, praising and thanking them, he disbanded the army.

§280. Then, with the notable men, and his courtiers, he went through the City. First he planned how to repopulate it, not merely as it formerly was but more completely, if possible, so that it should be a worthy capital for him, situated, as it was, most favorably by land and by sea. Then he donated to all the grandees, and to those of his household, the magnificent homes of the rich, with gardens and fields and vineyards inside of the City. And to some of them he even gave beautiful churches as their private residences.

§281. For himself, he chose the most beautiful location in the center of the City for the erection of a royal palace. After this, he settled all the captives whom he had taken as his portion, together with their wives and children, along the shores of the city harbor, since they were sea-faring men whom they previously had called Stenites. He gave them houses and freed them from taxes for a specified time.

§282. He also made a proclamation to all those who had paid their own ransom, or who promised to pay it to their masters within a limited time, that they might live in the City, and he granted them, also, freedom from taxes, and gave them houses, either their own or those of others.

§283. He wanted those of the nobility whom he approved of to live there with their wives and children. Accordingly he gave them houses and lands and provisions for living, and tried in every way to help them. This was his intention and purpose, as has been stated.

The Safavid Challenge

In Muslim opinion, the Ottomans' right to rule rested on their success in war against the Christians and on their implementing the Holy Law in their lands. But this did not entitle them to dominate other Sunnî Muslim states and when Ottoman arms first attempted to overthrow rival Muslim rulers throughout Asia Minor, religious resistance developed. In 1502 the threat increased when the head of the Safavid family, Ismâ'îl, proclaimed himself shâh and quickly built an empire directly to the east of the Ottoman frontier.

Ismâ'îl's success depended on his followers' belief that his descent (probably fictitious) from Muhammad's son-in-law 'Alî made him the true and only legitimate successor to the Prophet. Such a claim implied that all other Muslim rulers were usurpers, including the Ottoman sultâns. This doctrine was especially explosive because large numbers of people in Asia Minor were predisposed to accept such an idea. For generations a semi-secret Shî'ite propaganda had taught that the rulers of Islâm were all illegitimate, and that the true head of the Muslim community, the Imâm, would appear someday to overthrow the mighty and set all things right. Ismâ'îl's meteoric career seemed to match such expectations, and the many views which had developed about how and when the Imâm would manifest himself tended to coalesce around his person.

Sultân Selîm I responded to this challenge by resorting to terror against those in his domains suspected of sympathizing with Shâh Ismâ'îl. He massacred many thousands in eastern Asia Minor and then marched on Tabrîz, Ismâ'îl's new capital. Selîm's Ottoman forces defeated Ismâ'îl and his army at Chaldirân (1514) and occupied Tabrîz, but could not hold it because the town was too far from Constantinople. The result was a stand-off, each ruler remaining supreme within his own frontiers.

Before the battle of Chaldirân, Selîm and Ismâ'îl exchanged a number of letters. The two of these letters translated below are not dated, but were probably written sometime in 1514. Ismâ'îl's letter, apparently the only one he wrote, came in reply to three Selîm had written, one of which is translated below. The letters were, in fact, a form of propaganda. Selîm set out to defend his right to rule by quoting from the Qur'ân and alluding to examples from history which buttressed his claims. Ismâ'îl, who based his claims on heredity, had no need of such learning; rather he quotes from seemingly contemporary Persian poetry and appears almost casual, if not insolent, in addressing his rival.

LETTERS FROM SELÎM AND ISMÂ'ÎL

I

Selîm to Ismâ'îl (undated, ca. 1514)

"It is from Solomon and it is: 'In the Name of God, the Merciful, the Compassionate. Rise not up against me, but come to me in surrender.' "

[Qur'ân XXVII:30-31]

God's blessings upon the best of his creatures, Muhammad, his family, and his companions all.

"This is a Scripture We have sent down, blessed; so follow it, and be godfearing; haply so you will find mercy." [Qur'ân VI:156]

This missive which is stamped with the seal of victory and which is, like inspiration descending from the heavens, witness to the verse "We never chastise until We send forth a Messenger" [Qur'ân XVII:15] has been graciously issued by our most glorious majesty—we who are the Caliph of God Most High in this world, far and wide; the proof of the verse "And what profits men abides in the earth" [Qur'ân XIII:17) the Solomon of Splendor, the Alexander of eminence; haloed in victory, Farîdûn[1] triumphant; slayer of the wicked and the infidel, guardian of the noble and the pious; the warrior in the Path, the defender of the Faith; the champion, the conqueror; the lion, son

From *Asnâd va nâmehâye tarîkhî va ijtimâiyye dowreye safaviyye*, edited by Z. Sabitiyân, Tehran: Ibn-i Sînâ, 1964, pp. 112-17. Trans. especially for this volume by John Woods. Reprinted by permission of Mr. Woods.

1. An ancient and celebrated king of Persia, who began to reign about 750 B.C.E.

and grandson of the lion; standard-bearer of justice and righteousness, Sultân Selîm Shâh, son of Sultân Bayezîd, son of
Sultân Muhammad Khân—and is addressed to the ruler of the
kingdom of the Persians, the possessor of the land of tyranny
and perversion, the captain of the vicious, the chief of the mali-
cious, the usurping Darius[2] of the time, the malevolent Zahhâk[3]
of the age, the peer of Cain, Prince Ismâ'îl.

As the Pen of Destiny has drawn up the rescript "Thou
givest the kingdom to whom Thou wilt" [Qur'ân III:26] in our
sublime name and has signed it with the verse "Whatsoever
mercy God opens to men, none can withhold" [Qur'ân XXXV:
2], it is manifest in the Court of Glory and the Presence of
Deity that we, the instrument of Divine Will, shall hold in force
upon the earth both the commandments and prohibitions of
Divine Law as well as the provisions of royal proclamations.
"That is the bounty of God; he gives it unto whomsoever He
will." [Qur'ân LVII:21]

It has been heard repeatedly that you have subjected the upright community of Muhammad (Prayers and salutations upon
its founder!) to your devious will, that you have undermined the
firm foundation of the Faith, that you have unfurled the banner
of oppression in the cause of aggression, that you no longer up-
hold the commandments and prohibitions of the Divine Law,
that you have incited your abominable Shî'î faction to unsancti-
fied sexual union and to the shedding of innocent blood,[4] that
like they "Who listen to falsehood and consume the unlawful"
[Qur'ân V:42] you have given ear to idle deceitful words and
have eaten that which is forbidden:[5]

> He has laid waste to mosques, as it is said,
> Constructing idol temples in their stead,

2. Darius: Probably Darius III (r. 336-330 B.C.E.), who was defeated three
times by Alexander the Great before his assassination by the satrap of Bac-
tria. Selîm is alluding to current Ottoman-Safavid relations.

3. Zahhâk: A mythological king of Irân, notorious for blood-thirstiness.

4. Reference to uncanonical practices, such as temporary marriage. The
shedding of blood could be a reference to Shî'î massacres of Sunnîs at
Tabrîz and elsewhere.

5. Further reference to uncanonical (from Sunnî perspective) practices
condoned by Shî'ites.

that you have rent the noble stuff of Islâm with the hand of tyranny, and that you have called the Glorious Qur'ân the myths of the Ancients. The rumor of these abominations has caused your name to become like that of Hârith deceived by Satan.[6]

Indeed, as both the *fatwa*s of distinguished *'ulamâ*[7] who base their opinion on reason and tradition alike and the consensus of the Sunnî[8] community agree that the ancient obligation of extirpation, extermination, and expulsion of evil innovation must be the aim of our exalted aspiration, for "Religious zeal is a victory for the Faith of God the Beneficent"; then, in accordance with the words of the Prophet (Peace upon him!) "Whosoever introduces evil innovation into our order must be expelled" and "Whosoever does aught against our order must be expelled," action has become necessary and exigent. Thus, when the Divine Decree of Eternal Destiny commended the eradication of the infamously wicked infidels into our capable hands, we set out for their lands like ineluctable fate itself to enforce the order "Leave not upon the earth of the Unbelievers even one." [Qur'ân LXXI:26] If God almighty wills, the lightning of our conquering sword shall uproot the untamed bramble grown to great heights in the path of the refulgent Divine Law and shall cast them down upon the dust of abjectness to be trampled under the hooves of our legions, for "They make the mightiest of its inhabitants abased. Even so they too will do" [Qur'ân XXVII:34]; the thunder of our avenging mace shall dash out the muddled brains of the enemies of the Faith as rations for the lion-hearted *ghâzîs*. "And those who do wrong shall surely know by what overthrowing they will be overthrown." [Qur'ân XXVI:227]

> When I the sharp-edged sword draw from its sheath,
> Then shall I raise up doomsday on the earth.

6. Hârith: Possibly a reference to Hârith ibn Suwayd, who pretended to convert to Islâm in Muhammad's time, apostasized, and was ordered executed by Muhammad when he tried to rejoin the young Muslim community. Selîm is alluding to parallels between Hârith's and Ismâ'îl's career.

7. *Fatwa*s: legal opinions; *'ulamâ*: learned men.

8. Sunnî community: those who follow the practice of Muhammad, i.e., not those like Shî'îtes who followed 'Alî.

Then shall I roast the hearts of lion-hearted men,
And toast the morning with a goblet of their blood.
My crow-feathered arrow will fix the eagle in his flight;
My naked blade will make the sun's heart tremble.
Inquire of the sun about the dazzle of my rein;
Seek news of Mars about the brilliance of my arms.
Although a Sûfî[9] crown you wear, I bear a trenchant sword:
The owner of the sword will soon possess the crown.
O Mighty Fortune, pray grant this my single wish:
Pray let me take both crown and power from the foe.

But "Religion is Counsel," and should you turn the countenance of submission to the *qibla* of bliss and the Kaʿba[10] of hope—our angelic threshhold, the refuge of the noble—moreover, should you lift up the hand of oppression from the heads of your subjects ruined by tyranny and sedition, should you take up a course of repentance, become like one blameless and return to the sublime straight path of the Sunna[11] of Muhammad (Prayers and salutations upon him and God's satisfaction upon his immaculate family and his rightly-guided companions all!). For "My companions are like the stars: whomever you choose to follow, you will be guided aright."[12] and finally should you consider your lands and their people part of the well-protected Ottoman state, then shall you be granted our royal favor and our imperial patronage.

He whose face touches the dust of my threshold in submission
Will be enveloped in the shadow of my favor and my justice.

How great the happiness of him who complies with this!

On the other hand, if your evil, seditious habits have become a part of your nature, that which has become essential can never again be accidental.

---

9. Allusion to Safavî origins as mystical order. The "crown" was their special headgear. Though the meter is that of the old famous *Shâhnâmeh* of Firdawsî, such topical references mark it as contemporary composition.

10. *Qibla*: direction of prayer for Muslims, i.e., the Kaʿba or holy building in Mecca.

11. *Sunna*: practice, example, custom.

12. Reference to Shîʿî practice of cursing the first three caliphs.

What avail sermons to the black-hearted?

Then, with the support and assistance of God, I will crown the head of every gallows tree with the head of a crown-wearing Sûfî and clear that faction from the face of the earth—"The party of God, they are the victors" [Qur'ân V:56]; I will break the oppressors' grip with the power of the miraculous white hand of Moses, for "God's hand is over their hands." [Qur'ân XLVIII:10] Let them remove the cotton of negligence from the ears of their intelligence and, with their shrouds on their shoulders, prepare themselves for "Surely that which you are promised will come to pass." [Qur'ân VI:134] The triumphant troops "As though they were a building well-compacted" [Qur'ân LXI:4] crying out like fate evoked "When their term comes they shall not put it back a single hour nor put it forward" [Qur'ân VII:34] and maneuvering in accordance with "Slay them wherever you find them" [Qur'ân IV:89], will wreak ruin upon you and drive you from that land. "To God belongs the command before and after, and on that day the believers shall rejoice." [Qur'ân XXX:4] "So the last roots of the people who did evil were cut off. Praise be to God, the Lord of the Worlds." [Qur'ân VI:45]

II
Ismâ'îl to Selîm (undated, ca. 1514)

May his godly majesty, the refuge of Islâm, the might of the kingdom, he upon whom God looks with favor, the champion of the sultanate and of the state, the hero of the faith and of the earth, Sultân Selîm Shâh (God grant him immortal state and eternal happiness!) accept this affectionate greeting and this friendly letter, considering it a token of our good will.

Now to begin: Your honored letters have arrived one after another, for "No sooner has a thing doubled than it has tripled." Their contents, although indicative of hostility, are stated with boldness and vigor. The latter gives us much enjoyment and pleasure, but we are ignorant of the reason for the former. In the time of your late blessed father (May God enlighten his proof!) when our royal troops passed through the lands of Rûm[13]

13. Rûm, i.e., eastern Anatolia. Selîm's father was Bayezîd II (r. 1481-1512).

to chastise the impudence of ʿAlâʾ al-Dawla Dhûʾl-Qadr,[14] complete concord and friendship was shown on both sides. Moreover, when your majesty was governor at Trebizond [i.e., before his accession] there existed perfect mutual understanding. Thus, now, the cause of your resentment and displeasure yet remains unknown. If political necessity has compelled you on this course, then may your problems soon be solved.

> Dispute may fire words to such a heat
> That ancient houses be consumed in flames.

The intention of our inaction in this regard is twofold:

(1) Most of the inhabitants of the land of Rûm are followers of our forefathers (May God the All-Forgiving King have mercy upon them!).

(2) We have always loved the *ghâzî*-titled[15] Ottoman house and we do not wish the outbreak of sedition and turmoil once again as in the time of Tîmûr.

Why should we then take umbrage at these provocations? We shall not.

> The mutual hostility of kings is verily an ancient rite.

> Should one hold the bride of worldly rule too close,
> His lips those of the radiant sword will kiss.

Nevertheless, there is no cause for improper words: indeed, those vain, heretical imputations are the mere fabrications of the opium-clouded minds of certain secretaries and scribes. We therefore think that our delayed reply was not completely without cause for we have now dispatched our honored personal companion and servant Shâh Qulî Âghâ (May he be sustained!) with a golden casket stamped with the royal seal and filled with a special preparation for their use should they deem it necessary. May he soon arrive so that with assistance from above the mysteries concealed behind the veil of fate might be disclosed. But one should always exercise free judgment not bound solely

14. ʿAlâʾ al-Dawla Dhûʾl-Qadr: ruler of partially Shîʿite Dhûʾl-Qadr Turkomans in Elbistan and Marʿash, buffer state between Ottomans and Safavids. Ismâʿîl had attacked them in 1507.

15. An allusion to the Ottoman origin as frontier warriors for the faith.

by the words of others and always keep in view that in the end regrets avail him naught.

At this writing we were engaged upon the hunt near Isfahân;[16] we now prepare provisions and our troops for the coming campaign. In all friendship we say do what you will.

> Bitter experience has taught that in this world of trial
> He who falls upon the house of 'Alî[17] always falls.

Kindly give our ambassador leave to travel unmolested. "No soul laden bears the load of another." [Qur'ân VI: 164; LIII: 38]

When war becomes inevitable, hesitation and delay must be set aside, and one must think on that which is to come. Farewell.

Portraits of Three Monarchs
I. The Ottoman Sulaymân

Sulaymân I (r. 1520-1566) conquered most of Hungary for the Ottoman empire, and carried the Turkish frontier close to its final limits. After his time rapid expansion ceased, so that in retrospect Sulaymân's reign looked like the peak of Ottoman greatness, both to Turks and to their Christian enemies.

Sulaymân's high reputation in western Europe also owed a good deal to Ghislain de Busbecq (1522-1592) who published a series of letters describing Turkish government and society in rather favorable terms, praising Sulaymân as almost a model ruler. Busbecq was in a position to know, for he went to Constantinople in 1555 to act as ambassador for the Hapsburg ruler, Ferdinand I, and remained in Turkey until 1562. Extracts from his report are included here.

Busbecq intended these letters for publication. He wanted to inform the Western public about exotic Turkish institutions and customs; and for the most part his observations are correct, constituting

16. City in Persian Irâq, later (1598) to become the Safavid capital.
17. House of 'Alî, i.e., the Shî'îtes.

one of the earliest as well as one of the most vivid foreign accounts of the empire. Yet he had an axe to grind too. One of his purposes was to frighten European rulers and governments into reforming themselves by emphasizing the Turkish threat. Hence his report of the good order and discipline of Turkish troops was exaggerated; and his emphasis upon the rationality of Turkish institutions was enhanced by a desire to draw a contrast with the states of Christian Europe. One should take what follows with a reservation—not because what he says was untrue, but because he skipped over the seamier side of Ottoman reality.

BUSBECQ: FROM THE TURKISH LETTERS

.   .   .   .

On reaching Amasia[1] we were taken to pay our respects to Achmet, the Chief Vizier, and the other Pashas (for the Sultan himself was away), and we opened negotiations with them in accordance with the Emperor's injunctions. The Pashas, anxious not to appear at this early stage prejudiced against our cause, displayed no opposition but postponed the matter until their master could express his wishes. On his return we were introduced into his presence; but neither in his attitude nor in his manner did he appear very well disposed to our address, or the arguments, which we used, or the instructions which we brought.

The Sultan was seated on a rather low sofa, not more than a foot from the ground and spread with many costly coverlets and cushions embroidered with exquisite work. Near him were his bow and arrows. His expression, as I have said, is anything but smiling, and has a sternness which, though sad, is full of majesty. On our arrival we were introduced into his presence by his chamberlains, who held our arms—a practice which has always been observed since a Croatian sought an interview and

From *The Turkish Letters of Ogier Ghiselin de Busbecq, Imperial Ambassador at Constantinople, 1554-1562*, trans. by Edward E. Foster, Oxford: The Clarendon Press, 1927, pp. 58-62, 65-66, 109-14, Reprinted by permission of The Clarendon Press, Oxford.

1. April 7, 1555.

murdered the Sultan Amurath[2] in revenge for the slaughter of
his master, Marcus the Despot of Serbia. After going through
the pretence of kissing his hand, we were led to the wall facing
him backwards, so as not to turn our backs or any part of them
towards him. He then listened to the recital of my message, but,
as it did not correspond with his expectations (for the demands
of my imperial master were full of dignity and independence,
and, therefore, far from acceptable to one who thought that his
slightest wishes ought to be obeyed), he assumed an expression
of disdain, and merely answered "Giusel, Giusel," that is,
"Well, Well." We were then dismissed to our lodging.

The Sultan's head-quarters were crowded by numerous attendants, including many high officials. All the cavalry of the
guard were there . . . , and a large number of Janissaries. In
all that great assembly no single man owed his dignity to anything but his personal merits and bravery; no one is distinguished from the rest by his birth, and honour is paid to each
man according to the nature of the duty and offices which he
discharges. Thus there is no struggle for precedence, every man
having his place assigned to him in virtue of the function which
he performs. The Sultan himself assigns to all their duties and
offices, and in doing so pays no attention to wealth or the empty
claims of rank, and takes no account of any influence or popu-
larity which a candidate may possess; he only considers merit
and scrutinizes the character, natural ability, and disposition of
each. Thus each man is rewarded according to his deserts, and
offices are filled by men capable of performing them. In Turkey
every man has it in his power to make what he will of the position into which he is born and of his fortune in life. Those who
hold the highest posts under the Sultan are very often the sons
of shepherds and herdsmen, and, so far from being ashamed of
their birth, they make it a subject of boasting, and the less they
owe to their forefathers and to the accident of birth, the greater
is the pride which they feel. They do not consider that good
qualities can be conferred by birth or handed down by inheritance, but regard them partly as the gift of heaven and partly as
the product of good training and constant toil and zeal. Just as

2. Murad II.

they consider that an aptitude for the arts, such as music or mathematics or geometry, is not transmitted to a son and heir, so they hold that character is not hereditary, and that a son does not necessarily resemble his father, but his qualities are divinely infused into his bodily frame. Thus, among the Turks, dignities, offices, and administrative posts are the rewards of ability and merit; those who are dishonest, lazy, and slothful never atttain to distinction, but remain in obscurity and contempt. This is why the Turks succeed in all that they attempt and are a dominating race and daily extend the bounds of their rule. Our method is very different; there is no room for merit, but everything depends on birth; considerations of which alone open the way to high official position. On this subject I shall perhaps say more in another place, and you must regard these remarks as intended for your ears only.[3]

Now come with me and cast your eye over the immense crowd of turbaned heads, wrapped in countless folds of the whitest silk, and bright raiment of every kind and hue, and everywhere the brilliance of gold, silver, purple, silk, and satin. A detailed description would be a lengthy task, and no mere words could give an adequate idea of the novelty of the sight. A more beautiful spectacle was never presented to my gaze. Yet amid all this luxury there was a great simplicity and economy. The dress of all has the same form whatever the wearer's rank; and no edgings or useless trimmings are sewn on, as is the custom with us, costing a large sum of money and worn out in three days. Their most beautiful garments of silk or satin, even if they are embroidered, as they usually are, cost only a ducat to make.

The Turks were quite as much astonished at our manner of dress as we at theirs. They wear long robes which reach almost to their ankles, and are not only more imposing but seem to add to the stature; our dress, on the other hand, is so short and tight

---

3. This passage is an overstatement. It was not the case that birth counted for nothing, since gradually certain offices tended to become the preserves of certain families or patrons. However it was the case that a lowly man could rise on the basis of merit. In a system in which the ruler wished to hold the sole allegiance of those in his employ, a man of slave origin, owing everything to his master, was an ideal candidate for office.

that it discloses the forms of the body, which would be better hidden, and is thus anything but becoming, and besides, for some reason or other, it takes away from a man's height and gives him a stunted appearance.

What struck me as particularly praiseworthy in that great multitude was the silence and good discipline. There were none of the cries and murmurs which usually proceed from a motley concourse, and there was no crowding. Each man kept his appointed place in the quietest manner possible. The officers, namely, generals, colonels, captains, and lieutenants—to all of whom the Turks themselves give the tile of Aga—were seated; the common soldiers stood up. The most remarkable body of men were several thousand Janissaries, who stood in a long line apart from the rest and so motionless that, as they were at some distance from me, I was for a while doubtful whether they were living men or statues, until, being advised to follow the usual custom of saluting them, I saw them all bow their heads in answer to my salutation. On our departure from that part of the field, we saw another very pleasing sight, namely, the Sultan's bodyguard returning home mounted on horses, which were not only very fine and tall but splendidly groomed and caparisoned.

You will probably wish me to describe the impression which Soleiman made upon me. He is beginning to feel the weight of years, but his dignity of demeanour and his general physical appearance are worthy of the ruler of so vast an empire. He has always been frugal and temperate, and was so even in his youth, when he might have erred without incurring blame in the eyes of the Turks. Even in his earlier years he did not indulge in wine or in those unnatural vices to which the Turks are often addicted. Even his bitterest critics can find nothing more serious to allege against him than his undue submission to his wife[4] and its result in his somewhat precipitate action in putting Mustapha to death, which is generally imputed to her employment of love-potions and incantations. It is generally agreed that, ever

4. Roxalana: a favorite wife of Sulayman, said to have been of Russian descent, who led him to suspect his first-born (by another wife) son Mustapha, and to have him strangled.

since he promoted her to the rank of his lawful wife, he has possessed no concubines, although there is no law to prevent his doing so. He is a strict guardian of his religion and its ceremonies, being not less desirous of upholding his faith than of extending his dominions. For his age—he has almost reached his sixtieth year—he enjoys quite good health, though his bad complexion may be due to some hidden malady; and indeed it is generally believed that he has an incurable ulcer or gangrene on his leg. This defect of complexion he remedies by painting his face with a coating of red powder, when he wishes departing ambassadors to take with them a strong impression of his good health; for he fancies that it contributes to inspire greater fear in foreign potentates if they think that he is well and strong. I noticed a clear indication of this practice on the present occasion; for his appearance when he received me in the final audience was very different from that which he presented when he gave me an interview on my arrival.

The Sultan, when he sets out on a campaign, takes as many as 40,000 camels with him, and almost as many baggage-mules, most of whom, if his destination is Persia, are loaded with cereals of every kind, especially rice. Mules and camels are also employed to carry tents and arms and warlike machines and implements of every kind. The territories called Persia which are ruled by the Sophi,[5] as we call him (the Turkish name being Kizilbash), are much less fertile than our country; and, further, it is the custom of the inhabitants, when their land is invaded, to lay waste and burn everything, and so force the enemy to retire through lack of food. The latter, therefore, are faced with serious peril, unless they bring an abundance of food with them. They are careful, however, to avoid touching the supplies which they carry with them as long as they are marching against their foes, but reserve them, as far as possible, for their return journey, when the moment for retirement comes and they are forced to retrace their steps through regions which the enemy has laid waste, or which the immense multitude of men and baggage ani-

5. I.e., Sûfî, Ismâ'îl II, Safavid Shâh. The Turks called the Safavids Kizilbash (red-headed or hatted) because of their distinctive red headgear.

mals has, as it were, scraped bare, like a swarm of locusts. It is only then that the Sultan's store of provisions is opened, and just enough food to sustain life is weighed out each day to the Janissaries and the other troops in attendance upon him. The other soldiers are badly off, if they have not provided food for their own use; most of them, having often experienced such difficulties during their campaigns—and this is particularly true of the cavalry—take a horse on a leading-rein loaded with many of the necessities of life.[6] These include a small piece of canvas to use as a tent, which may protect them from the sun or a shower of rain, also some clothing and bedding and a private store of provisions, consisting of a leather sack or two of the finest flour, a small jar of butter, and some spices and salt; on these they support life when they are reduced to the extremes of hunger. They take a few spoonfuls of flour and place them in water, adding a little butter, and then flavour the mixture with salt and spices. This, when it is put on the fire, boils and swells up so as to fill a large bowl. They eat of it once or twice a day, according to the quantity, without any bread, unless they have with them some toasted bread or biscuit. They thus contrive to live on short rations for a month or even longer, if necessary. Some soldiers take with them a little sack full of beef dried and reduced to a powder, which they employ in the same manner as the flour, and which is of great benefit as a more solid form of nourishment. Sometimes, too, they have recourse to horseflesh; for in a great army a large number of horses necessarily dies, and any that die in good condition furnish a welcome meal to men who are starving. I may add that men whose horses have died, when the Sultan moves his camp, stand in a long row on the road by which he is to pass with their harness or saddles on their heads, as a sign that they have lost their horses, and implore his help to purchase others. The Sultan then assists them with whatever gift he thinks fit.

All this will show you with what patience, sobriety, and economy the Turks struggle against the difficulties which beset them, and wait for better times. How different are our soldiers,

6. This refers to those irregular "feudal" troops called up during a general mobilization and responsible for their own supplies.

who on campaign despise ordinary food and expect dainty dishes (such as thrushes and beccaficoes) and elaborate meals. If these are not supplied, they mutiny and cause their own ruin; and even if they are supplied, they ruin themselves just the same. For each man is his own worst enemy and has no more deadly foe than his own intemperance, which kills him if the enemy is slow to do so. I tremble when I think of what the future must bring when I compare the Turkish system with our own; one army must prevail and the other be destroyed, for certainly both cannot remain unscathed. On their side are the resources of a mighty empire, strength unimpaired, experience and practice in fighting, a veteran soldiery, habituation to victory, endurance of toil, unity, order, discipline, frugality, and watchfulness. On our side is public poverty, private luxury, impaired strength, broken spirit, lack of endurance and training; the soldiers are insubordinate, the officers avaricious; there is contempt for discipline; licence, recklessness, drunkenness, and debauchery are rife; and, worst of all, the enemy is accustomed to victory, and we to defeat. Can we doubt what the result will be? Persia alone interposes in our favour; for the enemy, as he hastens to attack, must keep an eye on this menace in his rear. But Persia is only delaying our fate; it cannot save us. When the Turks have settled with Persia, they will fly at our throats supported by the might of the whole East; how unprepared we are I dare not say!

But to return to the point from which I digressed. I mentioned that baggage animals are employed on campaign to carry the arms and tents, which mainly belong to the Janissaries. The Turks take the utmost care to keep their soldiers in good health and protected from the inclemency of the weather; against the foe they must protect themselves, but their health is a matter for which the State must provide. Hence one sees the Turk better clothed than armed. He is particularly afraid of the cold, against which, even in the summer, he guards himself by wearing three garments, of which the innermost—call it shirt or what you will—is woven of coarse thread and provides much warmth. As a further protection against cold and rain tents are always carried, in which each man is given just enough space to lie down, so that one tent holds twenty-five or thirty Janissaries. The material for the garments to which I have referred is provided at the public expense. To prevent any disputes or suspicion of favour, it is distributed in the following manner. The soldiers are summoned by companies in the darkness to a place chosen for the purpose—the balloting station or whatever name you like to give it—where are laid out ready as many portions of cloth as there are soldiers in the company; they enter and take whatever chance offers them in the darkness, and they can only ascribe it to chance whether they get a good or a bad piece of cloth. For the same reason their pay is not counted out to them but weighed, so that no one can complain that he has received light or chipped coins. Also their pay is given them not on the day on which it falls due but on the day previous.

The armour which is carried is chiefly for the use of the household cavalry, for the Janissaries are lightly armed and do not usually fight at close quarters, but use muskets. When the enemy is at hand and a battle is expected, the armour is brought out, but it consists mostly of old pieces picked up in various battlefields, the spoil of former victories. These are distributed to the household cavalry, who are otherwise protected by only a light shield. You can imagine how badly the armour, thus hurriedly given out, fits its wearers. One man's breastplate is too small, another's helmet is too large, another's coat of mail is too heavy for him to bear. There is something wrong everywhere; but they bear it with equanimity and think that only a coward finds fault with his arms, and vow to distinguish themselves in the fight, whatever their equipment may be; such is the confidence inspired by repeated victories and constant experience of warfare. Hence also they do not hesitate to re-enlist a veteran infantryman in the cavalry, though he has never fought on horseback, since they are convinced that one who has warlike experience and long service will acquit himself well in any kind of fighting. . . .

Portraits of Three Monarchs
II. The Mughal Akbar

The Mughal rulers of India claimed descent from Chîngîz Khân and Tamerlane. The founder of the dynasty was Babar (r. 1526-1530) who, having been driven from Fârghanâ, built a new empire for himself in northwestern India. Akbar (r. 1556-1605), his grandson, was the first Mughal emperor to establish the family power firmly on the basis of a relatively stable administrative machine, alliances with native Rajput rulers and a policy of religious tolerance and universalism.

Akbar was a generous and discriminating patron of art and letters, as were his predecessors and successors. Among those he supported was Abû'l Fazl ibn Mubârak (1550-1602), author of the history of Akbar's reign from which extracts are reproduced here.

The flowery flattery that almost obscures the meaning of some of Abû'l Fazl's passages was strictly conventional. Persian literature had elaborated the praise of princes into an art form prodigal in words, hyperbolic beyond credibility, and admired for skillful variations on familiar similes, metaphors, and rhetorical turns of phrase. Abû'l Fazl's skill is lost to readers unfamiliar with such language. What should be remembered is that the flowers of rhetoric did not conceal the kernel of meaning from his readers. To them it would be clear that Abû'l Fazl was really praising not Akbar so much as his attempt to unite the various religions and cultural groups then dividing India. Moreover, the verbal arabesques recorded in such a text are themselves indicative of the refined and effete atmosphere of the Persian-Turkish-Mongol court life out of which this literary-artistic tradition had grown.

ABÛ'L FAZL: FROM THE BOOK OF AKBAR

[INTRODUCTION]

So long as the spiritual supremacy over the recluse which is called Holiness and the sway over laymen which is called Sovereignty, were distinct, there was strife and confusion among the children of Noah (mankind). Now that in virtue of his exaltation, foresight, comprehensive wisdom, universal benevolence, pervading discernment and perfect knowledge of God, these two great offices . . . which are the guiding thread of the spiritual and temporal worlds, have been conferred on the opener of the hoards of wisdom and claviger of Divine treasuries, a small portion at least,—if his holy nature grant the necessary faculty,— may be brought from the ambush of concealment to the asylum of publicity. Knowest thou at all who is this world-girdling luminary and radiant spirit? Or whose august advent has bestowed this grace? 'Tis he who by virtue of his enlightenment and truth, is the world-protecting sovereign of our age, to wit, that Lord (*Shâhanshâh*)[1] of the hosts of sciences,—theatre of God's power,—station of infinite bounties,—unique of the eternal temple,—confidant of the daïs of unity,—jewel of the imperial mine,—bezel of God's signet-ring,—glory of the *Gûrgân*[2] family,—lamp of the tribe of Timur,—lord of incomparable mystery,—heir of Humâyûn's[3] throne,—origin of the canons of world-government,—author of universal conquest,—shining forehead of the morning of guidance,—focus of the sun of holiness,—sublime concentration of humanity,—heir-apparent of the sun,—anthology of the books of fate and destiny,—protago-

---

From The *Akbarnâmâ*, by Abul-l-Fazl ibn Mubârak, trans. by H. Beveridge, Calcutta: The Asiatic Society, 1905-39, Vol. I, pp. 16-17, 56-57, 132; Vol. II, pp. 92-93, 113-14, 234-35, 246-47, 372-73, 581-82; Vol. III, pp. 116-19, 157-59, 364-66, 398-400; Vol. III, pp. 1258-61. Reprinted by permission.

1. Exalted title for Akbar.

2. *Gûrgân* is said to mean son-in-law or near relation in Mongolian; it was a title taken by Tîmûr to indicate his connection with the house of Chîngîz Khân. (Tr.)

3. Akbar's father (r. 1530-1556).

nist of triumphant armies,—quintessence of the commingling of
nights and days,—cream of the progeny of the elements[4] and
the heavenly bodies,—world's eye (sun) of benevolence and
bounty. . . .
[Four pages of similar epithet follow.]

. . . .

[THE BIRTH OF AKBAR]

Among the strange circumstances which occurred near the
time of the appearance of the light of fortune,[5] there was this,—
that before the auspicious moment above-mentioned, the mother
felt a pressing urgency to bring forth the child. Maulânâ Când,
the astrologer, who by the king's order, had been stationed by
the chaste threshold in order that he might cast the horoscope,
was perturbed, as the moment was inauspicious. "In a short
time, a glorious moment will arrive, such as does not happen
once in a thousand years. What an advantage if the birth could
be delayed." Those who were present made light of it and said,
"What is the good of your agitation? Such things are not under
control."

At this very instant the impulse to bring forth passed off and
the astrologer's mind was set at rest somewhat by the transit of
the unlucky moment. The ostensible cause of this supreme blessing was that a country midwife had been just brought in to perform her office, and as her appearance was repulsive, the holy
soul of Miryam Makânî felt disgusted and her even temper was
rebuffed and so the urgency for parturition left her. But when
the chosen time came, the Maulânâ became disturbed, lest it
should accidentally pass by. The confidants of the harem said to
him, "Her Majesty, has after much suffering, got an interval of
relief and is now slumbering. It would not be right to waken
her. Whatever Almighty God, in His good pleasure, has determined, must happen." Just as they were speaking, the pains of
travail came upon her Majesty, Miryam Makânî, and awoke

4. The elements are called the earthly mothers, and the planets, the heavenly fathers. (Tr.)

5. I.e., Akbar; astrology seems to have been unusually important at the
Tîmûrid court, as at many other contemporary courts.

her and in that auspicious moment, the unique pearl of the vice-regency of God (*Khilâfat*) came forth in his glory.

They spread the carpet of joy under the canopy of chastity and curtain of honour, and made ready a feast of joy and exultation. The veiled ones of the pavilion, and the chaste inmates of the royal harem anointed the eye of hope with the collyrium[6] of rejoicing and coloured the eyebrows of desire with the indigo of merriness. They decked the ear of good tidings with the earring of success, painted the face of longing with the vermilion of pleasure, encircled the fore-arm of wish with the bracelet of purpose, and donning the anklet of splendour on the dancing foot, stepped into the theatre of delight and joy and raised the strain of praise and gratulation. Fan-wavers sprinkled otto of roses, and winnowed the air with sandal-scented arms. Dark-haired maidens freshened the floor by rubbing it with perfumes. Rose-cheeked damsels gave a new lustre to joy by sprinkling rose-water. Red-garmented, sweetly-smiling nymphs enveloped the silver-bosomed ones in gold, by scattering saffron. Rose-scented, jasmine-cheeked ones soothed the rapid dancers with camphor-ated sandal-wood. Gold in thuribles on the borders of the carpet, gave off fumes of incense. They uncovered the stoves which were filled with lign-aloes and ambergris. Musicians created enchanting ecstacy, and melodious minstrels breathed forth magic strains.

. . . .

Among other wondrous indications there was this, that contrary to the way of other infants, his Majesty, the king of kings, at his birth and at the first opening of his eyes on the visible world, rejoiced the hearts of the wise by a sweet smile. Penetrating physiognomists recognized the smile as the herald-augury of the smiles of the spring of dominion and fortune and saw in it, the opening bud of hope and peace.

. . . .

[ONE OF AKBAR'S MYSTICAL EXPERIENCES]

At this time a strange thing happened in relation to the Lord of the Earth, who was keeping himself in the disguise of an in-

6. Kohl, for decorating the eyes.

cognito, and was giving attention to the concealment of his idio-
syncrasy—a mystery which has already been conveyed, as far
as my capacity would allow, from the heart to paper. The event,
of which the following is an account, was the cause of some
well-instructed minds coming to a knowledge of truth. One day
the world-adorning Shâhinshâh[7] felt constrained by the presence of short-sighted men, and began to chafe. The power of indignation which in a disposition innately equable is an ingre-
dient deposited by the Lord of power broke out into anger. He
became averse to the servants of fortune's threshold who always
attended on his stirrup and separated from them, and issued an
order that no one of his retinue should be in attendance on him.
He even sent away his grooms and such like persons that the
solitude of his retirement might not be contaminated by the
crowd of this class of men and went out unattended and alone
from the camp of fortune. In reality he was engaged in prayer-
ful communion with his God, ostensibly he was angered with
men. Among his special horses there was a noble 'Irâqî horse
called Hairân which Khizr Khwâja Khân had presented to him.
It had not its like for spirit and swiftness, and was also un-
equalled for viciousness. When he was left loose no one could
come near him, and it was with difficulty that he could be re-
caught. The divine hero of the world, owing to his strength and
courage, rode him constantly. In this period of solitude he
mounted upon this auspicious steed, and set off rapidly, leaving
society aside and increasing his glory by the presence of God.
When he had gone some distance he dismounted for some purpose, and, becoming heedless of the nature of his steed, assumed
the posture of communing with his God. That swift and fiery
horse acted according to its custom and rushed off rapidly so
that it disappeared from the far-searching gaze of His Majesty.
When his holy heart was again disposed to mount, there was
no one in attendance, and no horse at his service. For a little
while he was perplexed what to do, when suddenly he saw that
this very horse was coming from a distance and galloping towards him. It ran on till it came back to him and stood quietly
waiting for him. His Majesty was astonished and again mounted

7. Akbar. Shâhinshâh is an old Persian title, meaning "Lord of Lords."

the noble animal. It must be considered as one of the strange faculties of this throne-adorning dominion that a horse, whose habit was not to allow himself to be readily mounted, and who, when he ran off, could with difficulty be re-caught, and who had gone off and disappeared in such a plain, should, merely on the attention of the Shâhinshâh being directed towards him come back of his own accord and quietly submit to be re-mounted. Bravo! what apprehension can there be from solitude to him whom the incomparable Deity favours, and of whom he takes charge? And what improbability is there in such things happening to him? Although it may seem as if the wisdom-erecting Deity makes the world-adorning beauty of this spiritual and temporal visible to him alone, yet in reality it is the setting forth of sundry lamps in the highway of guidance for the direction of the short-sighted and superficial, in that they who know in him a visible lord and king may, what is more and better, know him as a spiritual ruler, and recognising that the pleasing of him is the pleasing of God may arrive at the rose-rendezvous of eternal happiness.

.   .   .   .

[A DEMONSTRATION OF AKBAR'S BLESSEDNESS]

. . . One day he mounted the elephant called Lakhna, which was an exhibitor of terrific rage, at a time when it was at the height of its ferocity, evil nature and man-killing, and made it engage with an elephant like itself, so that the proudest were surprised. The elephant Lakhna, on which H.M. was riding, was victorious and was madly pursuing the other when suddenly its foot, which resembled a great pillar, fell into a deep ditch, and in its furious condition, and when the fumes of wrath were circulating in its brain, it made great struggles and movements. At this time an athlete who was riding on the elephant's rump, for the rule is that a lion-hearted, skilful man rides crupper on these mountain forms, and such a one is called in Hindi Bhoi, could not sit the sky-high rearings of the elephant, and fell to the ground. Then, when cries awoke on every side, and the hearts of the loyal melted within them, the holy personality was also moved from its place, and his sky-brushing foot became fixed in the rope of the elephant's neck, which in Hindi is called Kalâwa. H.M. with a heart which can throw the noose of courage on the heavens, and a palm which had God's help in its fingers, firmly seized the rope, and having hold of the strong cable of this Divine protection remained strong of heart and serene in soul. In that tumult and uproar which produce an earthquake in the terrene, and a riot in time, and while the elephant with his great strength was extricating his feet from the abyss, and was making marvellous struggles and inclining from side to side to the ground, and while on one hand there were the cries of the people, and on the other the efforts of the elephant for getting rid of H.M.'s sacred personality, a number of intrepid, loyal and alert men came and released H.M. from the elephant. The disturbed heart of the world was appeased, and the commoved life of the age became stationary again. I do not know if this beauty under the aspect of terror displayed itself without the intention of this chosen one, in order that the far-reaching thoughts of the wicked might be shortened by seeing such (Divine) guardianship, or whether that spiritual and temporal Khedive, that king of the visible and invisible, knowingly and designedly exhibited such glory, so that by one splendid act might be manifested the blindness of weak-sighted malevolents, and the illumination of the loyal. In a short time, when H.M. had put himself in order, the elephant by his own efforts brought out his foot from the hole and began to be riotous. H.M. with the same open view, and serene soul again mounted the elephant and proceeded, encompassed by the Divine protection, to his fixed abode.

. . . Several times when this fortunate writer has had the privilege of private conversation with His Majesty the Shâhin-shâh he has heard from his holy lips that "our knowingly and intentionally mounting on *mast*, murderous elephants when they have a moment previously brought their drivers under their feet and killed them, and when they have slain many a man, has this for its cause and motive that if I have knowingly taken a step which is displeasing to God or have knowingly made an aspiration which was not according to His pleasure, may that elephant finish us, for we cannot support the burden of life under God's displeasure." Good God, what an insight is this! and what a calculation with oneself! In fine, at all times, whether that of holy privacy, or that of engrossment in business, in time of battle, and in time of banquet, he is ever regardful of the real, guiding thread, and while he is outwardly with the creature, and inwardly with the Creator, he is at one and the same moment the arranger of the sections of the outward and inward and acts as the leader of both those great parties, and while deriving pleasure from both of those pleasant products adorns the throne both of the spiritual and the temporal universe.

.   .   .   .

[SOME OF AKBAR'S REFORMS AND ACCOMPLISHMENTS]

One of the glorious boons of His Majesty the Shâhinshâh which shone forth in this auspicious year was the abolition of enslavement. The victorious troops which came into the wide territories of India used in their tyranny to make prisoners of the wives and children and other relatives of the people of India, and used to enjoy them or sell them. His Majesty the Shâhin-shâh, out of his thorough recognition of and worship of God, and from his abundant foresight and right thinking gave orders that no soldier of the victorious armies should in any part of his dominions act in this manner. Although a number of savage natures who were ignorant of the world should make their fastnesses a subject of pride and come forth to do battle, and then be defeated by virtue of the emperor's daily increasing empire, still their families must be protected from the onset of the world-conquering armies. No soldier, high or low, was to enslave them, but was to permit them to go freely to their homes and relations. It was for excellent reasons that His Majesty gave his attention to this subject, for although the binding, killing or striking the haughty and the chastising the stiff-necked are part of the struggle for empire—and this is a point about which both sound jurists and innovators are agreed—yet it is outside of the canons of justice to regard the chastisement of women and innocent children as the chastisement of the contumacious. If the husbands have taken the path of insolence, how is it the fault of the wives, and if the fathers have chosen the road of opposition what fault have the children committed? Moreover the wives and innocent children of such factions are not munitions of war! In addition to these sound reasons there was the fact that many covetous and blindhearted persons from vain imaginings or unjust thoughts, or merely out of cupidity attacked villages and estates and plundered them, and when questioned about it said a thousand things and behaved with neglect and indifference. But when final orders were passed for the abolition of this practice, no tribe was afterwards oppressed by wicked persons on suspicion of sedition. As the purposes of the Shâhinshâh were entirely right and just, the blissful result ensued that the wild and rebellious inhabitants of portions of India placed the ring of devotion in the ear of obedience, and became the materials of world-empire. Both was religion set in order, for its essence is the distribution of justice, and things temporal were regulated, for their perfection lies in the obedience of mankind.

Among the principal events of the year was the founding of the fort of Agra. It is not concealed from the minds of the mathematical and the acquainted with the mechanism of the spheres that since the world-adorning creator hath decked Time and the Terrene[8] with the existence of the Shâhinshâh in order that the series of creations might be perfected, that wise-hearted one has exercised himself in bringing each individual life from the secrecy of potentiality to the theatre of performance. At one time he has prepared the constituents of rule by perfecting the earth for animated nature by improving agriculture by irrigation and the sowing of seeds. At another time he establishes spiritual and temporal dominion by building fortresses for the protection of products and the guarding of honour and prestige. Accordingly, he at this time gave directions for the building in Agra—which by position is the centre of Hindustan—of a grand fortress such as might be worthy thereof, and corespond to the dignity of his dominions. An order was then issued that the old fort which was

8. Earth.

built on the east bank of the Jamna, and whose pillars had been shaken by the revolutions of time and the shocks of fortune, should be removed, and that an impregnable fort should be built of hewn stone. It was to be stable like the foundation of the dominion of the sublime family and permanent like the pillars of its fortunes. Accordingly, lofty-minded mathematicians and able architects laid the foundations of this great building in an hour which was supreme for establishing a fortress. The excavations were made through seven strata of earth. The breadth of the wall was three yards and its height sixty yards. It was provided with four gates whereby the doors of the dominion were opened towards the four quarters of the world. Every day 3 to 4,000 active builders and strong-armed labourers carried on the work. From the foundations to the battlements, the fortress was composed of hewn stone, each of which was polished like the world-revealing mirror, and was ruddy as the cheek of fortune. And they were so joined together that the end of a hair could not find place between them. This sublime fortress, the like of which had never been seen by a fabulous geometrician, was completed with its battlements, breastwork, and its loop-holes in the space of eight years. . . .

.   .   .   .

One of the occurrences was the testing of the silent of speech. . . . There was a great meeting, and every kind of enlightenment was discussed. In the 24th Divine year H.M. said that speech came to every tribe from hearing, and that each remembered from another from the beginning of existence. If they arranged that human speech did not reach them, they certainly would not have the power of speech. If the fountain of speech bubbled over in one of them, he would regard this as Divine speech, and accept it as such. As some who heard this appeared to deny it, he, in order to convince them, had a *serai* built in a place which civilized sounds did not reach. The newly born were put into that place of experience, and honest and active guards were put over them. For a time tongue-tied . . . wetnurses were admitted there. As they had closed the door of speech, the place was commonly called the Gang Mahal (the dumb-house). On the 29th (Amardâd—9th August 1582) he went out to hunt. That night he stayed in Faizâbâd,[9] and next day he went with a few special attendants to the house of experiment. No cry came from that house of silence, nor was any speech heard there. In spite of their four years they had no part of the talisman of speech, and nothing came out except the noise of the dumb. What the wise Sovereign had understood several years before was on this day impressed on the hearts of the formalists and the superficial. This became a source of instruction to crowds of men. H.M. said, "Though my words were proved they still are saying the same things with a tongueless tongue. The world is a miserable abode of sceptics. . . . To shut the lips is really to indulge in garrulity. They have hamstrung the camel of the Why and Wherefore, and have closed the gate of speech with iron walls."[10]

. . . .

[AKBAR AS SPIRITUAL GUIDE AND PATRON]

At this time the writer of this glorious record, Abul Fazl, the son of Mubârak was, in accordance with a sublime indication and mysterious message, exalted by prostrating himself at the holy Court of the Shâhinshâh. By the Divine assistance there was a beginning of the cure of his self-worshipping pride. The brief account of this matter is as follows. After coming from the hidden chamber of the womb to the crowded inn of existence he [*i.e.* the author] in his fifth year attained to conventional discretion. Under the educating eye of his spiritual and physical father he in his fifteenth year became acquainted with the rational and the traditional sciences. . . . Though these opened the gate of knowledge and gave him the entry to wisdom's antechamber, yet by his ill-fortune he became egotistic and self-conceited. The foot of his energy rested for a while in admiration of his own excellences, and the throng of students around him augmented his presumption. Their indiscriminate agitation

9. Not found. (Tr.)
10. Cf. the account given by Akbar himself to Father Jerome Xavier. . . . A. F. represents Akbar as making the experiment in order to prove that speech was not spontaneous with children, and as having proved his point. But Xavier's account shows that Akbar had an idea that he might find out the sacred language. It was a cruel experiment. Akbar's comment on his critics is obscure. Apparently, it means that though he proved his case, they still are unconvinced. (Tr.)

and lack of judgment put into his head the thought of asceticism
and retirement. Though during the day his cell was made bright
by teaching science, yet at night he would take the path of the
fields and approach the enthusiasts of the "Way of Search." He
would implore inspiration from those treasure-holding paupers.
I was kept in the defiles of astonished perturbation by the contrary views of the superficially learned, and by the vogue of
imitative formalists. I had neither power to be silent nor
strength to cry out. Though the exhortations of my honoured
father kept me from the desert of madness, yet no helpful
remedy reached the troubled spot of my soul. Whiles my heart
was drawn towards the sages of the country of Cathay, . . .
whiles it felt inclined towards the ascetics of Mount Lebanon
(the Druses) (?). Sometimes a desire for conversation with the
Lamas of Thibet broke my peace, and sometimes a sympathy
with the *padres* of Portugal pulled at my skirt. Sometimes a
conference with the *mubids* of Persia, and sometimes a knowledge of the secrets of the Zendavesta robbed me of repose, for
my soul was alienated from the society both of the sobered and
the (spiritually) drunken of my own land. Though the foodless-
ness of search was broken by the emporium . . . of outward
and inward perfections, by which is meant my advantageous attendance on my honoured father, yet as that unique product of
creation's workshop lived under the veil of seclusion, there was
no remedy for my distress. Owing to my own ignorance I
thought that my outward position was incompatible with the
final state, . . . and was much disturbed in consequence, and
sought to be remote from the society around me. At last fortune
favoured me, and mention was made in the holy assemblage
(Akbar's religious meetings) of the acquirements of this one
(himself) who was bewildered in life's society. My honoured
brother, my well-wishing friends, my loving relatives, and my
disciples were unanimous in saying, "You should obtain the
boon of serving the spiritual and temporal Khedive." I was not
inclined to do this, and my atrabilious apprehensions of the social state disturbed my soul, which was inclined to solitude. For
I had not opened a farseeing eye, and my genius was bent upon
breaking the bonds of restraint. After the fashion of the ignorant

and superficial I looked upon external circumstances as destructive of inwardness, and limitation as opposed to absoluteness. At length my father withdrew the veil and guided me to truth. He made clear to me the wondrous working of the authors of destiny, and withdrew from my head the hood of self-conceit. By delightful discourses in private interviews and in judicious assemblies, he impressed upon me the spiritual perfections of the sitter on the throne of fortune (Akbar). By sage expositions he made it clear that "The piety and knowledge of God possessed by this divinely born jewel are imperfectly known by any one. At this day he is the leader of the caravans both of Society and of Seclusion, the meeting of the oceans of Realm and Religion, the dawn of the lights of form and substance. The multiplicity of external associations does not withhold him from essential unity. Outwardly bound, he is inwardly free. From him comes the solution of spiritual and temporal matters." Of necessity I preferred the pleasing of him (his father) to my own desires, and as my heart's treasury, rich in spiritualities, was empty of the world's goods, I wrote a commentary on the verse of the Throne as an offering to the sublime court, and I presented the writing as an excuse for my being empty-handed. The Shâhinshâh received it graciously. He cast special glances on me, and by the wealth of service which is indeed the elixir of worth, he calmed my troubled mind. Love for that holy personality took possession of my heart. At this time the expedition to the eastern provinces engaged his mind. My disposition did not permit me, the sitter in the dust, to seek association with the great ones of the court, and those who were attached to the threshold of honour had not, when engrossed by the affairs of the Sultanate, leisure to take notice of unknown and humble persons. I was debarred from entering the service. Though my old notions still lurked in my soul, yet the spiritual tie between me and that great one of realm and religion continued to bind me, and when the lord of the earth returned, after conquering the eastern provinces, to the capital of Fathpûr, he remembered me, the anchorite. I had the good fortune to kiss the threshold, and this bewildered one came to find his face on the path.

· · · · · · · · · ·

[AKBAR'S RELIGIOUS UNIVERSALISM]

At this[11] time when the capital was illuminated by his glorious advent, H.M. ordered that a house of worship . . . should be built in order to the adornment of the spiritual kingdom, and that it should have four verandahs. . . . Though the Divine bounty always has an open door and searches for the fit person, and the inquirer, yet as the lord of the universe, from his general benevolence, conducts his measures according to the rules of the superficial, he chose the eve of Friday, which bears on its face the colouring . . . of the announcement of auspiciousness, for the out-pouring. . . . A general proclamation was issued that, on that night of illumination, all orders and sects of mankind—those who searched after spiritual and physical truth, and those of the common public who sought for an awakening, and the inquirers of every sect—should assemble in the precincts of the holy edifice, and bring forward their spiritual experiences, and their degrees of knowledge of the truth in various and contradictory forms in the bridal chamber of manifestation.

Wisdom and deeds would be tested, and the essence of manhood would be exhibited. Those who were founded on truth entered the hall of acceptance, while those who were only veneered with gold went hastily to the pit of base metal. There was a feast of theology and worship. The vogue of creature-worship was reduced. The dust-stained ones of the pit of contempt became adorners of dominion, and the smooth-tongued, empty-headed rhetoricians lost their rank. To the delightful precincts of that mansion founded upon Truth, thousands upon thousands of inquirers from the seven climes came with heart-felt respect and waited for the advent of the Shâhinshâh. The world-lord would, with open brow, a cheerful countenance, a capacious heart and an understanding soul, pour the limpid waters of graciousness on those thirsty-lipped ones of expectation's desert, and act as a refiner. He put them into currency, sect by sect, and tested them company by company. He got hold of every one of the miserable and dust-stained ones, and made

11. The order for the building of the House of Worship was given in . . . February-March, 1575. (Tr.)

them successful in their desires,—to say nothing of the be-cloaked and the be-turbaned. From this general assemblage H.M. selected by his far-reaching eye a chosen band from each class, and established a feast of truth. Occasionally he, in order to instruct the courtiers, sent perspicuous servants who could discriminate among men, and these reflective and keen-sighted men brought every description of person to perform the *kornish*.[12] Then that cambist and tester of worth examined them anew and invited some of them.

. . . .

. . . His sole and sublime idea was that, as in the external administration of the dominion, which is conjoined with eternity, the merits of the knowers of the things of this world had by profundity of vision, and observance of justice, been made conspicuous, and there had ceased to be a brisk market for pretence and favouritism, so might the masters of science and ethics, and the devotees of piety and contemplation, be tested, the principles of faiths and creeds be examined, religions be investigated, the proofs and evidences for each be considered, and the pure gold and the alloy be separated from evil commixture. In a short space of time a beautiful, detached building was erected, and the fraudulent vendors of impostures put to sleep in the privy chamber of contempt. A noble palace was provided for the spiritual world and the pillars of Divine knowledge rose high.

At this time, when the centre of the Caliphate . . . was glorified by H.M.'s advent, the former institutions were renewed, and the temple of Divine knowledge was on Thursday nights illuminated by the light of the holy mind.[13] On 20 Mihr, Divine month, 3 October 1578, and in that house of worship, the lamp of the privy chamber of detachment was kindled in the banqueting-hall of social life. The coin of the hivers of wisdom in colleges and cells was brought to the test. The clear wine was separated from the lees, and good coin from the adulterated. The wide capacity and the toleration of the Shadow of God were unveiled. Sûfî, philosopher, orator, jurist, Sunnî, Shîa, Brahman,

12. Ritual greeting of respect.
13. The meaning is that Akbar was present at the discussions. (Tr.)

Jatî, Sîûrâ Cârbâk, Nazarene, Jew, Sâbî (Sabîan), Zoroastrian,[14] and others enjoyed exquisite pleasure by beholding the calmness of the assembly, the sitting of the world-lord in the lofty pulpit, . . . and the adornment of the pleasant abode of impartiality. The treasures of secrets were opened out without fear of hostile seekers after battle. The just and truth-perceiving ones of each sect emerged from haughtiness and conceit, and began their search anew. They displayed profundity and meditation, and gathered eternal bliss on the divan of greatness. The conceited and quarrelsome from evilness of disposition and shortness of thought descended into the mire of presumption and sought their profit in loss. Being guided by ignorant companions, and from the predominance of a somnolent fortune, they went into disgrace. The conferences were excellently arranged by the acuteness and keen quest of truth of the world's Khedive. Every time, eye and heart gained fresh lustre, and the lamp of vigils acquired new glory. The candle of investigation was lighted for those who loved darkness and sequacity. The families of the colleges and monasteries were tested. The handle of wealth and the material of sufficiency came into the grasp of the needy occupants of the summit of expectation. The fame of this faith-adorning method of world-bestowing made home bitter to inquirers and caused them to love exile. The Shâhinshâh's court became the home of the inquirers of the seven climes, and the assemblage of the wise of every religion and sect. The veneer and the counterfeitness of all those who by feline tricks and stratagems had come forth in the garb of wisdom were revealed. A few irreverent and crafty spirits continued their old tactics after the appearance of Truth and its concomitant convictions, and indulged in brawling. Their idea was that as in the great assemblies of former rulers the purpose of science and the designs of wisdom had been but little explored owing to the crowd of men, the inattention of the governor of the feast, the briskness of the market of praters, etc., so perhaps in this august assemblage they might succeed by the length of their tongues, and a

14. For Yati, the clergy or ascetics among the Jains. Sîûrâ. A general name for the Jains. For Charvaka. They are Nâstiks or infidels of Hindu philosophy. Sabîan. Also called the Christians of St. John. (Tr.)

veil might be hung over the occiput . . . of truth. The Khedive of wisdom by the glory of his mind carried out the work to a conclusion deliberately and impartially, and in this praiseworthy fashion, which is seldom found in the saints of asceticism,—how then is it to be found in world-rulers?—tested the various coins of mortals. Many men became stained with shame and chose loss of fame, while some acquired wisdom and emerged from the hollow of obscurity to eminence. Reason was exalted, and the star of fortune shone for the acquirers of knowledge.

. . . .

[THE REACTION TO UNIVERSALISM]

. . . A set of evil-thoughted, shameless ones imagined that the Prince of horizons regarded with disfavour the Muhammadan religion. . . . The sole evidence which those wrongheaded wicked ones, whose understanding was rusted, had for this was that the wise sovereign out of his tolerant disposition and general benevolence, and extensive overshadowing, received all classes of mankind with affection. Especially did he search for evidence in religious matters from the sages of every religion and the aescetics of all faiths. Nor did he accept the replies of the headstrong and uninquiring. Above all, at this time Christian philosophers assailed the orthodox . . . , (those in agreement) of the day in the sublime assemblies, and learned discussions were carried on. The calumniators of the enlightened who by pretences had claimed for themselves a learning that did not exist, made a clamour in the court of sovereignty. They were put to shame in the holy market of justice and the heyday of discrimination, and lowered their heads into the folds of ignorance, but in the privy chambers of darkness they joined their confederates in the cry that they were mourning the loss of Faith, and that the king of the Age had, out of partiality, not accepted their replies. In their wickedness they cast suspicion upon that choice one of truth and that inwardly enlightened one. In their black-heartedness and shamelessness, they gave no heed to the fact that the honour and respect which this appreciative throne-occupant used to show to the family of the prophet had been rarely exhibited by other monarchs. Many good

Saiyyids[15] had been raised to dignities and high offices by the favour of H.M., and from time to time they were still farther promoted and the garden of their wishes kept watered and verdant. Nor did he permit that any member of this family should lay his head on the holy feet, or rub the forehead on the threshold of fortune. A set of squint-eyed, wicked people taxed him with Shî'ism; and so led astray simple-minded Sunnîs. The cause of the stumbling of this set was that in the sublime assemblies the proofs of those two sects, like those of other sects, were discussed, and that the Shâhinshâh from equity selected what was preferable.

Verse.
When a statement is strong in argument,
It is unfortunate if you do not listen to it.

His likes or dislikes, the greater or lesser numbers of the disputants, their being acquaintances or strangers, raised no dust of difference. The short-sighted and irreflecting on seeing his fondness for discussion indulged in idle talk. The favour shown to Persians, most of whom belonged to that sect (the Sh'îa), increased the evil thoughts of the turbulent. Out of ignorance, and worship of routine they did not remember the precept about accepting the explanation that was conformable to reason. And either the promotion of Turanians was hidden from the bigoted eyes of this set, or they wilfully remained ignorant of it and sought for pretexts. An impure faction reproached the caravan-leader of God-knowers with being of the Hindu (Brahman) religion. The ground for this improper notion was that the prince out of his wide tolerance received Hindu sages into his intimacy, and increased for administrative reasons the rank of Hindus, and for the good of the country showed them kindness. Three things supported the evil-minded gossips. First—The sages of different religions assembled at court, and as every religion has some good in it, each received some praise. From a spirit of justice the badness of any sect could not weave a veil over its merits. Second—The season of "Peace with all" was honoured at the court of the Caliphate, and various tribes of

15. Descendants of the Prophet.

mankind of various natures obtained spiritual and material success. Third—The evil nature and crooked ways of the base ones
of the age.

By the right thinking and truthful conduct of the world's lord,
they were soon put to shame for their ignorance, and set about
endeavouring to amend the days of their ignorance, but many
ask retribution for their evil deeds descended into the tortures of
failure.

.   .   .   .

[AKBAR'S DEATH]

Of the last events and of the final catastrophe, namely the
soul-piercing, sense-destroying, heart-rending occurrence of
the passing of the empire-adorning Khâqân,[16] and of the march
of the caravan-leader of Truth's highway from this perishable
caravansarai to the Holy world and to the everlasting kingdom.

In the beginning of winter, when the air was cold, and the
constitution became torpid.

Verse.

From the cold blasts of Mihrgân (autumn)
The life of the garden congealed,
Recuperative powers remained imbedded,
There was no start of vegetation,
The rose was bared of her silken kerchief,
The hearts of the trees were congealed,
The rose garden . . . was congealed into clay . . . ,
The hundred lamps of the house of mourning died out,
In the garden the glory of the jasmine faded
As when the face of the moon is eclipsed,
The market of flowers and spring broke up,
The world's grandeur was dissolved,
Both the tulip's diadem was reversed
And the cypress's standard laid low.

The wind of autumn blew on the house-garden of world-rule,
and the cold blast of Mihrgân passed over the rose-garden of
fortune. The ever-vernal flower of the parterre of sovereignty

16. I.e., Akbar.

was touched by the hand of decay, and the verdant tree of the garden of the Caliphate lost its foliage. Why should I not speak plainly. The throne-adorner, the world's fortune withdrew his skirt from realm and clime. The sitter on the *masnad* of glory shook out his sleeve over throne and diadem. The world-lighting luminary which, contrary to the sun and moon, shed his light day and night, became in a moment dark, and the constellation of fortune, the centre of the world's light, which, contrary to the fixed stars and the planets, bestowed its rays night and day, suddenly became extinguished. The sound of the drum of dominion which for years had filled the spheres with joy, at once ceased. The notes of the flute of joy, on hearing which Venus used to dance with joy during the night-time, altogether died away.

. . . .

. . . On the eve of Wednesday, 4th Abân, 15th October, 1605, H.M. withdrew the shade of his heavenly self from the heads of mortals, and spread out the shadow of his beneficence over the heads of the celestials. The men of this world sate down in the dark days of failure, while the inhabitants of the other world attained their long-cherished wishes. The report of this disaster caused lamentation in heaven and earth. There was a daily-bazaar of consternation and terror, and sorrow and affliction became active. Darkness took possession of the earth, and the evening of sorrow fell upon mortals in the midday of contentment. The lightning of labour and sorrow struck mankind's harvest of joy. The stone of violence and oppression smote on the vases of the hearts of the sincere. Good God! What a personality he was! He was pure from every stain and endowed with all perfections. What a jewel free from every blemish and pure of every stain! Lofty prestige, a happy horoscope, an awakened fortune, complete auspiciousness, a daily-increasing dominion, mounting victoriousness, pleasant friendship, a love of pleasantry, friend-cherishing, foe-destroying, a kingdom-bestowing liberality, a might that overthrew enemies, a world-embracing majesty, a world-conquering resolution, a firmness and gravity together with the working of conspicuous miracles, lofty converse, an il-luminated mind, a God-given understanding, an enlightened soul, a taste for knowledge, an expounder of mysteries, and an opener of mysteries, conquest over difficulties, etc., etc.—all these were gathered together in that sublime personality and created astonishment among the lords of insight.

Portrait of Three Monarchs
III. The Safavid 'Abbâs

Shâh 'Abbâs the Great (r. 1588-1629) inherited a state that had been built upon fervent religious faith. The Safavid family claimed to be the sole legitimate heirs to the Prophet Muhammad and as such demanded that all good Muslims submit to their leadership. This claim, of course, made enemies of all other Muslim rulers, but by 'Abbâs' time, fervor had cooled, at least in court circles. Peace with the Ottoman empire became possible, and 'Abbâs himself was more interested in how to get hold of competent gunsmiths—if need be, from as far away as England—than in fine points of Muslim doctrine.

In order to cement relations with Europeans, whose skills in war and technology had begun to matter very much, Shâh 'Abbâs was willing even to admit to his country missionaries, whose professed aim was to convert Muslims to Christianity. The following extract comes from a report written by two Carmelite missionaries sent by the Pope to Irân in 1604: Father Simon was the leader and superior of the mission; Father Vincent is described in the text.

REPORT OF THE CARMELITE MISSION
(FROM FATHER SIMON: REPORT ON PERSIA, PERSIANS AND 'ABBÂS I)

. . . The country which I saw is sparsely inhabited, for the most part all flat, with little water and much uncultivated land;

From *A Chronicle of the Carmelites in Persia and the Papal Mission of the XVIIth and XVIIIth Centuries*, compiled by H. G. Chick, London: Eyre and Spottiswoode, 1939, vol. I, pp. 155-61, 248-55.

while that which is cultivated has a great abundance of all sorts
of produce, such as we have in Italy, and cheap. For less than a
real[1] seven pounds of white bread could be had in Isfahan,[2] and
at the time there was a scarcity. . . . There is an abundance of
wine, rice, grapes, melons and other fruit—all the year round
fresh can be seen—of meat and oxen sufficiently so. The Persians do not eat the flesh of cows and calves, but mutton to a
vast extent and horseflesh, which is the most esteemed and by
the nobles. The climate is very temperate: last winter there was
little cold. In Isfahan, where I was, no snow fell, except for a
little at the end of February. The heat of summer is not great:
and on account of the clemency of the climate all sleep in the
open on the roofs, and those who are sick similarly. The Persians have few doctors, yet there are many old men among
them. Their garb is a long garment, different from that of the
Turks: they tie shawls round their waists, and almost all of
them go clothed in cotton stuffs of various colours in imitation
of the king. Their chief food is rice with meat, and they do not
use such variety, nor dainties as in these countries [of Europe]:
and they are frugal and satisfied with little food. At their ban-
quets they display great sumptuousness, both in the great quantity of viands, as in the preparation and serving of them: Allah
Virdi Khan, captain-general of the king of Persia, in a banquet
he gave to certain Kurdish ambassadors, put on the table 3,000
dishes all of gold with lids of the same, as I was informed by
some Turks who were present. Almost all of them drink wine:
they sit and eat on the ground on rich carpets. The houses are
of stone, remarkable inside for the great amount of stucco work
ornamenting the ceilings and the walls: so they do not employ
tapestries. On the street side they have no windows, so that their
women should not be seen: and thus the streets are not attractive, nor is the city fine. The Persians are white (skinned), of
fair stature, courteous, friendly towards foreigners and tracta-
ble: they set store on nobility of birth, which the Turks do not
do. They are very ceremonious and use many forms of politeness after their own fashion. There are some of them, who pro-

1. A small Persian coin.
2. City to which 'Abbâs had moved his capital.

fess to be philosophers and mathematicians, almost all of them
to be poets: and they continually have books in their hands.
They have many large mosques, where they go to say their
prayers, and they allow any nation whatsoever to enter them.
. . . Thrice daily, morning, noon and evening, they say their
prayers: first they wash, then they spread a carpet or their outer
garment on the ground, placing on it a stone . . . and they
make many prostrations, calling on God and 'Ali, in which con-
sist all their devotions. They make profession of cleanliness in
respect of their bodies, clothes and in everything. They have
two kinds of persons dedicated to God's service: one they call
"Mullas," which is to say "learned men" or "doctors" . . . they
are esteemed by the lords and the rest, and have mosques in
their charge. The other kind of persons devoted to God's service
they call "Darwish," and they profess to abandon the world
more (than the other). They have only one miserable garment,
full of patches, over which they wear a sheepskin crosswise over
the shoulders: they go barefoot, they profess to disdain money,
and some of them will not even take it when given to them as
alms: they have no homes, and do not trouble to prepare food
for themselves, but sleep wherever night may overtake them
and eat whatever be given them as alms. They use some kinds
of penances, such as piercing their ears and hanging heavy
weights to them: they make a great practice of a rule of life,
and in their "lenten" periods[3] they fast, do not drink wine, make
a point of great charitableness, and to practise it in the summer-
time they stand in the public squares with cold water, which
they give gratis to anyone wanting it. Many of them do not
marry, and they remain in a community obedient to a superior.
These latter have good mosques and pleasant places outside the
towns after the guise of our hermits, to which the Muhamma-
dans resort out of piety. They sleep all together in one room on
a carpet, and their sheepskins, without anything else [as bed-
ding]: and, when they die, they are considered heavenly spirits,
and some of them even while alive by the common people, especially if mentally deranged, because then it is said of them
that God has deprived them of the use of reason, so that they

3. I.e., Ramadân, the Muslim month of fasting from sunrise to sunset.

may be always with Him and not sin. When they come into the towns, both men and women kiss their garments. Nowadays there are hardly any of them who observe that mode of life and, although they may do so outwardly to some extent, in the matter of poverty in particular, they are very sensual and marry, receive money, drink wine, do not observe the fasts, and have many other vices, for which reason the Shah does not esteem them, nor does any person of quality, but only the common people. The Persians have one wife, and pay no attention to first and second degrees of relationship in matrimony: they have as many concubines as they can afford: and so they have special places for their wives which they call "saraglios," into which they allow no man to enter, not even their own sons. The walls of the saraglios are very high; they have no windows looking on the streets, and those women are more closely cloistered than our nuns. They hardly ever go out, not even to the mosques, nor are they allowed to see anyone except the relatives: so that few respectable women are to be found in the streets. When women travel they do so on the backs of camels in certain great baskets covered with cloth or silk, according to their standing, while the men ride on horseback: there are no vehicles. The nobles in their saraglios have many women, some 200, some 300 or more, whom they take with them when on campaign with the army or wherever they go, and I think that to have so many may be more out of pomp and show than for any other reason, because men of 70 and 80 years old have them and take them about with them, and, when they want to extol a rich man, they say "he has a large saraglio, or that he takes about with him so many camel-loads of women." Almost all the women who are to be seen in the squares, both in the clothes they wear and in other matters, comport themselves with much modesty; besides the long dresses they wear a kerchief of white linen which covers them completely and they never let their faces or their hands be seen. For the rest they go about and ride through the city.

The Persians were formerly very superstitious and abhorred Christians, as if these latter were a foul race: thus they would not eat with them, nor from the vessels from which a Christian had eaten, nor did they allow them to tread on their carpets, nor to touch them: if a Christian were to touch the garment of one, the man would take it off and have it washed. Nowadays, because the Shah shows great regard for Christians, passes his time with them and sets them at his table, they have abandoned all this and act towards them as they do towards their own people: only in some distant districts and among the common folk is it still kept up.

. . . The king, Shah 'Abbâs . . . is 34[4] years old . . . of medium height, rather thin than fat, his face round and small, tanned by the sun, with hardly any beard: very vivacious and alert, so that he is always doing something or other. He is sturdy and healthy, accustomed to much exercise and toil: many times he goes about on foot, and recently he had been forty days on pilgrimage, which he made on foot the whole time. He has extraordinary strength, and with his scimitar can cut a man in two and a sheep with its wool on at a single blow—and the Persian sheep are of large size. He has done many other feats and has found no one to come up to him in them. In his food he is frugal, as also in his dress, and this to set an example to his subjects; and so in public he eats little else than rice, and that cooked in water only. His usual dress is of linen, and very plain: similarly the nobles and others in his realm, following suit, *whereas formerly they used to go out dressed in brocade with jewels and other fopperies*: and if he see anyone who is overdressed, he takes him to task, especially if it be a soldier. But in private he eats what he likes. He is sagacious in mind, likes fame and to be esteemed: he is courteous in dealing with everyone and at the same time very serious. For he will go through the public streets, eat from what they are selling there and other things, speak at ease freely with the lower classes, cause his subjects to remain sitting while he himself is standing, or will sit down beside this man and that. He says that is how to be a king, and that the king of Spain and other Christians do not get any pleasure out of ruling, because they are obliged to comport themselves with so much pomp and majesty as they do. He

4. I.e., he had been born in 1574—as pointed out previously, this must be an error, for it would make 'Abbâs only 55 at his death in 1629: it is perhaps a manuscript reversal of the figures, and these should read 43. (Tr.)

causes foreigners to sit down beside him and to eat at his table. With that and accompanying all such condescension he requires that people shall not want in respect towards him and, should anyone fail in this regard, he will punish the individual severely. So the more he demonstrates kindliness to his subjects and the more familiarly he talks with them, they tremble before him, even the greatest among them, for, while joking, he will have their heads cut off. He is very strict in executing justice and pays no regard to his own favourites in this respect; but rather is the stricter with them in order to set an example for others. So he has no private friends, nor anyone who has influence with him. Formerly there was in his service a great favourite of his, employed in removing manure from the stables. The Shah promoted him, and the man got to become very rich. In a chest of porphyry he preserved the patched garments which he had used to shake out the manure and the harness of a mule. The Shah went to his house and wanted to see all the riches he possessed. The man showed him (the Shah) everything. When they came to the chest of porphyry, he said that he did not want to open it, because all that he had exhibited belonged to his Majesty, only what was inside that chest was his own property. Finally he opened it: and the Shah commended him for it. He had kept those articles because he knew the king's temperament. While we were at his Court, he caused the bellies of two of his favourites to be ripped open, because they had behaved improperly to an ordinary woman. From this it comes about that in his country there are so very few murderers and robbers. In all the time I was at Isfahan, i.e. 4 months, there was never a case of homicide. He is very speedy in dispatching business: when he gives audience, which he does at the gate of his palace, in the Maidan, he finishes off all the cases that are brought to him. The parties stand present before him, the officers of justice and his own council, with whom he consults when it pleases him. The sentence which he gives is final and is immediately executed. If the guilty party deserve death, they kill him at once: to this end, when he gives audience, twelve dogs and twelve men [? sic], who devour men alive, are kept ready: he keeps them in order to use the greater severity. Apart from the officials, once

the sentence is given, it is not permitted to anyone to make any
reply: for the person is at once driven off with blows of the
sticks of some 30 to 40 royal farrashes,[5] who stand ready to do
this. When he wants to stop giving audience, he causes it to be
proclaimed that no one, on pain of death, may bring him petitions, and, when he wants to go out of doors unaccompanied,
that no one should follow him.

The like speed in dispatching business is practised by his officials: and his Wazir, or chancellor, who has charge of all the
royal revenues, the dispatch of ambassadors, and all other affairs, and who is the first person after the Shah, used to dispatch
200 petitions in a morning and after having sat and given a
hearing for six or seven hours would go out as serene, as if he
were coming from taking his horse for a walk.

There are four councillors of the king—Allah Virdi Khan, his
general: 'Ata Baig his Wazir: the Qurchi Bashi: and one who
was his "governor" and preceptor. The three last are always
with the Shah, and when he gives audience are standing next
to him. He has to be obeyed absolutely: anyone failing in the
slightest will pay for it with his head. And so he has had most of
the old nobles of Persia killed off and put in their stead low-bred
persons whom he has aggrandized. In the whole of Persia there
are only two of the old-time governors. To one of them, while
with the army in the field, the Shah said that he was to post a
battalion[6] so many paces distant from a river (for he—'Abbas—
gives all orders of importance). Afterwards he (the Shah) summoned him, and the grandee declared that he had the battalion
in such and such a position. Others present said that he had not:
the Shah orderd that, if it (the battalion) were not found there,
the grandee's head should be brought back to him. The messenger went and found him in the position assigned him by the
king; because, although on the previous night, when they told
him in the Shah's name to put his battalion there, he had said
that it would be better in another position, he had not however
dared to go against the king's order. Because of the great obedience they pay him, when he wills to have one of the nobles

5. Farrâsh: Palace chamberlain.
6. The word *battaglione* is used in the Italian in 1608.

killed, he dispatches one of his men to fetch the noble's head: the man goes off to the grandee, and says to him: "The Shah wants your head." The noble replies: "Very well," and lets himself be decapitated—otherwise he would lose it and, with it, all his race would become extinct. But, when they [i.e. the grandees] allow themselves to be decapitated, he aggrandizes the children.

.   .   .   .

He is very valiant and has a great liking for warfare and weapons of war, which he has constantly in his hands: we have been eye-witnesses of this because, whenever we were with him, he was adjusting scimitars, testing arquebuses, etc.: and to make him a present that will give him pleasure is to give him some good pieces of arms. This is the great experience which he has obtained of warfare over so many years, that he makes it in person and from the first it has made him a fine soldier and very skilled, and his men so dexterous that they are little behind our men in Europe. He has introduced into his militia the use of and esteem for arquebuses and muskets, in which they are very practised. Therefore it is that his realm has been so much extended on all sides. . . .

His militia is divided into three kinds of troops: one of the Georgians, who will be about 25,000 and are mounted: they are entitled to pay throughout the year, and have a general commanding: this is the old-time militia of the kings of Persia for the guarding of their persons. The present king has introduced the second force, which is made up of slaves of various races, many of them Christian renegades: their number will be as many again, and they are more esteemed than the first cited, both because they are servants of the king, and he assigns posts to them and promotes them. His captain-general and other grandees belong to this corps: they serve mounted and each of them has servants according as he can afford. The third body consists of soldiers whom the great governors of Persia are obliged to maintain and pay the whole year: they will be about 50,000. The captain-general is obliged to keep up and pay 12,000 of them annually: others more or less, and to this end the king grants them, as it pleases him, the territories he captures, and all the revenue these produce: as, for instance, he gave the province of Shiraz to his captain-general and the province of Lar, which will produce many hundreds of thousands of scudi[7] in revenue, of which he does not give a penny to the king. When they (the great governors) accomplish something signal in war, he gives them a governorship which produces greater revenue and sometimes the territory they capture is left to them. All the above-mentioned soldiers, who will total some 100,000, receive pay for the whole year. Then, according to the campaign and enterprise the king wishes to undertake, he enlists others, and, when it be necessary to make a great effort, he has it proclaimed throughout his country that whosoever is his well-wisher should follow him. Then everyone takes up arms.

. . . .

(FROM FATHER VINCENT: AN AUDIENCE WITH 'ABBÂS)

In May 1621 there returned to Persia, as first Visitor General of the Carmelite Missions in Persia and the East, Fr. Vincent of S. Francis, one of the three pioneers of 1607, and founder of the Residence at Hurmuz, who after reverting to work in Italy about 1616 had become prior of the convent at Palermo, and of that of S. Paul in Rome. . . .

. . . A striking account has been left on record by the Visitor General of an audience [with 'Abbâs; the English Agent Monox was also present] at which he was present, 5.6.1621. . . .

There are in Persia some English merchants, Lutherans and of other sects, here to buy silk: and one of them who is the Chief and whom the rest obey resides in the city of Isfahan: the merchants in England choose him to receive the money, which they remit him in order to purchase the silk, which each year may attain a total quantity of 600,000 ducats,[8] which is shipped and exported from Jashk, a port on the Persian Gulf, in English

7. Scudi: Singular *scudo*, Italian gold or silver coins.
8. A Venetian gold coin of considerable value.

ships which come out each year. This English Agent is treated by the Shah like an ambassador.

At the season when the Fr. Visitor General arrived in the city of Isfahan, the English had some articles, which had reached them by the ships that year, and they had asked an audience of the king in order to offer them as gifts, and so his Highness sent for them on that day and also summoned our Fr. Vincent, whom together with his companion, the king of Persia received inside the Haram or Saraglio, where no one may enter without special permission from his Majesty.

With his back to the wall of the farther side of the room, his Highness was sitting, as was his wont, on the floor, which was covered with rich carpets: he was eating alone from off a silken tablecloth. He had in front of him a single, but very large silver dish, on which there was a variety of foods made from rice of various hues, all cooked differently and each arranged in its compartment, in the separate compartments of rice there being buried partridges, pigeons, quails, and all sorts of boiled and roasted meats. He had also in front of him some Chinese porcelain bowls of rather small size, filled with the juice of lemons and oranges sweetened with sugar and flavoured with spices, from which to take a spoonful or two from time to time while he ate. For it is the Persian custom, while they are eating, not to drink water or wine, and in order to be able to digest the food . . . they use these juices while feeding: when they have finished, after a short time they begin to drink. . . .

Round the same apartment were also seated and eating off tablecloths of silk some of the principal among the king's subjects and two envoys from the king of Tatary, who had come from Caffa [Crimean peninsula] and also the English Agent mentioned above together with his Lutheran chaplain attired in a flowing gown of black damask, having wide and long sleeves . . . as well as their interpreter with four other English heretics.

The Fr. Visitor entered and made the proper obeisance to the Shah, who bade him sit down, together with his companion, at the same tablecloth and dish, from which he himself was eating. He (the Shah) said that he was welcome and that he remembered seeing him in Persia on two previous occasions, and knew him very well: then he enquired about the Visitor's health and the date of his arrival in Isfahan. Next, Fr. Vincent presented the letters he had brought: two Briefs from His Holiness (one in reply to a letter, in which the Shah had written to the Pope) another letter from the Grand Master of Malta, who had handed it to the Fr. Visitor General on his passage by Malta. The Shah replied graciously and, taking the letters, gave them to Mir Abul Ma'ali, his chief secretary of state, to have translated.

Two days previously the English had been with the king and discoursed at great length on the matter of religion and spoken ill of the Catholics saying that they were idolaters, who adored pictures and images, and made the sign of the cross, etc. The Shah had said that he would bring the Fathers together with them, so that they might hold a disputation on these matters.

This was the motive why the king of Persia asked the Fathers about the difference there is between Catholics and English.

The Fr. Visitor answered that the English are heretics and false Christians, and that Roman Catholics are the true Christians. The Shah continued on this topic of religion and touched in the course of it on four main points, which were:

(*a*) fasting and good works, (*b*) about the Cross, and its adoration and images, (*c*) on free-will, (*d*) on the antiquity of the Roman Catholic religion, and the primacy of the Sovereign Pontiff.

The occasion for the first topic, that of fasting and good works, arose from the Shah asking the Fathers why they were not eating. They replied that it was Ember Saturday in Pentecost. The king enquired of the English what fasts they kept. Their "Chief" replied that God had not commanded men to fast, and, although the English Agent spoke through his interpreter, still the king asked the Fathers what he was saying, and they answered in Persian that the Englishman said that God had not commanded men to fast and the Fathers continued: "See, your Highness, what an absurd falsehood and error it is, as it is true that by their religious laws Christians, Muslims, Jews and Gentiles have fasts of obligation."

Here there was small controversy since the matter was manifest and clear. With one voice the Shah and the grandees sitting with him said that it was a very great error and falsehood, because fasts, prayer, penitential exercises and good works are recommended in the law of Moses, in the Gospel, and the Quran, and in fine by all the prophets.

Second point: on the Cross, its adoration, and on images. The Shah enquired of the Fathers whether the English made the sign of the Cross to bless themselves. The Fathers answered "no." He asked further whether they had images of the saints and adored them: the reply was given him: "no." He asked the Fathers: "Why do the Franks venerate them, as in this they resemble the Idolaters?" (Persians, in praying, prostrate themselves repeatedly, and with their head and forehead venerate certain seals or counters of earth, of the size of a doubloon, and the beads, on which they recite their prayers, are made from earth from Mecca.)

In order to convince him the Fathers put the question to the king: "Because your Highness and your people prostrate yourselves and worship seals and beads made of earth would it be right for us to call your Highness and your people idolaters? Certainly not, because we know that, when you perform that of act of adoration, you do not mean by it that that seal and stone are God, but do it out of piety and reverence for that soil, as it comes from the places of sepulture of your ancestors and the great men whom you consider saints." The Shah answered: "That is not the chief reason and intention we have for worshipping on earthen seals[9] and beads, but rather in that act of veneration we make an act of recognizing that we are clay, and that from earth God created us, and we adore the Creator of this: and the reason why in the mosques and in our houses whilst we say our prayers on matting and carpets our prayers would not be lawful and acceptable, unless we said them on" (i.e. touching) "the earth. With this in view, for more convenience and cleanliness we use the earthen medallions and beads: and that

9. *Muhreh*, which Shî'îs touch with their foreheads in the prostrations during prayer. (Tr.)

they are of this or that soil is an accidental matter: it suffices that it be earth. And so, when we have any other sort of stone, even if it be a piece of rock, we have no need of a seal. It is also true that we venerate it (the seal) as a memorial and a pious object, as thou sayest, but not mainly for that reason."

To this the Fathers replied: "Very good! And thus our Christian religion does not adore nor serve images, as if they were gods, nor does it expect from them the future judgment (God preserve us from such a thing!), but it venerates images for the things they represent. They serve us also as memorials to remind us of the virtues of those saints they represent, in order that we may imitate them and beg them to intercede by their prayers with our Lord God, that He will grant us what we ask and that we may be good and his servants, as they have been, so that we may attain the glory which they now enjoy. So that, just as your Highness and your people do not say that that earthen medallion is God, no more do we say that the statues of the saints are gods, nor do we adore them as such." With these reasonings the Shah and his courtiers remained content.

The king said that Christians do not make the cross properly because there are only three nails, and we make the sign of it in four places: and, thus speaking, the Shah made the sign as a proof of what he said. The Fr. Visitor replied that it is not done on account of the nails of the Cross, but in order to signify the Trinity of Persons and unity of God and the incarnation of the Son of God: and so it is done at His name, signifying that there is one God alone, Father, Son and Holy Ghost, who are the three Persons; and the Father is signed on the head, to signify that He is the beginning of the other Persons, the Son on the body to signify that He became man in the virginial womb of S. Mary, and the Holy Ghost is signed on the two shoulders to signify that the Third Person proceeds from the Father and the Son. The king was pleased to have heard this explanation and said: "I believed that you made the cross in order to signify that Christ, the Lord, Son of God and man, died on the cross in order to save and redeem all men." The king then said: "We hold that the Lord Jesus is the Spirit of God and was not crucified by the Jews, but that God, seeing that the Jews wanted to crucify him, drew him up as the Spirit into heaven, putting the features of Jesus on Judas, who had sold him and whom, because he appeared to be so like Him, they took and crucified."

The Father said, "We hold in the Gospel that Jesus Christ is the Word of God, and that He himself as a man was crucified for the salvation of men and the third day rose from the dead and after 40 days ascended into heaven in the sight of all his disciples, who were afterwards witnesses of these truths for all the world."

The king asked whether the English believe this. The Fr. Visitor replied "yes." The Shah put the question to the minister (clergyman) of the English who was present, and who confirmed that it was the case, because in this particular they believe the same as the Roman Catholics: and then, in order to show courtesy to the Fathers, with his hand the king poured out and gave them to drink, making a sign of the cross over the cup.

The third point concerned free-will. The king turned to question the Fathers—who were the better, the English or the Roman Christian. The Fathers replied that by its fruit the goodness and quality of the tree are known: that the king should enquire about the things the English did and the examples they gave, and from those he would be able to judge. The Agent of the English rejoined that they were the better Christians, and that they had the right Faith. On this the Fathers observed: "Shah, we do not want to say more to your Highness than this, that the English are heretics and of a like sect as the Turks, who deny free-will and say that all the evil men do and the demons do is done of necessity, and they cannot do less, because God so wills: and so they (the English) say that God does everything, whether good or evil."

Here the grandees of the king looked at each other, and the Shah in particular jumped from his seat (as the saying goes) and began to make a sermon to all present, very earnestly as he detested that theory. He spoke with great gusto, so that the Tatar envoys from Caffa, who were there and who are of the same sect as the Turks, should hear him. After the king finished his arguments, the Fathers said: "This is the reason, your Majesty, why the English, who have no consciences nor fear of God, are pirates, rob, slay, destroy, and one cannot rely on their word, because they say that they cannot do anything else, seeing that they have no option."

The English did not know what reply to make during all this harangue of the Shah, which lasted for the space of more than three-quarters of an hour, during which his Highness brought forward many arguments and examples in opposition to the English who deny free-will, and in particular he said that it was most false. . . .

Regarding the fourth and last point, the antiquity of the Roman Catholic religion and the primacy of the Sovereign Pontiff, the Shah enquired how long the English had been separated from the Romans and the Pope. The Fr. Visitor told him "70 or 80 years." The Agent of the English said that *they* were the primitive Christians. The Fathers asked him whether previous to those 70 or 80 years the English and Romans were all one and whether all England paid obedience to the Roman Pontiff. The English answered "yes: it was the truth that formerly they yielded obedience to the Pope." When this had been admitted and translated to the Shah by the interpreter of the English themselves, his Highness remarked that, just as the Sunnis and Turkish heretics will not ascribe the primacy to Husain, son of Amir-ul-Mu'minin [i.e. 'Ali], but instead to 'Umar,[10] so the English do not obey the vicar of Jesus, who is the Pope of Rome: and for this they are heretics.

The sun was entering through a window and troubled the king: so he got up and made a sign to the Fathers to follow him. Together with his Highness they entered a smaller, but cooler apartment, and all sat down in this order: on the right hand he caused the minister (clergyman) to sit and on the left near himself the Fathers (the Persians consider the left-hand a more honoured seat, because, they say, it is on the side where the heart is, and the sword is worn). Then 'Ali Quli Khan, governor of _____ and the chief judge of the court of crimes; next the Georgians, and in another apartment, but very near by, so that they could see and converse with the Shah, were his other gentlemen. Below the minister, and beside him were the Tatars from Caffa,

10. 'Ali: fourth Caliph (656-661); 'Umar: second Caliph (634-644).

and last of all the rest of the English, near whom in a little closet were the king's minstrels playing on musical instruments and singing.

The English wanted to discuss the business of the silk and to ask for it to be finished and for the Shah's mandate for them to go and purchase it in Gilan and Shirwan. The Shah made signs to one of his officials, who then told the interpreter that by no manner of means was their business to be discussed, because it was not the time for it, giving it to be understood that it was not suitable to talk of business in front of the Fathers.

The Shah returned once more to talk about the nails [in the cross] of Christ, asking whether they were three or four. The answer was given him that some Saints said there were four, but that the majority conclude that there were three. This opinion pleased the Shah: and he crossed his legs, saying that with a single nail they had nailed both feet, and that was how he had seen it in pictures. Here the English Agent wanted to cast ridicule on the Catholics and asked the Fathers how many wounds Christ had in His body. The Fr. Visitor answered him that there were five. He [the English Agent—Monox] laughed a great deal and said: "No: there were four." The Fr. Visitor enquired which they were. He (the English Agent) replied: "one wound only in the two feet, because a single nail had transfixed them, and the rest in the two hands and the side." The Fr. Visitor, remarking that he (the Agent) was a layman and would know little about philosophy, turned to the minister, and asked whether he too held that opinion: to which the minister said "yes." So then the Fr. Visitor enquired once more of the minister whether the wounds in the feet were continuous or contiguous: the latter answered that they were continuous and for that reason were one wound. Our Religious remarked that that was contrary to philosophy, because something "continuous" is that which is joined by a common end. But the wounds in Christ's feet were not coupled by a common end: therefore they were not continuous, and in consequence they were two wounds, and not one. The minister did not know what to answer. The Shah and the grandees wanted to understand the point in dispute: it was explained to them, and they laughed at the English for saying

AN AUDIENCE WITH 'ABBÂS

that in the two wounded feet there was only one wound because
a single nail pierced them.

. . . .

The Fathers said to his Highness that, if he allowed, they
would put a problem before him: and the Shah bade them pro-
pound it. So they said: "Since it is true that in all countries and
states there are good and bad people, perforce among our Christian community there are also some bad men, who commit
crimes: and perhaps it might be necessary to punish them by
shedding their blood, by mutilation of their limbs, or by putting
them to death." So they enquired in such case who was to be the
judge to try the case and execute punishment, because it was
not lawful for Religious to be judges, or mix themselves up in
secular affairs. Taking in one hand a piece of his garment, like
a man shaking the dust from it, the Shah answered and said: "I
have nothing to do with any crime that any of your people may
commit contrary to your law; but my wish is that you punish
misdemeanours, and that you see to and keep your houses, people and community clean and free from such, so that there be
no disorder or scandal: and, as to criminal offences of which you
cannot be the judge, since you are priests, choose from among
the Franks residing here or staying temporarily here one to be
judge, with the authority of a consul,[11] and you as priests, knowing more of the law, would be able to tell the consul what in
conscience and justice he should do. So that it is our wish that
you Fathers from the Pope execute justice between your people
in conformity with the law of Christ and the orders that you
have from the Pope. I say the same to the English." 'Ali Quli
Khan, the chief judge and . . . the king's secretary and Wazir,
in loud voices extolled this decree of the Shah, telling the Fathers that his Highness had done them a great favour, on which
the Fathers duly tendered thanks.

The Shah asked the English whether their Gospel and ours
were all one. The Agent answered: "No." Thereupon the Fr.
Visitor said that the Agent was telling the truth, because our
Gospel was the real one, and theirs false, being full of the false-

11. This seems to be an authorization of the extra-territorial jurisdiction,
which prevailed in Persia till 1928. (Tr.)

hoods which they told. On this the Shah reproved the Fr. Visitor, saying that the English had not told him falsehoods and had always carried out their promises and were of much utility in his country. "But, you; yes," he said to the Visitor, "you have told me lies." In reply the Father asked: "What falsehood have I told your Highness?" The Shah answered: "This, that the king of Portugal and Spain has promised to make war on the Turks: when he has not done so." The Father remarked: "His Majesty the king of Spain and the Christian princes have warred all these years against the Turks," and then asked: "How many years is it that your Highness is making war on the Turks?" The Shah replied: "Twenty years." The Father rejoined: "Then, if in those twenty years the Emperor, aided by the Christian princes, had not been to war with the Turks and had not kept them occupied in Hungary and other parts (as he did in the years 1604–5–6 and 1607) at the request and instance of the Pope, would your Highness have captured after Tabriz and Julfa Erivan, Ganjeh, etc.? Later in the year 1607 did not your Highness take Shamakha and Demirkapu, called by its other name, "The Iron Gate" (Darband) together with all the very fertile province of Shirwan, and, finally, is it not the fact that your Highness had no further assault from the Turks until the year 1610, in which there came Murad Pasha, who had delayed more than 7 years in bringing assistance and relief to those provinces so that your Highness had been able so to consolidate your position in them, to great advantage in that you obtained a signal victory?" The Shah had nothing to say to this. The Fathers continued: "Majesty, the war which the king of Poland is making against the Turks, too, is that not by a Catholic king, obedient to the Pope, the vicar of Christ?" The Shah answered: "Tell me what the Pope is doing, not what others are doing." The Fathers rejoined: "What the Christian princes are doing may also be said to be what the Pope is doing, because, just as when the hand does any good action, it is the head which directs it and to it the praise is given, and, just as when Allah Virdi Khan, Amir Khan, etc., generals of your Highness, gain any victories or conquer any territory, the glory is attributed to your Highness, so also the victories won by the Christian princes are attributed to the Pope who is the head and father of all Christians."

. . . .

To that the Shah returned that, if the Pope were in person to go to fight against the Turks and to spend his treasure on it, all the rest of the Christian princes would go too and expend their money and resources. For, whoever does not obey the Pope, the vicar of Christ, is no good Christian.

Thereupon the Fathers said: "Well! that is why we said, your Majesty, that the English are no good Christians, because they do not obey the Pope, and they are the cause of the Christian Catholic princes not making war on the Turks. For these heretics, disobedient to the Pope, rebel against their Catholic princes, who are obedient to him, and make war on them, as in these last years the Palatine, son-in-law of the king of England, did against the Emperor, although, thanks to God, the Emperor has gained the victory over him and despoiled him of his lands and punished him as he deserved."

. . . .

It was already late, and the guests got up, and we too took our leave of the king, kissing his hand. As we went out, the English made apologies to the Fathers and begged their pardon for having exceeded the limits of politeness. The Fathers answered that in disputations on matters of religion neither politeness nor dissimulation nor compliments are to be used, and that they wished them well and no boon greater than the salvation of their souls, and for this had spoken so freely about Catholic truth.

. . . .

Within two months of those asseverations of respect for Jesus, the fickle monarch, presumably instigated, had let loose a persecution of Christians. . . .

V

The Crisis of Modernization
(19th and 20th Centuries)

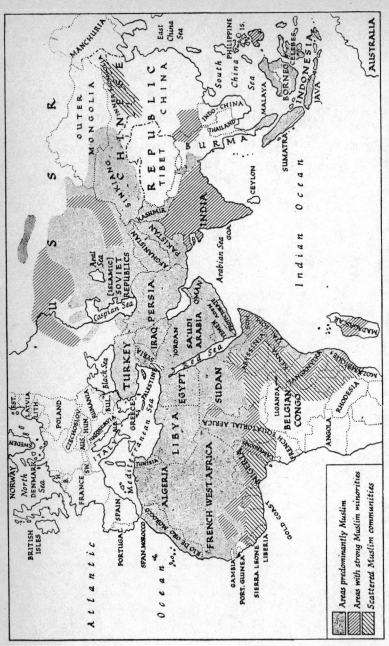

From *The Social Structure of Islam* by Reuben Levy (1971) by permission of Cambridge University Press.

Areas predominantly Muslim

Areas with strong Muslim minorities

Scattered Muslim communities

Introduction

By the beginning of the nineteenth century, Islâmic states and peoples had begun to feel pressure from western Europeans in more and more aspects of daily life. By the beginning of the twentieth century most Muslim states had lost their sovereignty to some form of foreign imperial control, and those that maintained independence did so precariously.

This situation presented Muslim thinkers and political leaders with great difficulties. Islâm required its adherent to believe that God ruled the world and that the Divine Will initiated and controlled political change along with all other changes among men. Why then should God abandon the true believers and favor Christians, who compounded their original religious errors by not remaining faithful to their own mistaken version of divine revelation?

One repsonse was to argue that God was punishing Muslims for failures to conform to the laws and instructions Allâh had revealed to Muhammad. The obvious cure was to revert to patterns of life prescribed by the Qur'ân and to purify religion of all innovations and corruptions. This was the path that recommended itself to the Wahhâbî reformers of Arabia, to the followers of the Mahdî in the Sudan, and to many less prominent Islâmic revivalist reforms in West Africa. The logical antithesis of these purist reactions was to view Islâm as a gigantic error and try to do away with the inheritance from the past entirely. This was the path undertaken by Mustapha Kemâl Atatürk in Turkey after World War I.

Most Muslims found these extremes unattractive and tried to combine the Islâmic inheritance from the past with whatever elements of modernity seemed necessary for the preservation of the Islâmic tradition. The problem existed on an intellectual level, as illustrated by our selections from Iqbâl, the poet inspirer of the movement to found Pakistan, and Afghânî, and on a practical level as illustrated by our selection from Hussein, nineteenth-century Muslim reformist. The political problem which had haunted Islâm since the disappearance of the caliphate as an effective imperial government was another critical problem. The competing demands of modern state-building and old-fashioned attachment to the community of the faithful as a whole remained logically irreconcilable, as our selections from Atatürk and Jinnah, the founder of Pakistan, suggest.

The Plight of Islâm: Poetry

The poem *Complaint and Answer*, a major portion of which is included here, directly confronts the dilemmas of Islâm in modern times. The author, Muhammad Iqbâl (1876-1938), was born in Lahore, India. Being of the upper classes he was educated both in traditional Islâmic cultures and in Western learning, represented in the India of his day by the British. He completed his studies in England, and after receiving a Ph.D. in philosophy he returned to India in 1905, where he taught philosophy and practiced law for a few years. Then, disgusted by official life, he retired to the life of a man of letters. It was at this stage of his life in 1912 that he wrote *Complaint and Answer*.

The language in which Iqbâl wrote was Urdu, a mixture of Persian and Hindi and the literary medium for most Indian Muslims. *Complaint and Answer* preserves some of the traditional Sûfî metaphors; in this respect Iqbâl maintained a traditional stance. Yet the thrust of his argument is strongly Western, and it echoes the style of the Victorian English poet Alfred Lord Tennyson almost as strongly as it recalls Rûmî and the later Persian poets. Iqbâl's poem thus reflects a poignant effort to reconcile two very alien words, which is central to the dilemma of contemporary Islâm.

IQBÂL: FROM COMPLAINT AND ANSWER

The Complaint

Why must I forever suffer loss, oblivious to gain,
Why think not upon the morrow, drowned in grief for
    yesterday?

From *Complaint and Answer* by Sir Muhammad Iqbâl, trans. by Arthur J. Arberry, Lahore: Ashraf Press, 1955, pp. 3-7, 9-10, 12-20, 32-33, 41-43, 45-59, 61-69. Reprinted by permission.

Why must I attentive heed the nightingale's lament of pain?
Fellow-bard, am I a rose, condemned to silence all the way?[1]
No; the burning power of song bids me be bold and not to faint;
Dust be in my mouth, but God—He is the theme of my
      complaint.
True, we are forever famous for our habit to submit;
Yet we tell our tale of grief, as by our grief we are constrained.
We are but a muted lyre; yet a lament inhabits it—
If a sigh escapes our lips, no more can sorrow be contained.
God, give ear to the complaint of us, Thy servants tried and
      true;
Thou art used to songs of praise; now hear a note of protest too.
.   .   .   .

Strange indeed the spectacle Thy world supplied before our[2]
      days,
Here men bowed them down to stones, there paid they rever-
      ence to trees;
Only to the visual image was attuned the human gaze—
How could hearts adore a God no eye percipient may seize?
Well Thou knowest, was there any anywhere to name Thy
      Name?
By the Muslim's strong right arm Thy purpose to fulfilment
      came.
Though the Seljuks had their empire, the Turanians their sway,
Though the Chinese ruled in China, the Sassanians in Iran,
Though the Greeks inhabited broad, fruitful acres in their day
And the Jews possessed their cubit, and the Christians owned
      their span,
Who upraised the sword of battle in Thy Name's most sacred
      cause,
Or who strove to right the ruined world by Thy most hallowed
      laws?
It was we and we alone who marched, Thy soldiers, to the fight,
Now upon the land engaging, now embattled on the sea,
The triumphant Call to Prayer in Europe's churches to recite,

1. The nightingale's singing to the rose is a common Sûfî image.
2. I.e., Muslims'. Iqbâl here claims identity with all Muslims, early and
late, throughout the world.

Through the wastes of Africa to summon men to worship Thee.
All the glittering splendour of great emperors we reckoned
    none;
In the shadow of our glinting swords we shouted, "God is One!"
All our life we dedicated to the dire distress of war;
When we died, we died exultant for the glory of Thy Name;
Not to win a private empire did we draw the swords we bore—
Was it in the quest of riches to earth's frontiers that we came?
Had our people striven for the sake of worldly goods and gold
Would they then have shattered idols they might gainfully have
    sold?
We were rocks immovable when in the field we took our stand,
And the bravest-hearted warriors by our thrust were swept
    away;
It sufficed us to enrage, if any gainsaid Thy command,
Then we hurled us on their cannons, took their swordpoints but
    for play.
Into every heart we struck the impress of Thy Unity
And beneath the dagger's lightning preached the Message,
    Lord, of Thee.

.   .   .   .

Strove there ever other nation in the cause of Thee alone,
Bore there ever other people battle's anguish for Thy sake?
Whose the sword that seized the world, and ruled it as its very
    own?
Whose the loud Allahu Akbar[3] that compelled the earth to
    wake?
Whose the dread that kept the idols cowering and terrified
So that, heads cast down and humbled, "He is God, the One,"
    they cried?
In the press of mortal combat if the hour of worship came
Then the people of Hejaz, to Mecca turning, bowed in prayer;
King Mahmud, Ayaz the slave—their rank in service was the
    same,
Lord and servant—at devotion never difference was there.
Slave and master, rich and needy—all the old distinctions gone,

3. "Allâhu Akbar" means "God is the greatest," a common Muslim battle
cry.

Unified in adoration of Thy Presence, they were one.[4]
In the Hall of Space and Being, at the dawn and eventide
Circulated we like goblets with the Wine of Faith replete;
Still we roved o'er plain and mountain, spread Thy Message far
    and wide—
Is it known to Thee, if ever we returned to own defeat?
Desert after desert spanning, faring on through sea on sea,
In the Ocean of the Shadows our strong coursers watered we.
We erased the smudge of falsehood from the parchment
    firmament,
We redeemed the human species from the chains of slavery;
And we filled the Holy Kaaba[5] with our foreheads humbly bent,
Clutching to our fervent bosoms the Koran in ecstasy.
Yet the charge is laid against us we have played the faithless
    part;
If disloyal we have proved, hast Thou deserved to win our
    heart?
Other creeds claim other peoples, and they have their sinners
    too;
There are lowly men among them, and men drunken with
    conceit;
Some are sluggards, some neglectful, some are vigilant and true;
Multitudes disdain Thy Name in loathing utter and complete;
But the showers of Thy mercy other thirsting souls assuage,
Only on the hapless Muslims falls the lightning of Thy rage.[6]
Hark, the idols in the temples shout, "The Muslims are no
    more,"
Jubilant to see the guardians of the Kaaba's shrine depart;
The world's inn is emptied of those singing cameleers of yore,
Vanished is their caravan, Koran close-pressed to reverent heart.
Disbelief is loud with laughter; art Thou deaf, indifferent?
Disregardest Thou Thy Unity, as if it nothing meant?

4. This is a criticism of the intense social distinctions common among Indian Muslims of Iqbâl's day. It was this disunity which the Muslim League,
as led by Muhammad Jinnah and inspired by Iqbâl, sought to ameliorate.
5. Muslim sacred building in Mecca.
6. This passage should be read in light of the minority status of Muslims
in India.

Not of this are we complaining, that their coffers overflow
Who have not the wit or grace of converse in society;
But that infidels should own the houris[7] and the palaces—ah,
   woe!
While the wretched Muslims must with promises contented be.
Now no more for us Thy favours and Thy old benevolence—
How and wherefore is Thy pristine kindliness departed hence?
Why no more are worldly riches among Muslims to be found,
Since Thy power is as of old beyond compute and unconfined?
If Thou willest, foaming fountains from the desert's breast can
   bound
And the rippling mirage may the traveller in the forest blind.
All we have is jeers from strangers, public shame, and
   poverty—
Is disgrace our recompense for laying down our lives for Thee?
So; it is on others only that the world its love bestows;
We, who walk Thy chosen path—to us a phantom world is left.
Be it so; bid us be gone, and let the earth belong to those,
Yet protest not that the earth of Unity is now bereft.
For no other cause we live but Thy remembrance to maintain;
When the saki is departed, can the winecup yet remain?[8]

.   .   .   .

Life is joyless now, and death no comfort promises to bring;
To remember ancient sorrows is the sole delight I know.
In the mirror of my mind what gems of thought are
   shimmering,
In the darkness of my breast what shining revelations glow!
Yet no witness in the garden may the miracle attest;
Not a tulip there lies bleeding with a brand upon its breast,
Break, hard hearts, to hear the carol of this nightingale forlorn;
Wake, dull hearts, to heed the clamour and the clangour of this
   bell;

7. The famed black-eyed maidens of the Muslim Paradise.
8. A plea to God, in the wine imagery of classical Sûfî poetry, not to
desert His people. "Saki" means "cup-bearer" or "wine-server"—a common
Sûfî metaphor for the spiritual master (here perhaps God himself or one
of His messengers) who bring God's inspiration and love, the "wine" of
spiritual "drunkenness."

Rise, dead hearts, by this new compact of fidelity reborn;
Thirst, dry hearts, for the old vintage whose sweet tang you
    knew so well.
Though the jar was cast in Persia, in Hejaz the wine first
    flowed;
And though Indian the song be, from Hejaz derives the mode.[9]

The Answer

Came a Voice: "Ah, pitiable is the story thou hast told;
Sure, thy cup is overflowing with the tears that never cease.
High as heaven has the loud thunder of thy cry impassioned
    rolled;
In what impudence of language thy distraction finds release!
Thanks at least for this, that thy complaint was beautifully
    phrased,
And the creature to his Maker has in conversation raised.
We would fain be bountiful, but no petitioner is there;
When no traveller approaches, how can We guide on the way?
Free to all Our loving kindness, none is worthy of Our care—
Even We could never fashion a new Adam of such clay.
Were there any to receive it, We would give a royal throne;
A new world We have to offer, were one earnest seeker known.
Hands are impotent and nerveless, hearts unfaithed and infidel,
The Community a heartbreak to their Prophet and a shame;
Gone the idol-breakers, in their places idol-makers dwell;
Abrahams their fathers were; the children merit Azar's[10] name.
New and strange the band of drinkers, and their wine is strange
    and new,
A new shrine to house their Kaaba, new and strange the idols
    too.

.   .   .   .

Very heavy on your spirits weighs the charge of morning
    prayer;
Leifer far would you be sleeping, than rise up to worship Me.

9. "Hejaz" (the area in Arabia where Islâm was born) is meant here to
show that, as far distant as Indian Muslims may be from their origins,
those origins are still in the prophecy of Muhammad.
10. Azar: Abraham's father, an idolater.

Ramadan[11] is too oppressive for your tempers free to bear;
Tell me now, do you consider *that* the law of loyalty?
Nations come to birth by Faith; let Faith expire, and nations die;
So, when gravitation ceases, the thronged stars asunder fly.
Why, you are a people utterly bereft of every art;
Not a nation in the world so lightly spurns its native place;
You are like a barn where lightnings nestle, and will not depart;
You would sell your fathers' graveyards, nor account such traffick base;
Making profit out of tombstones has secured you such renown—
Why not set up shop in idols, if you chance to hunt some down?
Who erased the smudge of falsehood from the parchment firmament?
Who redeemed the human species from the chains of slavery?
Who once filled the Holy Kaaba with their foreheads lowly bent,
Clutching to their fervent bosoms the Koran in ecstasy?
Who were they? They were your fathers; as for now, why, what are you,
Squatting snug, serenely waiting for to-morrow to come true?
Did you say that Muslims must with promises contented be?
That is a complaint unfounded, and by commonsense abhorred;
The Creator's law is justice, out of all eternity—
Infidels who live like Muslims surely merit Faith's reward.
There is scarcely one amongst you after Paradise aspires;
There is not a Moses living, though unquenched are Sinai's fires.
One and common are the profit and the loss the people bear.
One and common are your Prophet, your religion, and your creed,
One the Holy Sanctuary, one Koran, one God you share;
But to act as one, and Muslims—that would every bound exceed.
Here sectarianism triumphs, class and caste there rule the day;
Is it thus you hope to prosper, to regain your ancient sway?

11. The month of fasting from sunrise to sunset as prescribed in the Qur'ân.

Who abandoned the example of the Chosen Messenger?
Who took temporal advantage as their touchstone of success?
Who are dazzled by strange customs, alien usages prefer?
For the manners of their fathers who a faint disgust profess?
In your hearts there is no ardour, in your spirits feeling none;
As regards the Prophet's Message, why, with that you've long
      since done.

Now, if any stand to worship in the mosques, it is the poor,
And if any bear the pains of holy fasting, it is they;
They alone Our Name revere, and Our remembrance keep
      secure;
That your misdeeds may be hidden, still they labour and they
      pray.

Drunken with the pride of riches, wealthy men neglect God's
      due;
The communion of Islam lives on, because the poor are true.

Now no more the preacher's message from a ripened judgment
      springs,
Quenched the lightning of his spirit, out the lantern of his word;
Lifeless hangs the Call to Prayer, with no Bilal[12] to lend it
      wings;
While philosophy spins on, Ghazali's[13] lectures go unheard.

"Silenced is the voice of worship," the deserted mosques lament;
"Where are now the brave Hejazis men of godly, true intent?"
Loud the cry goes up, "The Muslims? They are vanished, lost
      to view!"

We re-echo, "Are true Muslims to be found in any place?"
Christian is your mode of living, and your culture is Hindoo;
Why, such Muslims to the Jews would be a shame and a
      disgrace.

Sure enough, you have your Syeds, Mirzas, Afghans, all the
      rest;[14]
But can you claim you are Muslims, if the truth must be
      confessed?

12. Muhammad's black *muezzin*, or caller to prayer.
13. Ghazâlî: (d. 1111) Muslim theologian, teacher, writer on mysticism,
criticized philosophy as heretical.
14. Persian-Muslim princely titles.

Ever truthful, ever fearless was the Muslim in his speech,
Strong and sure his sense of justice, clean of partiality;
High exalted was his courage, far above the common reach,
And sweet modesty the dew was that refreshed his nature's tree;
Of his wine the liquid essence by self-naughting was distilled.
And his joy was in self-emptying the flask his Maker filled.
Every Muslim was a lancet poised to sever falsehood's vein,
In the mirror of his being ceaseless action's lustre shone;
In his own right arm he trusted, by his strength he could attain,
And while you are scared of dying, he had fear of God alone.
If the child learns not the knowledge that has made his father
    sage,
Then what right has he by merit to his father's heritage?
You are all intoxicated with the joy of fleshly ease;
Are you Muslims? What, is this the way Islam would have you
    tread?
Ali's[15] poverty you will not, Uthman's[16] wealth you dare not
    seize—
What relationship of spirit links you to your glorious dead?
For the fact that they were Muslims they were honoured in
    their day;
You, who have abandoned the Koran, are spurned and cast
    away.
You are wroth with one another, they were kindly, merciful;
You, who sin, see sins in others, they concealed their brothers'
    sin;
Be the Pleiades your dwelling, if they are attainable,
Yet your souls must be in order, and with them you should
    begin.
They possessed the realm of China, they ascended Persia's
    throne;
You have not their manly honour, and are great in words alone.
Self-destruction is your fashion, noble self-esteem was theirs;
You would flee from brotherhood, a brotherhood for which they
    died;
Yours the tongue that idly blabs, theirs was the hand that
    greatly dares;

15. Muhammad's son-in-law, fourth Caliph (r. 656-661).
16. Third Caliph (r. 644-656).

You are fain to pluck a bud, they mastered all the garden wide.
Nations to this day rehearse the legend of their loyalty,
And their truth still stands inscribed upon the scroll of history.
On your people's far horizon like a star you shone so bright,
Till, by India's garish idols lured, to Brahmans you were
    turned;
You forsook the nest that nursed you, lifted by the love of flight,
But your youth were void of action, and to doubt the Faith they
    learned;
Education and refinement from all fetters set them free,
Brought them forth from their own Kaaba to embrace idolatry.

.   .   .   .

This new age is like a lightning, setting every stook ablaze;
Not a desert, not a garden is in safety from its blast;
The new fire elects for fuel peoples of the ancient days,
The communion of the Prophet joins the general holocaust;
Ah, but if the faith of Abraham again would brightly show,
Where the flames are at their fiercest, there a garden fair would
    grow!
Let the gardener not be downcast to descry the garden's plight;
Soon the starlight of the blossoms shall the naked boughs adorn,
And the choking weeds and brambles will have vanished out of
    sight,
And where martyrs shed their life-blood crimson roses will be
    born.
Look upon the deep vermillion flooding all the eastern sky—
It is your horizon, glowing to behold your sun arise.
There are nations in Life's garden that have gathered in their
    fruit,
Others shared not in the harvest, and are swept by autumn's
    gales;
Multitudes of trees there stand, some green, some withered to
    the root,
Myriads as yet lie hidden in the womb that never fails;
After centuries of tending soars Islam, a mighty tree,
Fruitful yet, a splendid symbol of immense vitality.

Now the onslaught of the Bulgars[17] sounds the trumpet of
    alarm,
Screaming to the heedless sleepers news of an awakening;
Thou supposest it the tiding of fresh grief and mortal harm,
Yet it can thy self-denial and thy pride to testing bring.
Wherefore fearest thou the neighing of the warsteeds of the foe?
Never shall Truth's light be doused, for all God's enemies may
    blow.
The reality thou art is hidden from the peoples' eyes;
The bright cavalcade of Being has most urgent need of thee;
It requires thy burning breath, Time's sinews to revitalise,
And thy kingdom is the star that rules the Future's destiny.
Where is now the time for leisure? Mighty labours yet await,
Ere the light of the One Godhead all the world irradiate.
Thou art like the scent imprisoned in a bud; thyself release!
Load thy pack upon thy shoulder, fan the meadow with thy
    breeze.
To a mighty desert let thy insubstantial mote increase.
From a murmuring wave become the roaring tempest of the
    seas.
With the power of love triumphant lift the lowly from their
    shame;
Light the world, too long in darkness, with Muhammad's
    radiant name.
Were it not for this fair blossom, songless were the nightingale,
The sweet rosebud in Time's garden would no more smile
    tenderly;
Without him to play the Saki,[18] wine and vessel both would fail,
Faith in God the One would perish, and yourselves would cease
    to be.
By this name the great pavilion of the skies is held in place,
To this name the pulse of Being quivers yet through boundless
    Space.

17. This refers to defeats suffered by Ottoman Turks in the First Balkan
War in 1912.
18. See note 8 above.

The Plight of Islâm: Prose

The impact of Western ideas and ideals, evident in the writing of
Iqbâl, is far more apparent in the autobiography of Tâhâ Hussein
(1889-   ). Hussein was born in a poverty-stricken village of upper Egypt and became blind in childhood. Nevertheless he attended the famous University of Al-Azhar in Cairo and went on
from there to the Sorbonne in Paris. He served as Minister of Education in Egypt, 1950-1952.

The first passage, from Hussein's autobiography (1920), recalls
the religious practices of his childhood. As an educated and sophisticated man, he found them superstitious and even corrupt. The
second passage, from a critique of education written in 1938, shows
how he hoped to correct his nation's past errors by emphasizing
Egypt's historical connections with Europe and by playing down
the ties with Islâm. In this way even radical westernization could
be portrayed as no more than a belated return to Egypt's real tradition. The shallowness of such an argument reflects the acuteness
of the dilemma in which a westernized Muslim like Hussein found
himself.

HUSSEIN: FROM THE STREAM OF DAYS

Sheikhs[1] of the Sufis[2]—What might they be? They were many
in number and scattered throughout the regions of the land. The
town was scarcely ever free from them. Their sects were different and they split up the people between them into schisms and
divided their affections to a very great degree. There was acute

From *An Egyptian Childhood; The Autobiography of Tâhâ Hussein,* trans.
by E. P. Patton, London: George Routledge and Sons, Ltd., 1932, pp. 95-102,
105.

1. Leaders.
2. Mystics.

rivalry in the province between two families of the Sufis; one held sway in the upper part of the province and other in the lower part.

However, since the people of the province move about and think nothing of migrating from village to village or from town to town within the province, it happened that the followers of one family would settle in a district where the other family held sway.

Now the leaders of the two families used to move about the province visiting their followers and adherents. And Ye Gods! what animosities were aroused when the chief of the upper region came down to the lower or the chief of the lower region visited the upper.

The lad's[3] father was a follower of the chief of the upper region and had taken the oath of allegiance to him, as his father had done before him. The lad's mother was also a follower of the chief of the upper region; in fact her father had been one of his assistants and intimate disciples. The chief of the upper region had died and had been succeeded by his son, the pilgrim. . . . This man was more active than his father and had a greater capacity for trickery, rapacity and arousing animosities. Moreover he was nearer to worldly things than his father and farther removed from the things of religion.

The lad's father had gone down to the lower part of the province and had settled there, and it was the custom of the chief of the upper part to visit him once every year. When he came he did not come alone or with a few people but with a mighty army, the number of which, if it did not reach a hundred, fell not far short of it. He did not take the train or any Nile boats, but instead he proceeded on his way, surrounded by his companions mounted on horses, mules and asses. As they passed through villages and small towns they alighted and mounted in strength and magnificence, victorious in a place where they alone held sway, and united in a place where their opponents were at all powerful.

Thus they came when they visited the lad's family, and when

3. I.e., Tâhâ Hussein, the subject of the autobiography.

they arrived the street was filled with them and their horses, mules and asses.

They occupied it from the canal to its southern extremity. Ere long a lamb was killed and tables laid out in the street, and soon they fell upon their food with a gluttony that was almost unbelievable.

Meanwhile the sheikh was sitting in the guest-room surrounded by his chosen friends and devotees, and the owner of the house and his household were in front of him carrying out his behests. When they had finished their lunch they went away and left him to sleep where he was. Later he got up and wished to perform the ceremonial ablutions (before prayer). Then see how the people vie with one another and quarrel as to who shall pour the water on him! And when that is done see how they race and quarrel to get a drink of the water of his ablutions! But the sheikh was too preoccupied to heed them. He prayed and made supplications at great length.

When at last he had finished all this he gave an audience to the people and they flocked to him, some kissing his hand and going away meekly, some holding conversation with him for a moment or so, and others asking him about some affair, and the sheikh would answer them with strange, vague expressions that they could interpret pretty much as they liked.

The lad was brought to him and he touched his head, quoting a verse from the Quran: "And he taught you what you knew not, and the grace of God was mighty upon you." From that day the lad's father was convinced that his son was destined to become great.

After the sunset prayer the tables were laid again and they ate. Then followed the evening prayer and then the assembly was held. The holding of the assembly is an expression for people assembled at a dervish circle for Zikr.[4] They perform the Zikr sitting in silence. Then they began to move their heads and raise their voices a little. Then a shudder runs through their bodies and lo! they are all standing, having leapt up into the air

---

4. "Dervish" means "sûfî," often a wandering mendicant. "Zikr" means "mentioning," "remembrance"; it is a Sûfî observance in which the name of God is "mentioned" repeatedly, having a hypnotic effect on participants.

like jacks-in-the-boxes. The sheikhs move about the circle, re-
citing the poetry of Ibn Farid and similar poems.[5]

Now this sheikh was particularly fond of a well-known ode
in which there is mention of the Prophet's Night Journey and
Ascent. It begins as follows:

"From Mecca and the Most Glorious House
To Jerusalem travelled by night Ahmad."[6]

The sheikhs used to chant this continually and the performers
of the Zikr used to move their bodies in time to this chant, bend-
ing and straightening themselves as though these sheikhs were
making them dance.

Whatever the lad forgets he will never forget the night on
which one of the reciters made a mistake and interpolated a
phrase in the place of a phrase of the ode. Forthwith the sheikh
got excited and boiled and foamed and frothed, crying at the
top of his voice, "You sons of bitches, may God curse your fathers, and your fathers' fathers, and your fathers' fathers' fathers as far as Adam! Do you want to bring destruction on this
man's house?"

And whatever the lad forgets he will never forget the effect of
this outburst of wrath upon the hearts of the performers of the
Zikr and the other people present. It was just as though the people were convinced that the mistake in this ode was a source of
bad omen without parallel.

The lad's father at first showed agitation and consternation,
but later appeared more confident and tranquil. When on the
morrow, after the sheikh had taken his departure, the family
talked about him and what had taken place between him and
the performers and reciters of the Zikr, the owner of the house
laughed in a way such as left no doubt in the lad's mind afterwards that the faith of his father in this sheikh was not free

5. Ibn Farid. 'Umar Ibn al-Farîd was the poet of Arabic mysticism. His
dîwân (collection of poetry) includes a Hymn of Divine Love, called Nazm
al-Sulûk or Poem on mystics' progress, also a Hymn of Wine, called the
Khamriyyah. (Tr.)
6. The Night Journey: an early vision Muhammad had (apparently in a
dream) which foretold the victory of Islâm.

from doubt and contempt. . . . Yes, doubt and contempt! Certainly the greediness and covetousness of the sheikh were too obvious for anybody with the slightest degree of discrimination or reflection to be taken in.

The person who loathed the sheikh most and was most indignant about him was the lad's mother. She hated his visit and found his presence unbearable. She performed what she performed, and prepared what she prepared with hatred and indignation, so much so that she managed to bridle her tongue only with the greatest difficulty. The reason was that the visit of the sheikh was a heavy burden on this family, which, although in comfortable circumstances, was on the whole poor.

The visit of the sheikh consumed a great deal of wheat, cooking fat, honey, and things like that. Moreover it put the owner of the house to the trouble of borrowing in order to buy what was necessary in the way of lambs and goats. For the sheikh never descended upon this family without staying until the following day; and when he took his departure he also took with him anything that took his fancy and pleased him. At one time he would take a carpet, at another a Kashmir shawl; and so on.

Yet the visit of him and his companions was something which the family heartily desired because it enabled them to boast, hold up their heads and outdo their neighbours. But still they hated it because it cost them what it did in the way of money and trouble.

In fact it was an ineluctable evil, established by custom and meeting the desire of the people.

Now the connection of the family with one of the Sufi sects was strong and lasting. It left among them many lasting traces in the way of information, stories and talk about miracles and supernatural events.

Both parents of the lad took great delight in relating all this information and talk to their children. . . .

. . . .

In this fashion the lad learnt all kinds of information about wonders and miracles, as well as Sufi mysteries.

And so it was that, whenever he wished to talk about anything like that to his companions and fellows at the school, they would

relate similar tales to him, which they attributed to the chief
of the lower region and in which they believed implicitly.

The country people, including their old men, youths, lads and
women, have a particular mentality in which is simplicity, mysticism and ignorance. And those who have had the greatest
share in producing this mentality are the Sufis.

HUSSEIN: FROM THE FUTURE OF CULTURE IN EGYPT

The subject to be treated in this discourse is the future of culture in Egypt, now that our country has regained her freedom
through the revival of the constitution and her honor through
the realization of independence. We are living in an age characterized by the fact that freedom and independence do not constitute ends in themselves, but are merely means of attaining
exalted, enduring, and generally practical goals.

Many peoples in various parts of the world have found their
freedom and independence to be meaningless and unproductive.
Indeed, these qualities did not prevent them from being attacked
by other peoples who also enjoyed them without regarding them
as ultimates. They had a civilization built on the basis of culture
and science together with the power and wealth engendered
thereby. Had not Egypt neglected culture and science, willingly
or unwillingly, she would not have lost her freedom and independence and would have been spared the struggle to regain
them.

There is no use in regretting what is past, for we cannot do
anything about it. Rather, we will sharpen our determination
and strengthen our hopes for the future by reflecting on the triumph that climaxed the long and arduous struggle for independence, acknowledged by the civilized world in admitting us
along with the other free peoples into the League of Nations.
Exult and hope we may, but not to the exclusion of action. We

From *The Future of Culture in Egypt*, by Tâhâ Hussein, trans. by Sidney
Glazer, Washington, D. C.: American Council of Learned Societies, 1954, pp.
1-5, 7-9, 15-17, 20, 25. Reprinted by permission.

must not stand before freedom and independence in contented admiration. Like all advanced nations, Egypt must regard them as a means of attaining perfection.

I know of nothing that causes me more worry than this newly won independence and freedom of ours. I fear that they may beguile us into thinking that we have come to the end of the road when in fact we have just reached the beginning. I am worried because we are now burdened with truly immense responsibilities toward ourselves and the civilized world which we may not fully appreciate. We may fail to make the progress we should, either through sheer neglect or insufficient determination. Such failure will be counted against us by Europeans in general and by our friends the English in particular, who will magnify our every shortcoming, however trivial, and say: they demanded their independence and struggled for it, but when they finally obtained it, they did not taste or enjoy it—they did not know how to use it!

Like every patriotic educated Egyptian who is zealous for his country's good reputation, I want our new life to harmonize with our ancient glory and our new energy to justify both the opinion we entertained of ourselves while we were seeking independence and the opinion held by civilized nations when they recognized our independence and cordially welcomed us to Geneva.

I do not want us to feel inferior to the Europeans because of our cultural shortcomings. This would cause us to despise ourselves and admit that they are not treating us unjustly when they are being arrogant. It is obnoxious for a man who is sensitive to dignity and honor to be compelled to acknowledge that he is not yet deserving of them. Let us keep this disgrace from ourselves and the nation. The way to do it is to take hold of our affairs with determination and vigor from today on, discard useless words for meaningful action, and establish our new life on a sound, constructive basis.

I do not like illusions. I am persuaded that it is only God who can create something from nothing. I therefore believe that the new Egypt will not come into being except from the ancient, eternal Egypt. I believe further that the new Egypt will have to be built on the great old one, and that the future of culture in Egypt will be an extension, a superior version, of the humble, exhausted, and feeble present. For this reason we should think of the future of culture in Egypt in the light of its remote past and near present. We do not wish, nor are we able, to break the link between ourselves and our forefathers. To the degree that we establish our future life upon our past and present we shall avoid most of the dangers caused by excesses and miscalculations deriving from illusions and dreams.

At the outset we must answer this fundamental question: Is Egypt of the East or of the West? Naturally, I mean East or West in the cultural, not the geographical sense. It seems to me that there are two distinctly different and bitterly antagonistic cultures on the earth. Both have existed since time immemorial, the one in Europe, the other in the Far East.

We may paraphrase the question as follows: Is the Egyptian mind Eastern or Western in its imagination, perception, comprehension, and judgment? More succinctly put—which is easier for the Egyptian mind: to understand a Chinese or Japanese, or to understand an Englishman or a Frenchman? This is the question that we must answer before we begin to think of the foundations on which we shall have to base our culture and education. It seems to me that the simplest way to do this is by tracing the complicated development of the Egyptian mind from earliest times to the present.

The first thing to note is that, so far as is known, we had no regular, sustained contacts with the Far East that could have affected our thinking and political or economic institutions. The available archaeological remains and documents reveal little more than that Egyptians at the end of the Pharaonic period evinced some desire to explore the Red Sea coasts, which they left only with great caution, chiefly for the sake of goods from India and South Arabia. Their attempts were tentative, unorganized, and ephemeral.

The contacts between ancient Egypt and the lands of the East scarcely went beyond Palestine, Syria, and Mesopotamia, that is, the East that falls in the Mediterranean basin, but there is no doubt that they were strong and continuous and that they exerted an influence on the intellectual, political, and economic life of all the countries involved. Our mythology relates that Egyptian gods crossed the Egyptian frontiers in order to civilize the people in these regions. Historians tell us that the kings of Egypt at times extended their sway over them. Ancient Egypt was a major power politically and economically not only in comparison with her neighbors, but with the countries that cradled the European civilization with which we are examining our kinship.

It would be a waste of time and effort to set forth in detail the ties binding Egypt to the ancient Greco-Aegean civilization. School children know that Greek colonies were established in Egypt by the Pharaohs before the first millenium B.C. They also know that an Eastern nation, Persia, successfully invaded our country at the end of the sixth century B.C. But we resisted fiercely until the Alexandrian era, having recourse at one time to Greek volunteers, and at another time allying ourselves with the Greek cities.

The meaning of all this is very clear: the Egyptian mind had no serious contact with the Far Eastern mind; nor did it live harmoniously with the Persian mind. The Egyptian mind has had regular, peaceful, and mutually beneficial relations only with the Near East and Greece. In short, it has been influenced from earliest times by the Mediterranean Sea and the various peoples living around it.

. . . .

History shows that religious and linguistic unity do not necessarily go hand in hand with political unity, nor are they the props on which states rely. The Muslims realized this a long time ago. They established their states on the basis of practical interests, abandoning religion, language, and race as exclusively determining factors before the end of the second century A.H. [eighth century of the Christian Era] when the Umayyad dynasty in Andalusia was in conflict with the Abbassids in Iraq. In the fourth century A.H. [tenth century of the Christian Era] the Islamic world replaced the Islamic empire. Various national blocs and states emerged everywhere. They were built on eco-

nomic, geographical, and other interests and differed in strength
and stability.

Egypt was one of the earliest among the Islamic states to recover her ancient, unforgotten personality. History tells us that
she violently opposed personality. History tells us that she violently opposed the Persians and Macedonians, the latter being
eventually absorbed into the local population. Egypt yielded to
the Western and Eastern Roman rulers only under duress and
had to be kept under continuous martial law. History further
relates that she acquiesced most reluctantly even to Arab domination. The spirit of resistance and rebelliousness that followed
the conquest did not subside until she regained her independent
personality under Ibn Tûlûn[1] and the dynasties that followed
him.

. . . .

Islam arose and spread over the world. Egypt was receptive
and hastened at top speed to adopt it as her religion and to make
the Arabic of Islam her language. Did that obliterate her original mentality? Did that make her an Eastern nation in the present meaning of the term? Not at all! Europe did not become
Eastern nor did the nature of the European mind change because Christianity, which originated in the East, flooded Europe
and absorbed the other religions. If modern European philosophers and thinkers deem Christianity to be an element of the
European mind, they must explain what distinguishes Christianity from Islam; for both were born in the geographical East,
both issued from one noble source and were inspired by the one
God in whom Easterners and Westerners alike believe.

How is it possible for fair-minded persons to see no harm coming to the European mind from reading the Gospel, which trans-
ports this mind from the West to the East, and at the same time
to regard the Koran as purely Eastern, even though it has been
clearly and straightforwardly proclaimed that the Koran was
sent only to complete and confirm what is in the Gospel?

If it is true that Christianity did not transform the European

1. Independent governor of Egypt, reigned 868-883, after throwing off yoke
of Caliphate.

mind or eliminate either its inherited Hellenism or Mediterranean qualities, it must be equally true that Islam did not
change the Egyptian mind or the mind of the peoples who embraced it and who were influenced by the Mediterranean Sea.
Indeed, we may go much further and say quite confidently that
the spread of Islam into the Middle and Far East amplified the
power of the Greek mind and extended it into regions where it
had seldom reached before. The Europeans would certainly not
have disputed or denied the fact if Christianity had recorded
such an achievement.

Islam and Christianity came to resemble each other in another
way. Christianity influenced and was influenced by Greek philosophy before the rise of Islam. Philosophy became Christian
and Christianity became philosophical. The same thing happened when Islam came into contact with Greek philosophy.
Philosophy became Muslim and Islam became philosophical.
The history of the two faiths is one with respect to this phenomenon. Why does Christianity's association with philosophy make
it one of the props of the European mind, while Islam's association with this same philosophy fails to make it a prop of the
Muslim mind?

The essence and source of Islam are the essence and source of
Christianity. The connection of Islam with Greek philosophy is
identical to that of Christianity. Whence, then, comes the difference in the effect of these two faiths on the creation of the
mind that mankind inherited from the peoples of the Near East
and Greece?

When the barbarians attacked Greco-Roman Europe they
dealt a dangerous blow to its civilization, almost extinguishing
the torch of the Greek mind which had glowed there before the
collapse of the Roman Empire. While it was barely able to
flicker on in a few monasteries, Islam was translating, enlarging,
and propagating Greek philosophy, which was subsequently
transmitted to Europe. Here in Latin translation it led to an
intellectual revival that enabled the European mind to regain its
splendor in the twelfth century of the Christian Era. Why is
Europe's connection with Greek culture during the Renaissance
one of the props of the European mind, whereas her connection

with the same Greek culture through Islam is not so regarded? Can we seriously maintain the existence of important differences between the nations living on the eastern shore of the Roman Sea and the nations living on its western shore?

Several years ago I heard a lecture by the great Belgian historian Pirenne before a meeting of the Geographical Society of Egypt held under the auspices of the Faculty of Arts. His discussion of certain matters that were overlooked at the time left a deep impression upon me. He declared that the invasion of Europe by the barbarians would not have doomed her to intellectual retrogression during the Middle Ages had the sea lanes between East and West remained open. But the emergence of Islam and the ensuing rivalry with Christianity interrupted communications for a time, with the result that Europe was rendered economically prostrate first and then profoundlly ignorant. When the ties between East and West were restored, Europe cast off her shackles of poverty and darkness.

This means, if I understand Pirenne correctly, that the cornerstone of intellectual life in Europe rests on its connection with the East via the Mediterranean Sea. How can this sea create in the West an outstanding, superior mind and at the same time leave the East without any mind or with one that is weak and decadent?

No, there are no intellectual or cultural differences to be found among the peoples who grew up around the Mediterranean and were influenced by it. Purely political and economic circumstances made the inhabitants of one shore prevail against those of the other. The same factors led them to treat each other now with friendliness, now with enmity.

We Egyptians must not assume the existence of intellectual differences, weak or strong, between the Europeans and ourselves or infer that the East mentioned by Kipling in his famous verse "East is East and West is West, and never the twain shall meet" applies to us or our country. Ismâ'îl's statement that Egypt is a part of Europe should not be regarded as some kind of boast or exaggeration, since our country has always been a part of Europe as far as intellectual and cultural life is concerned, in all its forms and branches.

In order to become equal partners in civilization with the Europeans, we must literally and forthrightly do everything that they do; we must share with them the present civilization, with all its pleasant and unpleasant sides, and not content ourselves with words or mere gestures. Whoever advises any other course of action is either a deceiver or is himself deceived. Strangely enough we imitate the West in our everyday lives, yet hypocritically deny the fact in our words. If we really detest European life, what is to hinder us from rejecting it completely? And if we genuinely respect the Europeans, as we certainly seem to do by our wholesale adoption of their practices, why do we not reconcile our words with our actions? Hypocrisy ill becomes those who are proud and anxious to overcome their defects.

For our national defense we need a strong army, one equal in men and equipment to that of any potential aggressor. Our forces must be organized on the European pattern, particularly with respect to the training of soldiers, officers, and the various categories of specialists. I think all Egyptians would agree with this, although they might be chagrined to learn that certain practical considerations prevent the plans from being implemented with the desired speed.

"We have inherited from our ancestors a hit-and-run style of fighting and weapons such as swords, bows and arrows, and coats of armor. We have no need for a military organization such as the Europeans have or their instruments of destruction. Let us be satisfied with an army comparable in size and equipment to that commanded by Khalîd ibn al-Walîd or Baybars."[2] Needless to say, Egyptians would ridicule anyone who spoke this way. Probably the conservatives and antiquarians would turn upon him more violently than the rest. We want to be like the European nations in military power in order to repel the attack of any aggressor and to be able to say to our English friends: "Thank you, you may go; for we can now defend the Canal." Who wants the end must want the means; who wants power

2. Khalîd ibn al-Walîd was Muhammad's greatest general and leader of much of the conquest. Baybars was the Mamlûk ruler of Egypt who reigned 1260-1277.

must want the elements constituting it; who wants a strong European-type army must want European training.

We also need economic independence. No one doubts or disputes this. Indeed, we clamor for it and importune the government to do whatever it can as quickly as possible. We want this independence not for its own sake, but for the protection of our wealth and resources. I do not mean we should be independent of the Hejaz, Yemen, Syria, and Iraq, but independent of Europe and America. We must therefore use the same means that the Europeans and Americans use to defend their national economies. This would entail, among other things, the building of schools to train our youth for the purpose. Again, who wants the end must want the means. It is not enough, nor is it logical, for us to seek independence while we behave like slaves.

Further, we want scientific, artistic, and literary independence so that we may be equals, not slaves of the Europeans in these aspects of life too. Desiring this intellectual and concomitant psychological independence, we naturally must want the means, namely, studying, feeling, judging, working, and organizing our lives the way they do.

We want, finally, to be free in our country, free from both foreign pressure and domestic inequity and oppression. The former requires strength, the latter democracy. If we aim at these ends we must adopt the means to acquire them. These are the means by which the European and American countries acquired their independence and their democratic government. The genuineness of Egypt's perennial desire for independence is attested to by the fact that our national personality was never absorbed into any one of the numerous races that attacked us. On the contrary, we managed to keep this personality intact from earliest times. Now that we have succeeded in restoring the honor and self-respect that come with independence, it is our plain duty to protect what we have won.

We must rear a generation of Egyptian youth who will never know the humiliation and shame that was the lot of their fathers. This can be done only by building education on a solid foundation.

Some Egyptians object to Europeanization on the grounds that it threatens our national personality and glorious heritage. I who have long argued that we stoutly protect our independence naturally do not advocate rejection of the past or loss of identity in the Europeans, although occasional bewitched individuals and groups have done this very thing. The only time that we might have been absorbed by Europe was when we were extremely weak, ignorant, and possessed of the notion that the hat was superior to the turban and the fez because it always covered a more distinguished head! However, such fears are completely baseless now that we know our history and are aware of the essential similarities between ourselves and the Europeans.

Although great powers imposed their will on us for many centuries, they were unable to destroy our personality. In modern times Egypt stood up to the mightiest nation on earth, lacking every weapon except faith in itself and its cause. After emerging victorious from this struggle, does anyone imagine that it is likely to lose its identity to the English? Hardly! This could happen only if Egypt were unable or unwilling to fight Europe with its own weapons.

The controlling factors in Egypt's destiny are its geographical situation, religion, artistic heritage, unbroken history, and the Arabic language. To defend our country, with its geographical situation, against aggression necessitates adopting European weapons and technique. Our religion, I feel, will be best maintained by doing as our ancestors did and keeping it responsive to contemporary needs. Guarding and advancing our linguistic and artistic achievements have always been dear to my heart. We render sincere homage to the past only when we strive to make the present and future worthy of it.

I cannot be justly accused of advocating loss of Egyptian identity since I am merely asking that the preservatives of defense, religion, language, art, and history be strengthened by the adoption of Western techniques and ideas. These constitute as little danger to Egypt's personality as they do to Japan's, perhaps less so because her past cannot match ours.

It is an indisputable duty of the state to ensure that its boys and girls are provided with proper instruction in the national language. Language is both a vital component of the national personality and an instrument of communication among the people of a given country. Thus, the state is not unjust or tyrannical if it requires the foreign schools in Egypt to teach Arabic and checks to see that this is done satisfactorily. Similarly, Egyptian history and geography should be part of their basic curricula.

The question of religious education in the school is complex. It is, of course, our right as well as our duty to ascertain whether or not foreign institutions are subverting the parental religion of the students and treating them as subjects for propaganda and evangelization. Egyptians differ with regard to religion in the schools. Some want education to be completely secular, with religious instruction being left to the family. Others consider religion as much a part of the national personality as language or history and instruction in it equally necessary. This undoubtedly represents the majority view and must, therefore, be reflected in the curricula of all the schools.

I know that many foreign school administrations will experience considerable difficulty in accepting the logic of this kind of thinking. But we must follow through if we are genuinely desirous of attaining national unity. Foreigners who dislike the idea of teaching Islam in their schools, which are by nature Christian or secular, should realize that it is equally difficult for Egyptians to tolerate the mere existence of these schools on their soil, however necessary they may be.

My attitude toward the independent Egyptian schools is not wholly negative because any state that permits foreigners to found schools on its soil cannot prohibit its own citizens from doing the same. Moreover, I am eager to see the private enterprise of individuals and groups encouraged, not only in promoting education but in furthering all other types of civic endeavor. However, these schools too should be strictly supervised by the state in order to prevent the development of discordant elements at this crucial stage in our history.

Revival

Jamâl al-Dîn al-Afghânî (1839-1897) spent his life trying to stir the Muslim world to resist European encroachment. He was born in Persia, but went to India while still young. There he acquired an intense distaste for British imperialism and the conviction that only a concerted effort by all Muslims could hold the West at bay.

Afghânî began his political career in Afghânistân in 1866 while trying to stir up resistance to British infiltration. In 1868 he was expelled for political activities and went to Istanbul where he was again expelled on the same charges. He then turned up in Cairo, where he remained from 1871 to 1879, only to be expelled once again. After a visit to India and time spent in London (1882) and Paris (1884), where he edited an Arabic newspaper, Afghânî went to Istanbul. From 1891 until his death he lived there, having lost whatever political following he had ever enjoyed.

Afghânî wanted to combine Muslim truth with European science and skills in order to create a truly powerful Muslim state once more. The selection that follows was written 1880-1881, during his visit to India. It is a reply to a *Commentary on the Qur'ân*, published by Ahmad Khân, an Indian westernizer who had abandoned the Muslim faith.

AFGHÂNÎ: "COMMENTARY ON THE COMMENTATOR"

He who does not look
upon things with the eye
of insight is lost and
*to be blamed.**

From *An Islamic Response to Imperialism; Political and Religious Writings of Sayyid Jamâl ad-Dîn "al-Afghânî,"* ed. & trans. by Nikki R. Keddie. Originally published by the University of California Press, 1968, pp. 123-29. Reprinted by permission of the Regents of the University of California.

* In Arabic. (Tr.)

Man is man because of education. None of the peoples of mankind, not even the savage, is completely deprived of education. If one considers man at the time of his birth, one sees that his existence without education is impossible. Even if we assumed that his existence were possible without education, his life would in that state be more repulsive and vile than the life of animals. Education consists of a struggle with nature, and overcoming her, whether the education be in plants, animals, or men.

Education, if it is good, produces perfection from imperfection, and nobility from baseness. If it is not good it changes the basic state of nature and becomes the cause of decline and decadence. This appears clearly among agriculturalists, cattle raisers, teachers, civil rulers, and religious leaders. In general, good education in these three kingdoms [human, animal, and plant] is the cause of all perfections and virtues. Bad education is the source of all defects and evils.

When this is understood, one must realize that if a people receives a good education, all of its classes and ranks, in accord with the natural law of relationships, will flourish simultaneously and will progress. Each class and group among that people, according to its rank and degree, tries to acquire the perfections that are appropriate to it, and does obtain them. The classes of that people, according to their rank, will always be in a state of balance and equilibrium with each other. This means that just as great rulers will appear among such a people because of their good education, so there will also come into existence excellent philosophers, erudite scholars, skilled craftsmen, able agriculturalists, wealthy merchants, and other professions. If that people because of its good education reaches such a level that its rulers are distinguished beyond the rulers of other peoples, one can be certain that all its classes will be distinguished above the classes of other countries. This is because perfect progress in each class depends on the progress of the other classes. This is the general rule, the law of nature, and the divine practice.

When, however, corruption finds its way into that people's education, weakness will occur in all its classes in proportion to their rank and to the extent of the corruption. That is, if weakness appears in the ruling circles, this weakness will surely overtake the class of philosophers, scholars, craftsmen, agriculturalists, merchants, and the other professions. For their perfection is the effect of a good education. When weakness, disorder, and corruption are introduced into a good education, which is the causative factor, inevitably the same weakness, disorder, and corruption will enter into the effects of that education. When corruption enters a nation's education it sometimes happens that, because of the increase of corruption in education and the ruin of manners and customs, the various classes, which are the cause of stability, and especially the noble classes, are gradually destroyed. The individuals of that nation, after removing their former clothes and changing their name, become part of another nation and appear with new adornments. This happened to the Chaldeans, the Phoenicians, the Copts, and similar people.

Sometimes Eternal Grace aids that people, and some men of high intelligence and pure souls appear among them and bring about a new life. They remove that corruption which was the cause of decline and destruction, and rescue souls and minds from the terrible malady of bad education. And through their own basic luster and brightness they return the good education and give back life once more to their people. They restore to them greatness, honor, and the progress of classes.

This is why every people who enter into decline, and whose classes are overtaken by weakness, are always, because of their expectation of Eternal Grace, waiting to see if perhaps there is to be found among them a wise renewer, experienced in policy, who can enlighten their minds and purify their souls through his wise management and fine efforts, and do away with the corrupt education. By the policies of that sage they could return to their former condtion.

There is no doubt that in the present age, distress, misfortune, and weakness besiege all classes of Muslims from every side. Therefore every Muslim keeps his eyes and ears open in expectation—to the East, West, North, and South—to see from what corner of the earth the sage and renewer will appear and will reform the minds and souls of the Muslims, repel the unforeseen corruption, and again educate them with a virtuous education. Perhaps through that good education they may return to their former joyful condition.

Since I am certain that the Absolute Truth (*haqq-i mutlaq*) will not destroy this true religion and right *shari'a*, I more than others expect that the minds and souls of the Muslims will very soon be enlightened and rectified by the wisdom of a sage. For this reason I always want to keep abreast of the articles and treatises that are now appearing from the pens of Muslims, and be thoroughly acquainted with the views of their authors. I hope that in these readings I may discover the elevated ideas of a sage who could be the cause of good education, virtue, and prosperity for the Muslims. I would then hope, to the extent of my ability, to assist him in his elevated ideas and become a helper and associate in the reform of my people.

In the course of discussions and investigations about the ideas of the Muslims, I heard of one of them who, mature in years and rich in experience, took a trip to European countries. After much labor and effort he wrote a Commentary on the Koran in order to improve the Muslims. I said to myself, "Here is just what you wanted."

And as is customary with those who hear new things, I let my imagination wander, and formed various conceptions of that commentator and that commentary. I believed that this commentator, after all the commentaries written by Traditionists, jurists, orators, philosophers, Sufis, authors, grammarians, and heretics like Ibn Râwandî[1] and others, would have done justice to that subject, unveiled the truth, and achieved the precise goal. For he had followed the ideas of both Easterners and Westerners. I thought that this commentator would have explained in the introduction to his commentary, as wisdom requires, the truth and essence of religion for the improvement of his people. That he would have demonstrated the necessity of religion in the human world by rational proofs, and that he would have set up a general rule, satisfying the intellect, to distinguish between true and false religions. I imagined that this commentator had undoubtedly explained the influence of each of the prior, untrue religions on civilization and the social order and on men's souls and minds. I thought he would have explained in a philosophical way the reason for the divergence of religions on some matters,

1. Ibn Râwandî: ninth-century heretic who criticized prophecy in general and Muhammad's prophecy in particular.

along with their agreement on many precepts, and the reason for the special relation of each age to a particular religion and prophet.

Since he claims to have written this commentary for the improvement of the community, I was certain he had in the introduction of his book described and explained in a new manner, with the light of wisdom, those divine policies and Koranic ethics that were the cause of the superiority and expansion of the Arabs in every human excellence. I was sure he had included in his introduction those precepts that were the cause of the unity of the Arabs, the transformation of their ideas, the enlightenment of their minds, and the purification of their souls; and all that when they were in the extremity of discord, savagery, and hardship.[2]

When I read the commentary I saw that this commentator in no way raised a word about these matters or about divine policy. In no manner are Koranic ethics explained. He has not mentioned any of those great precepts that were the cause of the enlightenment of the minds and purification of the souls of the Arabs. He has left without commentary those verses that relate to divine policy, support the promulgation of virtuous ethics and good habits, rectify domestic and civil intercourse, and cause the enlightenment of minds. Only at the beginning of his commentary does he pronounce a few words on the meaning of "sura," "verse," and the separate letters at the beginning of the suras. After that all his effort is devoted to taking every verse in which there is mention of angels, or *jinns*,[3] or the faithful spirit [Gabriel], revelation, paradise, hell, or the miracles of the prophets, and, lifting these verses from their external meaning, interpreting them according to the specious allegorical interpretations of the heretics of past Muslim centuries.

The difference is that the heretics of past Muslim centuries were scholars, whereas this unfortunate commentator is very ignorant. Therefore he cannot grasp their words correctly. Taking the subject of man's *nature* as a subject of discourse, he pro-

2. Afghânî believed in the Muslim religion as a basis for political unity among Muslims of his day.

3. Spirits.

nounces some vague and meaningless words, without rational demonstrations or natural proofs. He apparently does not know that man is man through education, and all his virtues and habits are acquired. The man who is nearest to his nature is the one who is the farthest from civilization and from acquired virtues and habits. If men abandoned the legal and intellectual virtues they have acquired with the greatest difficulty and effort, and gave over control to the hands of nature, undoubtedly they would become lower than animals.

Even stranger is the fact that this commentator has lowered the divine, holy rank of prophecy and placed it on the level of the *reformer*.* He has considered the prophets to be men like Washington, Napoleon, Palmerston, Garibaldi, Mister Gladstone, and Monsieur Gambetta.

When I saw the commentary to be of this kind, amazement overtook me, and I began to ask myself what was the purpose of this commentator in writing such a commentary. If the goal of this commentator is, as he says, the improvement of his community, then why does he try to end the belief of Muslims in the Islamic religion, especially in these times when other religions have opened their mouths to swallow this religion?

Does he not understand that if the Muslims, in their current state of weakness and misery, did not believe in miracles and hell-fire, and considered the Prophet to be like Gladstone, they undoubtedly would soon abandon their own weak and conquered camp, and attach themselves to a powerful conqueror? For in that event there would no longer remain anything to prevent this, nor any fear or anxiety. And from another standpoint the prerequisites for changing religion now exist, since being like the conqueror, and having the same religion as he, is attractive to everyone.

After these ideas and reflections, it first occurred to me that this commentator certainly believes that the cause of the decline of the Muslims and of their distressed condition is their religion itself, and that if they abandoned their beliefs they would restore their former greatness and honor. Therefore, he is trying to re-

* In English. (Tr.)

move these beliefs, and because of his motivation he could be forgiven.

Having reflected further, however, I said to myself that the Jews, thanks to these same beliefs, rescued themselves from the humiliation of slavery to the pharoahs and rubbed in the dust the pride of the tyrants of Palestine. Has not the commentator heard of this.

And the Arabs, thanks to these same beliefs, came up from the desert lands of the Arabian peninsula, and became masters of the whole world in power, civilization, knowledge, manufacture, agriculture, and trade. The Europeans in their speeches referred aloud to those believing Arabs as their masters. Has not this fact reached the ears of this commentator? Of course it has.

After considering the great effects of these true beliefs and their followers, I looked at the followers of false beliefs. I saw that the Hindus at the same time that they made progress in the laws of civilization, and in science, knowledge, and the various crafts, believed in thousands of gods and idols. This commentator is not ignorant of this. The Egyptians at the times when they laid the foundations of civilization, science, and manufactures, and were the masters of the Greeks, believed in idols, cows, dogs, and cats. This commentator undoubtedly knows this. The Chaldeans, at the time that they founded observatories, manufactured astronomical instruments, built high castles, and composed books on agricultural science, were worshippers of the stars. This is not hidden from the commentator. The Phoenicians, in the age that they made manufacture and commerce on land and sea flourish, and colonized the lands of Britain, Spain, and Greece, presented their own children as sacrifices to idols. This is clear to the commentator.

The Greeks, in that century that they were rulers of the world, and at the time that great sages and revered philosophers appeared among them, believed in hundreds of gods and thousands of superstitions. This is known to the commentator. The Persians, at the time when they ruled from the regions of Kashgar to the frontiers of Istanbul, and were considered incomparable in civilization, had hundreds of absurdities engraved in their hearts. Of course the commentator remembers this. The modern

Christians, at the same time as they acknowledged the Trinity, the cross, resurrection, baptism, purgatory, confession, and transubstantiation, assured their domination; progressed in the spheres of science, knowledge, and industry; and reached the summit of civilization. Most of them still, with all their science and knowledge, follow the same beliefs. The commentator knows this well.

When I considered these matters I realized that the commentator never was of the opinion that faith in these true beliefs caused the decline of the Muslims. For religious beliefs, whether true or false, are in no way incompatible with civilization and worldly progress unless they forbid the acquisition of science, the earning of a livelihood, and progress in sound civilization. I do not believe that there is a religion in the world that forbids these things, as appears clearly from what has been said above. Rather I can say that the lack of faith results only in disorder and corruption in civil life, and in insecurity. Reflect—this is *Nihilism!**

If the lack of faith brought about the progress of peoples, then the Arabs of the Age of Ignorance would have had to have precedence in civilization. For they were mostly followers of the materialist path, and for this reason they used to say aloud: "Wombs push us forth, the earth swallows us up, and only time destroys us." They also always used to say: "Who can revive bones after they have decomposed?"[4] This despite the fact that they lived in the utmost ignorance, like wild animals.

After all these various thoughts and considerations, I understood well that this commentators is not a reformer, nor was his commentary written for the improvement and education of the Muslims. Rather this commentator and this commentary are for the Islamic community at the present time like those terrible and dangerous illnesses that strike man when he is weak and decrepit. The aim of his modifications has been demonstrated above.

The goal of this commentator from this effort to remove the beliefs of the Muslims is to serve others and to prepare the way for conversion to their religion.

* In English. (Tr.)
4. Qur'ân XXXVI:77. (Tr.)

These few lines have been written hastily. Later, by the power of God, I will write in detail about this commentary and the aims of the commentator.

Nationalism: The Case of Turkey

The Ottoman Empire lost most of its European provinces to insurgent Christian nations of the Balkans during the nineteenth and early twentieth century. In World War I the imperial government joined the Germans, and when defeat came in 1918 it was in no position to resist plans for partitioning the Asian provinces of the Ottoman state among the victors. The Arab provinces became "mandates" under French and British supervision; but within the heartland of Turkish Anatolia, projects for slicing off coastal portions of the peninsula for the benefit of Greeks and Armenians roused bitter resistance.

Mustapha Kemâl (1881-1938) was born in Salonika, and saw his native city taken over by the Greeks in 1912. He believed that a nation wins the right to live only by struggle, and in the crisis of 1918-1921, when the future of the Turkish nation seemed in jeopardy, he took command of a Turkish nationalist movement based at Ankara. War with the Greeks led to victory for Mustapha Kemâl's forces, and he was given the title ghâzî—linking his movement with the beginning of Ottoman greatness. To this was later added the honorific title Atatürk (Father of Turks).

Having won success on the battlefield, Mustapha Kemâl had next to reconstruct a government. In 1923 he invited the Grand National Assembly to declare a republic; in the next year the new government disestablished Islâm, abolished the office of Caliph/Sultan, and made the new Turkish republic into a thoroughly secular and strongly anti-Muslim state. In place of the age-old Muslim identity, Mustapha Kemâl proposed to instill a vivid sense of Turkishness among the people. Nationalism had to substitute for religion by becoming a religion, and the new secular state had to substitute nationalist schooling for the old Muslim education.

In 1927 Mustapha Kemâl delivered an account of his steward-

ship of the Turkish nation to the National Assembly in a speech
that lasted for an entire week. A short passage from this speech is
reproduced here.

ATATÜRK: FROM "SPEECH TO THE ASSEMBLY, OCTOBER, 1924"

. . . .

[THE JUSTIFICATION FOR MUSTAPHA KEMÂL'S ACTIONS]

Let us return to a closer examination of the facts, so that we
may rapidly review them as a whole.

Morally and materially, the enemy Powers were openly attacking the Ottoman Empire and the country itself. They were
determined to disintegrate and annihilate both. The Padishah-
Caliph[1] had one sole anxiety—namely, to save his own life and
to secure the tranquillity of himself and the Government. Without being aware of it, the nation had no longer any one to lead
it, but lived in darkness and uncertainty, waiting to see what
would happen. Those who began to understand clearly the ter-
rors and extent of the catastrophe were seeking some means
whereby to save the country, each guided by the circumstances
that surrounded him and the sentiments that inspired him. The
Army existed merely in name. The commanders and other officers were still suffering from the exhaustion resulting from the
war. Their hearts were bleeding on account of the threatened
dismemberment of their country. Standing on the brink of the
dark abyss which yawned before their eyes, they racked their
brains to discover a way out of the danger.

Here I must add and explain a very important point. The Nation and the Army had no suspicion at all of the Padishah-
Caliph's treachery. On the contrary, on account of the close
connection between religion and tradition handed down for centuries, they remained loyal to the throne and its occupant. Seek-

From *A Speech Delivered by Ghâzî Mustapha Kemâl. President of the
Turkish Republic, October 1927*, Leipzig: K. F. Koehler, 1929, pp. 15-17,
584-87, 590-93, 595-97, 721-24. Reprinted by permission of K. F. Koehler
Verlag, Stuttgart.

   1. Padishah: Persian title meaning "emperor."

ing for means of salvation under the influence of this tradition, the security of the Caliphate and the Sultanate concerned them far more than their own safety. That the country could possibly be saved without a Caliph and without a Padishah was an idea too impossible for them to comprehend. And woe to those who ventured to think otherwise! They would immediately have been looked down upon as men without faith and without patriotism and as such would have been scorned.

I must mention another point here. In seeking how to save the situation it was considered to be specially important to avoid irritating the Great Powers—England, France and Italy. The idea that it was impossible to fight even one of these Powers had taken root in the mind of nearly everybody. Consequently, to think of doing so and thus bring on another war after the Ottoman Empire, all-powerful Germany and Austria-Hungary together had been defeated and crushed would have been looked upon as sheer madness.

Not only the mass of the people thought in this strain, but those also who must be regarded as their chosen leaders shared the same opinion. Therefore, in seeking a way out of the difficulty, two questions had to be eliminated from discussion. First of all, no hostility was to be shown towards the Entente Powers; secondly, the most important thing of all was to remain, heart and soul, loyal to the Padishah-Caliph.

Now, Gentlemen, I will ask you what decision I ought to have arrived at in such circumstances to save the Empire?

As I have already explained, there were three propositions that had been put forward:

1. To demand protection from England;

2. To accept the United States of America as a mandatory Power.

The originators of these two proposals had as their aim the preservation of the Ottoman Empire in its complete integrity and preferred to place it as a whole under the protection of a single Power, rather than allow it to be divided among several States.

3. The third proposal was to deliver the country by allowing each district to act in its own way and according to its own capa-

bility. Thus, for instance, certain districts, in opposition to the theory of separation, would have to see that they remained an integral part of the Empire. Others holding a different opinion already appeared to regard the dismemberment of the Empire as an accomplished fact and sought only their own safety.

You will remember that I have already referred to these three points.

None of these three proposals could be accepted as the correct one, because the arguments and considerations on which they were based were groundless. In reality, the foundations of the Ottoman Empire were themselves shattered at that time. Its existence was threatened with extermination. All the Ottoman districts were practically dismembered. Only one important part of the country, affording protection to a mere handful of Turks, still remained, and it was now suggested also to divide this.

Such expressions as: the Ottoman Empire, Independence, Padishah-Caliph, Government—all of them were mere meaningless words.

Therefore, whose existence was it essential to save? and with whose help? and how? But how could these questions be solved at such a time as this?

In these circumstances, one resolution alone was possible, namely, to create a New Turkish State, the sovereignty and independence of which would be unreservedly recognised by the whole world.

This was the resolution we adopted before we left Constantinople and which we began to put into execution immediately we set foot on Anatolian soil at Samsoon.[2]

.   .   .   .

[DEBATES ON THE CALIPHATE]

If you wish it, I will now give you a short account of the debates that took place during a secret sitting when the Caliph was elected on the 18th November.[3]

2. Samsoon: city on the Black Sea coast where Mustapha Kemâl landed in 1919 to begin his campaign for Turkish independence.

3. The Republic had been declared October 29 of the same year, 1923, when Sultân Mehmed VI, who remained in Istanbul under Allied occupation, was replaced by his son Abdulmejîd.

There were many deputies in the Assembly who regarded the question as being very serious and important. The Hodjas,[4] in particular, were very attentive and alert, as they had at last found a subject that appealed to them.

The Caliph is a fugitive . . . he had to be deposed, another had to be elected. The new Caliph had not to be left in Constantinople, he had to be transferred to Angora,[5] so that he should be brought as near as possible to the Head of the nation and the State.

In short, following the flight of the Caliph, the whole of Turkey, the whole of Islam was overthrown, or was at least threatened to become so . . . they had to be on the watch. Such were the anxieties and fears that were uttered.

Some of the speakers on their part spoke of the necessity to define the character and powers of the Caliph who was to be elected.[6]

I also took part in the debates. Most of my statements were replies to the observations that had been put forward. They can substantially be summarised in the following sentences: "Surely it is possible to analyse and discuss the question for a long time. But the more we listen to one another and the more we loose ourselves in these discussions and analyses, the more difficulties and delays we shall encounter. I only want to draw your attention to this fact: This Assembly is the Assembly of the Turkish people. Your powers and authority can only extend to the Turkish people and our Turkish country and can only be effective in so far as the question concerns their lives and their destiny.

"Our Assembly, Gentlemen, cannot attribute to themselves powers that comprise the whole of the Islamic world.

"The Turkish nation and our Assembly, consisting of their representatives, cannot confide their existence to the hands of a person who bears, or will bear, the title of Caliph. No, they cannot do so.

4. Hodja: religious functionary, often a member of a dervish community.

5. Angora (Ankara): the inland Anatolian town chosen as capital of the new Turkish Republic.

6. Remember in what follows that the Caliph had been considered head of all Muslims. Mustapha Kamâl's attempt to create a nation-state obviously required an adjustment of that notion.

"We are told that through this question confusion will arise in the Mohamedan world. Whoever stated that has lied or is lying."

To one interrupter I said quite openly:

"You, you may well lie. You have learned to do so very well."

After having explained that there was no cause to make such a fuss about this affair I declared:

"Our greatest strength, our prestige in the eyes of the world depend on the new form and the new character of our régime. The Caliphate might be in a state of slavery. The persons who bear the title of Caliph might flee into foreign countries. Our enemies and the Caliph can join and together attempt any enterprise, but they can never shake the administrative system of New Turkey, nor her policy, nor her power.

"I state once more and in a formal manner that the Turkish nation is in full possession of their sovereignty without reservation and without restriction. This sovereignty does not suffer any partition in whatever form or colour it might be. Nobody, whether he is called Caliph or by any other title, can participate in the direction of the destiny of this nation. This nation cannot possibly allow this. There is no deputy of the people who could make such a proposition.

"We must, therefore, proclaim the deposition of the fugitive Caliph, elect a new one and proceed in everything that regards this question in conformity with the points of view we have expounded. It is quite impossible to act otherwise."

In spite of the somewhat tempestuous debates that took place we arrived at an agreement with the majority of votes in the Assembly as to the course to be followed.

.   .   .   .

[THE DRAWBACKS OF THE OLD ORDER]

The results of the Lausanne Conference,[7] which lasted for eight months in two sessions, are known to the world at large.

For some time I followed the negotiations of the Lausanne Conference from Angora.

7. Opened November 21, 1922.

The debates were heated and animated. No positive results regarding the recognition of Turkish rights were noticeable. I found this quite natural, because the questions brought forward on the agenda did not exclusively concern the new régime, which was only three or four years old.

Centuries-old accounts were regulated. It was surely neither a simple nor convenient task to find our way through such a mass of old, confused and rubbishy accounts.

We know that the Ottoman Empire, whose succession the new Turkish State had accepted, was fettered by the Capitulations which existed in the name of ancient Treaties. The Christian elements enjoyed numerous privileges and favours. The Ottoman Government could not exercise the administration of justice in regard to foreigners dwelling in the Ottoman Empire. It was forbidden to impose taxes on foreigners as were raised from our own citizens. The Government was also prevented from taking steps against those elements in the interior that undermined the foundations of the State.

The Ottoman Government was also prohibited from securing the means of carrying on their existence in a manner worthy of human beings by the Turkish people, the original element from which they emanated. They could not restore the country, could not build railways and were not even free to establish schools. If we tried to do so the foreigners immediately interfered. In order to secure a luxurious existence for themselves, the Ottoman sovereigns and their Courts had not only placed all the revenues of the country and the nation at their disposal, but they had in addition floated numerous loans, thereby sacrificing not only all the resources of the nation, but even the honour and dignity of the State. And this was done to such an extent that the Empire had become incapable of paying the interest on these loans and was regarded in the eyes of the world as being in a state of bankruptcy.

The Ottoman Empire, whose heirs we were, had no value, no merit, no authority in the eyes of the world. It was regarded as being beyond the pale of international right and was, as it were, under the tutelage and protection of somebody else.

We were not guilty of the neglect and errors of the past and, in reality, it was not ourselves from whom they ought to have demanded the settlement of accounts that had accumulated during past centuries. It was, however, our duty to bear the responsibility for them before the world. In order to procure true independence and sovereignty for the nation we had still to submit to these difficulties and sacrifices. As for myself, I was certain that we would achieve a positive result in any event. I had no doubt that the whole world would finally recognize the principles which the Turkish nation had to adopt and realise at all cost for their existence, their independence and their sovereignty; because the foundations had actually and in reality already been laid by strength and merit. What we demanded from the Conference was nothing more than the confirmation in a proper manner of what we had already gained. We only claimed our well-known and natural rights. In addition, we had the power to preserve and protect these rights. Our strength was sufficient for this purpose. Our greatest strength and our surest point of support was the fact that we had realised our national sovereignty, had actually placed it in the hands of the nation and had proved by facts that we were capable of maintaining it. These were the considerations that allowed me calmly to follow the course of the negotiations at the Conference without attaching undue importance to the vexatious agitations through which they passed.

The monarchy having been abolished and the Caliphate denuded of its powers, it had become very important to get into close touch with the people and once more to study their psychology and spiritual tendencies.

.   .   .   .

MUSTAPHA KEMÂL'S ARGUMENTS AGAINST THE PARTY WANTING TO MAINTAIN THE CALIPHATE

I must call attention to the fact that Hodja Shukri Effendi,[8] as well as the politicians who pushed forward his person and signature, had intended to substitute the sovereign bearing the title of Sultan or Padishah by a monarch with the title of Caliph.

8. Hodja Shukri Effendi: a pious Muslim who opposed Mustapha Kemâl's religious policy.

The only difference was that, instead of speaking of a monarch of this or that country or nation, they now spoke of a monarch whose authority extended over a population of three hundred million souls belonging to manifold nations and dwelling in different continents of the world. Into the hands of this great monarch, whose authority was to extend over the whole of Islam, they placed as the only power that of the Turkish people, that is to say, only from 10 to 15 millions of these three hundred million subjects. The monarch designated under the title of Caliph was to guide the affairs of these Mohamedan peoples and to secure the execution of the religious prescriptions which would best correspond to their worldly interests. He was to defend the rights of all Mohamedans and concentrate all the affairs of the Mohamedan world in his hands with effective authority.

The sovereign entitled Caliph was to maintain justice among the three hundred million Mohamedans on the terrestrial globe, to safeguard the rights of these peoples, to prevent any event that could encroach upon order and security, and confront every attack which the Mohamedans would be called upon to encounter from the side of other nations. It was to be part of his attributes to preserve by all means the welfare and spiritual development of Islam.

The absurd ideas which ignorant people like Shukri Hodja and his companions were disseminating about the actual condition prevailing in the world under the power of "religious prescriptions" with the intention of abusing our nation, are not worthy of being repeated here. In the course of centuries there have been people and there are still people to-day in the interior as well as in foreign countries who profited by the ignorance and fanaticism of the nations and try to make use of religion as a tool to help them in their political plans and personal interests. The fact that there are such individuals unfortunately compels us again to go into this question.

So long as the sentiments and knowledge of mankind with regard to religious questions are not yet freed from myths and purified in the light of true science, we shall find historians everywhere who play a religious comedy. We must actually belong to those "beings who live wholly in God," like Shukri

Hodja, not to be enlightened about the absurdities of the illogical ideas and impracticable prescriptions which they sow broadcast in all directions.

If the Caliph and Caliphate, as they maintained, were to be invested with a dignity embracing the whole of Islam, ought they not to have realised in all justice that a crushing burden would be imposed on Turkey, on her existence; her entire resources and all her forces would be placed at the disposal of the Caliph?

According to their declarations, the Caliph-Monarch would have the right of jurisdiction over all Mohamedans and all Mohamedan countries, that is to say, over China, India, Afganisthan, Persia, Irak, Syria, Palestine, Hedjas, Yemen, Assyr, Egypt, Tripolis, Tunis, Algeria, Morocco, the Sudan. It is well known that this Utopia has never been realised. The pamphlet itself signed by Hodja Shukri emphasises that the Mohamedan communities have always separated from one another under the influence of aims that were diametrically opposite to one another; that the Omayades of Andalusia, the Alides of Morocco, the Fatimides of Egypt and the Abbassides of Bagdad have each created a Caliphate, that is to say, a monarchy of their own. In Andalusia there were even communities embracing a thousand souls, each of which was "a Commander of the Faithful and a Torch of Faith." Would it have been logical or reasonable to pretend to be ignorant of this historic truth and to designate under the title of Caliph a ruler destined to govern all the Mohamedan States and nations, some of which were independent, while most of them were under a foreign protectorate? Particularly the fact that a mere handful of men consisting of the population of Turkey, burdened with the anxiety of supporting such a sovereign, would it not have been the surest means for strangling this people? Those who say: "The attributes of the Caliph are not of a spiritual kind," and "the basis of the Caliphate is material strength, the temporal power of the Government," proved thereby that for them the Caliphate was the State. And thereby it could easily be perceived that they pursued the aim of putting at the head of the Turkish Government some personality bearing the title of Caliph.

The attempts of Hodja Shukri Effendi and his political colleagues to conceal their political designs and to represent them under the form of a religious question which concerned the entire Mohamedan world had the only result that this puppet representing the Caliphate was still more speedily swept off the stage.

I made statements everywhere, that were necessary to dispel the uncertainty and anxiety of the people concerning this question of the Caliphate. I formerly declared: "We cannot allow any person, whatever his title may be, to interfere in questions relating to the destiny, activity and independence of the new State which our nation has now erected. The nation itself watches over the preservation and independence of the State which they have created, and will continue to do so for all time." I gave the people to understand that neither Turkey nor the handful of men she possesses could be placed at the disposal of the Caliph so that he might fulfill the mission attributed to him, namely, to found a State comprising the whole of Islam. The Turkish nation is incapable of undertaking such an irrational mission.

For centuries our nation was guided under the influence of these erroneous ideas. But what has been the result of it? Everywhere they have lost millions of men. "Do you know," I asked, "how many sons of Anatolia have perished in the scorching deserts of the Yemen? Do you know the losses we have suffered in holding Syria and the Irak and Egypt and in maintaining our position in Africa? And do you see what has come out of it? Do you know?

"Those who favour the idea of placing the means at the disposal of the Caliph to brave the whole world and the power to administer the affairs of the whole of Islam must not appeal to the population of Anatolia alone but to the great Mohamedan agglomerations which are eight or ten times as rich in men.

"New Turkey, the people of New Turkey, have no reason to think of anything else but their own existence and their own welfare. She has nothing more to give away to others."

To enlighten the people on still another point, I employed these expressions: "Let us accept for a moment that Turkey would take this mission upon herself and would devote herself to the aim of uniting and leading the whole Islamic world and that she would succeed in achieving this aim. Very good, but sup-

pose these nations whom we want to subject and administer
would say to us: 'You have rendered great services and assistance to us for which we are thankful to you, but we want to remain independent. We do not suffer anybody else to interfere in
our independence and sovereignty. We are capable of leading
and administering ourselves.'

"In such a case will the efforts and sacrifices made by the people of Turkey result in anything more than earning thanks and
a benediction?

"It is evident they intended that the people of Turkey should
be sacrificed to a mere caprice, to a fancy, to a phantom. To this
effect the idea of attributing functions and authority to a Caliph
and a Caliphate can be comprehended."

I asked the people: "Will Persia or Afganistan, which are
Mohamedan States, recognise the authority of the Caliph in a
single matter? Can they do so? No, and this is quite justifiable,
because it would be in contradiction to the independence of the
State, to the sovereignty of the people."

I also warned the people by saying that "the error of looking
upon ourselves as masters of the world must cease."

.   .   .   .

During the time we had been engaged on the question of the
Caliphate and of religion we had become clear with regard to
the fact that one point of the Constitution Act offered a problem
to public opinion and especially to that of the intellectuals.

Those who after the proclamation of the Republic became
aware that this contentious point of the law was not only maintained but that a second point of a similar nature had been added,
did not conceal their surprise either then or later.

Le me explain these two points to you:

Article 7 of the Constitution Act of the 20th January, 1921,
and Article 26 of the Constitution Act of the 21st April, 1924,
refer to the authority of the Grand National Assembly. In the
beginning of the Article we find it laid down as the first duty of
the Assembly that "the prescriptions of the Sheri should be put
into force."[9]

9. Shari'a (Sheri): legal rules and regulations of Islâm (see selection from
Shâfi'î, Section II).

But now there are people who cannot understand the nature of these prescriptions nor what is meant by the "prescriptions of the Sheri."

The Authorities of the Grand National Assembly referred to and enumerated in the same Article, that is to say, relating to the publication, amendment and interpretation of the laws, their repeal and cancellation, etc., as clear and comprehensible in themselves that the existence of an independent formula, such as "the putting into force of the prescriptions of the Sheri," cannot and are not intended to express anything other than the "prescriptions of the law."

Any other interpretation would be incompatible with the conception of modern law; unless a totally different meaning were to be attached to the expression "prescriptions of the Sheri."

I was myself in the chair when the first Constitution Act was drafted. Many attempts were made to explain that the expression "prescriptions of the Sheri" had nothing whatever to do with the law which we were drafting. But it was impossible to convince those who, guided by a wrong conception, attached quite another interpretation to this expression.

The second point consists of the sentence at the beginning of Article 2 of the new Constitution Act: "The State religion of Turkey is the Mohamedan religion."

Long before this sentence was incorporated in the text of the Constitution Act, during the course of long meetings and consultations with journalists from Ismidt and Constantinople, one of my interviewers at Ismidt put the following question: "Will the new State have a religion?"

I must confess that it was most undesirable that I should have to answer this question, because, in the circumstances then prevailing, I did not wish to be compelled to give an answer which was evident—incidentally, a very short one.

If a State having amongst its subjects elements professing different religions and being compelled to act justly and impartially towards all of them and allowing justice to prevail in its tribunals equally towards foreigners as well as its own subjects, it is obliged to respect freedom of opinion and conscience. It is surely not justified in making restrictions in this natural author-

THE CRISIS OF MODERNIZATION

ity of the State by attributing other qualities to it which are
capable of having an ambiguous meaning.

When we say that "the official language of the State is Turkish," everybody understands what this means; everybody understands that it is natural that the Turkish language should be
used in official affairs. But will the sentence "The State religion
of Turkey is the Mohamedan religion" be accepted and understood in the same way? It must naturally be criticised and
explained.

I could not answer the question put to me by the journalist,
my interviewer, with: "The State cannot have a religion." On
the contrary, I answered: "It has one—the Mohamedan
religion."

I immediately felt the need of commenting on and qualifying
my answer by the following sentence: "The Mohamedan religion includes the freedom of religious opinion."

Thereby I wanted to express that the State is obliged to respect freedom of opinion and freedom of conscience.

Undoubtedly my interviewer did not find my reply reasonable and repeated his question in the following form: "Did you
mean to say that the State will identity itself with a particular
religion?"

"I do not know," I said, "whether this will be the case or not."
I wanted to end the debate, but this was not possible. "Then,"
they told me, "the State will prevent me from expressing an
opinion that corresponds to my views and thoughts on any question. And if the case should arise I shall be punished for having
done so."

"But will everybody discover a way to silence his conscience?"

At that time I was thinking of two things. The first was: Will
not every grown up person in the new Turkish State be free to
select his own religion?

Then I recalled Hodja Shukri's proposal which was: "Some
of my colleagues among the Ulema[10] as well as myself, consider
it to be our duty to publish our common thoughts, as well the
prescriptions of Islam, which are confirmed and set forth in the

10. 'Ulamâ (sing. 'âlim): learnèd men.

books of the Sheri . . . to enlighten the minds of the Mohamedans, which have unfortunately been led astray."

I also recalled the following sentence: "The Caliphate of
Islam has been entrusted by the Prophet to protect and perpet-
uate the religious prescriptions and to be the representative of
the Prophet in the exercise of the Sheriade."

But to quote the words of the Hodja would be equivalent to
an attempt to abolish the national sovereignty.

But, on the other hand, we had not to consider the bulk of the
knowledge of the Hodjas comprised in formulae which had
been dictated in the time of Caliph Yesid[11] and which had been
appropriated to a régime of absolutism.

Consequently, who would be deceived if the expressions
"State" and "Government" were enwrapped in the cloak of religion and the Sheriade? Although the meaning of these expressions, as well as of the authorities of the Assembly, are now
clear to everybody, what need is there for this deception?

This was the actual truth; but I did not wish to discuss this
subject any longer with the journalist on that day at Ismidt.

. . . .

Honourable Gentlemen, when, in consequence of serious necessity we became convinced for the first time that it would be
useful for the Government to take extraordinary measures, there
were people who disapproved of our action.

There were persons who disseminated and sought to gain
credence to the thought that we were making use of the law for
Restoration of Order and the Courts of Independence as tools of
dictatorship or despotism.

There is no doubt that time and events will show to those who
disseminated this opinion how mistaken they were, and put
them to shame.

We never used the exceptional measures, which all the same
were legal, to set ourselves in any way above the law.

On the contrary, we applied them to restore peace and quiet-
ness in the country. We made use of them to insure the existence and independence of the country. We made use of them

11. Caliph Yazîd I, 680-683, is probably referred to. (Tr.)

with the object of contributing to the social development of the nation.

Gentlemen, as soon as the necessity for the application of the exceptional measures to which we had turned no longer existed, we did not hesitate to renounce them. Thus, for instance, the Courts of Independence ceased their activity at the given moment, just as the law regarding the Restoration of Order was re-submitted to the Assembly for examination as soon as its legislative term had elapsed. If the Assembly considered it necessary to prolong its application for some time this certainly happened because it saw therein the higher interest of the nation and of the Republic.

Can anyone be of the opinion that this decision of the High Assembly was intended to hand over to us the means for the carrying on of a dictatorship?

Gentlemen, it was necessary to abolish the fez, which sat on our heads as a sign of ignorance, of fanaticism, of hatred to progress and civilisation, and to adopt in its place the hat, the customary headdress of the whole civilised world, thus showing, among other things, that no difference existed in the manner of thought between the Turkish nation and the whole family of civilised mankind. We did that while the law for the Restoration of Order was still in force. If it had not been in force we should have done so all the same; but one can say with complete truth that the existence of this law made the thing much easier for us. As a matter of fact the application of the law for the Restoration of Order prevented the morale of the nation being poisoned to a great extent by reactionaries.

It is true that a deputy of Brusa,[12] who, during his whole time of being deputy, had not once appeared on the speaker's rostrum, nor ever spoken a word in the Chamber in defence of the interests of the nation and the Republic, the deputy of Brusa, I say, Nureddin Pasha, introduced a lengthy motion against wearing hats and mounted the rostrum to defend it.

He asserted that hat-wearing was a "contradiction of the fundamental rights of the national sovereignty, and of the principle

12. Brusa: northwestern Anatolian town near the Sea of Marmora.

of the integrity of personal freedom," and attempted "on no account to let this measure be forced upon the population." But the outbreak of fanaticism and reaction which Nureddin Pasha succeeded, from the tribune, in calling forth, merely led to the sentencing of a few reactionaries by the Courts of Independence.

Gentlemen, while the law regarding the Restoration of Order was in force there took place also the closing of the Tekkes,[13] of the convents, and of the mausoleums, as well as the abolition of all sects and all kinds of titles such as Sheikh, Dervish, "Junger," Tschelebi, Occultist, Magician, Mausoleum Guard, etc.

One will be able to imagine how necessary the carrying through of these measures was, in order to prove that our nation as a whole was no primitive nation, filled with superstitions and prejudices.

Could a civilised nation tolerate a mass of people who let themselves be led by the nose by a herd of Sheikhs, Dedes, Seids, Tschelebis, Babas and Emirs; who entrusted their destiny and their lives to chiromancers, magicians, dice-throwers and amulet sellers? Ought one to conserve in the Turkish State, in the Turkish Republic, elements and institutions such as those which had for centuries given the nation the appearance of being other than it really was? Would one not therewith have committed the greatest, most irreparable error to the cause of progress and reawakening?

If we made use of the law for the Restoration of Order in this manner, it was in order to avoid such a historic error; to show the nation's brow pure and luminous, as it is; to prove that our people think neither in a fanatical nor a reactionary manner.

Gentlemen, at the same time the new laws were worked out and decreed which promise the most fruitful results for the nation on the social and economic plane, and in general in all the forms of the expression of human activity . . . the Citizens' Law-book, which ensures the liberty of women and stabilises the existence of the family.

Accordingly we made use of all circumstances only from one point of view, which consisted therein: to raise the nation on to

13. Houses for dervish communities, a little like Christian monasteries.

that step on which it is justified in standing in the civilised world, to stabilise the Turkish Republic more and more on stead-fast foundations . . . and in addition to destroy the spirit of despotism for ever.

. . . .

These detailed descriptions, which have occupied you for so many days, are, after all, merely a report of a period of time, which will henceforth belong to the past.

I shall consider myself very happy if I have succeeded in the course of this report in expressing some truths which are calcu-lated to rivet the interest and attention of my nation and of fu-ture generations.

Gentlemen, I have taken trouble to show, in these accounts, how a great people, whose national course was considered as ended, reconquered its independence; how it created a national and modern State founded on the latest results of science.

The result we have attained to day is the fruit of teachings which arose from centuries of suffering, and the price of streams of blood which have drenched every foot of the ground of our beloved Fatherland.

This holy treasure I lay in the hands of the youth of Turkey.

Turkish Youth! your primary duty is ever to preserve and defend the National independence, the Turkish Republic.

That is the only basis of your existence and your future. This basis contains your most precious treasure. In the future, too, there will be ill-will, both in the country itself and abroad, which will try to tear this treasure from you. If one day you are compelled to defend your independence and the Republic, then, in order to fulfil your duty, you will have to look beyond the possibilities and conditions in which you might find yourself. It may be that these conditions and possibilities are altogether un-favourable. It is possible that the enemies who desire to destroy your independence and your Republic represent the strongest force that the earth has ever seen; that they have, through craft and force, taken possession of all the fortresses and arsenals of the Fatherland; that all its armies are scattered and the country actually and completely occupied.

Assuming, in order to look still darker possibilities in the face, that those who hold the power of Government within the country have fallen into error, that they are fools or traitors, yes, even that these leading persons identify their personal interests with the enemy's political goals, it might happen that the nation came into complete privation, into the most extreme distress; that it found itself in a condition of ruin and complete exhaustion.

Even under those circumstances, O Turkish child of future generations! it is your duty to save the independence, the Turkish Republic.

The strength that you will need for this is mighty in the noble blood which flows in your veins.

Nationalism: The Case of Pakistan

Muslims reached India as conquerors as early as the eighth century, but geographically deep penetration of the sub-continent began only after 1000. By the beginning of the eighteenth century the Mughals had pushed Islâmic dominion to the southernmost part of the land; but almost at once Hindu revolt on the one hand, and insubordination of provincial governors on the other, broke the Mughal empire into quarreling parts. This allowed the British East India Company to bring India under its jurisdiction by 1818; but in 1947 British India in turn gave way to two successor states: the Republic of India, in which most of the population is Hindu, and Pakistan, in which most people are Muslim.

For several centuries, from about 1000 to 1750, Indian Muslims remained a politically dominant minority. They found it harder to adjust to British rule than did the Hindus, for whom the coming of the British amounted only to a change of masters, not a change of status; thus the Hindus were able to play a more prominent role in initial responses to modern civilization. Only in the 1920's did a few Muslim leaders wake up to the threat of political mobilization of India's Hindu masses by Mohandas Gandhi and others; which

jeopardized the traditional status of Muslims among the populations of India.

The man who most vigorously expressed this consciousness was
Muhammad 'Alî Jinnah (1876-1948). Jinnah, son of a prosperous
merchant in Bombay, studied law in England (1892-1896) and on
his return built up a successful practice. He entered politics as an
associate of the National Congress Party, but split with the party in
1919 when Gandhi began his first mass disobedience campaign. For
some time, relations between the Moslem League, headed by Jinnah,
and the National Congress Party remained ambiguous; but by 1937
Jinnah concluded that cooperation with the Hindus was impossible,
and that the only way to secure the interests of the Muslims of
India was to give them a country of their own. Ten years later his
wishes were realized through the establishment of Pakistan, and
Jinnah served briefly before his death as the first governor-general
of the new state.

The excerpts from Jinnah's speeches that follow date from 1938 to
1940. This was a time when Jinnah had decided to press for independent nationhood but had still to convince the Muslims, the
British, and the Hindus that a pan-Islâmic identity on the one hand
and a common Indian-ness on the other hand was not preferable
to or easier to put up with than separate nationhood for the Muslims.

Jinnah prevailed in the end, but millions have died since 1947 as a
result of continuing frictions between the Indian and Pakistani
states and the rival religious-cultural communities each represents.

FROM JINNAH: PRESIDENTIAL ADDRESS
DELIVERED AT THE ANNUAL SESSION OF THE
ALL-INDIA MUSLIM LEAGUE HELD AT
PATNA ON 26-29 DECEMBER, 1938

.   .   .   .

I am convinced—I think you are also now convinced, and
many who are not yet convinced will soon be convinced, and
those who are honestly mistaken now, not those who are dishonest in their conviction, will also be convinced—that the Con-

From *Some Recent Speeches and Writings of Mr. Jinnah*, edited by Jamil-
ud-Din Ahmad, Lahore: Ashraf Press, 1942, vol. I, pp. 79-83. Reprinted by
permission.

gress is not a national body. It is a misfortune of our country; indeed, it is a tragedy that the High Command of the Congress is determined, absolutely determined, to crush all other communities and cultures in this country and establish Hindu raj.[1] They talk of Swaraj,[2] but they mean only Hindu raj. They talk of national government, but they mean only Hindu government. But the bubble has been pricked too soon. Intoxicated with power gained under the new Constitution, with the majority in six or seven provinces the Congress game has been exposed a little too soon. What did the Congress do when it got the power? With all its pretensions of nationalism, it straightway started with the *Bande Matram*. It is admitted that *Bande Matram* is not the national song, yet it is sung as such and thrust upon others. It is sung not only in their own gatherings, but Muslim children in Government and Municipal schools too are compelled to sing it. Muslim children must accept *Bande Matram* as their national song, no matter whether their religious beliefs permit them to do so or not. It is idolatrous and a hymn of hate against Muslims.

Take the case of the Congress flag. Admittedly it is not the national flag of India, yet that flag must be respected by everyone and hoisted on every Government and public building. It does not matter if the Muslims object to it, the Congress flag must be paraded as the national flag of India and thrust upon the Muslims.

Take next the case of Hindi-Hindustani. I need not add to what has already been said on the subject by the Chairman of the Reception Committee. Is there any doubt now in the mind of anyone that the whole scheme of Hindi-Hindustani is intended to stifle and suppress Urdu?[3] (Voices: "no doubt.")

GANDHI'S SCHEME OF HINDU REVIVAL

Take next the Wardha scheme of education. Were the Muslims taken into confidence when the scheme was under prepara-

1. I.e., Hindu rule, government power.
2. I.e., self-rule.
3. Persianate language of India, associated with Muslim rule under the Mughal dynasty.

tion? The whole scheme was conceived and its details worked out behind the back of the Muslims. Who is the author of the scheme? Who is the genius behind it? Mr. Gandhi. I have no hesitation in saying that it is Mr. Gandhi who is destroying the ideal with which the Congress was started. He is the one man responsible for turning the Congress into an instrument for the revival of Hinduism. His ideal is to revive Hindu religion and establish Hindu raj in this country, and he is utilising the Congress to further this object.

INTERFERING WITH MUSLIM LIFE

The reaction of the Muslims to such a scheme of education could not but be what it has been all over the country. You have seen the Pirpur Report and I need not add to what has been described in that document. The position may be summed up in one sentence. To-day Hindu mentality and outlook is being carefully nurtured and Muslims are being forced to accept the Hindu ideals in their daily life. Have Muslims anywhere done anything of the sort? Have they anywhere sought to impose Muslim culture on the Hindus? Yet whenever Muslims have raised the slightest voice of protest against the imposition of Hindu culture on them, they have been branded as communalists and disturbers of peace, and the repressive machinery of the Congress Governments have been set in motion against them. Take the cases that have occurred in Bihar. Who have suffered suppression of culture under the Congress Government? It is the Musalmans.[4] Against whom are the repressive measures taken, prohibitory orders issued and among whom are arrests made? It is the Muslims. I should like to know a single instance —I am prepared to learn and correct myself—a single instance where the Muslim League or Muslim individuals may have tried to force their own culture upon the Hindus in the last eighteen months. (Cries: nowhere.)

MUSLIMS STIRRED

I do not wish to dwell any longer upon this. I have done with it, so far as the Congress is concerned. As regards the Musal-

4. Variant spelling of Muslims.

mans I can say that it is a matter of great congratulation to All-India Muslim League that it has succeeded in awakening a remarkable national consciousness among the Muslims. Muslims, as I said before, were like men who had lost their moral, cultural and political consciousness. You have not yet got to the fringe of acquiring that moral, cultural and political consciousness. You have only reached that stage at which there has come awakening—your political consciousness has been stirred.

To-day you find—apart from the fact whether the Congress claims are right or wrong—to-day you find that the Hindus have to a very large degree acquired that essential quality, moral, cultural and political consciousness, and it has become the national consciousness of the Hindus. This is the force behind them. That is the force I want the Muslims to acquire. When you have acquired that, believe me, I have no doubt in my mind, you will realise what you want. The counting of heads may be a very good thing, but it is not the final arbiter of the destiny of nations. You have yet to develop a national self and national individuality. It is a big task, and, as I have told you, you are yet only on the fringe of it. But I have great hopes of our success. The developments that have already taken place are almost miraculous. I never dreamed we could make this wonderful demonstration which we see to-day. But even then we are only on the fringe of the problem.

JINNAH: SPEECH BROADCAST ON ÎD DAY, 13TH NOVEMBER, 1939

We, of the older generation, have had our trials, but I wish to forget them to-night in the company of my friends particularly the young, and to touch, if I may, the fresher springs of inspiration in their hearts, for it is they who will henceforth have to bear the burden of our aspirations.

The discipline of the Ramazan[1] fast and prayer will culminate to-day in an immortal meekness of heart, before God, but it

From *Some Recent Speeches and Writings of Mr. Jinnah,* pp. 105-9.
1. Variant spelling of Ramadan, the Muslim month of fasting.

shall not be the meekness of a weak heart, and they who would think so are doing wrong both to God and to the Prophet, for it is the outstanding paradox of all religions that the humble shall be the strong and it is of particular significance in the case of Islam, for Islam, as you all know, really means action.

This discipline of Ramazan was designed by our Prophet to give us the necessary strength for action. And action implies society of man. When our Prophet preached action he did not have in mind only the solitary life of a single human being, the deed he accomplishes only within himself, the prayer and all it involves spiritually.

According to the Holy Quran a very real connection exists between prayer and life. You will remember how many and wonderful are the opportunities given to us to meet our fellow beings, to study them, to understand them, and through understanding serve them and you will notice that all these opportunities have been created by laying down the law for prayers.

Five times during the day we have to collect in the mosque of our mohalla, then every week on Friday we have to gather in the Juma mosque; then again twice a year we have to congregate in the biggest mosque or *maidan*[2] outside the town on the Id[3] day, and lastly there is the Hajj to which Muslims from all parts of the world journey, once at least in their life-time, to commune with God in the House of God. You will have noticed that this plan of our prayers must necessarily bring us into contact not only with other Muslims but also with the members of all communities whom we must encounter on our way. I don't think that these injunctions about our prayers could have been merely a happy accident. I am convinced that they were designated thus to afford men opportunities of fulfilling their social instincts.

Man has indeed been called God's caliph[4] in the Quran and if that description of man is to be of any significance it imposes upon us a duty to follow the Quran, to behave towards others as

2. Square.
3. Annual festival among Muslims.
4. Literally "assistant," the title of Muhammad's successors as head of Muslim community.

God behaves towards His mankind. In the widest sense of the word, this duty is the duty to love and to forbear. And this, believe me, is not a negative duty but a positive one.

If we have any faith in love and toleration towards God's children, to whatever community they may belong, we must act upon that faith in the daily round of our simple duties and unobstrusive pieties. On this day of Id, there will be no more worthy manifestation of the spirit that is kindled in us through fast and prayer than to resolve to bring about a complete harmony within our household, within our community and within our country with all its variety of religions and creeds and to work whether in private life or public, for no selfish ends but for the greater good of all our countrymen and finally of all human beings.

It is a great ideal and it will demand effort and sacrifice. Not seldom will your minds be assailed by doubts. There will be conflicts not only material which you perhaps will be able to resolve with courage, but spiritual also. We shall have to face them, and if to-day, when our hearts are humble, we do not imbibe that higher courage to do so, we never shall. All our leaders both Muslim and Hindu continue to be pained at communal strifes. I shall not enter into the history of their causes but there will arise moments when the minds of men will be worked up and when differences will assume the character of a conflict. It is at such moments that I shall ask you to remember your Id prayer and to reflect for a while if we could not avoid them in the light of the guidance given to us by our Quran and that mighty spirit which is Islam. I would ask you to remember in these moments that no injunction is considered by our Holy Prophet more imperative or more divinely binding than the devout but supreme realisation of our duty of love and toleration towards all other human beings.

All social regeneration and political freedom must finally depend on something that has a deeper meaning in life. And that, if you will allow me to say so, is Islam and Islamic spirit. It is not great speeches and big conferences only that make politics. Several young men have been coming to me to know how they could serve their country.

Well, young friends, if I touch upon politics to-night it is only to tell you, as a word of advice, that we have our rights and our claims in a future India. But we shall not be obstinate about them, for obstinacy will be the negation of that spirit of love and toleration which should fall upon us this Id day and whose blessings the Prophet commands us to communicate to others. But each one of us can serve our country by disciplining himself and discipline is the essence of this holy period.

Is one regular in one's habits? Does one sleep at the proper time? Does one keep to the left of the road or abstain from throwing litter on the road? Is one honest and sincere in one's work? Does one render such help as one can to others? Is one tolerant? They may seem small matters but in them is the nucleus of a self-discipline which will be of immense value in the combined efforts of all communities and all creeds towards a greater India. This will be a service to our country which may not bring you into the limelight of politics but it will assure you a lasting peace in your hearts in the knowledge that you have contributed your share to making the politician's task easier.

I am coming to the end of my brief talk. As I do so, I remember John Morley's book on "Compromise." I usually dislike recommending books to young people, but I think you all ought to read that book not only once but over and over again. There is a good chapter in it on the limits of compromise, and the lesson it teaches regarding the pursuit of truth and the limitation on our actions in practice are worth pondering over.

In the pursuit of truth and the cultivation of beliefs we should be guided by our rational interpretation of the Quran and if our devotion to truth is single-minded, we shall, in our own measure, achieve our goal. In the translation of this truth into practice, however, we shall be content with so much, and so much only, as we can achieve without encroaching on the rights of others, while at the same time not ceasing our efforts always to achieve more.

Finally, I would urge you never to forget that "Islam expects every Muslim to do his duty by his people."

JINNAH: PRESIDENTIAL ADDRESS AT THE
ALL-INDIA MUSLIM LEAGUE LAHORE SESSION,
MARCH, 1940 (?)

. . . .

Now, I should like to put before you my views on the subject
as it strikes me taking everything into consideration at the present moment. The British Government and Parliament, and more
so the British nation, have been for many decades past brought
up and nurtured with settled notions about India's future, based
on developments in their own country which has built up the
British constitution, functioning now through the Houses of
Parliament and the system of cabinet. Their concept of party
government functioning on political planes has become the ideal
with them as the best form of government for every country,
and the one-sided and powerful propaganda, which naturally
appeals to the British, has led them into a serious blunder, in
producing the constitution envisaged in the Government of India Act of 1935. We find that the most leading statesmen of
Great Britain, saturated with these notions, have in their pronouncements seriously asserted and expressed a hope that the
passage of time will harmonise the inconsistent elements in
India.

A leading journal like the London *Times* commenting on the
Government of India Act of 1935, wrote, 'Undoubtedly the differences between the Hindus and Muslims are not of religion in
the strict sense of the word but also of law and culture, that they
may be said, indeed, to represent two entirely distinct and separate civilisations. However, in the course of time, the supersti-
tion will die out and India will be moulded into a single nation.'
So, according to the London *Times*, the only difficulties are superstitions. These fundamental and deep-rooted differences, spiritual, economic, social and political, have been euphemised as
mere 'superstitions.' But surely it is a flagrant disregard of the
past history of the subcontinent of India as well as the fundamental Islamic conception of society *vis-a-vis* that of Hinduism

From *Some Recent Speeches and Writings of Mr. Jinnah*, pp. 175-81.

to characterise them as mere 'superstitions'. Notwithstanding a thousand years of close contact, nationalities, which are as divergent today as ever, cannot at any time be expected to transform themselves into one nation merely by means of subjecting them to a democratic constitution and holding them forcibly together by unnatural and artificial methods of British Parliamentary Statute. What the unitary government of India for 150 years had failed to achieve cannot be realised by the imposition of a central federal government. It is inconceivable that the fiat or the writ of a government so constituted can ever command a willing and loyal obedience throughout the subcontinent by various nationalities except by means of armed force behind it.

The problem in India is not of an inter-communal character but manifestly of an international one, and it must be treated as such. So long as this basic and fundamental truth is not realised, any constitution that may be built will result in disaster and will prove destructive and harmful not only to the Musalmans but to the British and Hindus also. If the British Government are really in earnest and sincere to secure peace and happiness of the people of this sub-continent, the only course open to us all is to allow the major nations separate homelands by dividing India into 'autonomous national states'. There is no reason why these states should be antagonistic to each other. On the other hand, the rivalry and the natural desire and efforts on the part of one to dominate the social order and establish political supremacy over the other in the government of the country will disappear. It will lead more towards natural good-will by international pacts between them, and they can live in complete harmony with their neighbours. This will lead further to a friendly settlement all the more easily with regard to minorities by reciprocal arrangements and adjustments between Muslim India and Hindu India, which will far more adequately and effectively safeguard the rights and interests of Muslims and various other minorities.

It is extremely difficult to appreciate why our Hindu friends fail to understand the real nature of Islam and Hinduism. They are not religions in the strict sense of the word, but are, in fact, different and distinct social orders, and it is a dream that the

Hindus and Muslims can ever evolve a common nationality, and this misconception of one Indian nation has gone far beyond the limits and is the cause of most of your troubles and will lead India to destruction if we fail to revise our notions in time. The Hindus and Muslims belong to two different religious philosophies, social customs, literatures. They neither intermarry nor interdine together and, indeed, they belong to two different civilisations which are based mainly on conflicting ideas and conceptions. Their aspects on life and of life are different. It is quite clear that Hindus and Musalmans derive their inspiration from different sources of history. They have different epics, different heroes, and different episodes. Very often the hero of one is a foe of the other and, likewise, their victories and defeats overlap. To yoke together two such nations under a single state, one as a numerical minority and the other as a majority, must lead to growing discontent and final destruction of any fabric that may be so built up for the government of such a state.

History has presented to us many examples, such as the Union of Great Britain and Ireland, Czechoslovakia and Poland. History has also shown to us many geographical tracts, much smaller than the sub-continent of India, which otherwise might have been called one country, but which have been divided into as many states as there are nations inhabiting them. Balkan Peninsula comprises as many as 7 or 8 sovereign states. Likewise, the Portuguese and the Spanish stand divided in the Iberian Peninsula. Whereas under the plea of unity of India and one nation, which does not exist, it is sought to pursue here the line of one central government when we know that the history of the last 12 hundred years has failed to achieve unity and has witnessed, during the ages, India always divided into Hindu India and Muslim India. The present artificial unity of India dates back only to the British conquest and is maintained by the British bayonet, but termination of the British regime, which is implicit in the recent declaration of His Majesty's Government, will be the herald of the entire break-up with worse disaster than has ever taken place during the last one thousand years under Muslims. Surely that is not the legacy which Brittain would bequeath to India after 150 years of her rule, nor would Hindu and Muslim India risk such a sure catastrophe.

Muslim India cannot accept any constitution which must necessarily result in a Hindu majority government. Hindus and Muslims brought together under a democratic system forced upon the minorities can only mean Hindu raj. Democracy of the kind with which the Congress High Command is enamoured would mean the complete destruction of what is most precious in Islam. We have had ample experience of the working of the provincial constitutions during the last two and a half years and any repetition of such a government must lead to civil war and raising of private armies as recommended by Mr. Gandhi to Hindus of Sukkur when he said that they must defend themselves violently or non-violently, blow for blow, and if they could not, they must emigrate.

Musalmans are not a minority as it is commonly known and understood. One has only got to look round. Even to-day, according to the British map of India, 4 out of 11 provinces, where the Muslims dominate more or less, are functioning notwithstanding the decision of the Hindu Congress High Command to non-co-operate and prepare for civil disobedience. Musalmans are a nation according to any definition of a nation, and they must have their homelands, their territory and their state. We wish to live in peace and harmony with our neighbours as a free and independent people. We wish our people to develop to the fullest our spiritual, cultural, economic, social and political life in a way that we think best and in consonance with our own ideal and according to the genius of our people. Honesty demands and the vital interest of millions of our people impose a sacred duty upon us to find an honourable and peaceful solution, which would be just and fair to all. But at the same time we cannot be moved or diverted from our purpose and objective by threats or intimidations. We must be prepared to face all difficulties and consequences, make all the sacrifices that may be required of us to achieve the goal we have set in front of us.

Ladies and gentlemen, that is the task before us. I fear I have gone beyond my time limit. There are many things that I should like to tell you, but I have already published a little pamphlet containing most of the things that I have been saying and

I think you can easily get that publication both in English and in Urdu from the League office. It might give you a clearer idea of our aims. It contains very important resolutions of the Muslim League and various other statements. Anyhow, I have placed before you the task that lies ahead of us. Do you realise how big and stupendous it is? Do you realise that you cannot get freedom or independence by mere arguments? I should appeal to the intelligentsia. The intelligentsia in all countries in the world have been the pioneers of any movements for freedom. What does the Muslim intelligentsia propose to do? I may tell you that unless you get this into your blood, unless you are prepared to take off your coats and are willing to sacrifice all that you can and work selflessly, earnestly and sincerely for your people, you will never realise your aim. Friends, I therefore want you to make up your mind definitely and then think of devices and organise your people, strengthen your organisation and consolidate the Musalmans all over India. I think that the masses are wide-awake. They only want your guidance and your lead. Come forward as servants of Islam, organise the people economically, socially, educationally and politically and I am sure that you will be a power that will be accepted by everybody. (Cheers.)

Reform in the Hinterland

In many areas where Muslims lived in the nineteenth and twentieth centuries the problems of rejuvenating Islâmic life evoked a very different response from those exemplified by the preceding selections. In much of Africa (excluding North Africa), though Islâm had been introduced centuries before, Muslims lived as minorities within pagan or religiously mixed societies. In West Africa, as in the Arabian peninsula, the late eighteenth century saw the beginnings of a series of revivalist and reformist movements which sought to purify Islâm and to substitute Muslim government for non-Muslim. The impetus was religious as well as economic and political, and was sometimes connected with the increasing strength and militancy of Sûfî orders, whose members traveled from one outlying area to another, preaching, converting, exhorting to action. In several cases a religious order provided the initial organizational structure and necessary network of interpersonal connections.

Movements of protest against the *status quo* were almost as old as Islâm itself, often involving expectations of a *mahdî* or savior who would fill the world with righteousness and justice; these movements were especially frequent in areas like Africa where the situations of the Muslim minorities approximated the conditions of Muhammad's early life.

In the eastern Sudan, the first protest movement did not emerge until late in the nineteenth century. It was inspired by Muhammad Ahmad ibn Sayyid 'Abdallâh (*ca.* 1843-1885), the son of a poor schoolmaster whose family claimed descent from the Prophet. After early theological studies, Muhammad joined a Sûfî order, and in 1870 retired to a remote island in the White Nile to devote himself to solitary religious exercises in a cave. (Muhammad the Prophet made a similar retreat at one stage of his life.) His stern puritanical principles attracted disciples, and about 1880 Muhammad proclaimed himself the long-awaited *mahdî*, divinely appointed to restore religion and righteousness. This excited widespread response in the lands of the upper Nile, but looked like rebellion in Cairo, where a British protectorate over the Egyptian government was still being formed. It was, indeed, the willingness of the nominally Muslim ruler of Egypt to submit to British control that lent much of the cutting edge to the Mahdî's movement. Muhammad himself died in 1885; but his movement continued to gain momentum under 'Abdallâh et Taaisha, the "Khalîfa" (*ca.* 1846-1899) until British troops intervened, and the Mahdî's followers met crushing defeat in battle (1898).

Authentic records from the Mahdî's movement are rare, since most communication was by word of mouth. What follows is a pastiche of quotations and proclamations attributed to him. They do not pretend to be verbatim; rather, they sum up the main doctrines he preached.

THE MAHDÎ: FROM LETTERS AND
PROCLAMATIONS

In 1881, after a series of militant protests, the Mahdî rejected
a summons from the governor-general of the Sudan and openly
declared Holy War. A small Egyptian expedition in August
failed to rout him and his followers, and another expedition was
sent out under al-Shallalî, who first demanded submission.

The Mahdî's reply, written 22 May 1882, showed how he,
like all Muslim reformers of his kind, compared his situation
with the Prophet's. He could well have compared his victory
over the Egyptian force to the Prophet's victory at Badr, out-
numbered as they both were:

> You say that Our only followers are the Baqqâra, the ignorant,
> the nomads and the idolators. Know then that the followers of the
> prophets before Us and of Our Lord Muhammad were the weak and
> the ignorant and the idolators, who worshipped rocks and trees. As
> for the kings and the rich and the people of luxury, they did not
> follow them until they had ruined their places, killed their nobles
> and ruled them by force. . . . And whereas you say, "Arise and
> come to us; go with us to the place of the Mahdi, that is Mecca";
> know that Our going is only by the command of the Apostle of God,
> in the time that God will. We are not under your command but you
> and your superiors are under Our Command. . . . For there is
> nothing between Us and you save the sword; . . . let him who will
> believe and let him who will disbelieve. Take heed, take heed of
> writing again, for We shall send you no reply though you were to
> write for years so long as you persist in denial.

A victory over al-Shallalî's troops yielded large booty and
gained for the Mahdî more and more supporters. In September,
1882, he besieged the Egyptian garrison of el-Obeid, which surrendered on January 18, 1883. After making el-Obeid his residence, the Mahdî announced his decision to conquer the Sudan
and neighboring lands:

From *The Mahdist State in the Sudan, 1881-1898*, by Peter Malcolm Holt,
Oxford University Press, second edition 1970, pp. 50, 73-74, 85, 101, 106-7,
110-12. Reprinted by permission of the Clarendon Press, Oxford.

The Apostle of God gave me good tidings in the prophetic vision and said to me, "As thou didst pray in El Obeid, thou shalt pray in Khartoum, then thou shalt pray in the mosque of Berber, then thou shalt pray in the Holy House of God (Mecca), then thou shalt pray in the mosque of Yathrib (Medina), then thou shalt pray in the mosque of Cairo, then thou shalt pray in Jerusalem, then thou shalt pray in the mosque of al-'Irâq, then thou shalt pray in the mosque of al-Kûfa."[1]

In a letter appointing one 'Uthman Diqna *amir*, or viceroy, of the tribes of the Suakin region, the Mahdî makes it clear how he viewed the purposes of his Holy War. Note that the Turks, though Muslims, were viewed as part of the enemy:

Know that I am sending to you an amîr from this place to establish the Faith and revive the *Sunna* of the Lord of the Prophets and Apostles. He is Shaykh 'Uthmân Diqna, the son of Abû Bakr al-Sawâkinî. If he stays in your territories, gather around him, assist him and swear to hear and obey him. Assist him and go out with him to the war (*al-ghazw*) and the *jihâd*,[2] and purify the earth of the Turks and the corrupters.

In November, 1883, the Mahdî was in a position to take the whole of the Sudan; and the British (who had already occupied Egypt) were prepared to relinquish it to him. With this in mind they sent General Gordon to escort the Europeans still living in Khartoum to Egypt. Gordon wrote to the Mahdî offering the "Sultanate of Kordofan," the Mahdî's original center in the western Sudan, among other things, urging him at the same time to release his European prisoners. This was the Mahdî's reply:

Know that I am the Expected Mahdi, the Successor of the Apostle of God. Thus I have no need of the sultanate, nor of the kingdom of Kordofan or elsewhere, nor of the wealth of this world and its vanity. I am but the slave of God, guiding unto God and to what is with Him . . . and God has succoured me with the prophets and the apostles and the cherubim and all the saints and pious men to revive His Faith. . . . As for the gift which you have sent Us, may God reward you well for your good-will and guide you to the

1. In southern Irâq.
2. Holy war.

right. . . . It is returned to you herewith with the clothing We wish for Ourself and Our Companions who desire the world to come.[3]

As the Mahdî, Muhammad ibn 'Abdallâh continued to make a covenant with his followers as he had done before when simply a Sûfî *shaykh*. The oath of allegiance, below, summarizes the major components of the Mahdist movement at this stage. The assertion of the unity of God had always been a fundamental tenet of reformers, especially those who found themselves surrounded by what they considered idolatry. The most basic sins were those which most commonly prevented social unity.

We swear allegiance to God and His Apostle, and we swear allegiance to you, upon the unity of God, and that we will not associate anyone with Him, we will not steal, we will not commit adultery, we will not bring false accusations and we will not disobey you in what is lawful. We swear allegiance to you upon the renunciation of this world and its abandonment, and being content with what is with God, desiring what is with God and the world to come, and that we will not flee from the *jihâd*.[4]

The Mahdî's investiture of his successor (January 26, 1883), the man to be caliph after his death, and his equating him to Muhammad's successor, further illustrates how reformers often tried to justify themselves by showing that their situation and actions conformed to the history of Muhammad's community.

Know . . . that the Khalifa 'Abdallâhi, *Khalîfat al-Siddîq*, commander of the Army of the Mahdia, was designated in the prophetic vision. . . . Since you know, my beloved, that the Khalifa 'Abdallâhi is of me and I am of him and that the Lord of Being[5] has designated him, be conformable unto him as ye are conformable unto me, and submit unto him outwardly and inwardly as ye submit unto me. Believe in his words and do not be suspicious of his deeds, for all that he does is by command of the Prophet or by permission from Us, not by his mere independent judgment, nor is

3. The clothing referred to by the Mahdî was a patched garment (*jubba*), which, with a turban, a rosary, and other accoutrements, served as the uniform of an Ansari. Gordon had sent the Mahdî a robe of honor.

4. Holy war.

5. The Lord of Being, i.e., the Prophet Muhammad.

it foolishness, but he is the representative of the Prophet in executing his command and judgment is by his instruction. So his action
towards you and decision among you is in accordance therewith.
So know of a certainty that his judgment among you is the judgment of the Apostle of God . . . . Whosoever discusses his right,
even to himself, silently, has lost this world and the world to come
. . . for he is the Khalifa of al-Siddîq. . . . Inasmuch as ye have
understood this, he ['Abdallâhi] is now in his [Abû Bakr al-Siddîq's] place, for Our Companions are as the Companions of the
Apostle of God. He whom we have mentioned is Our Khalifa and
his *khilâfa* is by a command from the Prophet. Whoever of you believes in God and the Last Day and has faith in my Mahdiship, let
him submit to the Khalifa 'Abdallâhi both outwardly and inwardly.
If you see him apparently transgressing in a matter, leave it to be
judged by the knowledge of God and a good interpretation. . . .
The Khalifa is the Leader of the Muslims and Our Khalifa, Our
representative in all matters of the Faith. Beware of murmuring
against his right, thinking evil or failing to obey him. . . . This is
the declaration of the command of God and His Apostle, so let those
who transgress His command be warned lest chastisement or sore
punishment befall them.

The following proclamations from 1883 show how the Mahdî
tried to adhere to the Prophet's practice in financial and legal
matters:

It was incumbent upon Us to collect for the Muslims what would
satisfy their need. I have found no-one like Ahmad Sulaymân to
act as my assistant with integrity, austerity, trustworthiness, good-
will in service, and high zeal. So I have established him as a commissioner (*amîn*) over the stores of the Muslims and the treasury.
So he is commissioner over it on my behalf and is trusted in what
he does therein. . . . He may therefore appoint anyone to assist
him and dismiss anyone who does not respond to his command and
judge anyone where judgment is due. . . . Whoever betrays him,
betrays me; whoever harms him, harms me and shall be liable to
the appropriate judgment. . . . He has received permission from
the Lord of Being and if he gives judgment in any due of the treasury or matter concerning it, let him judge only with justice and
truth.[6]

6. Ahmad Sulaymân was the man put in charge of the treasury after the
victory at el-Obeid.

. . . .

You have given me your covenants and promises of obedience to my command. . . . I am pleased with no-one who is fraudulent in anything of the booty. Let him be sincere to God and His Apostle and to Us and bring it to Us at the place where it is due, so that the Fifth may be taken from it and the rest divided among you in accordance with the commandment of God and His Apostle. . . . We know that in this expedition were great wealth and innumerable possessions, all of which has fallen into your hands.

. . . .

It is my resolution that all the Companions and especially the khalifas should assist the Khalifa 'Abdallâhi in gathering the booty and the zakâh[7] for the treasury. He shall, according to his knowledge, disperse the agents in this and they themselves and their followers shall be assistants. . . . Since duty demands adherence to the oath of allegiance, let all the Brethren levy the tithe and the zakâh and the booty for the treasury, and let no-one take anything for himself or his company. Let relief for all the Ansâr[8] be from the treasury. Let him who has relatives and family, whether many or few, disclose this; also he who has but little, and he shall be allotted sufficient from the treasury. . . . If the treasury is empty, have patience until God gives the treasury sufficiency.

. . . .

And levy among your families the zakâh; camels, cattle, sheep and goats in accordance with the ordinance imposed by God in regard to the beasts mentioned. Take from the owners of arable land the zakâh of grain. Everything which accrues to you from zakâh or booty is to be set out in lists which are to be sent here in succession, with a letter from you, so that it may be brought into the treasury of the Muslims and thence distributed to the weak, the poor and the Party of God, the warriors. Do not be in any way remiss in gathering the dues of God and do not neglect to send them speedily. If anyone refuses them to you, take them even against his will and tell Us at once for Our information.

When matters required particular guidance, the Mahdî claimed direct inspiration from the Prophet and unique authority.

7. Tax.
8. Ansâr: helpers, as with Muhammad in Medina.

Information came from the Apostle of God that the angel of inspiration is with me from God to direct me and He has appointed him. So from this prophetic information I learnt that that with which God inspires me by means of the angel of inspiration, the Apostle of God would do, were he present.